Confronting Identities in the Roman Empire

Also available from Bloomsbury

Female Mobility and Gendered Space in Ancient Greek Myth, Ariadne Konstantinou
The Roman Castrati, Shaun Tougher
Women's Life in Greece and Rome, Maureen B. Fant and Mary R. Lefkowitz

CENTRO DE ESTUDOS CLÁSSICOS E HUMANÍSTICOS DA UNIVERSIDADE DE COIMBRA

fct Fundação para a Ciência e a Tecnologia

REPÚBLICA PORTUGUESA

This work is financed by funds through FCT – Fundação para a Ciência e a Tecnologia, I.P., in the framework of the project *Rome our Home: (Auto)biographical Tradition and the Shaping of Identity(ies)* (PTDC/LLT-OUT/28431/2017) and *Projeto Geral do Centro de Estudos Clássicos e Humanísticos* (UIDB/00196/2020 e UIDP/00196/2020).

Confronting Identities in the Roman Empire

Assumptions about the Other in Literary Evidence

Edited by
José Luís Brandão,
Cláudia Teixeira
and
Ália Rodrigues

BLOOMSBURY ACADEMIC
LONDON • NEW YORK • OXFORD • NEW DELHI • SYDNEY

BLOOMSBURY ACADEMIC
Bloomsbury Publishing Plc
50 Bedford Square, London, WC1B 3DP, UK
1385 Broadway, New York, NY 10018, USA
29 Earlsfort Terrace, Dublin 2, Ireland

First published in Great Britain 2024

Cover design: Terry Woodley
Cover image: Trajan's column in Rome. © BGStock72/Adobestock

A catalogue record for this book is available from the British Library.

A catalog record for this book is available from the Library of Congress.

ISBN: HB: 978-1-3503-5398-5
ePDF: 978-1-3503-5399-2
eBook: 978-1-3503-5423-4

Typeset by RefineCatch Limited, Bungay, Suffolk

To find out more about our authors and books visit www.bloomsbury.com and sign up for our newsletters.

Contents

Contributors

Ália Rodrigues obtained her PhD in Classical Studies from the University of Coimbra, Portugal. More recently, she worked as a postdoctoral researcher in the project *Rome our Home: (Auto)biographical Tradition and the Shaping of Identity(ies)*, at the Centre for Classical and Humanistic Studies. Over the past few years, her primary research focus has been the intellectual history of political ideas, with a specific emphasis on the Greek and Roman political traditions.

Claudia Beltrão is Professor of Ancient History at the Federal University of Rio de Janeiro – UNIRIO, Brazil. Her research and teaching interest is the intellectual life of late Republican Rome, with special emphasis on the study of Roman religion in the philosophical works of Cicero. She has recently co-edited, with Federico Santangelo, the volumes *Cicero and Roman Religion* (2020) and *Estátuas na Religião Romana* (2020).

Cláudia Teixeira is Associate Professor in Literature at the University of Évora, Portugal, and Co-PI of the project *Rome our Home: (Auto)biographical Tradition and the Shaping of Identity(ies)*. Her research interests focus on biography, epic, and novel. She has been working on Virgil, Petronius, Apuleius, and the *Historia Augusta*. She is also interested in the intellectual context of the University of Évora in the sixteenth and seventeenth centuries. Her latest publication was as co-editor of *Roman Identity: Between Ideal and Performance* (2022).

Denis Álvarez Pérez-Sostoa is Assistant Professor in the Department of Classical Studies and Vice Dean for International Relations and Mobility Programmes at the University of the Basque Country, Spain. His main research has focused on the middle and late Roman Republic, including ancient diplomacy, warfare, and post-war settlements and agreements. He has been a member of several research projects. His work has been published in both Spanish and international journals, including *Veleia*, *Athenaeum*, *Revue des Études Anciennes*, and *Epigraphica* and has also given some fifteen talks and lectures at congresses. His latest work, *Suicidio vs rendición en la República romana* (2020), analyses suicide as a counterpart to diplomatic failure.

Eleni Bozia is Associate Professor of Classics and Digital Humanities in the Department of Classics at the University of Florida. Her research interests include identity and belonging in the high Roman Empire and digital humanities. She has published on translingualism, transculturalism, computational linguistics, and digital preservation. Her most recent book is *Lucian and His Roman Voices* (2015).

Filomena Giannotti is Researcher in Latin language and literature at Siena University, Italy. Her research interests relate to Late Antiquity, Classical reception, and the *Aeneid*. Her most recent book is *Scrinia Arverna: Studi su Sidonio Apollinare* (2021). She is also the author of a commentary on Sidonius' third book of letters, *Sperare meliora* (2016), and of the chapter 'Sidonius Reception: Late Nineteenth to Twenty-First Centuries' in the *Edinburgh Companion to Sidonius Apollinaris* (2020). In 2021, she was awarded the prestigious prize *Virgilio – sezione Mantua*, for her commentary on the *Aeneid* and several works on Virgil's poem and its reception.

Francisco Martínez Sánchez is a PhD student in the Department of Ancient History at the University of Seville, Spain. His research is focused mainly on Graeco-Roman culture, especially everything related to piracy, trade, and ancient navigation.

José Luís Brandão is Associate Professor in Classic Studies at the University of Coimbra, Portugal, and PI of the project *Rome our Home: (Auto)biographical Tradition and the Shaping of Identity(ies)*. He is interested in epigram, novel, biography, and historiography. He has been working on Martial, Suetonius, *Historia Augusta*, and Plutarch, authors on whom he has published studies and translations into Portuguese. He has also edited, with F. Oliveira, two volumes on the history of Rome. He has developed an interest in translation and production (actor, director, and consultant) for the theatre group *Thíasos* and coordinated the Festival of Classical Theatre *FESTEA*.

Louise Revell is Associate Professor in Roman Studies at the University of Southampton. Her research focuses on Rome's western provinces, looking at questions of imperialism, identity, and incorporation. She is the author of *Roman Imperialism and Local Identities* (2009) and *Ways of Being Roman: Discourses of Identity in Rome's Western Provinces* (2015), and co-editor of *The Oxford*

Handbook of Roman Britain (2016). She is currently working on urban citizenship as a mode of integration into the Roman Empire.

Mario Lentano is Professor of Latin literature at the University of Siena, Italy. His main research interests involve comedy, school declamation, Roman family relationships, and the legends on the origins of Rome. His most recent book is *Virgilio* (2022).

Martina Gatto has a PhD in Ancient Classics and their Fortune from the University of Rome 'Tor Vergata' and has conducted her research at the KU Leuven University, Belgium, for one year as a visiting PhD student. Her main research interests are Spartan history and tradition, Sparta in modern thought, and Greek historiography.

Nuno Simões Rodrigues is Associate Professor in the Department of History at the University of Lisbon, Portugal. His main research interests include Greek myth and religion, Roman social history in the late Republic and early Roman Empire, and reception studies. He has published on women and identity in the age of Augustus. He is a co-author of a book about the reception of Euripides' *Iphigenias* in eighteenth-century Portuguese culture (2022). He is currently co-editing a book on Roman identity and contemporaneity.

Paolo Desideri was Full Professor of Roman History in the University of Florence, Italy. Retired since 2011, he continues to research widely in the fields of ancient (Greek and Roman) historiography, Greek literature in Roman imperial times, and the tradition of the classics in modern European political thought. His most recent book is *Ellenismo imperiale: Nuovi studi su Dione di Prusa* (2019).

Pedro David Conesa Navarro is Assistant Professor of Ancient History in the Department of Prehistory, Ancient History and Archaeology at the Complutense University of Madrid, Spain. He held a predoctoral fellowship granted by the Seneca Foundation and completed his PhD under international co-supervision (University of Murcia and University of Rome 'Tor Vergata'). He has obtained the highest qualification in both institutions and the extraordinary doctoral prize. He has completed several research stays in international centres (Cambridge, Rome, Heidelberg, Hamburg) and has participated in national and international seminars. He has published several scientific papers and book chapters about Roman history.

Ralph Moore recently completed his doctorate in Classics at Trinity College Dublin. His research interests are in Roman imperialism, class and ethnicity in Antiquity, and history and archaeology of ancient Western Europe. His most recent publication is *Friends in High (and Low) Places: The Allobroges and the Politics of Patronage and Provincial Society in the Late Roman Republic* (2021).

Rúben Henrique de Castro is a researcher at CHAM – Centre for Humanities and a doctoral student in Ancient History at the University of Seville, Spain, and at the Nova University Lisbon, Portugal; his thesis is titled *Gods and Men: Omens, Legitimacy and Power in Imperial Rome*. His research interests include Roman cosmovision, Roman religion, and Roman divination. He has published mostly about Roman imperial omens. His latest publication was a book chapter titled *The Year of the Four Emperors: Perspectives on Civil War and Imperial Legitimacy in the Omens of 68 and 69* AD (2021).

Sara Casamayor Mancisidor teaches Ancient History at the University of La Rioja, Spain. She obtained her PhD at the University of Salamanca, Spain, with a dissertation on women's old age in ancient Rome. Her research focuses on the intersection between gender and old age in Rome. She has also worked on other topics such as disability in the imperial period and the reception of Antiquity in the contemporary digital world.

Selena Ross is a PhD candidate in the Department of Classics at Rutgers University. Her research focuses on Roman social history, with an emphasis on agriculture, animal husbandry, and rural craft. Her recent projects have investigated herdsmen, the parameters of domestic labour, and the rhetoric and reality of self-sufficiency.

Serena Connolly is Professor in the Department of Classics at Rutgers University. She has research interests in Roman law, Roman social history, and the history of ancient Mediterranean science and technology. Her most recent book is *Wisdom from Rome: Reading Roman Society and European Education in the Distichs of Cato* (2022).

Introduction

José Luís Brandão, Cláudia Teixeira and Ália Rodrigues

I

This volume stems directly from the activities of the BioRom project – *Rome our Home: (Auto)biographical Tradition and the Shaping of Identity(ies).*[1] Following the publication of a previous volume from the project, which reported the results developed in Task 1,[2] this volume is the result of Task 2, which focused on the relationship between Rome and the 'other' and included a series of workshops, seminars, and a congress. Arising from these outputs, the current volume brings together a set of essays discussing perceptions of the 'other(s)' in literature produced in ancient Rome.

Addressing what the 'other' entails for one's own time is no easy task, doubly so for times far distant. In fact, the apparent binary nature of the concept as a relational category that implies an 'I' and an 'other',[3] has been the target of various critiques across many fields and frameworks. There are a vast array of disciplinary and interdisciplinary studies, the wide latitude of which extends from discussion of abstract dimensions of the concept and the methods that operate the mediations between the 'I' and the 'other', to the analysis of the socio-political impacts of the construction of otherness in the context of social relations and organizations.

These models of analysis have favoured an approach centred on communities or groups and have focused on issues such as the affirmation and defence of identities (social justice, the economic, social, and political impacts of alterity and diversity, mechanisms of shaping, maintaining or concealing identities and of cultural appropriation, etc.). These issues have been explored according to distinct paradigms focusing on the problem of the 'other' within the framework of their own sociabilities, daily interactions, practices, conflicts, tensions, and deviations, emphasizing the cultural context of these identities, as well as the social representations that emerge from this diversity and their effects (estrangement, exoticization, stigmatization, simplification, objectification, criminalization, etc.).

II

In parallel, the relationship between identity and otherness has also been undergoing re-examination among historians, classicists, and archaeologists, both for the ancient world and in the context of reception studies. On the one hand, the relations that were established in the Roman world in the framework of the formation and development of a culture that hegemonically aggregated a multitude of peoples with very distinct cultural backgrounds, have proven to be a fertile field of analysis. In many ways, the creation and hegemony of a 'global' Roman identity culture, which had both the power to 'integrate', unify, and to annihilate difference, provided, in many registers, a cognitive model for the understanding of similar phenomena that occurred later both in colonial empires and in the globalized world.[4] On the other hand, the acute theoretical lenses that post-colonial studies, among others, has applied to the study of the relationship of colonial powers with colonized peoples has resulted in a massive shift in how we approach the study of identity construction in the premodern age. By focusing on the experiences that led to the construction of the subaltern or subjected 'other' as a silenced, marginalized, and hierarchised other,[5] studies, such as that of Said, have exposed the ethnic, geographical, economic, linguistic, and political identities of the colonized as something socially constructed by the dominating centre, which used them not only as a mechanism to promote 'separation' but also to validate systems of domination. This new framework was embraced by studies focused on Antiquity, insofar as it offered possibilities for the analysis of hitherto unexplored realities and a more complex and adjusted framework for understanding the 'silences' to which many 'others' who formed part of ancient societies were historically subjected.

Moreover, constructivism, by emphasizing the dynamic nature of identities, also favoured the questioning of perspectives that saw Roman identity in the framework of an identity essentialism, affiliated with elements such as race, ethnicity, language, and shared symbolic heritages (values and beliefs), i.e. with elements whose definition tended to persist as such over time.

The abandonment of the essentialist perspective – nourished by a new theoretical framework that emphasized the idea of the construction of identities as a dynamic process susceptible to change according to the circumstances that determine the experience of individuals and communities throughout life – brought new epistemological and methodological principles to the study of the issue. In the first place, greater understanding was arrived at by internalizing the principle that identities, as they are subject to a framework of interactions, both group and individual, of a transformative nature, are not impermeable, fixed or uniform, but rather formed in a complex way over time through innumerable processes of negotiation and renegotiation. Secondly, the principle that identity is made up of multiple strata, both on the paradigmatic axis – that is, on the level where individuals and groups are at a given point in the historical chain – and on the syntagmatic axis – that is, on the level of the multiple states of identity that individuals and groups assume throughout life, according to the evolution of their affinities, ways of thinking and social, economic, and religious practices, also brought a fresh perspective to the study of ancient identities, separate from us only in time.

As far as the ancient world and Rome in particular are concerned, this new way of approaching and studying identity brought consequences not only for Roman cultural identity studies – which came to be perceived as the result of a long process mediated by multiple influences[6] that intervened dynamically in its construction over the centuries – but also for the construction of identities in an imperial context, in which the 'other' played an undeniably central role. Notions such as 'imposition', 'forced acculturation', and 'monolithic centralization of civilization' implied in the concept of Romanization have been widely reconsidered in various studies.[7] Such studies have highlighted that the process of cultural supra-unification was not only more flexible than the previous paradigm would let us suppose but was mediated by processes that implied more than the monolithic and non-dialogic replacement of a significantly distinct set of regional cultures. Thus, although citizenship, ways of life, urbanization, material culture, language, religion, dress, and practices became indicators of Romanness that replaced equivalent indicators from previous states of culture, the process of cultural change that mediated this transition came to be seen as a dynamic process in which multiple responses occurred, both group and individual. In particular, the combined analysis of political, legal, religious, and economic aspects and of practices, discourses, ways of life, etc., showed disparate experiences, leveraged in multiple processes of negotiation and renegotiation. Study of these processes has revealed hybrid and successively negotiated and renegotiated states of identity shifting according to contexts, interactions, and conditioning factors and interests,[8] which, temporally and geographically,[9] mediated the relationship of individuals and groups with the Roman world. This new perception implied a revision in the concept of the 'other'. Not only because the 'other' was recognized as actively implicated in the process of cultural change, but also because it led to a redefinition of the role that elements such as ethnicity,[10] culture,[11] and power[12] played in it.

III

Although the perspectives centred on local and regional realities allow us to consider the existence of multiple forms of relating to the 'other' and to extract frameworks in relation to social practices that show either the adoption of new values, behaviours, and practices or patterns of resistance and the maintenance of elements of native cultures, the perception of identities on a literary level – the main objective of this book – is based on different assumptions. In fact, to speak of the 'other' within the framework of a temporally distant society, privileging literary access, presents challenges to an integrated interpretation of realities. First, because literature, despite the universalizing visions it transmits (or the way in which they have been taken as universalizing models), constitutes a limited access to a complex society whose written texts translate neither the totality nor the diversity of experiences. Secondly, because literature, which is both a product and producer of culture, conveys beliefs, values, myths, and collective representations, embodies visions of cultural identity and otherness from the centre of the cultural system and, in this condition, is mediated by filters associated with the values and beliefs of the ingroup. This dominant position determines, therefore, that the perceptions derived from it are mostly adjusted to the system of cultural representations and historically shared symbolic heritages (namely beliefs and values), which, at each period of time, these ingroups project onto themselves and the surrounding world. This has a consequence: the expression of concepts such as identity (understood as the feeling of belonging to a community shared by the individuals within it) or otherness gains an objective existence, albeit mediated by mechanisms of inclusion and exclusion operated from the ideological cultural centre of the narratives. In this respect, literature tends to be consolidated as an element of expression of the 'grand narrative',[13] that is, as a totalizing and justifying discourse about the 'essence' of communities and their place in history.

The texts that embody the great Roman narrative are no exception in this respect, for they not only nurtured a teleological vision of history but also generally supported the narrative of domination. In fact, they conveyed an imaginary in which *Romanitas* equated to order and civilization and in which the definition of what it was to 'be Roman' implied the adoption of a strict cultural code, composed of social norms and moral principles. That is, the sharing not only of a set of principles and models of action, but also of a historically constructed reality, to which the common ancestry and the values of the *mos maiorum* provided authority and cohesion. For these reasons, literature tended to constitute a discursive mechanism that separated, hierarchized, and polarized the division between the centre and the cultural and identity periphery(ies).

Moreover, literature has not given much space to the 'other', as the transmitter of its experience as 'differentiated', reducing it to the protagonist of an absent history, or, when it does, it does so through the filter of the dominant culture, activating prejudices and pre-judgements that, in the end, reinforce the feeling of sameness. Such is the case in Plautus' *Poenulus*, where the primary prejudices and generalizations about the Carthaginian enemy are projected and Roman morality is used as a yardstick.[14]

However, and despite these limitations, the texts and their contexts constitute a privileged stage for the analysis of the tensions and conflicts between the centre and the periphery(ies), as well as the processes of legitimation and delegitimation, which have led some of these peripheries to become part of the cultural system and others to become subject to stigmatization, stereotyping, discrimination, exotification, and objectification.

Evidently, these processes are not always clear or homogeneous. For example, formulations of ethnical othering present themselves as disparate even in works that embody the traditional imaginary of Roman cultural identity. As an example, the identity narrative that emerges in Virgil's *Aeneid* as a result of the mythogenesis presented in book 6 highlights the complex relationship played by identity elements, such as ethnicity(ies), with the meaning of origin, and culture. From this relationship stems the idea that the incorporation and integration of individuals with 'ethnically multiple origins' resulted, almost by fiat, in the construction of a 'culturally bound group'.[15]

That said, assuming that the text also points to the ideology underlying the plan of cultural unification and identity that was taking place at the historical level, such ideology finds its evaluative counterpoint in the description of the barbarian peoples on the edge of the empire in a pose of submission before Augustus (*Aen.* 8). This image not only conflicts with the mythological vision of the ethnically multi-polar creation of Rome, but also brings into the narrative the more objective circumstances of Augustan *Realpolitik*, which allows for, among other things, the contrast to be equated and the perceptions, processes, mechanisms, and forms that shaped the relationship with the various 'others' to be investigated.

Similarly, dominant cultural systems are not immune to identity tensions, which, in the Roman case, arose from aspects as varied as those resulting from the acculturation of a multitude of radically distinct peoples or from the social promotion mechanisms that included the possibility of natives, slaves, and freedmen ascending to citizenship and to the highest ranks of the empire's political and military hierarchy. It is true that we cannot attribute to the multiculturalism that emerged in the Roman sphere all the aspects that we attribute today to that concept. We may certainly include under its umbrella the institutional policies that responded to that diversity (e.g. the policy of citizenship), but not the recognition and valorization of group identities that the concept implies today. It is also true that we cannot disconnect the mechanisms of social promotion from the circumstances of the time, subjecting them to an evaluation by the standards of current societies. Yet it is no less true that societies with the complexity of the Roman world are indeed subject to evolution and this evolution also conditions the modification of their social and identity perceptions[16] and, consequently, the categorizations, practices of acceptance and rejection, and the feelings of belonging, inclusion, and exclusion, of which literature is one repository.

To reconsider the 'other' on the basis of literary texts does not imply, for all that has been said, a defence of the neutrality of narrative discourse as a means of symbolic representation of the dominant culture or a subversion of its status as an ideological or evaluative object. But neither does it imply the removal of their importance as an object that characterizes an era and a culture, adding substance to the idea that only material culture or, at best, hybrid objects such as inscriptions, are reliable indicators of historical and cultural realities.

Despite the recognition that Latin texts present 'Romanocentric, centralising and elitist'[17] perspectives, we cannot forget that the place of truth in literature is, above all, the place of perspective or, as eloquently stated by Todorov, 'the truth of literary texts is not narrowly referential; it is intersubjective and consists in the adherence of readers far beyond centuries or national borders'.[18]

IV

In this sense, the aim of this book is to explore the 'perspectives', angles, and interests expressed by the texts in order to explore practices of relation, inclusion, exclusion, and transformation that confirm or refute traditional views concerning the concepts of otherness and cultural identity.

It is clear that Roman identity has a contextual character, depending on the times and the places in which it is considered. The 'other' shifts according to these dimensions. Consequently, there is no single 'other', but many 'others' (some more consistent than others, some more permeable than others), as well as a series of records of interactions and mutual influences resulting therefrom.

The contributions are thus organized as case studies that propose complementary visions of the 'other', in their customs, activities, and locations. These complementarities attempt to answer questions centred on the following oppositions: white-Black, traditional-innovative, moral-immoral, legal-illegal, Roman/Greek-barbarian, man-woman, central-peripheral, global-regional, Italy-provinces, enemy-ally, authentic-spurious, normal-abnormal, cult-incult.

In Part One, 'Confronting Identities: Othering Communities and Groups', we present a selection of perspectives addressing the topic of Roman perceptions on community identity, taking into account the ethnic, geographical, religious, occupational, and social issues which comprise the important dimensions for the creation of the contextual 'other'. As a more general material evidence-based approach, in Chapter 1, Louise Revell addresses the relationship between identity, othering, and performativity through a case study of civic identities. Focusing on the peoples of the western provinces of the empire, Revell argues that a more nuanced and richer picture of Rome's impact on these societies can be constructed by re-constructing the kinds of lives they lived and the ways in which they formed and maintained their sense of self on a daily basis.

Moving further into the realm of literary sources, we find two frequent identifiers of the identity of the 'other': skin colour and religion. In Chapter 2, Mario Lentano considers the question of skin colour in Roman culture. Lentano demonstrates the untenable nature of claims that Classical texts reflect white supremacy through a close reading of texts and engagement with a wealth of recent scholarship on this topic. In Chapter 3, Claudia Beltrão investigates the religion of the 'other' and considers the gradual increase in reluctance among the Roman elite to welcome other religions at the end of the Republic. She focuses on the important perspective of Cicero, occupying both a voice for the Roman elite but also that of an individual within that group, and considers the topic of religious inclusivity in various of his dialogues, especially *De natura deorum*, in order to explore the tension between Romanness and foreignness.

As often definers of more or less organized, more or less integrated groups, we have activities that can be identitary or transgressive. In Chapter 4, Selena Ross addresses visions of the 'other' and their integration into the empire taking Varro as a starting point. Varro provides a reliable and proven model for understanding the integration of certain stakeholders within his contemporary milieu. The integration his text most speaks to is that of farmers (associated with ideas of a traditional Roman identity) and shepherds (associated with strong cultural ties to Greece and the 'other'). In Chapter 5, Francisco Martínez interrogates views on piracy in a non-Roman author, Plutarch, under Roman rule and entirely integrated in the empire. This is the romanticized *topoi* about the 'other' as transgressor and obstacle to the normal functioning of the empire, but also a way of fragmenting the ingrained association in the Roman mentality between piracy and the Greek world.

Several analyses follow dealing with the notion of the barbarian and the confrontation with Roman customs, mainly in two related literary genres (biography and autobiography), crossed with the importance of peoples and gender from the point of view of Roman rulers, beginning with Caesar and Augustus. In Chapter 6, Ralph Moore analyses the othering stereotypes in Caesar's accounts of diplomacy with Gauls and Germans, in order to illuminate the 'construction and reaffirmation of Roman cultural values and ethnic selfhood against othered groups'. Likewise, in Chapter 7, Denis Álvarez Pérez-Sostoa addresses the question of the value of the 'other' through the acquisition and manipulation of hostages in public fora, in this case, the value of foreign women as hostages, *contra mores maiorum*, in the context of Augustus' relations with the Germans, taking Suetonius' biography as a source. Following in this vein, in Chapter 8, Pedro David Conesa Navarro and Sara Casamayor Mancisidor consider the integration of a foreign practice – that of wet-nurses – that went against the *mores maiorum* that marked Roman tradition and identity.

The concluding chapters of Part One consider shifting views of the 'other' in relation to geographical identity in the empire, at a time when a global cultural identity could increasingly be considered alongside a multiplicity of local identities. In Chapter 9, Eleni Bozia addresses the geography of exile, gathering a profile of exilic views across the work of Ovid, Juvenal, Plutarch, Musonius Rufus, Favorinus, and Aelius Aristides. In the Roman Empire, while space could be defined in socio-cultural terms, *paideia* (learning) had the capacity to build new cultural worlds born of globalized culture sometimes allowing natives and foreigners to rethink that geography and use literature as the space to develop their own senses of belongingness. In Chapter 10, Paolo Desideri looks at the sophist-philosopher Dio's sympathy for the Dacians and their admirable customs in a work that is considered to be a kind of ideological parallel to Tacitus' *Germania* – proximity which helps to understand the differences between the Greek and the Roman writer regarding Trajan's policy towards the 'barbarian' populations of Central Europe. Part One concludes with a chapter by Filomena Giannotti on intellectual reactions to the end of Roman rule as well as the importance of *paideia* and the preservation of erudite Latin in a fragile globalized world.

Part Two, 'Confronting Identities: Othering Individuals', goes further in surfacing the perspectives of famous foreigners from Classical and post-Classical texts, understanding their polyvalent roles as models, enemies and allies, and transgressors who deviate from traditional identity models. It additionally considers traditionally more 'invisible' Romans, examining anonymous people who stood out for their special occupations or for escaping from bodily normality.

With regard to import foreigners who were welcomed as grounds for Roman identity, in Chapter 12, Martina Gatto addresses the question of the identification of Roman morality with the 'other' by positing the Greek legislator Lycurgus as an example of Roman traditional values. Considering the lawgiver as a kind of 'mirror statesman', Gatto explores Justin's admiration for a foreign figure from the past as an example of a process of changing but ongoing confirmation/consolidation of Roman moral identity – a kind of 'mirror' statesman (a tradition that will be extensively developed).

Texts about the enemies of Rome are effectively master classes in Roman constructions of the 'other'. In Chapter 13, based mainly on Livy, Nuno Simões Rodrigues reveals the construction of the profile of female alterity in a Roman context – the image of the vengeful, treacherous, and manipulative woman, but also of a capable and worthy enemy (i.e. mirroring the qualities of the victor). Livy portrays Sophoniba as an *exemplum* of gender and ethnic diversity in Roman culture, one which can define the woman of the 'other', but also shape Roman values. Additionally, in Chapter 14, Rúben Henrique de Castro presents to us the 'other' as the enemy of Rome. Through case studies of the portrayals of Viriathus, Boudica, and Arminius, the author seeks to provide a better understanding of the political, philosophical, and narrative elements and their relationship to authorial and wider Roman self-fashioning.

Because of the way the imperial court can influence fashions, the reaction of the biographical tradition to the introduction of exotic customs by emperors defines a (more or less fictional) image of the emperor, but also conveys the elite's perception of such customs. In Chapter 15, José Luís Brandão analyses the Suetonius' processes of recreating certain emperors' characters and behaviours that go beyond what is permitted in Roman citizens and in a ruler, namely those traits that diverge from the values and marks shaping Roman identity. Next, in Chapter 16, Cláudia Teixeira analyses Zenobia's biography in the *Historia Augusta*, arguing that the encomiastic construction of Zenobia's portrait does not reflect a laudatory conceptualization of the 'other'. Conditioned by the programmatic intention to demean Gallienus, the author of the *Historia Augusta* instrumentalizes Zenobia's biography and manipulates the construction of the figure by resorting to exceptionality, hybridity, and dualization.

In the concluding chapter of Part Two, we consider the institutionalization and integration of anonymous individuals seen as 'others'. So, in Chapter 17, Serena Connolly asks us to reflect on the abnormal and interesting 'other'. The chapter looks at offers of abnormal elements to the emperor: animals or individuals with abnormal bodies. It reveals the interest and curiosity (and erudition) of the emperor or the court in what is not normal, in 'a desire for a public-facing cultivation of intellectualism through discerning appreciation of otherness'.

As one can see, this volume gathers perspectives from several ancient and modern authors that illustrate how the concept of the 'other' is subtle and subject to appreciations that vary and are reformulated in space and time and depend on the subjectivities surrounding the moment of literary creation. Obviously, this is not a complete depiction of the 'other', but an approximation to its fragmented nature.

Notes

1 *Rome our Home: (Auto)biographical Tradition and the Shaping of Identity(ies)* (PTDC/LLT-OUT/28431/2017): https://www.uc.pt/en/cech/research/secondary-projects/biorom/

We would like to thank Guilherme Marques, to whom we are greatly indebted, for the editorial support given to the BioRom Project and, in particular, for the contribution made to this volume.

2 Lanzillotta et al. 2022.

3 On this relationship, see Given 2008: 587–9.

4 On this topic, see Pitts and Versluys 2016 on various approaches to the theme of globalization and in the Roman world.

5 See Bhabha 1994; Said 1978; Spivak 1985.

6 See Gruen 2011; Dench 2005.

7 Hingley 2005; Woolf 1992; Revell 2009; Wallace-Hadrill 2008.

8 On this topic, see Woolf 1992, 1997, 2004; Hingley 2005.

9 On the interactions within the provinces, see Mattingly 1997, 2004; Millett 1990, 2004; Revell 2009; Woolf 1992, 1994.

10 See Isaac 2017; Gruen 2010.

11 See Hingley 2005.

12 See Mattingly 2013, esp. part two, chapter 3.

13 See Lyotard 1984.

14 Initially portrayed with the stereotypes of an ethnic group reputed to be perjured and licentious, this unique Punic *senex* of Plautus – Hanon – turns out to be a paradoxical but essentially positive model. While anonymous, he is connoted with the commonplaces of the Punic race: the prologue (vv. 104–113), the slave (vv. 975–981, 1008–1009), and the soldier Antaménides (vv. 1309–1314) initially replicate the primary reaction of the Roman audience; but after he reveals himself, he becomes a model of Roman *pietas*. See Brandão 2016.

15 On the theme of integration and its various manifestations in the Roman world, see Kleijn 2013; Roselaar 2015.

16 Isaac 2017.

17 Dench 2010.

18 Todorov 2001: XI.

Bibliography

Bhabha, H. K. (1994), *The Location of Culture*, New York: Psychology Press.

Brandão, J. L. (2016), 'O *Poenulus* de Plauto e o seu tempo', in M. F. Silva, M. C. Fialho, and J. L. Brandão (eds), *O livro do tempo: escritas e reescritas. Teatro Greco-Latino e sua recepção I*, 285–301, Coimbra: Imprensa da Universidade de Coimbra.

Dench, E. (2005), *Romulus' Asylum: Roman Identities from the Age of Alexander to the Age of Hadrian*, Oxford: Oxford University Press.

Dench, E. (2010), 'Roman Identity', in A. Barchiesi and W. Scheidel (eds), *The Oxford Handbook of Roman Studies*, 266–80, Oxford: Oxford University Press.

Dench, E. (2018), *Empire and Political Cultures in the Roman World*, Cambridge: Cambridge University Press.

Galinsky, K. (1998), *Augustan Culture: An Interpretive Introduction*, Princeton, NJ: Princeton University Press.

Given, L. M., ed. (2008), *The Sage Encyclopaedia of Qualitative Research Methods*, Thousand Oaks, CA: Sage.

Gruen, E. (2011), *Rethinking the Other in Antiquity*, Princeton, NJ: Princeton University Press.

Gruen, E. (2020), *Ethnicity in the Ancient World: Did it Matter?*, Berlin: de Gruyter.

Hingley, R. (2005), *Globalizing Roman Culture: Unity, Diversity and Empire*, London: Routledge.

Honoré, T. (1987), 'Scriptor Historiae Augustae', *JRS*, 77: 156–76.

Huskinson, J., ed. (2013), *Experiencing Rome: Culture, Identity and Power in the Roman Empire*, London: Routledge.

Isaac, B. (2017), *Empire and Ideology in the Graeco-Roman World: Selected Papers*, Cambridge: Cambridge University Press.

Kleijn, G. de (2013), *Integration in Rome and in the Roman World*, Leiden: Brill.

Lanzillotta, L. R., J. L. Brandão, C. Teixeira, and A. Rodrigues, eds (2022), *Roman Identity. Between Ideal and Performance*, Turnhout: Brepols.

Lawrence, R. and J. Berry (1998), *Cultural Identity in the Roman Empire*, London: Routledge.

Lyotard, J. F. (1984), *The Postmodern Condition: A Report on Knowledge*, Minneapolis, MN: University of Minnesota Press.

Mattingly, D. J., ed. (1997), *Dialogues in Roman Imperialism: Power, Discourse and Discrepant Experience in the Roman Empire*, Journal of Roman Archaeology Supplement Series #23, Portsmouth, RI: JRA.

Mattingly, D. J. (2004). 'Being Roman: Expressing Identity in a Provincial Setting', *Journal of Roman Archaeology*, 17: 5–25.

Mattingly, D. J. (2013), *Imperialism, Power, and Identity: Experiencing the Roman Empire*, Princeton, NJ: Princeton University Press.

Millett, M. (1990), *The Romanization of Britain: An Essay in Archaeological Interpretation*, Cambridge: Cambridge University Press.

Millett, M. (2004), 'The Romanization of Britain: Changing Perspectives', *Kodai*, 13/14: 169–73.

Pitts, M. and M. J. Versluys, eds (2016), *Globalisation and the Roman World: World History, Connectivity and Material Culture*, Cambridge: Cambridge University Press.

Revell, L. (2009), *Roman Imperialism and Local Identities*, Cambridge: Cambridge University Press.

Revell, L. (2016), *Ways of Being Roman: Discourses of Identity in the Roman West*, Oxford: Oxbow Books.

Roselaar, S. T., ed. (2015), *Processes of Cultural Change and Integration in the Roman World*, Leiden: Brill.

Said, E. W. (1978), *Orientalism: Western Representations of the Orient*, London: Routledge.

Spivak, G. C. (1985), 'Can the Subaltern Speak?', *Wedge*, 7 (8): 120–30.

Todorov, T. (2001), *Life in Common: An Essay in General Anthropology*, trans. Katherine Golsan and Lucy Golsan, Lincoln, NE: University of Nebraska Press.

Tomlinson, J. (1991), *Cultural Globalization and Cultural Imperialism*, London: Continuum.

Tomlinson, J. (1999), *Globalisation and Culture*, Cambridge: Polity Press.

Wallace-Hadrill, A. (2008), *Augustan Cultural Revolution*, Cambridge: Cambridge University Press.

Welsch, W. (1999), 'Transculturality: The Puzzling Form of Cultures Today', in M. Featherstone and L. Scott (eds), *Spaces of Culture: City, Nation, World*, 194–213, London: Sage.

Woolf, G. (1992), 'The Unity and Diversity of Romanization', *Journal of Roman Archaeology*, 5: 349–52.

Woolf, G. (1994), 'Becoming Roman, Staying Greek: Culture, Identity and the Civilizing Process in the Roman East', *Proceedings of the Cambridge Philological Society*, 40: 116–43.

Woolf, G. (1997), *Becoming Roman: The Origins of Provincial Administration in Gaul*, Cambridge: Cambridge University Press.

Woolf, G. (2004), 'Cultural Change in Roman Antiquity: Observations on Agency', *Kodai*, 13/14: 157–67.

Part One

Confronting Identities: Othering Communities and Groups

1

Performing Identities in Rome's Western Provinces

Louise Revell

Introduction

For over thirty years, identity has been a key issue in Roman Studies as it has in the wider humanities and social sciences. Research has focused on ethnicity, gender, age, rank and, more recently, occupation. Texts have been critically deconstructed to tease out the rhetoric of the 'other', and material culture analysed to understand its meaning. Approaches have been adopted from other disciplines, including anthropology, social sciences, and philosophy. Inevitably, as we develop such approaches and engage with the ensuing debates, earlier assumptions have been questioned and problematized. In particular, the idea of essentialist identities has been rejected, assumptions about the easy transfer of present approaches to a past context have been challenged, and ideas of intersectionality have made everything a little more complicated. For those of us working with material evidence, there have been challenges as to whether we can even attempt to answer such questions without the confirmation of explicit textual statements.[1]

This complexity and the instability of self-identification and othering are a dominant theme in other chapters in this volume and demonstrate that, as a discipline, we have lost some of the earlier naivety about how to apply these ideas. In this chapter, I want to build on this and think about two questions in particular. The first addresses the two key themes of the conference: the relationship between performativity and the process of othering. The second derives from this performative approach, and examines how specific discourses become moments when multiple aspects of othering are worked through, creating a blurring between the polarities inherent in the creation of the 'other'. I will focus on the creation of local communities through urbanism and urban citizenship, using evidence predominantly from Baetica.

Identity, performativity, and the 'other'

Research into identity has formed an important component of Ancient History scholarship, whether explicitly stated or not. It forms part of a series of approaches that have sought to decentre the elite male narratives of these past societies and democratize them through the articulation of other experiences. Its foundations lay in the search for the invisible peoples, whether women, slaves, or homosexuals, and in Roman archaeology, it has formed part of a search for a subaltern perspective on Roman imperialism. Within the Anglophone world in particular, it has provided a route to talk about cultural change within the provinces in a context where 'Romanization' has become a problematic term.

Nevertheless, although identity has become a popular starting point for many studies or part of an on-trend title for their publication, in reality there are a variety of uses of the term. At one end of the scale, identity can be seen as a descriptor, be it man, woman, child, Roman, barbarian, soldier. The designation is taken as absolute and unproblematic, and once the person, the site, or the piece of material culture has been labelled, no further enquiry is needed. At the other end of the scale, identity is taken as problematic and changeable: it is not enough to allocate the label, it is necessary to interrogate what it meant and how it was manifested. My own work adopts this second approach: that as Roman archaeologists or historians we cannot say how any single person might have described themselves, but we can understand the conditions within which these labels were given a meaning.[2] It is impossible to provide a universal experience of 'the Roman woman'; instead, we can reconstruct the ideologies and discourses through which the experience of 'being a Roman woman' was both enabled and constrained.

At its most fundamental, identity is bound up in our sense of self: who we are and which groups we share an affinity with. At the same time, there is a second element: how we are viewed by others. These two perspectives may be the same, but there may also be differences, particularly in how an aspect of identity is judged. This becomes particularly apparent when we look at the question of professional or occupational identities in the Roman world. When viewed from the perspective of someone of higher status, an occupation may be seen as a sign of shame or a marker of a lesser social position. In contrast, to those who carry out such work, it may be a source of pride, through the required skills acquired through an apprenticeship or the generation of income to provide for their family. This potential dissonance can make research into identities of the past problematic as so often in the textual sources, the point of view presented is that of the more powerful.

A further complication is that a single person does not have a single aspect to their identity, but rather, multiple aspects. These may well encompass age, gender, sexuality, status, ethnicity, but also occupation, religion. These are not fixed, but may change over a lifetime, most obviously during the process of ageing from child to adult to elder, and various substages in between, but there may be other factors, such as change of profession, change in legal status, or change in religion. These elements will interact, breaking down the homogeneity within any specific identity group. An individual's sense of self will be a complex interplay of these different aspects, creating subgroups or subcultures. At times, this interaction may lead to an apparent rejection of one aspect of their identity, or the accusation from others of betrayal if their behaviours are deemed to contravene the expected social norms.

These problems have led to a complaint against research into identity that it is a form of palaeopsychology, and in reality we can never know what anyone thought their own identity was. However, this somewhat misunderstands the nature of any individual's identity, and arguably misapplies the individualization of the contemporary world to the past. In particular, it downplays the role of wider social structures on the individual. Identity is not an absolute nor a personal choice, but formed within the discourses at play within a particular society. By reconstructing these discourses and the positions within them, it then becomes possible to understand how identity in the past is formed. Therefore, an alternative approach is to use the range of evidence available to reconstruct such discourses or ideologies. From this starting point, it is possible to understand the expected behaviours for aspects of identity, how they intersected with other aspects, and how they might be contested and subverted.

Our sense of self, and other peoples' reading of our place within wider society is based on social encounters, whether the mundane routines of everyday living, or highly ceremonial encounters connected with politics or religion.[3] These are governed by social norms or informal rules which tie into the wider social discourses. They are based on a series of shared expectations about what is appropriate within these situations, in terms of behaviours, dress, speech, and so forth. To not know them, or to ignore them, is to be judged for that transgression, whether as an outsider, someone not expected to conform to them, or a rebel. Through these, we communicate who we are, our position within the various social structures, and which groups we belong to. At the same time, the other participants in the encounters will read off this information, and so decide how we relate to them, and how to treat us. Consequently, as we go into such encounters, we self-monitor. However, performativity is more than a mere show:

the internalization of these norms and behaviours by an individual creates this sense of self, and so they are part of the socialization into the wider group.

This brings us to the idea of othering or alterity. The discourses underpinning any aspect of identity rely on a definition of what is deemed appropriate or acceptable, but also what is inappropriate and unacceptable. A boundary is created, not a physical boundary, but rather a discursive boundary, expressed through behaviours, beliefs, and materials. Those who do not share these elements are seen as different. These oppositions can serve to bind one community together in the face of other communities, but they also serve to create groups within that society.[4] Consequently, an individual's identity is not formed in opposition to a single 'other', but as it is composed of multiple elements, so it requires multiple 'others'. Much of this is played out subconsciously in daily life, but there will be particular moments when the context highlights a particular aspect, whether it be ethnic/cultural identity, gender, religion, or any other aspect. At such moments, the associated boundaries and otherings will be more prominent. In this way, performativity involves the creation of ties of allegiance, but also statements of difference and othering.

Identity, performativity, and otherness are powerful elements of how any society operates. The communal identity gives coherence to a group, through a series of shared discourses. At the same time, the internal divisions with that society create complexity and subcultures. With the concept of othering, the group is given additional coherence by defining what it is not, something which is often less problematic than defining the ties which bind it. The shared beliefs and worldviews can be explicitly articulated, but often they underpin other elements of culture, such as myths or stories. Statements of belonging and difference are worked into the routines of shared experience and so analysing these routines can allow us to understand the structures of any particular society, but also how they are reproduced and recreated on a continuous basis. It is only through these repetitive activities that identities and groups are continually remade.

Creating a community of citizens

As argued, understanding such activities of identity maintenance can allow us to understand how past societies functioned. In this section, I want to explore how ethnic identities were articulated in the world and the outsider constructed. By ethnic identities, I do not mean the empire-wide invisible community of Roman versus non-Roman, but rather, the more localized ethnic identity based on membership of an urban community. This responds to work carried out on modern ethnic identities based on the nation-state, and the argument that in certain circumstances, these co-exist with nested identities – that is, an ethnic identity below that of the national identity.[5] This situation should not be entirely unfamiliar to scholars of the ancient world, as a similar situation has been argued for the ancient Greek world.[6] These local urban allegiances were an important element within Roman identities, but how were they given meaning as an element of an individual's identity, and what was the 'other' in these circumstances?

The changes brought by the incorporation into the Roman provinces have been extensively researched and documented, and it is not my intention here to go into them in any depth. Most pertinent to this chapter is the transformation of the western provinces from communities based on a tribe and tribal identity to one based on urban settlements and urban communities. The appearance of Roman-style towns has been extensively documented, but perhaps less discussed are the wider socio-political changes. The conquered areas were reorganized into provinces but from the second half of the first century BCE onwards, there was an increasing reorganization at a local level into communities dependent on an urban centre. This does not mean the entire community lived within the boundaries of the town but that they looked to the town as the centre of political authority, administration, and justice. Further attractions of the urban centres included religious worship, spectacular entertainments, and bathing.[7] From the time of Augustus, the physical urban centres were formalized through legal charters that created a political and legal structure in the image of Rome, but also envisaged a social structure similar to that of Rome.

Although it is usual to focus on the administrative and judicial impact of this urbanization, it is important to remember that it also resulted in a profound social transformation. The local communities ceased to be based around the ethos of the warrior and the warrior elite and instead were organized around the idea of citizenship with magistrates as leaders. This would have impacted on wider ideologies, such as political morality replacing martial valour as the model of masculinity. The potential continuity of authority for those at the top of the local hierarchies masks the disruption for those lower down the social ranks.[8] The internalization of this shift amongst these provincial communities can be seen in the language of citizenship and urban centres in defining both the community and the individual. Local identities became those of the urban centre, as demonstrated by the number of inscriptions in which a person self-identifies or is identified through their urban citizenship. This does not sit in opposition to a wider Roman identity but as I have argued elsewhere, here we are seeing nested ethnic identities.[9]

Work on citizenship in Rome has increasingly stressed the performative aspect: to be a citizen was to take part in public activities located within key spaces of the city. These took a variety of forms, such as the political acts of elections or taking part in assemblies, the ritual ceremonies of civic religion, or the militaristic celebrations of the triumph.[10] Through these communal activities citizenship was internalized as one criterion of being Roman. At the same time, not everyone within the group took the same role within these activities and so a difference was created. Within Rome's citizen body, the most immediate difference was between the equestrian/senatorial ranks and plebs through eligibility for personal political authority through the various magistracies and priesthoods. The visible authority of the senatorial elite performing their various duties made visible such status differences. At the same time, exclusion from political activity created further oppositions: between male and female, child and adult, freeborn and slave-born, citizen and non-citizen. These differences were not innocent, but were embedded in and legitimized the inherent inequalities within the urban community. Citizenship was seen to justify the authority of men over women, adult over child, and freeborn over slave, while the immigrant was reminded that they were not born into the community. Viewing rather than participating was a reminder of their otherness.

This idea of citizenship was promoted in the western provinces through the urban charters used for the provincial towns. A number of these exist but for the western provinces outside of Italy, the most important are from the Iberian provinces. These cover the two most frequent forms of urban constitution: towns given the status of *colonia* or *municipium*. One relates to a *colonia*: the *Lex Colonia Iulia Genetiva*, alternatively known as the *Lex Ursonensis*.[11] This is a Flavian copy of the charter for a *colonia* originally planned by Julius Caesar although potentially modified. The other charter, or group of charters, relates to the Flavian *municipia*, a major moment of urbanization in the peninsula. A number of these have been found, and together they suggest that there was a master charter which was then adopted for each town as appropriate. The text as it stands is a combination of the charters of Irni, Salpensa, and Malacitana.[12] Neither type of charter is complete, yet enough survives to understand the underpinning ideology of local urbanism. Furthermore, from these we can reconstruct the concept of citizenship as applied to these communities. In the following analysis, I draw mainly on the surviving chapters from the municipal charter, but much of the argument is likely to also apply to the *coloniae*.

Many of the extant chapters and much of the resulting academic literature focuses on the organization and administration of justice. However, for the purposes of this chapter, the elements of interest are those which outline the ceremonies surrounding citizenship. In particular, the municipal charter contains the guidance for holding the annual elections for magistrates. The detail allows us to reconstruct how such an event should be organized, and consequently, one moment when citizenship was performed. In these moments, each person internalized and reconfirmed their membership of the citizen group, and consequently this aspect of their identity. Furthermore, this was also when otherness from the urban community was expressed, creating insiders and outsiders. Not all of the urban community were citizens, and so the exclusion from active participation in the vote became a way of creating difference, and ultimately, formed part of the process of othering within the community. Therefore, we can use the detail of the elections to explore the two processes of performativity and othering.

Elections were held on an annual basis for the various ranks of local urban magistrates: duovirs, aediles, and quaestors. In the run up to the election, the presiding magistrate was required to gather nominations for candidates. These had to be made in his presence, and once he had a list of candidates, he was to publish them in a place where the list could be read from ground level. It is not stated where this list was to be set up: the forum would be the most likely, or a similar public space. It was clearly considered important that the election be contested: if not enough candidates were nominated, then those who were nominated could in turn nominate someone to stand against them. On the day of the election, the older of the two serving duovirs would usually take charge. Those eligible to vote were organized into curiae, and each curia had its own voting enclosure. Three scrutineers for each curia, chosen from a different curia, would swear an oath to act honestly and legally, and the candidates provided guarantees. All the citizens came together at the same time, and divided into the voting enclosures for their own curia. Each would cast their vote into the ballot box for their curia, watched by the three scrutineers and a representative for each candidate. Once the voting had taken place, the scrutineers counted the ballots for their curia and the results were declared. The first stage was to report who had gained the most votes in each curia, and lots were drawn to decide in what order the curiae would declare. The first would declare its choices, then the second, and so on until a candidate had achieved a majority of the curiae. At this point the presiding magistrate administered an oath to the successful candidate that he would act according to the charter and not intentionally do anything illegal. The oath was to be sworn before the *contio*, that is, in front of the assembled citizenry.

Such annual elections formed an event when membership of that community was reaffirmed, when a man who possessed the necessary qualification for urban citizenship acted as a citizen in the company of the rest of the citizen body. This was an act of communication: stating that he was a citizen and part of this group. At the same time, it was a moment when he was able to internalize that sense of who he was and how he fitted into this group. He was part of this urban community; his fellow citizens were those he stood with in the voting enclosures; the moment when he dropped his ballot for a specific candidate, he was reaffirming an ideology of membership through political activity. If he were selected to play a part in the scrutiny of the election process, he was responsible for ensuring the efficacy of the process, reaffirming its importance in the definition of the urban community. At the same time, this differentiated him from those who were not part of this system: the non-citizen. This created a form of performative othering: the exclusion from participating in the election created the perceived differences in identity which underlie the formation of the 'other', and the exclusion from the citizen body created a hierarchy between those who could participate and those who could not.

One group who were differentiated from the citizen were the *incolae*: those resident within the town, but not actually citizens.[13] *Incolae* are attested epigraphically in two main ways. The first is when an individual is identified as an *incola*, such as in the case of Quintus Cassius. His epitaph, which was found in Aurgi, describes him as being from the nearby town of Tucci, presumably possessing citizenship of that town, and as being an *incola* of Aurgi.[14] The two towns are set in opposition: he was from one, from which he would take his citizenship and *origo* (place of birth), and he was resident in the other. The second way in which *incolae* are attested is in inscriptions that record them acting alongside the local citizens, who may be described as *cives*, *municipes*, or *coloni*. Using the two terms together to stipulate the whole community is particularly pronounced in the dedication to Marcus Valerius Proculinus:

> M(arco) Valerio M(arci) f(ilio) / M(arci) n(epoti) G(ai) pron(epoti) Quir(ina) / Proculino IIvir(o) m(unicipum) m(unicipii) / liberi Singiliensis / cives et incolae ex aere conlato / hic in IIviratu publicos ludos et / totidem dierum privatos dedit / item populum universum in municipio / habitantem et incolas oleo et balineo / gratuito dato pervocavit / item quo die ludos iu(v)enum in theatro / dedit gymnasium et balinea viris et / mulieribus gratuita praestitit / huic cives et incolae pr(idie) K(alendas) Ianuarias / abeunti e IIviratu ob rem publicam / bene atministratam consensu omnium / in foro publice gratias egerunt et / hostias

> quas inmolaret item / statuam ex aere conlato dederunt / ordo decreto locum eligere / permisit / IIvir A(ulo) Cornelio Palma Front(on)iano II / P(ublio) Calvisio Tullo co(n)s(ulibus).[15]

Within this text, the *incolae* are explicitly mentioned three times, twice in relation to the donation of the honorific statue, and once as the recipients of Proculinus' largesse. The coupling of the two groups within the texts (*cives et incolae*) creates a difference between them while simultaneously giving the impression of the recipient earning the respect of the whole community.

The mechanism behind such dedications is unclear. Were there separate representatives of the two groups who agreed the dedication between them? Alternatively, and arguably more likely, these were set up at the instigation of the decurions generally (as they were required to give permission) or the duovirs themselves. If this second scenario was the case, then the use of the two terms together was presumably to emphasize that this was an honour on behalf of the whole community. To avoid the ambiguity that it was on behalf of one part of the community, *cives et incolae* makes this explicit, arguably amplifying the honour. The activities associated with the dedication are interesting: that citizens and the *incolae* gave public thanks in the forum and burnt offerings as he finished his year in office.

In the ancient world, an urban community was in most circumstances a small community. Cities such as Rome and Alexandria were very much the exception. Consequently, civic events formed an important definition of that community, who was a member, and who was not. Political activity was one way in which membership was acted out, but not the only way. The urban charters also allow for communal religious festivals and games in the theatre and amphitheatre. Inscriptions also record public banquets, and the judicial elements of the charter assume some form of judicial proceedings in the town. These different types of events were moments when being a citizen and part of that urban community were restated. It created a series of shared experience that tied the citizen body together at the same time as it tied them into the imaginary community of being Roman. In these circumstances, the 'other' was composed of those who were not part of the same urban community. The majority were distant others, but some lived in the same community as *incolae*. Their exclusion from political activity was symbolic of this distinction, but raises the question of whether religious and other types of events also marked them out. There is some suggestion that in theatres and amphitheatres, where seating was segregated according to social group, *incolae* might be allocated their own zone.[16]

The complexity of identity and the 'other'

Thus far I have presented a picture of a uniform body of citizens forming an urban community, reinforced by various forms of civic events. However, just as no person's identity can be reduced to a single element, likewise such encounters cannot be tied to the reproduction of a single element of identity. Whilst citizenship was a shared experience emphasizing the unity of the *cives* and the otherness of the *incolae*, in reality it was also part of the perpetuation of other aspects of belonging and difference. During the holding of an election, other forms of identity were also played out as political activity was also used in the creation and maintenance of other forms of identity and power hierarchies within the community. As a discourse, political participation served to legitimize the ideologies that underpinned them, creating a complex web of positions into which any one person fitted. This operated in two different ways. The intersection between the community-based identity and the other elements of personhood resulted in the different experiences of citizenship. Political performativity became tied up in the expression of other types of differences, and consequently the construction of different forms of othering. The second is that these intersections created a fuzziness to the boundary between politically active citizen and non-politically active citizen, opening a gap for certain types of people to transcend the apparent rigidity of these categories.

The first aspect to consider is how different levels of authority were maintained through political activity. One element of this was who was eligible to stand as a candidate for election. The urban magistracies were confined to a specific group within the community and not all citizens could stand for election. Some of the criteria are laid out in chapter fifty-four of the municipal law: to be eligible a candidate had to be male, he had to be freeborn, and he had to be over twenty-five years of age. This chapter does not stipulate a wealth qualification but from other evidence we can assume that one existed. Eligibility for election provided a means of distinguishing between wealthy and non-wealthy citizens. Service as a magistrate was something which brought authority and standing within the community, and this was perpetuated through membership of the *ordo* or town council. This created a separate social class of decurions who were marked not only by wealth but also by the assumption that they possessed greater political ability, which was channelled into the good of the town, as seen in the dedication to Proculinus (above): *ob rem publicam bene atministratum consensus omium*.

In the election and its aftermath, the magistrate was differentiated from the rest of the population in a number of ways. The authority of his role was confirmed by the presiding officer having to be a magistrate, thus making him the most visible person within the election. Magistrates were visibly marked out from the rest of the population as they were accorded certain privileges due to their position. They dressed differently as magistrates were allowed to wear the toga praetexta with its broad purple stripe, in contrast to the other *cives* wearing the plain white toga or local dress. He would probably be attended by an entourage provided by the town. We do not have the details of this within the municipal charter but from the colonial charter we can surmise that this might include lictors, scribes, messengers, a herald, a flute player, and general servants.[17] These may have been community slaves, but some may have been freemen appointed by the magistrate.[18] The incoming newly elected magistrate swore an oath attesting to his responsibility for the good management of the town, which visibly confirmed his membership of this magisterial elite as the election was announced. The oath accorded with an ideology of political authority reserved for the wealthy elite and, conversely, the elite justifying their position through their perceived service to the community. It added a moral element to this, in that a member of the elite class deemed unworthy of office could be challenged in court according to the colonial charter.[19]

The second aspect of complexity raised by the intersection between different elements of an individual's identity was where the power and authority accorded to one aspect contradicted that of another aspect. One example of this was the intersection between legal status and the criteria for magisterial status. Those who were born slaves were banned from magisterial service once they had been freed, yet in terms of wealth, they were eligible for membership of the decurial class. The freedman, as has been demonstrated in recent research, formed a difficult category between slave and freeborn.[20] One means used to accommodate their otherness was through the priesthoods associated with the imperial cult, the Augustales and the Sevires, which brought some of the privileges of the magisterial class.[21] Another way was to award the *ornamenta* (accoutrements) of a decurion to specific individuals. Both means were used to bring Marcus Helvius Anthus from the status of 'other' to a more prominent part of the citizen community. The inscription recoding the dedication of a statue to him gives an insight into some of the ways his otherness was masked through the language of the magistracies:

> M(arcus) Helvius Anthus Lucurg(entinus) / IIIIIvir Aug(ustalis) edito spec/taculo per quadridu/um ludorum scaeni/corum et dato gym/nasio per eosdem / dies item mulie/ribus balineum gra/tis huic ordo splen/didissimus Lucurgentin/

orum petente populo orna/menta decurionatus decrevit / Helvius Anthus ob honorem / statuam tan(t)i patris cum basi s(ua) p(ecunia) d(onum) d(edit) / p(opulus)q(ue) f(ecit).[22]

Some of the similarities between this and the Proculinus inscription are striking: both donated games and access to bathing to the townspeople, and both were honoured by both the town council and the plebs. As a sevir, Anthus would have held a religious authority similar to that wielded by Proculinus as part of his role as duovir. On public occasions, both would have carried out similar roles. For example, as the producer of games of various kinds, both would have had some form of prominent role, such as leading any procession to the games, or having a position of prominence in the tribunal of the theatre or amphitheatre. During public sacrifices and other religious festivals, each may have acted as an officiating priest, again taking a visible position of authority, their heads covered with their toga as an act of reverence or *pietas*. Finally, here we see the honour of *ornamenta decurionatus* granted to Anthus by the *ordo* at the request of the *populus*. This might refer to specific seats at games and public banquets, for example, which diminished the visible difference between them and other decurions, granting them the indicators of the highest form of urban citizenship.[23] We usually discuss such honours in abstract terms, but viewing these honours through the lens of performativity allows us to understand the very visible means of blurring the boundary between political insider and outsider.

The problems of reconciling contradictory levels of legal status can also be seen if we return to the case of the *incolae*. As argued above, these were defined as different by excluding them from political activity. For most *incolae*, this would not have been incongruent, but for those who were Roman citizens, there was a contrast between the respect due to their legal status as Roman citizen and their lack of inclusion in the local citizen community. This was reconciled by some of the means we have already seen with respect to the granting of *ornamenta* or priesthoods. There was also the possibility of being adopted into the citizen body/decurionate, as seen in the case of Lucius Aemilius Rectus, mentioned in a series of inscriptions from Carthago Nova.[24] His place of origin is unknown, although it has been suggested that it was somewhere in central Italy. He was part of the imperial administration, serving as a *scriba* (scribe) in Rome and in a number of provinces. At some point he presumably came to Iberia and settled in Carthago Nova, where he was granted local citizenship. Even without this formal process of *adlectio*, it was possible for a Roman citizen such as Rectus to participate in local politics if he was resident within the town. The municipal charter stipulates that in the magisterial elections, Roman citizens resident in the town were to be enrolled as a group into one of the curiae, and vote as part of the curia as though they were a citizen.[25]

The idea of creating difference between who was and who was not an active citizen can be taken beyond the divisions according to status and extended to gender and age. Women and children were legally regarded as citizens of the community, yet at the same time they were excluded from participation in the political life of the town. In this way, citizenship was incorporated into ideologies connected with other forms of identity, and became part of the justification for the hierarchies within these. For example, women could not vote because they were considered feeble minded and in need of guardianship. Children and adolescents could not vote because they did not yet have the necessary maturity, although if male and freeborn, there was the knowledge that this would be their future role.[26] Nevertheless, for women and the young, their exclusion from political activities such as the vote became a way to internalize their position as the 'other' to the more privileged adult, male citizen who was allowed to participate.

Nevertheless, as with the *incolae*, the complex intersection between gender, rank, and group identities blurred these oppositions. For women from families of rank, it was possible for them to take a more active role in local politics, although not an equal one to their male relatives. One of the most prolific women in Roman Iberia was Acilia Plecusa, who resided in Singilia Barba. She dedicated a series of six statues: to a provincial magistrate and his wife, and to her own husband, son, and daughter.[27] She is also mentioned on three family inscriptions, including her own tombstone. Her name on this series of statues placed her in the public arena, to be viewed by the townspeople. The two statues to women would also have created an impression of them being honoured in a similar fashion to the leading men of the town. However, in terms of thinking through the performative aspects of these dedications, there are a number of uncertainties. Did Acilia need to petition the *ordo* of decurions, especially in the case of the three dedications to her family? There is no mention in these inscriptions of any acts of munificence linked to their dedications, reducing the opportunity for Acilia and her family to interact with the citizen population as donors. This is in marked contrast to the dedication to Proculinus discussed earlier, which had clear indications of a relationship with the citizen body through his generosity and through their (apparent) desire to honour him. This leaves Acilia in an ambiguous position: apparently participating in the system of honouring others for political service, but not able to actively exercise political authority herself. Her otherness to the male citizens is reaffirmed, whilst her wealth sets her apart from other women.

Consequently, whilst political activity as part of the acts of the citizen created a sense of the community, it was not necessarily a uniform community. The realities of citizenship varied according to other social structures, such as gender or legal status. These fed into each other, and so we can view citizenship and the associated performances such as elections, games, and public sacrifices as locales when identities were acted out, differences from other types of identities shown, and the complex intersecting identities for any one individual person negotiated and internalized.

The shifting significance of urban citizenship – the case of Conventus Astigitanus

I have argued that membership of the urban community, as defined through citizenship and participation in community-based events, provides an important form of identity in the Roman world, whilst at the same time, being a point where the intersection with other forms of group identities enables distinctions to be made. These rest upon the creation of differences between groups through the daily rituals of urban life. In this final section, I want to add in a further layer of complexity: the shifting significance and meaning of these differences across space and time. The mutability of othering has been argued for the construction of the 'other' from textual sources. Edith Hall, for example, argues that the Greek creation of the Persian 'other' in the fifth century BCE came to the forefront after the Persian Wars.[28] Similarly, Andrew Wallace-Hadrill has argued for the creation of a Roman identity during the Augustan period as a shifting negotiation between the Greek and the Italic others.[29] The question can then be posed as to whether we can identify something similar within these provincial identities. Understanding this from the epigraphic and material evidence is more problematic on a number of fronts. The broad dating of these expressions of identity makes tying them into known historical events difficult, and in many cases, the detailed narrative is missing due to the Rome-centric focus of our sources.[30] The explicit display of identity is situational and the dominant characteristic will depend on the nature of the interaction. In certain circumstances, membership of a particular gender may be more important, in others it may be a professional group. This does not obliterate the other aspects, which still form part of an individual's underlying sense of self.

One issue facing the study of the Roman provinces is that the dominance of the Romanization has led to an emphasis on Roman with the 'other' as the native/barbarian/indigenous. The model of the modern nation-state and national identity have been applied with limited questioning of their applicability. Instead, we can argue for a Roman world much closer to the Greek.[31] An individual may tie their sense of belonging into the wider Roman koine through Roman citizenship or through shared cultural norms such as the authority of the emperor or methods of worshipping the gods.[32] Nevertheless, this was not at odds with membership of other groups; the work of sociologists and anthropologists has pointed to such nested identities, where a national identity can co-exist with other cultural attachments.[33] Within the civilian world, we might look for the existence of a provincial identity, or a more regional-based one, perhaps derived from former tribal regions. The development of these urban-based communities, expressed through citizenship and formalized through the urban charters, was a key part of an individual's self-identification, as demonstrated by the number of inscriptions recording the urban *origo* of individuals, not only in Iberia, but throughout the western provinces. However, we cannot treat this as a timeless and homogeneous phenomenon.

If we take the process of othering as a complex and unstable phenomenon, we can use the material discussed here to understand elements of the variability in its meaning. The first is to take an idea proposed by Greg Woolf in respect of Roman Gaul.[34] In the formation of provincial cultures, the initial difference was not between the community and the barbarian, but between the community and their own tribal past. The 'other' was their ancestors, who did not live in urban settings and therefore lay outside an idea of civilization based upon political authority and systems of justice residing in an urban context.[35] For the earliest generations living under Roman rule and within Roman-style towns, the adherence to a Roman form of identity, however imperfectly to their imperial rulers, was a prominent part of their sense of self. However, the epigraphic evidence demonstrates that, over time, this was replaced by the importance of local origin. Where we see statements of an ethnic identity, it is in terms of urban citizenship, and in most cases, it is in places where the individual was a stranger or *incola*.[36] For the inner provinces, they would rarely meet anyone who was not part of the Roman Empire (in contrast to the frontier regions) and consequently the 'other' became those who were from a different town. This did not eradicate a feeling of being part of the Roman community, but this was arguably a more important part of the daily encounters.

This picture would be recognizable in most of the western provinces, but it was not the case in one particular region of Iberia: the Conventus Astigitanus. Here there is a different pattern in the use of ethnonyms. There are the expected cases of individuals who are not from the area and state which town they are a citizen of. However, these are fewer in number than those which state their *origo* within that very town. For example, if we look at the town of Ilurco, there are four examples of ethnic statements on inscriptions found in the town and its territory, all referring to an *origo* of Ilurco itself. These were all funerary inscriptions, and the epitaphs for three men and one woman refer to them as *Ilurcensis*.[37] This phenomenon of using ethnonyms in the town they were derived from is also seen in Nescania, where all personal ethnonyms refer to the individuals as being from Nescania. The importance of explicitly stating this allegiance is evident in the inscription commemorating the dedication of a statue to the *Genius* of the *Municipium*.[38] The name of the town is given four times in the inscription: the *Genius* is named as the *Genius Municipi Nescaniensis*; the dedicator and the heir who carried out his wishes are both described using the ethnonym, and it is stated that the statue was set up in the forum in Nescania. The accumulation of the naming of the town within this single inscription is remarkable in stressing the importance of the local identity.

In total, over half of the recorded personal ethnic statements in the Conventus recorded the same ethnicity as the place where they were set up.[39] Here, a far more explicit contrast is being set up between the citizens and the *incolae*. Why this was the case was unclear. Work on inscriptions and more recent techniques within bioarchaeology are making it clear that mobility was much greater than previously assumed within the Roman Empire.[40] Perhaps here we are seeing a population feeling overwhelmed by incomers and so emphasizing their legal status as citizens of that town in contrast to the otherness of the incomers. This would certainly tie in with the density of urban settlement in the area and so the small size of each town's territory. Stating this membership of the community suggests that marking out differences has greater significance than elsewhere in the western provinces.

Both examples here of different intensities and meanings in the processes of othering warn against taking an essentialist approach to the 'other' within the provinces. This accords with wider perspectives which see far more variability in provincial social and political dynamics. As we move away from a homogenizing approach, we need to apply this finer-grained analysis and accept that not everything can be viewed through a Roman/barbarian lens. In these cases, the process of othering may have been applied to neighbouring communities and the past itself.

Conclusions

In this chapter, I have addressed the relationship between identity, othering, and performativity through a case study of civic identities. An important element of this has been the complex interplay of different elements of identity, how they create multiple others, and how they are enacted through regular routines such as the local elections when various groups play out their particular roles. In this examination, the focus has been on the identities of the group rather than the individual. Although named individuals from the epigraphic record have been used in the reconstruction of some of these civic events, they stand as representative of the group or of the 'other'. Through this focus on the group and the way in which the differences were enacted which ultimately produced the 'other', it has been possible to reconstruct the variety of experiences of a single event. However, although these have been presented in somewhat neutral terms, it is important to remember that othering or the creation of difference is rarely an innocent activity. In reality, othering is a process connected with power and the inequality of power relations. Discourses of otherness have been used to claim moral superiority and greater authority, legitimizing and justifying such claims. At their extremes, they are used to dehumanize the 'other' and have been tied into acts of intolerance and violence. This is clearly the case when there is conflict, armed or otherwise, between large political groups and nations. This has been clearly argued in the case of the fifth-century BC conflict between the Greeks and the Persians, and can also be seen in the western construction of the oriental.[41] It can also be seen on a more local scale as structuring relationships within communities. Here, it is tied into the inequalities of a society, often almost unsaid. Nevertheless, these discourses have been used to justify the authority of elite over non-elite, male over female, adult over child.

In thinking through these power relations and the way discourses of identity and otherness create such positions, there has been a tendency in the past to focus on those with authority or power. One reading of the account of the annual elections for the magistrates is to focus on the dominant position: that of the magistrate, through his acquisition of power, and his proclamation of that status through media such as inscriptions and statues. However, as I have demonstrated, this is not the only experience of these civic events. For the crowds of unnamed non-elite citizens, such moments also reaffirmed their roles within the society and their sense of self. We cannot put a name to them, as we can for Proculinus, but we can understand the social structures which led to them identifying as a *civis* of that town. At the same time, we can also reconstruct how this shared citizenship broke down under the intersections with wealth, legal status, gender or age, and further, how some people were able to claim greater visibility whilst others were rendered more invisible. The contribution of this form of analysis of the past is that it allows us to understand how the less powerful members of these societies were excluded from authority, and how that was justified and internalized. Ultimately, it has the potential to allow a more complete exploration of these provincial communities.

Notes

1 Hall 1997; Antonaccio 2010.
2 Revell 2009, 2015.
3 For performativity as a concept, Butler 1999; similar ideas underpin Goffmann 1959 and Bourdieu 1977.
4 For example, Barth 1969; Nash 1989.
5 Eriksen 1991, 2001.
6 Malkin 2001; Crielaard 2009.
7 Laurence et al. 2011.
8 Woolf 1998.
9 Revell 2015.
10 For example, Patterson 2000; Sumi 2005; Beard 2007.
11 Crawford 1996.
12 González 1986.
13 Mackie 1983.
14 CIL II^{2}/5.41.
15 CIL II^{2}/5.789.
16 Kolendo 1981.
17 Lex Ursonensis: Crawford 1996: §62.
18 As outlined in the colonial charter.
19 Lex Ursonensis: Crawford 1996: §129.
20 Petersen 2006; Mouritsen 2011.
21 Mackie 1993: 63–4.
22 CIL II.1209
23 Mackie 1983.
24 CIL II.3423, 3424, 5951, 5942; Abascal Palazón and Ramallo Asensio 1997.
25 Lex Malacitana: González 1986: §53.
26 Laurence 2006.
27 CIL II^{2}/5 780–781 to Publius Magnius Rufus Magonianus, 782 to his wife, 784 to her husband, 795 to her son, and 796 to her daughter.
28 Hall 1989.
29 Wallace-Hadrill 2008.
30 As argued in Revell 2002.
31 Malkin 2001.

32 This forms the basis of Revell 2009.
33 Eriksen 1991, 2001.
34 Woolf 1998.
35 For example, Cic., *de Inv. Rhet.* 1.2–3, *pro Sestio* 91–92.
36 Derks 2009.
37 CIL II^2/5 682–684, 707.
38 CIL II^2/5838.
39 The inscriptions analysed were taken from CIL II^2/5 and the data exclude those which relate specifically to political institutions such as the *ordo*, the decurions, or the plebs as a whole.
40 Haley 1991; Eckardt 2010.
41 Said 1979.

Bibliography

Abascal Palazón, J. M. and S. Ramallo Asensio (1997), *La Ciudad de Cathago Nova: la documentación epigrafíca*, Murcia: Universidad de Murcia.

Antonaccio, C. M. (2010), '(Re)defining Ethnicity: Culture, Material Culture and Identity', in S. Hales and T. Hodos (eds), *Material Culture and Social Identities in the Ancient World*, 32–53, Cambridge: Cambridge University Press.

Barth, F. (1969), 'Introduction', in F. Barth (ed.), *Ethnic Groups and Boundaries: The Social Organization of Cultural Difference*, 9–38, Oslo: Universitetsforlaget.

Beard, M. (2007), *The Roman Triumph*, Cambridge, MA: Harvard University Press.

Bourdieu, P. (1977), *Outline of a Theory of Practice*, Cambridge: Cambridge University Press.

Butler, J. (1999), *Gender Trouble: Feminism and the Subversion of Identity*, London: Routledge.

Crawford, M. (1996), *Roman Statutes*, Bulletin of the Institute of Classical Studies #64, London: Univerisity of London.

Crielaard, J. P. (2009), 'The Ionians in the Archaic Period: Shifting Identities in a Changing World', in T. Derks and N. Roymans (eds), *Ethnic Constructs in Antiquity: The Role of Power and Tradition*, 37–84, Amsterdam: Amsterdam University Press.

Derks, T. (2009), 'Ethnic Identity in the Roman Frontier: The Epigraphy of Batavi and Other Lower Rhine Tribes', in T. Derks and N. Roymans (eds), *Ethnic Constructs in Antiquity*, 239–82, Amsterdam: Amsterdam University Press.

Eckardt, H., ed. (2010), *Roman Diasporas: Archaeological Approaches to Mobility and Diversity in the Roman Empire*, Journal of Roman Archaeology Supplementary Series #78, Portsmouth, RI: JRA.

Eriksen, T. H. (1991), 'Ethnicity versus Nationalism', *Journal of Peace Research*, 28 (3): 263–78.

Eriksen, T. H. (2001), *Small Places, Large Issues: An Introduction to Social and Cultural Anthropology*, London: Pluto Press.
Goffmann, E. (1959), *The Presentation of the Self in Everyday Life*, New York: Doubleday.
González, J. (1986), 'The Lex Irnitana: A New Copy of the Flavian Municipal Law', *Journal of Roman Studies*, 76: 147–243.
Haley, E. W. (1991), *Migration and Economy in Roman Imperial Spain*, Barcelona: Publicacions Universitat de Barcelona.
Hall, E. (1989), *Inventing the Barbarian: Greek Self-definition through Tragedy*, Oxford: Clarendon Press.
Hall, J. M. (1997), *Ethnic Identity in Greek Antiquity*, Cambridge: Cambridge University Press.
Kolendo, J. (1981), 'La répartition des places aux spectacles et la stratification sociale dans l'Empire Romain: à propos des inscriptions sur les gradins des amphithéâtres et théâtres', *Ktema*, 6: 301–13.
Laurence, R. (2006), *Roman Pompeii: Space and Society*, 2nd edition, London: Routledge.
Laurence, R., S. Esmonde-Cleary and G. Sears (2011), *The City in the Roman West, c. 250 BC–c. AD 250*, Cambridge: Cambridge University Press.
Mackie, N. (1983), *Local Administration in Roman Spain, AD 14–212*, Oxford: BAR Publishing.
Malkin, I. (2001), 'Introduction', in I. Malkin (ed.), *Ancient Perceptions of Greek Ethnicity*, Cambridge, MA: Harvard University Press.
Mouritsen, H. (2011), *The Freedman in the Roman World*, Cambridge: Cambridge University Press.
Nash, M. (1989), *The Cauldron of Ethnicity in the Modern World*, Chicago, IL: University of Chicago Press.
Patterson, J. (2000), *Political Life in the City of Rome*, Bristol: Bristol Classical Press.
Petersen, L. H. (2006), *The Freedman in Roman Art and Art History*, Cambridge: Cambridge University Press.
Revell, L. (2002), 'Story-telling in Roman Archaeology', *Archaeological Dialogues*, 9 (1): 44–47.
Revell, L. (2009), *Roman Imperialism and Local Identities*, Cambridge: Cambridge University Press.
Revell, L. (2015), *Ways of Being Roman: Discourses of Identity in the Roman West*, Oxford: Oxbow Books.
Said, E. (1979), *Orientalism*, London: Routledge.
Sumi, G. S. (2005), *Ceremony and Power. Performing Politics in Rome between Republic and Empire*, Ann Arbor, MI: University of Michigan Press.
Wallace-Hadrill, A. (2008), *Rome's Cultural Revolution*, Cambridge: Cambridge University Press.
Woolf, G. (1998), *Becoming Roman: The Origins of Provincial Civilization in Gaul*, Cambridge: Cambridge University Press.

2

Decolor heres: Dark Skin in the Roman Cultural Imagination[1]

Mario Lentano

On 30 May 2021, news appeared online that those intending to graduate in Classics at Princeton University would no longer be required to know Greek and Latin, 'in a push to create a more inclusive and equitable program'. In the view of the professors who shared this decision, students entering the Department of Classics without 'previous exposure' to the classical languages 'will make it a more vibrant intellectual community'. What is more, the department's role 'in the long arc of systemic racism' is evident in their view.[2] To tell the truth, the examples given to justify these contrite affirmations relate more to the utilisation of slaves by the founders and benefactors of the University, on whose largesse the institution's financing then partly rested, than to racism strictly conceived. In any case, there can be no doubt that Princeton University's choice takes place in the context of a wider tendency that appears to be gathering pace in the United States and United Kingdom, which imputes to the classics – I mean, in this case, ancient Latin and Greek authors, not the departments that study them – the status of pathogens that should be kept at a distance, apparently because they are still considered capable of exercising a sort of contaminating effect on students who might come into contact with them. Even the choice of a term like 'exposure' to indicate the study of ancient languages in high schools is telling in this regard, since it is the same term used, for instance, to denote exposure to radiation or to the harmful effects of environmental pollutants.

This contribution offers too small a space to confront questions of such complexity and about which, besides, a sizeable bibliography has already accumulated in recent years.[3] Nevertheless, what I would like to try to suggest is that although Rome's history – for Greece the story would be different, at least in part – has been marked undeniably by much that is appalling (at least according to how our contemporary culture classifies behaviours), among these we do not find racism, systemic or otherwise, at least if we understand by this term the belief that the members of certain human groups possess characteristics that make them inferior and that legitimize discrimination against them, simply on account of belonging to this or that group.[4]

To begin with, the geo-climatic doctrine – theorized for the first time, in my understanding, at the end of the fifth century BCE in the Pseudo-Hippocratic treatise *Airs, Waters, and Places*, and diffused in Rome already in the late Republican period as the dominant paradigm for describing the differences between people and ethnicities – attributes differences above all to environmental factors. In the simplified version of the model that developed in the Roman world (probably thanks to Posidonius' ethnography), the theory clearly distinguished between peoples of the North and peoples of the South – the former being marked by light skin, large bodies, straight and light-coloured head and body hair, deep voices, and abundant blood; the latter, by contrast, because of their proximity to the sun, being marked by smaller bodies, curly hair, darker pigmentation, and a general prevalence of the dry element, resulting in scarcer blood. This distinction, based largely on corporal features, was associated with a second, psychological and attitudinal feature, which opposed the excessive martial courage of northern populations – valorous but tending to be reckless in the face of danger – to the excessive prudence of southern peoples, a vice that was only in part compensated for by their greater intellect. Between these extremes, Greece – and later Rome – presented an ideal balance of characteristics, which allowed its inhabitants to impose their hegemony on the rest of the world and simultaneously legitimated the position of primacy that they enjoyed.[5]

In other words, the characteristics of human communities do not come from any intrinsic (and so structural and indelible) features, but from external factors, as shown by the fact that changing such external factors could bring about a modification of characteristics and attitudes.[6] To give only one example: the Galatians or Gallo-Greeks, inhabitants of a region of Asia Minor which took from them the name of Galatia, were a Celtic tribe, originally from the Transalpine region, who emigrated to Anatolia during the third century BCE. According to the Roman historians, however, the environmental context of their new homeland brought it about that the Galatians lost some of the features associated with northern populations (especially their unthinking aggressiveness in war). The mild climate of Asia and the abundant resources available in their new territory in fact altered the nature of the Gallo-Greeks, clouding and cancelling the *feritas* (ferocity) that had characterized them previously.[7] The Roman sources explain this metamorphosis by analogy to the plant world, likening what happened to the Galatians to what happens to seeds when they are planted in soil different from customary.[8] At the same time, a similar way of posing the question highlights how, for ancient cultures, the traits that identify a people are not tied to innate and immutable characteristics, but can be modified to a significant extent, if the context in which its members find themselves living has changed. Not by chance, the opposite of what happened to the Galatians happened to the inhabitants of Massalia (modern Marseille), an ancient Greek outpost on the Mediterranean coast of Gaul, in the heart of the Celtic zone. Through continual contact with their barbarian neighbours, Livy observes, the Massaliotes 'took on a certain aggressiveness', which evidently the original Greek inhabitants of the city did not possess.[9]

But what to say of those dark-skinned peoples, to which the pronouncements of Princeton University specifically refer, and which constitute the preferred target of modern-day racisms? In this case, too, the information that can be found scattered throughout ancient sources does not appear to indicate the existence of any special stigma.[10] Let's begin with something that has not often attracted the attention of scholars, but that appears – to me – to be meaningful. At no moment in their history do the Romans, as the Greeks before them, ever appear to be collectively defined as 'white'. In Latin, the adjective *albus* can be used as an antonym of 'person of colour', but it does not ever appear to have been used in the plural to designate individuals of light complexion collectively.[11] This is not some mere terminological subtlety. In a passage of surpassing insight at the beginning of his *Histories*, Thucydides reflects on the absence of the term 'barbarian' in the Homeric poems, and justifies this absence by observing that during the period in which the poems were composed, the Greeks 'had not yet been marked off from the rest of the world by one distinctive appellation'.[12] Thus, according to the great Athenian historian, conceptions of 'Greek' and of 'barbarian' emerged together, and the latter had no reason to exist except in opposition to the former. If 'barbarians' do not appear in Homer, it is because the 'Greeks' themselves do not appear, either (or, at least, they were not yet endowed with a unique name that encompassed them all as a whole). Thucydides' reflection is striking for its understanding of how categories take form only through their relations and dialectically. Now, for the opposition 'white' vs. 'Black', an analogous process can be imagined. The two terms make sense only in relation to one another, as poles of a single dichotomy. So, the fact that the Romans did not define themselves in terms of the colour of their skin (that is, that they never call themselves *albi* –whites) appears to exclude that, in their eyes, another analogous category existed that included those who did *not* share that colour, identified as a separate and opposed grouping.

Second, in order to describe individuals of dark skin, Latin normally uses ethnonymic terms: *Maurus* and above all *Aethiops*. *Aethiops*, in particular, refers properly to the inhabitants of Ethiopia, the vast area that ancient geography located at the extreme edge of the world and that over the course of time was identified specifically with the area south of Egypt. This choice is interesting for several reasons.[13] To begin with, *Aethiops* is a compound adjective, which in its Greek matrix alludes to the appearance of skin 'burnt' by the sun. In respect to modern designations like *ne(g)ro*, *noir*, Black, and so on, it is not so much, then, a chromatic feature of the skin that comes to be emphasized, as its origin, which is again traced back to the influence of an environmental or climatic factor: close exposure to the heat of the sun. This is precisely what encouraged Lucretius, in two passages of the *De rerum natura*, to speak of the Ethiopians' 'completely cooked colour (*percoctus color*)'.[14] Furthermore, in ancient literature the Ethiopians are a familiar and indeed highly valourized people, already in Homer.[15] So far as we can tell, when they are tired of Olympus – or, more concretely, when the poet needs to free the scene of their cumbersome presence – the gods betake themselves, collectively or individually, to banquet among the Ethiopians, as Poseidon does at the beginning of the *Odyssey*. Poseidon is not present when it is agreed, in Zeus' vast hall, that Odysseus will return home – something he had long tried to prevent – and Homer justifies his absence by explaining:

> now the distant Ethiopians,
> who live between the sunset and the dawn,
> were worshipping the Sea God with a feast,
> a hundred cattle and a hundred rams.
> There sat the god, delighting in his banquet.[16]

In the *Iliad*, the gods spend a total of twelve days in Ethiopia, requiring Thetis, the mother of Achilles, to wait before meeting Zeus, before she can argue to him in favour of her son, who has been embarrassed by Agamemnon's arrogance. At the end of the poem, moreover, Iris goes to the Ethiopians to take part in the hecatombs offered to the gods.[17] So the Ethiopians, at the extreme edge of the world, enjoy the same commensality with the gods that Odysseus will enjoy in another margin space, the island of the Phaeacians, but that is unattainable by common man. Not by chance, the Ethiopians are described repeatedly by the ancients as a flawless people, specially devoted to the gods, whose benevolence they acquired by being the first to introduce sacrifices, festivals, and celebrations in their honour.[18] Furthermore, none of this made the Ethiopians weaklings or cowardly hedonists, devoted exclusively to dinner parties and religious festivals.

The hero Memnon, son of Aurora, came from Ethiopia, who with his band of dark-skinned warriors fought bravely by the side of the Trojans in one of the many narrative developments that flourished around the famous war, finally to be killed by Achilles. And in a well-known passage of the third book of Herodotus, the king of the Ethiopians 'of long life', scoffs at the threat of Cambyses to march against his country, giving a scornful response to the ambassadors who came to ask, on behalf of the Persians, for their submission.[19] Even in the garb of slaves the Ethiopians seem to be appreciated, even if only as an exotic curiosity. In a comedy of Terence – and already, presumably, in its Greek original – the young man Phaedria claims among his titles of merit that of having brought as a gift to his beloved courtesan a young Ethiopian slave-girl, whom the woman had insisted on having.[20]

We understand that the bodily traits of people of colour – curly hair, full lips, flat nose, to which are sometimes added thin and bowed legs, flat feet and, for women, abundant breasts – were well known to Greeks and Romans and recur often in their descriptions or iconographic representations of individuals belonging to these populations. In this case, too, however, a negative value does not seem to have been attributed to these features, except perhaps on a purely aesthetic level.[21] Already in the sixth century BCE the poet and philosopher Xenophanes of Colophon, in a famous passage in which he stresses how every human culture has elaborated an image of the gods beginning from its own physical characteristics, and after the striking claim that cows, lions, or horses, if they possessed hands, would depict the gods according to the model of their own bodies, goes on to explain that the Ethiopians venerate dark-skinned, snub-nosed gods, while the Thracians, on the other side of the world, depict them with blue eyes and red hair.[22] In a text like this, it is the same radical relativism that inspires reasoning to exclude that Xenophanes wanted to give the Ethiopians any negative connotation because of their skin colour.

In an entirely different period and context, similar conclusions are suggested by a brilliant but biting epigram of Martial:

> You have become a father, Cinna, from Marulla of seven
> not children: for not any are yours
> nor is one a son of your friend or neighbor,
> but conceived on pallets and mats
> they reveal their mother's indiscretions by their heads.
> This one with curled hair, who moves in a Mauritanian way
> shows himself to be the progeny of the cook Santra.
> But that one with a flat nose, and swollen lips

is the spitting image of Pannychus, director of the wrestling school.
Who is unaware that the third boy is the baker's,
whoever recognizes and sees bleary-eyed Dama?[23]

The epigram continues, mentioning other sons and daughters of Cinna, but its meaning is already clear from the part we have just cited. The unchaste Marulla has conceived seven times by so many different fathers, none of whom happens to be her actual husband. To her misfortune, however – and above all by means of the ancient understandings of transmission of appearances, which recognize the determining role of the paternal imprint – the features all come to be reproduced in their faces of the man from whom they were conceived, inevitably unmasking the woman's *materna furta*.[24] Among the many partners identified securely by Martial, it seems certain that the *palaestrita* Pannychus was imagined as a man of colour, given the recurrence of conventional descriptive elements like the snub nose and full lips.[25] A man of colour is in all likelihood (even if in this case there is not full agreement among scholars) also the son of Santra the cook, whose curly hair Martial mentions and whom he describes as *Maurus*, properly 'of the colour of the Mauritanians': a North African ethnic group that one part of the sources connected precisely with the Ethiopians and considered a kind of eastern offspring of that 'Black' people *par excellence*.[26] In any case – and this is what most counts in our perspective – in the eyes of the epigrammatist, the sexual relations enjoyed by Marulla with partners of colour do not seem to have brought the woman any particular opprobrium. Her two 'Black' lovers are cited by Martial on equal footing with the others, without their ethnic origin being attributed any special emphasis. What is important in his eyes is only the servile status that they share, as the initial pun shows on the double meaning of *liberi* (legitimate children and free individuals).

It is true, however, that at least in some cases adultery consummated with an individual of dark skin appears to bring an additional element of degradation, especially when the woman involved in that relation is not any Marulla but the irreprehensible Lucretia, that national heroin and unquestionable model of matronly chastity. The night on which Sextus Tarquinius entered her bedroom with the intention of raping her, Lucretia's resistance, as is known, was conquered by the threat of killing her and of placing in her bed, beside her body, a nude slave, and then accusing her of having been caught *in flagrante delicto* in the course of a sordid adultery.[27] Now, it is interesting that in one probably late version of this tale, cited in a note of Servius' commentary on Vergil, the slave in question becomes an 'Ethiopian', that is, a man of colour: a modification that is justified, apparently, by the supposition that this detail conferred on Tarquin's argument additional constrictive efficacy, to the degree it would have cast stronger discredit on Lucretia's reputation.[28] It is true, however, that the determining element of Tarquin's threat nevertheless remains, as already in the case of Martial's epigram, the servile status of the partner and not the colour of his skin, so much so that only the first element appears unchanged in all the versions of the story of Lucretia. At Rome, slave men and slave woman are a sexual toy at the disposition of their masters, but for a woman it is shameful to have intimate relations with one of them.

Similar considerations hold for a widespread scholastic theme that sees a matron accused of adultery after having given birth to a child of colour. The task, an ample extract of which has reached us in the declamatory collection of Calpurnius Flaccus, meant to offer a test of extreme difficulty to the students of rhetorical schools, who were called upon to defend the woman, more than to feed in them a stigmatizing vision of people of dark skin. And it is a fact that, in the quite lengthy surviving text of Calpurnius, the rhetor who takes the role of accuser does not appear to have emphasized the element of dark skin at all, except as an undeniable proof that the adultery actually took place.[29]

If anything, it can be useful to emphasize a further passage, which again refers to the specific mental framework of ancient cultures, like the association between skin colour and omens of bad augury. Black was in fact consistently connected in both Greece and Rome with the sphere of death, the underworld, and the dead, to whom not by chance were offered sacrificial victims of dark skin, while animals with white skin were reserved for the gods of the heavens.[30] Thus, speaking of a matron not much more inclined to marital fidelity than Martial's Marulla, in the so-called satire against women, Juvenal puts his interlocutor on guard against the possible birth of a baby of colour – the *decolor heres* mentioned in the title of this piece – alluding to the pigmentation of the skin with the statement that its father would never have wanted to see it in the morning:

> Rejoice, poor wretch; give her the stuff to drink whatever it be, with your own hand: for were she willing to get big and trouble her womb with bouncing babes, you might perhaps find yourself the father of an Ethiopian; and some day a coloured heir, whom you would rather not meet by daylight, would fill all the places in your will.[31]

Such a description does not refer at all to a presumed racist attitude on the part of this involuntary father, whose wife, moreover, does not seem to show any repugnance at joining with a man of dark skin. If anything, it alludes to the widespread popular belief, attested, almost contemporaneously to Juvenal, in

Lucian of Samosata and present in the folklore of many cultures until recent times: at its heart, to encounter something ill-omened, especially if it happens at the beginning of the day, represents an unlucky presage and suggests therefore the opportunity of not leaving home or of quickly returning home. This holds for a great variety of encounters considered of bad auspice, which include among other things an individual who stumbles on his right foot, a eunuch, a monkey, or, as the satirist's verses show, an individual of dark skin.[32] Once more, in short, the ancient text does not present any evidence of attitudes that can be described as racist, and the modern scholar ought to pay attention to not imposing interpretive categories that *seem* self-evident, because they are familiar to us, on a culture that must be studied instead according to its own standards.[33]

In the same way, a widespread historiographic tradition recounted that on the eve of the battle of Philippi, in 42 BCE, the imminent defeat of Caesar's killers had been presaged among other unlucky signs by the appearance at the gate of their camp of a Black man. The historian Florus speaks in this regard of an 'all too obvious signal of mourning', while Plutarch affirms that there had been a casual encounter between the man in question and the flagbearer who carried the eagle in battle, the standard of the legion and for this reason endowed with a strong symbolic value. Not by chance, the soldiers had seen to immediately eliminate this unfortunate circumstance, in demonstration of the vast diffusion of certain cultural models.[34] Something similar happened, later, to Septimius Severus on the eve of his death. While he was busy in military operations on the front of Britain, the emperor sees coming towards him a Black soldier, crowned by a wreath of cypress. If this were not enough, the 'Ethiopian' addresses Septimius Severus and calls him *deus victor* (winning god). Becoming angry, the emperor immediately orders the man to be taken from his sight, shaken by the triple bad omen represented by the man's skin colour, the plant used for the crown (traditionally associated with the sphere of mourning), and his invocation as a god, which could be considered an omen of his imminent apotheosis.[35]

Even evidence like this, however, does not necessarily imply a vision of 'Blacks' rooted in racism. In all likelihood, the Ethiopian killed at Philippi was a slave who normally followed the army, whose misfortune was only that of having been noticed at the moment in which the gates of the camp were being opened and the soldiers were heading towards the field of battle, as in fact all the sources do not fail to specify, in a situation, in short, that appears not too different from that of someone who sees a scene of bad omen precisely at the moment in which he leaves home and prepares to begin his day. As for the 'Ethiopian' who encountered Septimius Severus, the biographer of the *Historia Augusta* takes care to specify that this was a famous *scurra*, known among the soldiers for his jokes and witticisms, and who belonged to a *militaris numerus*, that is, an auxiliary unit of the army, enrolled on an ethnic basis, according to a technical meaning that the term *numerus* takes on beginning from the age of Trajan: both facts that confirm that the man enjoyed the full trust of the emperor.[36] Once more, it is the circumstances of the encounter, and not the colour of the skin as such, that takes on an ominous value, justifying Septimius's harsh reaction, like that of Brutus' soldiers.

A picture like the one we have briefly traced is however destined to change in significant part beginning with Late Antiquity, when the increasing establishment of Christianity enriches, and at the same time complicates, the network of symbolic associations tied to the colour of skin. Black becomes then consistently an attribute of Satan, the monkey of God and icon of evil, already in Greek authors often defined simply as *ho mélas*, and by extension this colour comes to be attributed to those who share a status somehow 'demonic', from the idolator to the sinner to the heretic. A 'symbolic Blackness', as it has recently been defined, that colonizes the imaginary promoted by the new creed and becomes rapidly dominant in late imperial culture.[37] As for Ethiopia, it often occurs as the emblem of sinning nations in the works of Christian thinkers, and before that in the production of an author of Jewish culture like Philo of Alexandria, thanks also to the presence in biblical texts diligently interpreted by the Fathers of the Church: to cite only one example, in his commentary on the Old Testament book of Sophonia, Jerome states that 'in all sacred scripture they are called "Ethiopians" who are completely immersed in vice'.[38] In this sense, Ethiopia is often likened to Egypt, whose negative characterization derived obviously from the circumstance of having long held in slavery the chosen people.

If one considers that in the eyes of the Greeks and Romans the Egyptians were renowned for their ancient wisdom and their religious devotion and that the Ethiopians, as we have seen, entered into and remained for a long time in the literary tradition as a blessed nation, beloved of and sharing a table with the gods, the reversal of perspective is total and contributes to laying the foundations of a transformation destined sooner or later to move from the world of metaphorical expressions to that of real discrimination.

Notes

1 I am grateful to the organisers of the conference *Othering and the Other: Performing Identity in the Roman Empire* for offering me the chance to take part in their work,

and to those who participated in the discussion that followed my talk for their precious suggestions and comments.

2 I cite Bernstein 2021. This is naturally not the first stance of its kind: in a 'Statement on Police Brutality, Systemic Racism, and the Death of George Floyd' published online on 3 June 2020 (Cullyer 2020), the American Society for Classical Studies 'recognizes and acknowledges the complicity of Classics as a field in constructing and participating in racist and anti-Black educational structures and attitudes'; and the positions taken in this respect in particular by Dan-el Padilla Peralta, a scholar of Ancient History at Princeton, are well known (see Bond 2019). For sensible criticisms of these positions, cf. Rebenich 2021.

3 I refer in particular to the studies of Frank M. Snowden, Jr., Lloyd A. Thompson, Gay L. Byron and Benjamin Isaac, which are cited in the following pages and are in any case presupposed even when no explicit reference is made.

4 In my view, the same holds true for the notion of 'proto-racism' as defined by Isaac 2004: 38: 'the term proto-racism, then, may be used when Greek and Latin sources attribute to groups of people common characteristics considered to be unalterable because they are determined by external factors or heredity', taken up again in Isaac 2006. Recently, Marcone 2018: 91 has observed that 'i concetti di "razzismo" e di "razzista" devono essere utilizzati quanto meno con cautela per non incorrere in forme di anacronismo', because in the ancient world 'è assente il presupposto che la differenza etnica abbia un fondamento biologico', and that, at least in respect to Greek culture, it would be more correct to speak of 'ethnocentrism'.

5 For Greece, cf. above all Aristotle, *Pol.* 1327b20 ff.; for Rome, Vitr. 6.1. All information on the geo-climatic model and on its transformation over time can be found in Sassi 1992; Oniga 1998; Stok 1999; Borca 2003; Isaac 2004: 55–74 (will full bibliography); Isaac 2006: 35–37; Li Causi 2008; Parodo 2011. I speak of a 'simplified version' in respect to the Roman world because in it the element of distinction between political regimes seems to disappear entirely – and especially the difference between free Greek cities and eastern despotisms – which instead plays a central role in Hellenic formulations of the model as an explanatory factor of cultural differences.

6 Thus rightly Oniga 1988: 106, 'per quanto rigido e schematico, e in ultima analisi pseudoscientifico ed etnocentrico, il determinismo ambientale antico ha ben poco a che vedere con il razzismo moderno. Viene infatti escluso *a priori* il concetto di ereditarietà: la diversità umana è dovuta a fattori ambientali e culturali, non genetici'. Stok 1999: 265, among others, echoes him.

7 Liv. 38.17.9, *iam M. Manlius unus agmine scandentes in Capitolium detrusit Gallos. et illis maioribus nostris cum haud dubiis Gallis, in sua terra genitis, res erat; hi iam degeneres sunt, mixti, et Gallograeci vere, quod appellantur.* Cf. for this passage, and for the passage of Florus cited in n. 8, where the term *feritas* appears, Lentano 2007:

201–5, with further bibliography; I find unacceptable Isaac's 2006: 38 interpretation of the Livian passage.

8 Flor. 1.27.11, *ceterum gens Gallograecorum, sicut ipsum nomen indicio est, mixta et adulterata est:... uti frugum semina mutato solo degenerant, sic illa genuina feritas eorum Asiatica amoenitate mollita est.*

9 Liv. 38.17.2, *Massilia, inter Gallos sita, traxit aliquantum ab accolis animorum.* Cf. Momigliano 1975: 51–7.

10 On the ancient world's representation of people of colour and the suitability of the concept of 'racism' to Greek and Roman culture, cf. Snowden 1970, 1983 (anticipated in other studies by the same author, such as Snowden 1947, 1960), Salmon 1984, and, with specific reference to Rome, Thompson 1989 and more recently Gruen 2006: 472–4; 2011: 197–220. A vast collection of translated and commented texts, including from Christian authors, is given in the dissertation of Diatta 2017. Bartůněk and Dadák 2015 is untrustworthy.

11 Cf., e.g., Varr., *Ling.* 8.41, *si alter erit puer, alter senex, aut unus albus et alter Aethiops* ('if the one is a boy and the other an old man, or one is white and the other an Ethiopian'; trans. R. G. Kent); 9.42, *si alter est Aethiops, alter albus* ('if the one is an Ethiopian and the other is a white man'); Iuv. 2.23, *loripedem rectus derideat, Aethiopem albus* ('let the straight-legged man laugh at the club-footed, the white man at the Blackamoor'; trans. G. G. Ramsay). On use of *Aethiops* to designate people of colour, cf. immediately following in the text.

12 Thuc. 1.3.3 (trans. R. Crawley).

13 According to Snowden 1997: 30, '"Ethiopians" is the *only* word regularly used by Greeks and Romans as the equivalent of "Negroes" or "Blacks" in twentieth-century usage' (original emphasis).

14 Lucr. 6.722, *inter nigra virum percocto saecla colore* ('among the tribes of people Blackened by the scorching sun'; trans. M. Ferguson Smith) and 6.1109, *usque ad nigra virum percocto saecla colore* (right on the tribes of people Blackened by the scorching sun), for which I refer to the observations of Nadeau 1977: 76–7 (I am grateful to Anna Maria Urso for having brought these passages to my attention). An alternative explanation for the Ethiopians' darker colouring is given by Ovid (*Met.* 2.235–236), who attributes it to an abundance of blood under the skin. It is telling that in this case, too, the ultimate reason is their close encounter with the chariot of the sun driven by Phaethon. In this respect, Plin., *Nat.* 2.189 speaks instead of humors attracted by heat towards the upper parts of the body, *illis in supera sucum revocari natura vaporis* ('the fluid, like vapour, are forced into the upper parts of the body'; trans. J. Bostock, H. T. Riley).

15 A useful survey and careful discussion of passages is given in Ryan 1997 (esp. 19–26 for Homer). Cf. also Snowden 1960, 1970: 144–55, 1983: 46–55; Desanges 1975: 408–11; Cracco Ruggini 1979; Zadi 1996; Byron 2002: 29–41. A treatment of the

Ethiopians is expressly excluded by Isaac 2004, as the author explains in his introduction (49–50).

16 Hom., *Od.* 1.22–26 (trans. E. Wilson). Cf. also 5.282–287. For commentary on these passages, cf., among others, MacLachlan 1992.

17 Cf., respectively, Hom., *Il.* 1.423–427 and 23.205–207.

18 Diodorus Siculus insists specially on this point. For Diodorus, divine benevolence allowed the Ethiopians to escape all those who tried to subjugate them, and to continue to live in peace and harmony (3.2).

19 For Memnon, central to the lost poem *Aithiopis* of the epic cycle, it is sufficient to refer to West 2013: 129–62. The episode of Cambyses' embassy and the reaction of the Ethiopians is recounted in Hdt. 3.17–25 and appears frequently in later texts, both in Greek and Latin.

20 Ter., *Eun.* 165–166, *mi dixti cupere te ex Aethiopia / ancillulam* ('you told me that you wanted a slave girl from Ethiopia'; trans. J. Barsby).

21 We can add, as well, the description of the African slave Scybale in the Pseudo-Vergilian *Moretum*, esp. vv. 31–35, and the observations of Giton in Petr. 102.

22 Xenoph., 11 B 16 Diels-Kranz (trans. J. S. Kirk, J. E. Raven): 'the Ethiopians say that their gods are snub-nosed and Black, the Thracians that theirs have light blue eyes and red hair'.

23 Mart. 6.39 (trans. J. R. Wells), *pater ex Marulla, Cinna, factus es septem / non liberorum: namque nec tuus quisquam / nec est amici filiusve vicini, / sed in grabatis tegetibusque concepti / materna produnt capitibus suis furta. / Hic qui retorto crine Maurus incedit / subolem fatetur esse se coci Santrae; / at ille sima nare, turgidis labris / ipsa est imago Pannychi palaestritae. / Pistores esse tertium quis ignorat, / quicumque lippum novit et videt Damam? / Quartus cinaeda fronte, candido voltu / ex concubino natus est tibi Lygdo: / percide, si vis, filium: nefas non est. / Hunc vero acuto capite et auribus longis, / quae sic moventur ut solent asellorum, / quis morionis filium negat Cyrtae? / Duae sorores, illa nigra et haec rufa, / Croti choraulae vilicique sunt Carpi. / Iam Niobidarum grex tibi foret plenus / si spado Coresus Dindymusque non esset.*

24 Bettini 1999: 217–18.

25 *Pannychus* is usually considered a kind of 'speaking name' that alludes to a lover capable of 'lasting' all night (hints in Soldevila et al. 2019: 445–6, s.v.); I would not exclude that it is also a reference to the dark colour of his skin, which makes him a kind of 'all night' (on the association of dark skin with shade, cf. e.g. Manil. 4.723–724). For Santra, cf. again Soldevila et al. 2019: 536–7, who do not comment on the presumable ethnicity of Marulla's lover, but note that the name is attested only in an epigraph of African provenance.

26 Cf. among others, Serv., *Aen.* 4.481, *Aethiopiae duae sunt, una circa ortum solis, altera circa occasum in Mauretania, quam nunc dicit* ('there are two Ethiopias, one in the

East and one in the West, in Mauretania, which is here referred to'; my trans.). The idea that there were two groups of Ethiopians, those of the setting sun and those of the rising sun, goes back to Homer and appears in the passage of the *Odyssey* cited above (1.23–24); on the reception and interpretation of this passage in ancient authors, cf. Nadeau 1970.

27 Thus the canonical version of Livy, cf. 1.58.4: *ubi obstinatam videbat et ne mortis quidem metu inclinari, addit ad metum dedecus: cum mortua iugulatum servum nudum positurum ait, ut in sordido adulterio necata dicatur* ('When he found her obdurate and not to be moved even by fear of death, he went farther and threatened her with disgrace, saying that when she was dead he would kill his slave and lay him naked by her side, that she might be said to have been put to death in adultery with a man of base condition'; trans. B. O. Foster).

28 Serv., *Aen.* 8.646: *per noctem stricto gladio eius ingressus cubiculum cum Aethiope, hac arte egit ut secum coiret, dicens: 'nisi mecum concubueris, Aethiopem tecum interimo, tamquam in adulterio deprehenderim* ('during the night, after holding a sword he entered her bedroom with an Ethiopian and by this stratagem he got her to lie with him, saying: If you don't sleep with me, I will kill the Ethiopian together with you as if I had caught you in the act of adultery'; my trans.). For interpretation of this passage, within the vast tradition on Lucretia, cf. Ramires 2010; Brescia 2019; Lentano 2020b, esp. 73–5.

29 I have discussed the *controversia* of Calpurnius Flaccus (2: 'Matrona Aethiopem peperit. Arguitur adulterii') in Lentano 2020a, with additional bibliography. The theme appeared also in a lost major declamation of Pseudo-Quintilian, not included in the collection that has reached us but whose content we can partially reconstruct (fr. 8 Lehnert = 4 Stramaglia).

30 On this last point, cf. Arnob., *Adv. gent.* 7.19–20. Generally, on the ominous associations of the colour Black, cf. Thompson 1989: 110–13.

31 Juv. 6.597–601 (trans. G. G. Ramsay; cf. also 5.52–55): *gaude, infelix, atque ipse bibendum / porrige quidquid erit; nam si distendere vellet / et vexare uterum pueris salientibus, esses / Aethiopis fortasse pater, mox decolor heres / impleret tabulas numquam tibi mane videndus.* On the theme of ethnic prejudice generally in Juvenal, see the works of Watts 1976 and more recently of Gellérfi 2019; on the meaning of *decolor* and its use 'to mark racial differences', cf. Snowden 1947: 280–1 and more recently Goldman 2015: 104–5 (the source of the citation); those who interpret the adjective in the sense of 'mulatto' are misled, as Watson and Watson 2014: 263 rightly observe.

32 Lucian, *Pseud.* 17 (trans. A. M. Harmon), 'We avoid those who are lame in the right foot, especially if we should see them early in the morning; and if anyone should see a cut priest or a eunuch or a monkey immediately upon leaving the house, he returns upon his tracks and goes back, auguring that his daily business for that day will not

be successful, thanks to the bad and inauspicious omen at the start'. The same in Lucian, *Eun.* 6, referring specifically to eunuchs.

33 This is the approach that in anthropological theory is termed 'emic' (in opposition to the 'etic' perspective, closer to the cultural categories of the observer); for application of this model to the ancient world, cf. Bettini and Short 2018: 11–17.

34 Cf., respectively, Flor. 2.17.7–8 (*nam et signis insedit examen et adsuetae cadaverum pabulo volucres castra quasi iam sua circumvolabant, et in aciem prodeuntibus obvius Aethiops nimis aperte ferale signum fuit* ('a swarm of bees settled on the standards; the birds which usually feed upon corpses flew round the camp, as though it were already their prey; and an Ethiopian who met the troops as they were marching to battle was only too clearly an omen of disaster'; trans. E. S. Forster) and Plut. *Brut.* 48.5 (trans. B. Perrin), according to whom the story was 'well known' ('And the story of the Ethiopian is well known, who, as the gate of the camp was thrown open, met the standard-bearer, and was cut to pieces by the soldiers, who thought his appearance ominous'). The same can be read in the later manual of omens by Julius Obsequens, who, as we know, drew on Livian material (70: *Brutianis in proelium egredientibus Aethiops in porta occurrit et a militibus confossus* ('as Brutus and his army were going out to battle an Ethiopian met them at the gate and was run through by the soldiers'; trans. A. Nice)), as well as in Appian (*Civ.* 4.134), who specifies that the encounter took place 'in front of the gates' (trans. H. White). Additionally, the death of Caligula (according to Suet., *Cal.* 57.4) was presaged, among other unlucky signs, by the fact that the night on which the emperor was stabbed, a theatrical production was given at the palace in which many Egyptian and Ethiopian actors took part, obviously characterised by their dark skin. On these episodes, cf., among others, Aubert 1999: 3–4.

35 SHA, *Sev.* 22.4–5, *Aethiops quidam e numero militari, clarae inter scurras famae et celebratorum semper iocorum, cum corona e cupressu facta idem occurit. quem cum ille iratus removeri ab oculis praecepisset et coloris eius tactus omine et coronae, dixisse ille dicitur ioci causa: 'totum fuisti, totum vicisti, iam deus esto victor'.*

36 Cf. *OLD*, *s.v. numerus*, 9b ('one of certain units of native troops employed as auxiliaries from Trajan's time onward').

37 I allude to Byron 2002. Amongst a vast bibliography, see esp. Aubert 1999 and Brakke 2001; for much useful information, cf. also Snowden 1960: 30–53, 1983: 44–6; Ullendorff 1968: 5–15; Cracco Ruggini 1979: 115–17 and 122–35; Wilson 2014. A partial reinterpretation of the Christian position can be found in Snowden 1997: 34–6.

38 Hier., *in Sophon.* 2.12: *in omnibus Scripturis Aethiopes eos appellari, qui penitus in vitia sunt demersi* (regarding a passage in which the oracle of Yahweh threatens kill the Ethiopians by sword). Other useful references in *ThLL*, vol. I, col. 1155: 27–34.

Bibliography

Aubert, J.-J. (1999), 'Du Noir en noir et blanc: éloge de la dispersion', *MH*, 56: 159–82.

Bartůněk, J. and P. Dadák (2015), 'Colours of the Roman Empire: Could Minorities be Authorities?', *Ad Alta. Journal of Interdisciplinary Research*, 5: 7–11.

Bernstein, B. (2021), 'Princeton Removes Greek, Latin Requirement for Classics Majors to Combat "Systemic Racism"', *National Review*, 30 May. Available online: https://www.nationalreview.com/news/princeton-removes-greek-latin-requirement-for-classics-majors-to-combat-systemic-racism/ (accessed 28 July 2022).

Bettini, M. (1999), *The Portrait of the Lover*, Berkeley, CA: University of California Press (or 1992, *Il ritratto dell'amante*, Torino: Einaudi).

Bettini, M. and W. M. Short (2018), 'Introduction', in M. Bettini and W. M. Short (eds), *The World through Roman Eyes: Anthropological Approaches to Ancient Culture*, 1–23, Cambridge: Cambridge University Press (or 2014, 'Introduzione', in *Con i Romani. Un'antropologia della cultura antica*, 7–22, Bologna: il Mulino).

Bond, S. E. (2019), 'A Roundup of Reports, Reactions, and Reflections After the SCS Annual Meeting', *Society for Classical Studies*, 18 January. Available online: https://classicalstudies.org/scs-blog/sarah-bond/blog-roundup-reports-reactions-and-reflections-after-scs-annual-meeting (accessed 28 July 2022).

Borca, F. (2003), *Luoghi, corpi, costumi. Determinismo ambientale ed etnografia antica*, Roma: Edizioni di Storia e Letteratura.

Brakke, D. (2001), 'Aethiopians Demons: Male Sexuality, the Black-Skinned Other, and the Monastic Self', *Journal of the History of Sexuality*, 10: 501–35.

Brescia, G. (2019), 'Uno schiavo etiope nel *cubiculum* di Lucrezia (Serv. *ad* Verg. *Aen.* 8.646)', in S. Condorelli and M. Onorato (eds), *Verborum violis multicoloribus. Studi in onore di Giovanni Cupaiuolo*, 51–72, Napoli: Paolo Loffredo.

Byron, G. L. (2002), *Symbolic Blackness and Ethnic Difference in Early Christian Literature*, London: Routledge.

Cracco Ruggini, L. (1979), 'Il negro buono e il negro malvagio nel mondo classico', in M. Sordi (ed.), *Conoscenze etniche e rapporti di convivenza nell'antichità*, 108–35, Milano: Vita e Pensiero.

Cullyer, H. (2020), 'Statement on Police Brutality, Systemic Racism, and the Death of George Floyd', *Society for Classical Studies*, 3 June. Available online: https://classicalstudies.org/scs-news/statement-police-brutality-systemic-racism-and-death-george-floyd (accessed 28 July 2022).

Desanges, J. (1975), 'L'Afrique noire et le monde méditerranéen dans l'Antiquité (Éthiopiens et Gréco-romains)', *Revue Française d'Histoire d'Outre-mer*, 62: 391–414.

Diatta, M. S. (2017), 'L'image de l'homme à la peau foncée dans le monde romain antique: constitution, traduction et étude d'un corpus de textes latins', PhD dissertation, Université de Bourgogne Franche-Comté.

Gellérfi, G. (2019), 'Xenophobic Utterances in Juvenal's *Satires*', *Graeco-Latina Brunensia*, 24: 81–91.

Goldman, R. B. (2015), 'The Multicolored World of the Romans', *Glotta*, 91: 90–111.

Gruen, E. S. (2006), 'Romans and Others', in N. Rosenstein and R. Morstein-Marx (eds), *A Companion to the Roman Republic*, 459–77, Oxford: Blackwell.

Gruen, E. S. (2011), *Rethinking the Other in Antiquity*, Princeton, NJ: Princeton University Press.

Isaac, B. (2004), *The Invention of Racism in Classical Antiquity*, Princeton, NJ: Princeton University Press.

Isaac, B. (2006), 'Proto-Racism in Graeco-Roman Antiquity', *World Archaeology*, 38: 32–47.

Lentano, M. (2007), *La prova del sangue: Storie di identità e storie di legittimità nella cultura latina*, Bologna: il Mulino.

Lentano, M. (2020a), 'Il colore che non ti aspetti: Per un commento alla seconda declamazione di Calpurnio Flacco', *BStudLat*, 50: 87–104.

Lentano, M. (2020b), 'Tutti gli uomini di Lucrezia: Sviluppi tardo-antichi e medievali di un mito romano', *Classica Vox*, 2: 55–79.

Li Causi, P. (2008), *Le immagini dell'altro a Roma e il determinismo climatico ambientale*, Trapani: Corrao.

MacLachlan, B. (1992), 'Feasting with Ethiopians: Life on the Fringe', *QUCC*, 40: 15–33.

Marcone, A. (2018), 'Idee di barbari a Roma tra la fine della Repubblica e il Principato', in C. Giuffrida, M. Cassia, and G. Arena (eds), *Roma e i 'diversi': Confini geografici, barriere culturali, distinzioni di genere nelle fonti letterarie ed epigrafiche fra età repubblicana e Tarda Antichità*, 91–101, Firenze: Le Monnier.

Momigliano, A. (1975), *Alien Wisdom: The Limits of Hellenization*, Cambridge: Cambridge University Press.

Nadeau, J. Y. (1970), 'Ethiopians', *CQ*, 20: 339–49.

Nadeau, J. Y. (1977), 'Ethiopians Again, and Again', *Mnemosyne*, 30: 75–8.

Oniga, R. (1998), 'I paradigmi della conoscenza etnografica nella cultura antica', *I Quaderni del Ramo d'oro*, 2: 93–121.

Parodo, C. (2011), 'Io è un altro: dinamiche di percezione dell'alterità in Roma antica', in A. Cannas, T. Cossu, and M. Giuman (eds), *Xenoi: Immagini e parola tra razzismi antichi e moderni. Atti del Convegno internazionale di studi, Cagliari, 3–6 febbraio 2010*, 17–32, Napoli: Liguori.

Ramires, G. (2010), 'Un'eroina nel racconto di Servio: Lucrezia', *DHA* suppl., 4.1: 61–75.

Rebenich, S. (2021), 'I classici "decolonizzati"', *QS*, 47: 5–11 (or 2020, 'Weisse Gelehrte unerwünscht. Was kann es heissen, die Wissenschaften vom Altertum zu "dekolonisieren"? In den Vereinigten Staaten wird unter dieser Losung ein umgekehrter Rassismus propagiert, der die internationale wissenschaftliche Gemeinschaft gefährdet', *Frankfurter Allgemeine Zeitung*, 26 November, 14).

Ryan, A. J. (1997), 'An Investigation into the Use of the Terms Αἰθίοψ and Αἰθιοπία in Greek Literature from Homer to Lycophron', MA dissertation, Department of Classics, University of Natal, Durban.

Salmon, P. (1984), '"Racisme" ou refus de la différence dans le monde gréco-romain', *DHA*, 10: 75–97.
Sassi, M. M. (1992), 'I barbari', in M. Vegetti (ed.), *Il sapere degli antichi*, vol. II, 262–78, Torino: Bollati Boringhieri.
Snowden, F. M., Jr. (1947), 'The Negro in Classical Italy', *AJPh*, 68: 266–92.
Snowden, F. M., Jr. (1960), 'Some Greek and Roman Observations on the Ethiopian', *Traditio*, 16: 19–38.
Snowden, F. M., Jr. (1970), *Blacks in Antiquity: Ethiopians in Greco-Roman Experience*, Cambridge, MA: Belknap Press.
Snowden, F. M., Jr. (1983), *Before Color Prejudice: The Ancient View of Blacks*, Cambridge, MA: Harvard University Press.
Snowden, F. M., Jr. (1997), 'Misconceptions about African Blacks in the Ancient Mediterranean World: Specialists and Afrocentrists', *Arion*, 4: 28–50.
Soldevila, R. M., A. M. Castillo and J. F. Valverde, eds (2019), *A Prosopography to Martial's Epigrams*, Berlin: De Gruyter.
Stok, F. (1999), 'Gli altri popoli visti da Roma: Cultura ed etnografia nel mondo antico', *Euphrosyne*, 27: 259–69.
Thompson, L. A. (1989), *Romans and Blacks*, Norman, OK: University of Oklahoma Press.
Ullendorff, E. (1968), *Ethiopia and the Bible: The Schweich Lectures*, Oxford: Oxford University Press.
Watson, L. and P. Watson, eds (2014), *Juvenal. Satire 6*, Cambridge: Cambridge University Press.
Watts, W. J. (1976), 'Race Prejudice in the Satires of Juvenal', *AC*, 19: 83–104.
West, M. L. (2013), *The Epic Cycle: A Commentary on the Lost Troy Epics*, Oxford: Oxford University Press.
Wilson, B. E. (2014), 'Neither Male nor Female: The Ethiopian Eunuch in Acts 8.26–40', *New Testament Studies*, 60: 403–22.
Zadi, G. (1996), 'L'imagerie grecque du monde négro-africain (Observations lexicales et littéraires)', *Faventia*, 18: 57–74.

3

Cicero on Foreign Religious Images and Practices

Claudia Beltrão

sua cuique civitati religio, Laeli, est nostra nobis

Cic., *Flac.* 69

Religious images, beliefs, institutions, and actions are all relevant to studying modes of perception and forms of thought and practices in the social construction of reality.[1] They contribute to shaping human lives and identities, expressing human beings' conscience of their world, and how to deal with and think of others. On a cultural level, this 'otherness' is reinforced or multiplied when we turn to foreign gods. Other people's deities, names, epiclesis, modalities and specialists of their worship, images, spaces reserved for them, and their followers' behaviour speak of 'strangeness'.

Gods, divine objects, and cults arrived in vast quantities in Rome from the fourth century BCE onwards. In the first phase of Roman expansion in central Italy, the practice of *evocatio* (evocation) and the dedication of temples to foreign deities suggest that the Romans perceived them religiously.[2] However, there is evidence that reverence in treating these foreign religious images and artworks diminished considerably as the conquests increased, especially after victories over enemies such as Carthage, Corinth, and Syracuse. In Cicero's time, the Romans had long been used to seeing the most precious and sacred cult statues of other peoples exhibited in triumphs, games, and other ceremonies led by magistrates; Roman nobles also had them displayed in their *domus* and *villae*.[3] The public display of these images, then decontextualized, would have deprived them of much of their former religious significance, creating new meanings for them. If foreign gods' inclusion matched the Middle Roman Republic into the sphere of power and dominance in religious affairs in Italy and beyond, in the mid-first century BCE, intellectual debates would assert the importance of traditional practices with a more inward-looking approach to religious matters.

Cicero has been increasingly recognized as an innovative agent in constructing religion and identity in the Late Roman Republic.[4] Here I am interested in how Cicero addresses foreign religious practices, gods, and divine images as relevant issues to intellectual debates in his lifetime. Focusing on *De natura deorum*, in which mentions of foreign gods and their images are sparse but rather revealing, briefly compared to mentions of foreign divinatory practices in *De divinatione*, I argue that Cicero's religious discourse, simultaneously shaping political, religious, and theological ideas, creates modes of seeing and perceiving religious contents for his contemporaries and beyond.[5]

'Closing' the Roman religious mind?

Ancient religions show significant porosity when compared with more recent ones, being capable of welcoming the different, even the strange, without blurring the borders between what falls under the hegemonic category of tradition and what belongs to innovation, integration, the distant, the different, often gathered under the modern label of 'otherness'. However, it does not mean that ancient religions had no limits or that divine integration had no specific logic. For instance, from the fourth to early second century BCE, Rome increased the number of the deities worshiped through the public cults of the city, a phenomenon well known to scholars, and the literary evidence presents this religious expansion as a response to a crisis such as wars or pestilences, or as a result of vows or divination.[6] It needs to be made clear whether these incorporations of new deities were based on established planning or on a case by case basis. However, at least one theological assumption is discernible: other people's gods are real gods, as well as the Roman ones. Thus, Roman practice, not theoretical speculation, seems to be the rule.[7]

Nevertheless, Greg Woolf has recently called attention to the fact that there is no scholarly consensus about why these incorporations of foreign gods to the public rites (*sacra publica*) stopped in the early second century, as wars, pestilences, vows, and divination continued to occur. Woolf also stresses the coincidence between the increasing regulation of private rites (*sacra privata*) and cases of, so to speak, religious repression, such as that of the *Bacchanalia* in 186 BCE.[8] It is what he called 'the closing of the Roman religious mind', actually a temporary phenomenon because new gods appeared in the public space and calendars from the mid-first century CE onwards, at the same time that expulsion of worshipers of foreign deities seems to come to an end. However, these new imperial cults were not introduced in the same way as the Republican ones, through religious and institutional processes controlled by the Senate, for religious authority and decision-making had also changed fundamentally in the principate.[9] So, between the second and the first century BCE, when Roman expansion was overly aggressive, such as during Augustan times, when more traditional religious contents were expressed, Rome seemed to be more hostile to foreign gods. According to Woolf, 'it looks more as if a sense of Roman exceptionalism was accompanied by a sense of the exceptional status of traditional Roman gods, relative that is to the gods of others',[10] asking if there is some connection between that massive expansion and hostility to foreign gods, a question open to debate.

There is a manifest and robust link between Roman religion and imperialism, and Cicero's *De haruspicum responso* offers some of the best evidence by far:

> etenim quis est tam vaecors qui aut, cum suspexit in caelum, deos esse non sentiat, et ea quae tanta mente fiunt ut vix quisquam arte ulla ordinem rerum ac necessitudinem persequi possit casu fieri putet, aut, cum deos esse intellexerit, non intellegat eorum numine hoc tantum imperium esse natum et auctum et retentum? quam volumus licet, patres conscripti, ipsi nos amemus, tamen nec numero Hispanos nec robore Gallos nec calliditate Poenos nec artibus Graecos nec denique hoc ipso huius gentis ac terrae domestico nativoque sensu Italos ipsos ac Latinos, sed pietate ac religione atque hac una sapientia, quod deorum numine omnia regi gubernarique perspeximus, omnis gentis nationesque superavimus.
>
> *Har. Resp.* 19

> Indeed, who is so witless that, when he gazes up into heaven, he fails to see that gods exist and imagines that chance is responsible for intelligence creations so transcendent that scarce can the highest artistry do justice to the immutable dispositions of the universe? Or who, once convinced that divinity does exist, can fail at the same time to be convinced that it is by its power that this great empire has been created, extended, and sustained? However good be our conceit of ourselves, conscript fathers, we have excelled neither Spain in population, nor Gaul in vigour, nor Carthage in versatility, nor Greece in art, nor indeed Italy and Latium itself in the innate sensibility characteristic of this land and its peoples; but in piety, in devotion to religion, and in that special wisdom which consists in recognition of the truth that the world is swayed and directed by divine disposal, we have excelled every race and every nation.[11]

Regardless of the highly political background of this statement, the uniqueness of Roman religion and the link between the Romans, their gods, and their empire was commonplace to Cicero's audience.[12] Moreover, considerable religious actions in the mid-first century played a relevant role in the Roman government.[13] Not surprisingly, theological debates and disputes about public norms, beliefs, and practices arise in Cicero's lifetime, concentrating on Roman religious content.[14] Nonetheless, in this time of 'closing the religious mind', different attitudes towards foreign gods emerged from intellectual debates, ranging from repudiation or mocking to indifference, tolerance or even defence.[15] Cicero's dialogues address non-Greek and non-Roman deities through a series of filters and codes expressing similarities and differences, distance or contiguity from implicit or explicit issues of foreign religions.

Criticizing Epicurean ethnocentric idle gods

Cicero subjects the gods to theological speculation firmly located in the first century BCE intellectual background.[16] Although most speakers in Cicero's dialogues refer to foreign gods and religious practices with disdain, there are nuances. For example, in *De natura deorum*, a theological dialogue from 45 BCE, the Epicurean character Velleius focuses on Greek and Roman deities and practices, broadening his scope at the end of his presentation:[17]

> exposui fere non philosophorum iudicia sed delirantium somnia. nec enim multo absurdiora sunt ea quae poetarum vocibus fusa ipsa suavitate nocuerunt ... cum poetarum autem errore coniungere licet portenta magorum Aegyptiorumque in eodem genere dementiam, tum etiam vulgi opiniones, quae in maxima inconstantia veritatis ignoratione versantur.
>
> *Nat. D.* 1.42–43

> I have given a rough account of the dreams of madmen than the verdicts of philosophers. For they are little less absurd than the outpourings of the poets, harmful as these have been owing to the charm of their style ... With the errors of the poets may be classed the portents of the Magi and the Egyptians, mad in their own way, and also popular opinions, which are more inconsistent owing to their ignorance of the truth.[18]

Velleius' Epicurean theology seems to promote gods 'as the image and likeness of human beings', apprehended by the sight of the mind.[19] The gods live in complete happiness in the *intermundia*, the empty spaces between the material worlds. They are not concerned with the world or human beings, which drives religious fear caused by myths and ignorance away.[20] Velleius had defined Epicurus' *prolepsis* as 'a sort of preconceived mental picture of a thing, without which nothing can be understood or investigated or discussed',[21] before affirming that the existence of anthropomorphic gods is a necessary inference generating a belief shared by nature, explained by the flow of the *simulacra*, the Epicurean atomic images.[22] In Epicurus' doctrine, it must be accepted to be true. Thus, the Epicurean anthropomorphic deity is intertwined with Graeco-Roman figurative patterns of the divine image.[23] According to this religious ethnocentrism, the Magi and the Egyptians are mad, and their religions are wholly flawed.

Replying to Velleius, the senator and pontiff Cotta, the Academic spokesman, denotes the insufficiency of Epicurean theology, delimiting a bias to unite the traditional divine images and a religious knowledge suitable not only for the Greeks and Romans.[24] Cotta's main argument is that the Epicurean definition of *prolepsis* is flawed by not integrating the cultural data that created different figurative and mental images of the gods, and this point is intensively exploited. It is indisputable that the human world has multiple divine images with different shapes and forms.

Throughout his critique, Cotta invests against Velleius' assertion that the divine anthropomorphic image is universal and discusses the difficulty of harmonizing restrictive theories about the gods with the world's various religious data and undeniable cultural diversity. So, if the anthropomorphic image is only one possibility of divine figuration, how could images reveal anything but the beliefs, knowledge, and convictions of the people who created them? Besides that, given the variety of divine images, how could one say that the anthropomorphic image constitutes the universal or natural form of divinity? Cotta often repeats these objections.[25] Closing his invective against the Epicurean theology, Cotta asks what about gods and goddesses in human form, as follows:

> et eos vituperabas qui ex operibus magnificis atque praeclaris, cum ipsum mundum, cum eius membra caelum terras maria, eumque horum insignia solem lunar stellasque vidissent, cuequeiro temporum maturitates mutationes vicissitudinesque cognovissent, suspicati essent aliquam excellentem esse praestantemque naturam quae haec effecisset moverem regeret gubernaret . . . tu quod opus tandem magnum et egregium habes quod effectum divina mente videatur, ex quo esse deos suspicere? 'habemus', inquis 'in animo insitam informationem quandam dei'. et barbati quidem Iovis, galeatae Minervae: num igitur esse talis putas? quanto melius haec vulgos imperitorum, qui non membra solum hominis deo tribuant sed usum etiam membrorum. dant enim arcum

sagittas hastam clipeum fuscinam fulmen, et si actiones quae sint deorum non vident, nihil agentem tamen deum non queunt cogitare. ipsi qui inridentur Aegyptii nullam beluam nisi ob aliquam utilitatem quam ex ea caperent consecraverunt; velut ibes maximam vim serpentium conficiunt, cum sint aves excelsae; avertunt pestem ab Aegypto, cum volucris anguis ex vastitate Libyae vento Africo invectas interficiunt atque consumunt, ex quo fit ut illae nec morsu vivae noceant nec odore mortuae. possum de ichneumonum utilitate de crocodilorum de faelium dicere, sed nolo esse longus. ita concludam, tamen beluas a barbaris propter beneficium nullum exstare sed ne factum quidem omino.

Nat. D. 1.100–101

Then you [Epicureans] censured those who argued from the magnificence and the splendid of the works, and who, observing the world itself, and the parts of the world, the sky and earth and sea, and the sun, moon and stars that adorn them and discovering the changes of the seasons and their periodic successions, conjectured that there must exist some excellent and outstanding nature who had created these things, and who imparted motion to them and guided and governed them . . . but as for you, what mighty masterpiece prayer do you adduce as apparently the creation of divine intelligence, leading you to conjecture that gods exist? 'We have an idea of god implanted in our minds', you say. Yes, and an idea of Jupiter with a beard and Minerva in a helmet, but do you, therefore, believe that those deities are really like that? The unlearned multitude is surely wiser here – they assign to god not only a man's limbs but the use of those limbs. For they give him bow, arrows, spear, shield, trident, thunderbolt; and if they cannot see what actions the gods perform, yet they cannot conceive of god as entirely inactive. Even the Egyptians, whom we laugh at, deified animals solely on the score of some utility which they derived from them; for instance, the ibis, being a tall bird with stiff legs and a long horny beak, destroys a great quantity of snakes; it protects Egypt from plagues, by killing and eating the flying serpents that are brought from the Libyan desert by the south-west wind, and so preventing them from harming the natives by their bite and their stench when dead. I might describe the utility of the ichneumon, the crocodile, and the cat, but I do not wish to be tedious. I will make my point thus: these animals are at all events deified by the barbarians for the benefits which they confer, but your gods not only do no service that you can point to, but they do not do anything at all.

Beginning with the Stoic idea, strongly criticized by Velleius, that the observation of the beauty and regularity of natural phenomena and celestial bodies led to the inference that there are gods, or a divine mind that creates, sustains, and governs the universe, Cotta challenges Velleius' notion of *prolepsis.*

After satirizing the Epicurean notion, Cotta asks: 'do you believe those gods are really like that?' Therefore, Cotta asks for the links between the human shape of Epicurean deities, well suited for Greeks and Romans, and the multifarious images of the gods in the world. Finally, he declares that ordinary people are wiser than philosophers, for they assign use and activity to divine bodies.[26] It is, obviously, a sharp criticism of the Epicurean divine *ataraxia*. Closing the point, the Egyptian theriomorphic gods address the function and benefit of the gods to human beings, which justifies their existence and is the criterion of the truth of the divine images, whatever they are.

It is relevant that Cotta mentions the Roman people followed by the Egyptians, 'those of whom we laugh at', but are characterized by common sense towards the gods, for they deify no animal that is not beneficial to them. Cotta argues that they have much more coherent opinions about the gods than Epicurus. This disqualification of the Epicurean doctrine recognizes the value of traditional beliefs. It refers to Velleius' disqualification of the Egyptians as demented and the Roman people as ignorant, a point taken up by Cotta as a critical aspect of the debate. Even more, Cotta argues that the Egyptian gods and those of others aroused more piety and veneration than the Roman ones:

> quid si etiam, Vellei, falsum illud omnino est, nullam aliam nobis de deo cogitantibus speciem nisi hominis occurrere? tamenne ista tam absurda defendes? nobis fortasse sic occurrit ut dicis: a parvis enim Iovem Iunonem Minervam Neptunum Vulcanum Apollinem reliquos deos ea facie novimus qua pictures fictoresque voluerunt, neque solum facie sed etiam ornatum aetate vestitu. at non Aegyptii nec Syri nec fere cuncta barbaria; firmiores enim videas apud eos opiniones esse de bestiis quibusdam quam apud nos de sanctissimis templis et simulacris deorum. et fana multa spoliata et simulacra deorum de locis sanctissimis ablata vidimus a nostris, at vero ne fando quidem auditam est crocodilum aut ibid aut faelem violating ab Aegyptio. quid igitur censes? apim illum sanctum Aegyptiorum bovem nonne deum videri Aegyptiis? tam, hercle, quam tibi illam vestram Sospitam. quam tu numquam ne in somnis quidem vides nisi cum pelle caprina, cum hasta, cum scutulo, cum calceolis repandis. at non est talis Argia nec Romana Iuno. ergo alia species Iunonis Argivis, alia Lanuinis. et quidem alia nobis Capitolini, alia Afris Hammonis Iovis. non pudet igitur physicum, id est speculatorem venatoremque naturae, ab animis consuetudine inbutis petere testimonium veritatis? isto enim modo dicere licebit Iovem semper barbatum, Apollinem semper inberbem, caesios oculos Minervae, caeruleos esse Neptuni . . . age et his vocabulis esse deos facimus, quibus a nobis nominantur? at primum, quot hominum linguae, tot nomina deorum.
>
> *Nat. D.* 1.81–83

> Furthermore, Velleius, what if your assumption that when we think of god, the only form that presents itself to us is that of a man is entirely untrue? Will you, nevertheless, continue to maintain your absurdities? Very likely, we Romans do imagine god as you say because, from our childhood Jupiter, Juno, Minerva, Neptune, Vulcan, and Apollo have been known to us with the aspect with which painters and sculptors have chosen to represent them, and not with that aspect only, but having that ornaments, age, and dress. But they are not so known to the Egyptians or Syrians, or any almost of the barbarians. Among these, you will find a belief in certain animals more firmly established than reverence for the holiest sanctuaries and images of the gods with us. For we have often seen temples robbed and images of gods carried off from the holiest shrines by our fellow countrymen, but no one ever heard of an Egyptian laying profane hands on a crocodile or ibis or cat. What therefore do you infer? That the Egyptians do not believe their sacred bull Apis to be a god? Precisely as much as you believe the Iuno Sospita of your native place to be a goddess, by Hercules! You never see her in your dreams unless equipped with goatskin, buckler, and slippers turned up at the toe. Yet that is not the aspect of the Argive Juno nor the Roman. It follows that Juno has one form for the Argives, another for the people of Lanuvium, and another for us. And indeed, our Jupiter of the Capitol is not the same as the Africans' Jupiter Ammon. Should not the physical philosopher, therefore, that is, the explorer and tracker-out of nature, be ashamed to go to minds besotted with the habit for evidence of truth? On your principle, it will be legitimate to assert that Jupiter always wears a beard and Apollo never, and that Minerva has grey eyes and Neptune blue . . . Tell me now, do we also make out the gods to have the same names as those by which they are known to us? But in the first place, the gods have as many names as humankind has languages.

Following Xenophanes' tropes on the various divine shapes, Cotta shows that the idea of active gods is a logical conclusion of the gods' *prolepsis*, found in the *vulgus imperitorum*, the uneducated people, and among the barbarians. Both Roman and foreign gods challenge the universalist pretension of the Epicureans.[27] So the Epicurean definition of *prolepsis* with its anthropomorphic gods is restrictive and fails to include religious experiences that give rise to different gods and divine images. In other words, Cicero favours the links between religions, gods, and the human experience in the world.

Against the Epicureans, Cotta points to the origin of religions and divine images, touching on sensitive points of the Epicurean doctrine that may also be perceived when we compare the *De natura deorum* with Philodemus' *De pietate* on the adjustment between the proleptic origin of the belief and the images of the gods on the one hand, and the fact of the world's religious diversity on the other.[28] Lastly, addressing the multiple divine names, Cotta refers to the links between the proleptic knowledge and the verbal language, as can be seen in Epicurus[29] and Diogenes Laertius.[30] Hence the variety of divine images and names reflects the diversity of human groups and their particular characteristics, a point taken by Cotta in a positive sense.

Cotta against the Stoic nonsense

In book 2, the Stoic Balbus did not mention foreign gods at all.[31] The Stoic idea of the divine is taken as derived from worldly experience, and belief in the gods is not formed from the *prolepsis* of divinity itself but rather from fear, admiration, or divinatory intuition.[32] The providential Stoic supreme god, the very cosmos, explicitly does not have the human form, but as for the Epicureans, for the Stoics, the 'natural' notion of the divine had been contaminated with irrationalities and misconceptions handed down by the same poets and artists who had also delivered correct ideas about the divinity.[33] As Balbus says:

> restat ut qualis eorum natura sit consideremus; in quo nihil est difficilius quam a consuetudine oculorum aciem mentis abducere ea difficultas induxit et vulgo imperitos et similes philosophos imperitorum, ut nisi figuris hominum constitutis nihil possent de dis inmortalibus cogitare; cuius opinionis levitas confutata a Cotta non desiderat orationem meam.
>
> *Nat. D.* 2.45

> It remains for us to consider the qualities of the divine nature, and on this subject, nothing is more difficult than to divert the eye of the mind from following the practice of bodily sight. This difficulty has caused both uneducated people generally and those philosophers who resemble the uneducated to be unable to conceive of the immortal gods without setting before themselves the forms of men: a shallow mode of thought that Cotta has exposed and which therefore calls for no discussion from me.

Balbus directly points to sculpture when dealing with religious beliefs and images. Divine images reiterated by the 'practice of bodily sight' had distorted the truth about the gods.[34] Moreover, Balbus broadens the point by arguing:

> videtisne igitur ut a physicis rebus bene atque utiliter inventis tracta ratio sit ad commenticios et fictos deos. quae res genuit falsas opiniones erroresque turbulentos et superstitiones paene aniles. et formae enim nobis deorum et aetates et vestitus ornatusque noti sunt, genera praeterea coniugia cognationes,

omniaque traducta ad similitudinem inbecillitatis humanae. nam et perturbatis animis inducuntur: accepimus enim deorum cupiditates aegritudines iracundias; nec vero, ut fabulae ferunt, bellis proeliisque caruerunt ... haec et dicuntur et creduntur stultissime et plena sunt futtilitatis summaeque levitates.

Nat. D. 2.70

Therefore, do you see how from a true and valuable physics has been evolved these imaginary and moulded gods? The perversion has been a fruitful source of false beliefs, crazy errors, and superstitions hardly above the level of old women's tales. We know what the gods look like and how old they are, their dress and equipment, and their genealogies, marriages, and relationships, and all about them is distorted into the likeness of human frailty. So, they are inculcated in the troubled spirits, and we accept their passions and emotions – we hear of their being in love, sorrowful, and angry; according to the myths, they even engaged in wars and battles ... these stories and these beliefs are utterly foolish; they are stuffed with nonsense and absurdity of all sorts.

Divine images and myths cannot ground religious knowledge, leading to nonsense, errors, and superstition. Even so, when expurgated of falsehoods through the Stoic interpretation of myths and divine names, they allow some support to humanity, integrating the traditional (Graeco-Roman) divine images in the Stoic theology.[35] Through the Stoic allegoresis and etymology,[36] it is possible to distinguish the beneficial and maleficent elements from the gods' images, helping ordinary people to know the divine properly. Then, Cotta argues against the Stoic notion of the gods. The Stoic rationalization of the divine made traditional gods nothing more than personifications of beneficial forces or aspects of nature, and even the Roman public gods were, after all, theologically disqualified. As allegories, if divine images and myths could be justified as a support for the ordinary people to reach religious knowledge, the Roman gods would not be living gods. Thus, Balbus' discourse does not satisfy the Academic criteria of verisimilitude. Cotta attacks the Stoic universalism and apriorism, for instance, in *Nat. D.* 3.39–40, in which he mentions the *vulgus*, the Syrians, the Egyptians, and the Greeks, declaring the multiplicity and variety of gods in the world, and even traditional Roman gods, such as Hercules and Romulus, are included in this picture of other people's beliefs:

nec vero volgi atque imperitorum inscitiam despicere possum, cum ea considero quae dicuntur a Stoicis. sunt enim illa imperitorum: piscem Syri venerantur, omne fere genus bestiarum Aegyptii consecraverunt; iam vero in Graecia multos habent ex hominibus deos, Alabandum Alabandis, Tenedi Tenen, Leucotheam quae fuit

> Ino et eius Palaemonem filium cuncta Graecia Herculem Aesculapium Tyndaridas Romulum nostrum aliosque compluris, quos quasi novos et adscripticios cives in caelum receptos putant. haec igitur indocti; quid vos philosophi, qui meliora? omitto illa, sunt enim praeclara: sit sane deus ipse mundus ... quare igitur pluris adiungimus deos? quanta autem est eorum multitudo?
>
> *Nat. D.* 3.39–40

> In fact, when I reflect upon the utterances of the Stoics, I cannot despise the stupidity of the vulgar and the ignorant. With the ignorant, you get superstitions like the Syrians' worship of a fish and the Egyptians' deification of almost every species of animal; nay, even in Greece, they worship a number of deified human beings, Alabandus at Alabanda, Tennes at Tenedos, Leucothea, formerly Ino, and her son Palaemon throughout the whole of Greece, as also Hercules, Aesculapius, the sons of Tyndareus; and with our own people Romulus and many others who are believed to have been admitted to celestial citizenship in recent times, by a sort of extension of the franchise! Well, those are the superstitions of the unlearned, but what of you, philosophers? How are your dogmas better? I pass over the rest of them, for they are remarkable indeed! ... Why then do we add so many gods? And what a crowd of them there is!

Consequently, the Stoics are as stupid as the ordinary people and the barbarians, making gods of the cosmos, the planets, stars, and constellations, naming them after beasts like Scorpio or Lion, and addressing a vast number of deified human beings and allegorical gods and goddesses. In Cotta's argument, the artistic creation and the conventions and beliefs of human societies are essential elements to consider. These choices fit each human group's beliefs and cultic practices, which are fundamental to religious knowledge. The gods' cultural, not natural, origin and identities do not affect their validity. Cotta stresses the conventionality and diversity of the divine. Human experience, artistic production, and tradition print forms in human minds, and therefore the religious practices of different peoples fix the shape and characteristics of their gods.

In a word, Epicurean and Stoic theologies do not present arguments logically valid for a piece of sound religious knowledge. For Cotta, both Epicurean and Stoic theologies are restrictive – one can also say ethnocentric – when one observes the world's great religious diversity. Clearly stating the unity of human eyes and mind,[37] Cotta points to the nature of cognition, which depends on the human localized experience of divinity, which forms the mind to perceive, conceive, and know the gods.

A senatorial view of religion(s)

When we briefly move on to Cicero's second theological dialogue, mentions of foreign religious practices and beliefs are also few but relevant. *De divinatione* was published in 44 BCE, depicting a fictional conversation between Marcus and his younger brother Quintus.[38] Cicero begins the dialogue by telling us that everyone has always believed in divination, its outcomes are often hard to disregard, and it has been an essential part of Roman culture and politics.[39] In a word, there are many arguments in its favour, but it seems complicated, or impossible, to explain its causes rationally, even if most philosophers have discussed divination. Moreover, if there is a risk of impiety by neglecting the divine signs, there is always a risk of superstition, which makes divination a subject worthy of intellectual scrutiny.[40] So, a careful rethinking of the question is welcome, in no small part, because divination played a significant role in Balbus' Stoic arguments in *De natura deorum*.[41]

In book 1, Quintus makes a case for divination based on *eventa*, an argument by example, mainly from a Stoic standpoint.[42] The foundation of his method of exposition is that divinatory art results from a long history of careful observation of signs and outcomes over a very long time.[43] In this way, arguing for the truth of divination, Quintus quotes examples from Persians, Assyrians, Chaldeans, Egyptians, Gauls, and other peoples in a vast geographic area, as in the initial passage of his long catalogue on the universal practice of divination:[44]

> eaque divinationum ratio ne in barbaris quidem gentibus neglecta est, siquidem et in Gallia Druidae sunt, e quibus ipse Divitiacum Haeduum hospitem tuum laudatoremque cognovi, qui et naturae rationem, quam fisiologian Graeci appellant, notam esse sibi profitebatur, et partim auguriis, partim coniectura, quae essent futura dicebat, et in Persis augurantur et divinant magi, qui congregantur in fano commentando causa atque inter se conloquendi, quod etiam idem vos quondam facere Nonis solebatis; nec quisquam rex Persarum potest esse, qui non ante magorum disciplinam scientiamque perceperit. licet autem videre et genera quaedam et nationes huic scientiae deditas. telmessus in Caria est, qua in urbe excellit haruspicum disciplina; itemque Elis in Peloponneso familias duas certas habet, lamidarum unam, alteram Clutidarum, haruspicinae nobilitate praestantes. in Syria Chaldaei cognitione astrorum sollertiaque ingeniorum antecellunt. Etruria autem de caelo tacta scientissume animadvertit, eademque interpretatur quid quibusque ostendatur monstris atque portentis. quocirca bene apud maiores nostros senatus, tum cum florebat imperium, decrevit ut de principum filiis x ex singulis Etruriae populis in disciplinam traderentur, ne ars tanta propter tenuitatem hominum a religionis auctoritate

abduceretur ad mercedem atque quaestum. Phryges autem et Pisidae et Cilices et Arabum natio avium significationibus plurimum obtemperant, quod idem factitatum in Umbria accepimus.

Div. 1.90–92

The same principle regarding divinatory procedures is not ignored even among barbarian nations, for in Gaul, there are the Druids, of whom I have known Divitiacus the Aeduan, your guest and admirer. He claimed that the science of nature, what the Greeks call physiologia, was known to him, and he used to foretell what would sometimes happen by augury and sometimes by interpretation. Among the Persians, augury and divination are practised by the Magi, who gather in a sacred place for discussion to meet each other, as you were once accustomed to doing on the Nones. No one could be king of the Persians who had not first learnt the art and lore of the Magi. It is possible to see families and people dedicated to this science. In Caria, there is Telmessus, in which city the art of the haruspices is pre-eminent; similarly, in the Peloponnese, Elis has two separate families, the Iamidae and the Clutidae, which are famed for their excellence in haruspicy. In Syria, the Chaldaeans excel in their knowledge of the stars and the sharpness of their minds. Etruria has the greatest knowledge of things struck by lightning and also interprets what is signified by each prodigy and portent. For this reason, in the time of our forebears, the Senate, at a time when our empire was thriving, decreed that the sons of leading citizens groups of ten should be handed over to the individual Etruscan peoples to be instructed in the discipline so that an art of such great importance should not, because of a lack of manpower, lose its religious authority to become an object of commerce and profit. The Phrygians, Pisidians, Cilicians, and the Arab nation are guided particularly by the signs given by birds, as we know was also regularly done in Umbria.[45]

According to Quintus, divination's many outcomes and universality are solid arguments for its veracity. In this way, the younger Cicero is open to foreign examples as equivalents, sometimes even superior, to the Roman ones.[46] By the logic of his argument, Quintus seems to state no religious differences between Romans and other diviners, as he connects foreign practices to the Romans and, in the case of the most famous Druid, Divitiacus, to Marcus himself. Even so, there is a moral difference when Quintus, anticipating Marcus' eventual criticism of his position, has implied the authority of Greek examples over other peoples by asking: 'Alright, barbarians are foolish and deceivers. But surely the history of the Greeks is not also falsified?'[47] However, there are a few occasions in book 2 on which Marcus doubts or denies the veracity of Quintus' examples.[48] The

Academic Marcus effectively rejects the possibility of drawing inferences from these anecdotes in favour of divination, arguing that the apparent connection between prediction and outcome results from chance. In a word, Marcus denies that it is possible to establish any causal relationship based on these examples to support the veracity of divination.

If Cicero notes that divination is widely diffused, not a Roman exclusivity in the proem,[49] foreign divination works differently in the debate between the brothers. Malcolm Schofield pointed out that Marcus consistently responds to Quintus by arguing based on forensic rhetoric, discrediting the supposed empirical basis of divination.[50] As Quintus argued based on examples rather than rational explanations, Marcus seeks to demonstrate that, despite much and varied evidence, Quintus' evidence was insufficient to establish the veracity of divination. Then Marcus defines foreign divination as superstitious while retaining Roman public divination for the benefit of the *res publica*:

> satis multa de ostentis; auspicia restant et sortes, eae quae ducuntur, non illae quae vaticinatione funduntur, quae oracla verius dicimus; de quibus tum dicemus, cum ad naturalem divinationem venerimus. restat etiam de Chaldaeis; sed primum auspicia videamus. 'difficilis auguri locus ad contra dicendum.' Marso fortasse, sed Romano facillumus. non enim sumus ii nos augures, qui avium reliquorumve signorum observatione futura dicamus. et tamen credo Romulum, qui urbem auspicato condidit, habuisse opinionem esse in providendis rebus augurando scientiam (errabat enim multis in rebus antiquitas), quam vel usu iam vel doctrina vel vetustate immutatam videmus; retinetur autem et ad opinionem vulgi et ad magnas utilitates rei publicae mos, religio, disciplina, ius augurium, collegio auctoritas.
>
> *Div.* 2.70

> Enough has been said of portents; auspices remain, and so do lots; I mean lots that are drawn and not those uttered by prophets and more correctly styled oracles. I shall speak of oracles when I get to natural divination. Also, I must discuss the Chaldeans. But first, let us consider auspices. 'To argue against auspices is a hard thing,' you say, 'for an augur to do.' Yes, for a Marsian, perhaps, but very easy for a Roman. For we Roman augurs are not the sort who foretell the future by observing the flights of birds and other signs. And yet, I admit that Romulus, who founded the city by the direction of auspices, believed that augury was an art useful in seeing things to come – for the ancients had erroneous views on many subjects. But we see that the art has changed due to experience, education, or the long lapse of time. However, out of respect for the opinion of the masses and the great service to the State, we maintain the augural practices, discipline, religious rites, laws, and authority of the augural college.[51]

Replying to Quintus, Marcus rejects foreign divination, stressing Roman practices of his times, creating a polarity between the reasonable practices of the Romans versus foreign superstitions.[52] Marcus, an augur himself, manipulates Quintus' examples to emphasize the senatorial control of public religious practices as a fundamental point of his argument. He notes that experience and education have improved Roman beliefs and practices in many respects, surpassing the erroneous views of the ancients. Nevertheless, he declares that the Roman augur does not foresee the future, based on the notion that the augury only appointed to divine approval or disapproval for a particular public action and because of popular opinion.[53] However, this argument is restricted, as one can see by comparing the above passage with Cicero's *De legibus* 2.21, in which a negative augury is taken as an announcement of a future disaster. Even so, Marcus' statement works soundly in the debate, distinguishing Roman and foreign practices and stressing the rational superiority of the former. In the peroration, Marcus reinforces the point, declaring that the worldwide diffused divination (*fusa per gentis*) has hindered the mind of almost everyone because of human weakness (*hominum imbecillitatem occupavit*).[54]

In some way, Quintus is open to foreign religious practices, while Marcus stresses Roman religious uniqueness, as seen in *De haruspicum responso* 19. Still, in *De natura deorum,* the Epicurean Velleius and the Stoic Balbus disregard or denigrate divine images divergent from Graeco-Roman beliefs and artistic formulas. At the same time, the senator and pontiff Cotta acknowledges the variety of religions and divine images in the Roman Empire. Therefore, these stylish and somewhat ambiguous references to foreign and peripherical gods and religions reveal Cicero's active engagement with theological questions brought by religious practices, images, and conceptions of the divine, opening a way to explore this issue through the tension between Romanness and foreignness, deepening the sense of its complexity.

Closing remarks

Cicero's statement at the beginning of this chapter shows a clue for his position about foreign religions and gods: 'Each people have its religion, Laelius, as we have ours'.[55] The imperative of upholding religious authority, adhering to tradition, and identifying with his community's values is what results from observing Cicero's theological discourse. Emphasizing the authority of the Senate, Cicero's Academic trend is wholly coherent with his senatorial background, in which consensus was established in debating each case particularly rather than by applying general rules – or philosophical dogmas. At the core of Cicero's discourse, religious beliefs can and should be subject to intellectual scrutiny. However, one must find a viewpoint in which reason does not undermine Roman public religion, neatly superior to the foreign ones. However, other people's practices, beliefs, gods, and images, even marginal or different from Roman standards, were deeply embedded in the empire's socio-political fabric to be ignored. The religious 'otherness' cannot be taken in isolation as if religious beliefs, practices, and ways of thinking respond to an autonomous logic, for they echo political, intellectual, and moral concerns. Hence, Cicero is an invaluable standpoint over a challenging moment in Roman religious history and a reminder of the complexity inherent in establishing comprehensive models or labels to deal with theological and cultural questions related to religion(s) in the Roman world.

Notes

1 On different conceptualization and figuration of the divine in the Roman Empire's theoretical reflection and religious practices, see esp. Belayche and Pirenne-Delforge 2015: 7–20; the studies collected in Estienne et al. 2014 and Belayche and Brulé 2010. See also the collection edited by Van Haeperen and Berthelet 2021.

2 On *evocatio*, see Ferri 2010. On the broad movement of buildings and dedications of temples in the Middle Republic, see Orlin 1997 and Ziolkowski 1992, and also the study by Padilla Peralta 2020, esp. part I.

3 On this topic, see Lazzeretti 2006; Stewart 2003, 2008; Hölscher 2004.

4 The innovations brought by Cicero and other late Republican writers to the field commonly defined as 'Roman religion' have been the subject of intense debate. See, e.g., Beltrão and Santangelo 2020; MacRae 2016; North 2014; Santangelo 2013; Rüpke 2012; Gildenhard 2011; Ando 2008. See esp. the study of the dialogues *De natura deorum* and *De divinatione* as critical pieces of Cicero's project for a philosophy of religion by Wynne 2019.

5 The study of this theme in Cicero's work is more exhaustive than the two selected dialogues. This selection is justified to ensure conciseness, but it is also rooted in the reading proposed by Wynne 2019, esp. 50–82, of *De natura deorum* and *De divinatione* as a unity in Cicero's intellectual project.

6 Orlin 2010 is an essential reference. On the *interpretatio Romana* and ancient literary evidence, see Ando 2008: 43–58, 184–6.

7 MacRae 2016: 13–52.

8 Woolf 2020: 119. On detached cases of Rome interfering with other people's religious practices, see Baudy 2006.
9 See, e.g., Várhelyi 2010.
10 Woolf 2020: 123.
11 English text by N. H. Watts, LCL.
12 See also Cic., *Nat. D.* 2.8, 3.5. On the political background and religious conflict between Cicero and Clodius, see Arena 2020 and Cairo 2017.
13 On the close links between religion and politics in the Roman Republic, see, e.g., Berthelet 2020; Belayche and Estienne 2020; Rüpke 2020; Berthelet 2015; Santangelo 2013: 10–15, 84–98, 107–14; Gildenhard 2011: 246–372; Montero 2006; Krostenko 2000: 385–9; Linderski 1982.
14 Cf. Rüpke 2014: 12–32.
15 See Ando 2020 on the Romans' principles and practices concerning foreign cults and gods and the conception of religion that these principles and practices presupposed. On the 'rationalization' of Roman religious contents, see Rüpke 2012. See also Habinek 1998; Feeney 1999; Moatti 1997.
16 For a substantial overview of Hellenistic theology, see Mansfeld 1999.
17 Velleius' point makes no moral distinction between traditional Greek and Roman gods.
18 English text by H. Rackham, LCL, slightly modified.
19 *Nat. D.* 1.103: *deus effigies hominis et imago* (god is the image and the likeness of man). See Long and Sedley 1987: 146–8 on the Epicurean god as an ethical paradigm. See also the analysis of Velleius' discourse in Wynne 2019: 83–110.
20 Lucretius, e.g., in *DRN* 1.110, clearly expresses this point.
21 *Nat. D.* 1.43: *anteceptam animo rei quandam informationem, sine qua nec intellegi quicquam nec quaeri nec disputari possit* (a sort of preconceived mental picture of a thing, without which nothing can be understood or investigated or discussed). See Cancik and Cancik-Lindemaier 2001.
22 See Schiesaro 1990 on the Epicurean *simulacrum*.
23 See, e.g., Algra 2007; Kleve 1978.
24 See Beltrão 2018 on Cotta's criticism of Velleius' discourse on the divine shape and body.
25 Cf. esp. 1.78, 81–84, 101. For a general view of the philosophical questions aroused in Cotta's critique, see Woolf 2015, esp. 34–48, and Graver 2009.
26 To the philosophers' detriment, Cicero also compares the *vulgus* and the philosophers in *Nat. D.* 1.77.
27 The Epicureans seem to think of divine *prolepsis* as a result of human culture, but Cicero obscures this point for the sake of his argument. See, e.g., Mansfeld 1999; Long and Sedley 1987; Kleve 1978.
28 See Obbink 2001, who argues that the Epicureans had not logically solved the question of the many and varied deities in the human world.

29 Epicurus, Hdt. 75, states that the attribution of names occurs in response to sensorial stimuli specific to each human group.

30 D. L. 10.33: when the word 'man' is pronounced, one thinks of man's image. This proleptic phenomenon occurs because sensations precede knowledge, and language allows the setting of general definitions.

31 See the analysis of Balbus' discourse in Wynne 2019: 138–64.

32 For a general view of Stoic theology, see Brennan 2009; Algra 2003; Long 1996.

33 On Stoic theology and the poets, see especially Long 1996: 58–85.

34 On the *consuetudo oculorum*, see Glucker 1996 (= 2020: 106–23).

35 Wynne 2019, esp. 138–64, is an illuminating analysis of Balbus' classification of two main kinds of gods: the paradigmatic gods (the cosmos, the sun, the moon, the planets, and fixed stars) and the cultural ones (subdivided into divine qualities such as Fides and Concordia, divinized human benefactors like Hercules and Romulus, and anthropomorphized physical entities such as Ceres and Liber, for the grain and the wine). See also Van Nuffelen 2011, Algra 2003, Long 1996.

36 *Nat. D.* 2.66–72. See, e.g., Brittain 2005 and Schofield 1980.

37 See, e.g., *Nat. D.* 3.20–21.

38 This dialogue has been heavily analysed in recent scholarship. See, e.g., Wynne 2019; Volk 2017; Santangelo 2013; Schofield 1986, 2009; Krostenko 2000; Beard 1986.

39 See a general view of divination at Rome in North 1990: 51–71.

40 *Div.* 1.7. See Guillaumont 2006 on Cicero and the ancient philosophical debates on divination. See also Setaioli 2018: 22–7.

41 The Stoics paid particular attention to divination, which could support the thesis that everything is fated and that the gods were interested in and cared for human beings, sending them messages through signs or dreams. This question was fundamental to religion and had political relevance in Cicero's time. On the public relevance of divination in the Late Roman Republic, see Berthelet 2015 and Santangelo 2012, 2013.

42 *Div.* 1.11–16. Even supporting Stoic arguments in *De divinatione*, Quintus was not a Stoic himself but theoretically linked to the Peripatetic Cratippus, a closer friend of both Cicerones (e.g. *Div.* 1.70–71, 113; *Div.* 2.107, 100; *Brut.* 250). On the Peripatetics Dicaearchus and Cratippus as supporters of natural divination (dreams and oracles), cf. *Div.* 1.70–72, 81, 113.

43 Tarrant 2000.

44 *Div.* 1.90–100.

45 English text by D. Wardle 2006. About this passage, see an innovative reading of the links between divination and environmental contexts by Padilla Peralta 2018.

46 See, e.g., *Div.* 1.25, 27–28, 37, 47.

47 *Div.* 1.37: *age barbari vani atque fallaces. num etiam Graiorum historia mentita est?*

48 Marcus doubts the veracity of the cases narrated by Quintus in *Div.* 2.58, 63, 66, and 112.

49 *Div.* 1.1–2.

50 Schofield 1986: 51–5. See also Krostenko 2000 on Marcus consistently rejecting foreign forms of divination.

51 English text by W. A. Falconer, LCL.

52 On the distinction of 'higher' and 'lower' divination in elite rhetoric, see Bendlin 2011.

53 In this way, Marcus narrows Roman divination to the *auspicia impetrativa*, seeking divine approval just for a specific action.

54 *Div.* 2.148.

55 *Flac.* 69.

Bibliography

Algra, K. (2003), 'Stoic Theology', in B. Inwood (ed.), *The Cambridge Companion to the Stoics*, 153–79, Cambridge: Cambridge University Press.

Algra, K. (2007), *Conceptions and Images: Hellenistic Philosophical Theology and Traditional Religion*, Amsterdam: Koninklijke Nederlandse Akademie van Wetenschappen.

Ando, C. (2008), *The Matter of the Gods: Religion and the Roman Empire*, Berkeley, CA: University of California Press.

Ando, C. (2020), 'Rites et religion, pluralisme et empire dans le monde romain', in N. Belayche and S. Estienne (eds), *Religion et pouvoir dans le monde romains. L'autel et la toge. De la deuxième guerre punique à la fin des Sévères*, 55–74, Rennes: Presses universitaires de Rennes.

Arena, V. (2020), 'Cicero, the Augures, and the Commonwealth in *De Legibus*', in C. Beltrão and F. Santangelo (eds), *Cicero and Roman Religion*, 23–44, Stuttgart: Franz Steiner.

Baudy, D. (2006), 'Prohibitions of Religion in Antiquity: Setting the Course of Europe's Religious History', in C. Ando and J. Rüpke (eds), *Religions and Law in Classical and Christian Rome*, 100–14, Stuttgart: Franz Steiner.

Beard, M. (1986), 'Cicero and Divination: The Formation of a Latin Discourse', *JRS*, 76: 33–46.

Belayche, N. and P. Brulé (2010), 'Introduction: Nomination et représentation du divin', *ARG*, 12: 3–5.

Belayche, N. and S. Estienne, eds (2020), *Religion et pouvoir dans le monde romain. L'autel et la toge*, Rennes: Presses universitaires de Rennes.

Belayche, N. and V. Pirenne-Delforge (2015), 'Fabriquer du divin: en guise de prélude', in N. Belayche and V. Pirenne-Delforge (eds), *Fabriquer du divin, Constructions et*

ajustements de la représentation des dieux dans l'Antiquité, 7–20, Liege: Presses universitaires de Liège.
Beltrão, C. (2018), 'Imágenes de los dioses en Cicerón: límites y contradicciones de la teología epicúrea sobre la imagen divina en *De natura deorum* I', *Auster*, 23: e042.
Beltrão, C. and F. Santangelo, eds (2020), *Cicero and Roman Religion: Eight Studies*, Stuttgart: Franz Steiner.
Bendlin, A. (2011), 'On the Uses and Disadvantages of Divination: Oracles and their Literary Representation in the Time of the Second Sophistic', in J. North and S. Price (eds), *The Religious History of the Roman Empire*, 175–250, Oxford: Oxford University Press.
Berthelet, Y. (2015), *Gouverner avec les dieux. Autorité, auspices et pouvoir, sous la République romaine et sous Auguste*, Paris: Les Belles Lettres.
Berthelet, Y. (2020), 'De la difference entre l'*auctoritas* des prêtres et celles de magistrats sous la République romaine', in J.-M. David and F. Hurlet (eds), *L'auctoritas à Rome. Une notion constitutive de la culture politique*, 121–43, Bordeaux: Ausonius.
Brennan, T. (2009), 'The Stoics', in G. Oppy and N. N. Trakakis (eds), *The History of Western Philosophy of Religion, vol. 1: Ancient Philosophy and Religion*, 105–17, London: Routledge.
Brittain, C. (2005), 'Common Sense: Concepts, Definition and Meaning In and Out of the Stoa', in B. Inwood and D. Frede (eds), *Language and Learning: Philosophy of Language in the Hellenistic Age*, 164–209, Cambridge: Cambridge University Press.
Cancik, H. and H. Cancik-Lindemaier (2001), 'The Truth of Images: Cicero and Varro on Image Worship', in J. Assmann and A. I. Baumgarten (eds), *Representation in Religion: Studies in Honor of Moshe Barash*, 43–61, Leiden: Brill.
Cairo, M. E. (2017), 'Autoridad religiosa y autoridad política en *De haruspicum responso* de Cicerón', *Maia*, 69: 486–500.
Estienne, S., V. Huet, F. Lissarrague and F. Prost, eds (2014), *Figures de dieux: construire le divin en images*, Rennes: Presses universitaires de Rennes.
Feeney, D. (1999), *Literature and Religion in Rome: Cultures, Contexts and Beliefs*, Cambridge: Cambridge University Press.
Ferri, G. (2010), *Tutela urbis: Il significato e la concezione della divinità tutelare cittadina nella religione romana*, Stuttgart: Franz Steiner.
Gildenhard, I. (2011), *Creative Eloquence. The Construction of Reality in Cicero's Speeches*, Oxford: Oxford University Press.
Glucker, J. (1996), '*Consuetudo oculorum*', in R. Katzoff (ed.), *Classical Studies in Honor of David Sohlberg*, 105–23, Ramat Gan: Bar-Ilan University Press.
Glucker, J. (2020), *Classics and Classicists: Selected Essays 1964–2000*, ed. A. Edelheit, Newcastle: Cambridge Scholars Publisher.
Graver, M. (2009), 'Cicero', in G. Oppy and N. N. Trakakis (eds), *The History of the Western Philosophy of Religion, vol. 1: Ancient Philosophy and Religion*, 119–32, London: Routledge.

Guillaumont, F. (2006), *Le* De Divinatione *de Cicéron et les théories antiques de la divination*, Brussels: Latomus.

Habinek, T. (1998), *The Politics of Latin Literature: Writing, Identity, and Empire in Ancient Rome*, Princeton, NJ: Princeton University Press.

Hölscher, T. (2004), *The Language of Images in Roman Art*, Cambridge: Cambridge University Press.

Kleve, K. (1978), 'On the Beauty of God: A Discussion between Epicureans, Stoics and Sceptics', *Symbolae Osloenses*, 53 (1): 69–83.

Krostenko, B. A. (2000), 'Beyond (Dis)Belief: Rhetorical Form and Religious Symbol in Cicero's *De Divinatione*', *TAPA*, 130: 353–91.

Lazzeretti, A. (2006), *M. Tulli Ciceronis In Verrem, action secundae Liber quartus (De signis): Commento storico e archeologico*, Pisa: ETS.

Linderski, J. (1982), 'Cicero and Roman Divination', *PP*, 37: 458–84.

Long, A. A. (1996), *Stoic Studies*, Cambridge: Cambridge University Press.

Long, A. A. and D. Sedley (1987), *The Hellenistic Philosophers*, Cambridge: Cambridge University Press.

MacRae, D. (2016), *Legible Religion: Books, Gods, and Rituals in Roman Culture*, Cambridge, MA: Harvard University Press.

Mansfeld, J. (1999), 'Theology', in K. Algra, J. Barnes, J. Mansfeld and M. Schofield (eds), *The Cambridge History of Hellenistic Philosophy*, 452–78, Cambridge: Cambridge University Press.

Moatti, C. (1997), *La raison de Rome: Naissance de l'esprit critique à la fin de la République*, Paris: Seuil.

Montero, S. (2006), *Augusto y las aves. Las aves en la Roma del Principado: prodigio, exhibición y consumo*, Barcelona: Universitat de Barcelona.

North, J. A. (1990), 'Diviners and Divination at Rome', in M. Beard and J. North (eds), *Pagan Priests: Religion and Power in the Ancient World*, 51–71, Ithaca, NY: Cornell University Press.

North, J. A. (2014), 'The Limits of the "Religious" in the Late Roman Republic', *History of Religions*, 53 (3): 225–45.

Obbink, D. (2001), 'Le livre I du *De natura deorum* de Cicéron et le *De pietate* de Philodème', in C. Auvray-Assayas and D. Delattre (eds), *Cicéron et Philodème: La polémique en philosophie*, 203–25, Paris: Ed. Rue d'Ulm.

Orlin, E. (1997), *Temples, Religion and Politics in the Roman Republic*, Leiden: Brill.

Orlin, E. (2010), *Foreign Cults in Rome: Creating a Roman Empire*, Oxford: Oxford University Press.

Padilla Peralta, D. (2018), 'Ecology, Epistemology, and Divination in Cicero *De Divinatione* 1.90–94', *Arethusa*, 51 (3): 237–67.

Padilla Peralta, D. (2020), *Divine Institutions: Religions and Community in the Middle Roman Republic*, Princeton, NJ: Princeton University Press.

Rüpke, J. (2012), *Religion in Republican Rome: Rationalisation and Ritual Change*, Philadelphia, PA: University of Pennsylvania Press.

Rüpke, J. (2014), *Superstitio: Devianza religiosa nell'Impero romano*, Rome: Carocci.

Rüpke J. (2020), 'Prêtres romains: sources et limites de l'autorité religieuse', in N. Belayche and S. Estienne (eds), *Religion et pouvoir dans le monde romain: L'autel et la toge*, 37–53, Rennes: Presses universitaires de Rennes.

Santangelo, F. (2012), 'Law and Divinations in the Late Roman Republic', in O. Tellegen-Couperus (ed.), *Law and Religion in the Roman Republic*, 31–54, Leiden: Brill.

Santangelo, F. (2013), *Divination, Prediction and the End of the Roman Republic*, Cambridge: Cambridge University Press.

Schiesaro, A. (1990), *Simulacrum et imago: Gli argomenti nel De rerum natura*, Pisa: Giardini.

Schofield M. (1980), 'Preconception, Argument and God', in M. Schofield, M. Burnyeat and J. Barnes (eds), *Doubt and Dogmatism: Studies in Hellenistic Epistemology*, 283–308, Oxford: Clarendon Press.

Schofield, M. (1986), 'Cicero For and Against Divination', *JRS*, 76: 47–65.

Schofield, M. (2009), 'Ciceronian Dialogue', in S. Goldhill (ed.), *The End of Dialogue in Antiquity*, 63–84, Cambridge: Cambridge University Press.

Setaioli, A. (2018), 'Divinazione e arte congetturali. Quinto e Marco (e Posidonio) nel *De diuinatione* ciceroniano', in E. Gavoille and S. Roesch (eds), *Diuina studia: Mélanges de religion et de philosophie anciennes offerts à François Guillaumont*, 13–28, Bordeaux: Ausonius.

Stewart, P. (2003), *Statues in Roman Society: Representations and Responses*, Oxford: Oxford University Press.

Stewart, P. (2008), *The Social History of Roman Art*, Cambridge: Cambridge University Press.

Tarrant, H. (2000), 'Recollection and Prophecy in the *De Divinatione*', *Phronesis*, 45 (1): 64–76.

Van Haeperen, F. and Y. Berthelet, eds (2021), *Dieux de Rome et du monde romain en réseaux*, Bordeaux: Ausonius.

Van Nuffelen, P. (2011), *Rethinking the Gods: Philosophical Readings of Religion in the Post-Hellenistic Period*, Cambridge: Cambridge University Press.

Várhelyi, Z. (2010), *The Religion of Senators in the Roman Empire: Power and the Beyond*, Cambridge: Cambridge University Press.

Volk, K. (2017), 'Signs, Seers, and Senators: Divinatory Expertise in Cicero and Nigidius Figulus', in J. König and G. Woolf (eds), *Authority and Expertise in Ancient Scientific Culture*, 329–47, Cambridge: Cambridge University Press.

Woolf, R. (2015), *Cicero, the Philosophy of a Roman Sceptic*, London: Routledge.

Woolf, G. (2020), 'Foreign Gods in the Age of Cicero', in C. Beltrão and F. Santangelo (eds), *Cicero and Roman Religion*, 117–33, Stuttgart: Franz Steiner.

Wynne, J. (2019), *Cicero on the Philosophy of Religion: On the Nature of the Gods and On Divination*, Cambridge: Cambridge University Press.

Ziolkowski, A. (1992), *The Temples of Mid-Republican Rome and their Historical and Topographical Context*, Rome: L'Erma di Bretschneider.

4

Non idem esse Romanos et Graecos: Varro's *De re rustica* and the Integration of the Roman World

Selena Ross

Introduction

In the preface to book 2 of his *De re rustica*, Varro insists to his audience that 'crop farming and animal husbandry are not the same' (non idem esse agri culturam et pastionem).[1] This idea, repeated twice more in this chapter alone, is central to understanding Varro's purpose in writing this book as he did. The idea that crop farming and animal husbandry are distinct industries is far from Varro's own invention. It is literally true – the two industries rely on different labour and require different knowledge and skills – and commonly referenced in literary and other sources. However, Varro is not merely repeating a familiar trope with a heavy hand, inserting rhetoric where it does not belong. As a highly skilled and educated writer, Varro balances literal fact with metaphor throughout his work, and this preface is no exception. While there is much nuance worthy of analysis, one message that comes out over the course of the preface to which this line belongs is quite clear. When Varro tells us that crop farming and animal husbandry, while not the same, are most effective when conducted in tandem, he presents a vision of productive coexistence – a vision much needed during the days of the late Republic.

This model of productive coexistence operates across the dual functions of the *Rust.* as an agricultural and philosophical work. As an agricultural treatise, it stresses the diversity and connectivity required to operate an estate that is not only functional but fits within the traditional moral bounds of Roman society. This is consistent with what we see in the *Rust.* and throughout related works on Roman agriculture, such as those by Cato the Elder, Columella, and Pliny the Elder. As a philosophical dialogue, it offers a vision of Roman *imperium* in which the Roman state governs a diverse and connected empire without compromising its past or its values. The peoples who have long been 'other' to Varro's Roman audience are now, to some extent, Romans themselves; the expansion of Roman power demands the integration of the many peoples both in and outside of Italy. I argue that Varro makes use of metaphor – equating crop farming with Rome and animal husbandry with the Greek world – to present these two interconnected models of Roman success. Through the choice of agriculture in general as a metaphor, and the dichotomy of crops versus animal husbandry in particular, Varro uses the familiar past to direct his audience towards the future.

Book 2: The preface

Book 2 of the *Rust.* discusses animal husbandry, *res pecuaria*. The book opens with a brief preface, introducing the topic and providing the framework for the dialogue itself. While books 1 and 3 are set at Rome – in the Temple of Tellus and the Villa Publica, respectively – book 2 takes place in Epirus, on the western coast of the Greek mainland directly across the Adriatic Sea from the southern heel of Italy, at the time when Varro was serving there under Pompey during his efforts to eradicate piracy. Suitable to Varro's punning nature, the scene is filled with people whose names remind the reader of the animals being discussed: among others, Scrofa speaks about swine, Vaccius on cattle. The conversation begins with Varro – in the past – speaking on the origin (*origo*) and dignity (*dignitas*) of animal husbandry. The remainder of the book moves through the eighty-one subcategories of animal husbandry which Scrofa identifies. These subcategories are based upon nine types of livestock: sheep, goats, swine, cattle, asses, horses, mules, dogs, and enslaved herdsmen. The care and breeding of each type is addressed briefly, the various participants speaking about their own areas of expertise.

In the preface, Varro establishes the ideological framework for this book. People living in towns are considered lazier (*desidiosiores*) than those working or even just living in the countryside.[2] Romans of his own day rely on imported goods instead of producing their own and even in the countryside they imitate the worst parts of city life: 'Therefore, as now nearly all the heads of families have crept back between the walls, with sickle and plough left behind they chose to busy their hands in the theatre and circus rather than in the grain fields and vineyards' (igitur quod nunc intra murum fere patres familiae correpserunt relictis falce et aratro et manus movere maluerunt in theatro ac circo, quam in segetibus ac vinetis).[3] There is a contrast between these contemporary men and their ancestors, who – like Varro himself, we are to believe – criticized those who preferred town life, having even constructed the very calendar to enable them to stay as much as possible on their farms. Varro presents farming as work that is not just necessary but innately moral.

It is noteworthy (though far from unique) that Varro's criticism of his contemporaries is blended with a disdain for Rome's reliance on imported goods. While the places mentioned by name – Africa, Sardinia, Cos, and Chios – are Roman territories, they are nonetheless considered foreign. The supposed decline in Italian agriculture and the accompanying reliance on imports is a matter of morality. Varro demonstrates this throughout the *Rust.*, and we see it reflected in other sources as well, especially through the use of exempla: notable and virtuous men of the Roman past who farmed alongside their military and political careers are cited in order to criticize the author's contemporaries for failing to do the same. Pliny the Elder and Columella both employ this technique, referencing Q. Cincinnatus, G. Serranus, G. Fabricius, and Curius Dentatus.[4] Following his use of these exempla, Columella acknowledges the debt of his own idea of the decline of the moral Roman farmer to Varro's work.[5] Varro's criticism of foreign luxury – especially in contrast with traditional, Roman humility – was and is viewed as a key focus of the *Rust.*

It is immediately following this complaint that Varro begins the passage with which this study is most concerned. Beginning with an attack on the greed of landowners in his own day, he quickly turns to the difference between crop farming – the subject of the previous book – and animal husbandry:

> And so in the land in which the herdsmen who founded the city [Rome] taught their descendants the cultivation of fields, in that place, contrary to that, because of greed their descendants – contrary to the law – made pastures from grain fields, ignoring the fact that the cultivation of fields and the raising of animals are not the same. For the shepherd is one thing and the ploughman another, and although oxen can be pastured in a field an oxherd is very different from a cowherd. For an ox does not produce that which is born in the field, but it bears it off with its teeth; contrary to this the tamed bull makes it so that grain is born more easily in the field and fodder is born more easily in the meadow. I say, the knowledge and science of the farmer are one thing, that of the herdsman another: what the cultivation of fields causes to be born from the earth is the domain of the farmer, while that which is born from the herd is the domain of the herdsman. Since then there is a great alliance between these, because it benefits the landowner more to feed the fodder on the estate than to sell it, and manure is most suited to the fruits of the earth, and livestock most of all are disposed to

that, one who own land ought to have knowledge of both the cultivation of fields and the raising of livestock, and even of *pastio villatica.*

> itaque in qua terra culturam agri docuerunt pastores progeniem suam, qui condiderunt urbem, ibi contra progenies eorum propter avaritiam contra leges ex segetibus fecit prata, ignorantes non idem esse agri culturam et pastionem. alius enim opilio et arator, nec, si possunt in agro pasci armenta, armentarius non aliut ac bubulcus. armentum enim id quod in agro natum non creat, sed tollit dentibus; contra bos domitus causa fit ut commodius nascatur frumentum in segete et pabulum in novali. alia, inquam, ratio ac scientia coloni, alia pastoris: coloni ea quae agri cultura factum ut nascerentur e terra, contra pastoris ea quae nata ex pecore. quarum quoniam societas inter se magna, propterea quod pabulum in fundo compascere quam vendere plerumque magis expedit domino fundi et stercoratio ad fructus terrestres aptissima et maxume ad id pecus appositum, qui habet praedium, habere utramque debet disciplinam, et agri culturae et pecoris pascendi, et etiam villaticae pastionis.[6]

Precise terminology is necessary for understanding this passage. While the word 'agriculture' is derived from the Latin *agri cultura* – the cultivation of fields – it is more expansive in meaning. It may refer equally to the growing of crops and animal husbandry. All the work that Varro describes throughout the *Rust.* falls under the modern umbrella of agriculture. For Varro, the tasks specific to *agri cultura* are much more limited; we see this outlined in the extensive debate on terminology at the start of the dialogue in book 1. For the purposes of clarity, when referring to what Varro considers *agri cultura* or the work of *coloni*, I will use the terms 'crop farming', 'cultivation', and 'farmer'.[7] When referring to what Varro terms *pastio* or *res pecuaria*, I will use the term 'animal husbandry', as defined above; I refer to all workers in animal husbandry as 'herdsmen'. Consistent with the modern usage, I will use the word 'agriculture' expansively, covering the broad range of work mentioned throughout the *Rust.* Lastly, I will use the word 'estate' to refer broadly to any landholding, parts of which are used for agriculture.

As this discussion of terminology suggests, it is easy to inadvertently blur the lines between different subsets of agriculture. We may anticipate that Varro, in emphasizing the diversity of agriculture, was in part responding to the same elision in his own day. It is true that there are many tasks on an agricultural estate that could be done by a non-specialized workforce.[8] However, especially on the larger estates considered by Varro and his peers, specialization was both necessary and beneficial. Within book 2 of the *Rust.*, Varro discusses the significance of specialization in the context of different types of herdsmen (e.g.

shepherds, swineherds, goatherds, oxherds).[9] Throughout his own agricultural treatise, Columella provides a more in-depth explanation of and justification for the specialization of agricultural workers, arguing that specialization leads workers to be more invested in their work, and therefore more efficient and profitable.[10] Varro makes it clear that carefully managed specialization is necessary for an estate to be as productive as possible.

As Varro suggests, there is great value in integrated, intensive agriculture, beyond the traditional ideal of the self-sufficient estate.[11] Manure is an incredibly valuable commodity: while crop rotation and the use of 'green manure' (the growing and ploughing under of nitrogen-fixing legumes) do much to improve soil composition, animal manure was unmatched as a fertilizer.[12] From the complementary perspective, money is saved by feeding livestock on pasture and with fodder grown on the estate. Both manure and fodder are valuable commodities which take up considerable space and are difficult to transport, making sources within the bounds of the estate even more desirable.[13] It is entirely logical for Varro to assert that animal husbandry and crop farming are compatible, and that anyone who wants to run a successful estate should have at least some degree of knowledge about both divisions of agriculture.

With this compatibility in mind, what is meant by the criticism of Romans who have 'made pastures from grain fields'? This may seem to imply that animal husbandry is driven by greed, being profit-driven and therefore incompatible with Roman morality.[14] However, this argument ignores the distinction between different models of animal husbandry. The animal husbandry criticized at the start of this passage is large-scale, extensive husbandry, most comparable to modern ranching. The animal husbandry which Varro describes elsewhere is integrated into a more diverse agricultural estate.[15] This criticism, then, has much in common with the criticisms we see elsewhere of vast estates which focus on extensive crop farming, including the *latifundia* referenced by authors such as Pliny the Elder.[16] It is not animal husbandry that is immoral but the excessive or otherwise improper use of it.

While it is the contents of the dialogue that inform the audience about the practices of animal husbandry, this preface frames the didactic agenda. Through his insistence on the complexity of agriculture, Varro justifies his choice to compose this work: the topic is one worth learning and writing about. By presenting himself as combatting the ignorance of his contemporaries, Varro argues that he is a suitable instructor. The softening of tone as the preface progresses guides the audience from the problem (greed and ignorance destroying agriculture) to the solution (employing the methods and approaches that Varro's work provides). With Varro as a guide, the audience not only comes to understand the underlying tensions at play but how to balance them and use them constructively.

Non idem esse agri culturam et pastionem

As Varro demonstrates, it is insufficient to say that crop farming and animal husbandry are not the same. They are complementary, each relying on, or at the very least benefiting from, the products of the other. They are united in how they contrast with other types of business, especially those that take place in urban settings. However, they are also in constant competition for valuable resources such as water and land. Even well-managed livestock pose a constant threat to crops, whether by trampling them or eating them. Varro references this in book 1 with the example of the notoriously destructive habits of goats, who, according to Fundanius, 'destroy all young crops by browsing, not least of all grapevines and olives' (omnia novella sata carpendo corrumpunt, non minimum vites atque oleas).[17] There is a distinct sense that animal husbandry poses a greater threat to crop farming than the reverse, although it offers significant benefits.

The relationship between crop farming and animal husbandry is consistent with what we see in Columella's work. While it is unlikely that Columella derives the idea solely from his predecessor, Varro's work – and especially the preface to book 2 of the *Rust.* – appears to have been quite influential. This dynamic is most overt in Columella's preface to book 6. Columella adapts words and phrases from Varro's preface for his own, and he presents the same relationship between crop farming and animal husbandry: they are simultaneously complementary and in competition. Columella was clearly influenced by Varro, and his choice to write a similar preface indicates that reference to this dichotomy was considered particularly useful when constructing a model of a successful estate.

Outside of the world of literature, we see this tension referenced in the Polla Inscription, *CIL* I2 638. Within a longer list of accomplishments, the magistrate commemorated states, 'I first made it so that the herdsmen ceded to the ploughmen concerning the public land' (*primus fecei ut de agro poplico aratoribus cederent pastores*). This references the ongoing competition over access to land; the tension at times grew to the extent that it warranted intervention.[18] This claim gains significance when we consider the location of the findspot in Lucania: not only was Lucania a hub of the sheep industry, it was one of the locations impacted by the Gracchan land distributions.[19] Given the degree of conflict that occurred surrounding public land, it is unsurprising that we find evidence of the tensions between crop farmers and herdsmen in areas where public land was a major resource for exploitation. It is perhaps significant that, as this dispute concerned public rather than private land, the benefits of combining the two industries – either in the form of savings on fodder or crop improvement through manure application – would not be felt by either side.[20] Outside of the structure of a private estate, it is difficult to reconcile the differences between the two industries, and both appear to have suffered as a result.

One last distinction between animal husbandry and crop farming merits discussion here, as Varro references it not only in the opening of book 2 but again in the preface of book 3: their chronology. Varro presents us with a progression through the ages of human development in his speech on the origins of animal husbandry near the beginning of the dialogue in book 2. First, we are told, 'men lived on those things which the untouched land bore plentifully' (*viverent homines ex his rebus, quae inviolata ultro ferret terra*), a familiar image of the golden age.[21] Following this came the pastoral age, in which men tamed animals and gathered fruits from the land, and then humans 'descended from the pastoral life to the cultivation of fields' (*a vita pastorali ad agri culturam descenderunt*).[22] There is a degree of ambiguity over whether Varro believes there is a fourth stage which he and his contemporaries occupy, though comparison with other passages in the work suggests that this is the case.[23] Regardless, Varro is clear that each stage retains portions of the past, integrating them into the present. Varro's model of an estate that combines crop farming and animal husbandry serves as an example of how this integration should be accomplished.

Varro complicates this model of the chronological progression of agriculture and humanity in the opening to book 3. While we cannot assume that Varro would expect his readers to apply what is said in book 3 to book 2, it nonetheless helps us to understand Varro's approach to the significance of the divisions of agriculture. The primary division in the opening to book 3 is that between countryside and city; this is not unexpected given the focus of book 3 on the more urban industry of *pastio villatica*. We are told that 'farmers preceded city-dwellers by a great number of years' (*immani numero annorum urbanos agricolae praestant*).[24] What follows seems to be a contradiction of the model presented in book 2:

> At first, due to poverty, people were practicing agriculture[25] largely without distinction, so that those who were descended from herdsmen were both sowing crops and pasturing livestock in the same fields; they separated the properties after they grew, and made it so that some were called farmers, and others herdsmen.

> agri culturam primo propter paupertatem maxime indiscretam habebant, quod a pastoribus qui erant orti in eodem agro et serebant et pascebant; quae postea creverunt peculia diviserunt, ac factum ut dicerentur alii agricolae, alii pastores.[26]

Varro presents here an image of small, impoverished estates combining crop farming and animal husbandry with no distinction. While this is certainly a messier image than what Varro provides in book 2, there is no contradiction; the reference to these people as descended from herdsmen makes this clear. This time of mixed forms of agriculture takes place at the transition from the pastoral life to the farming life, when the people were still maintaining a larger amount of their earlier ways. The eventual division is the state which Varro references throughout the *Rust.*

These discussions of the progress of humanity from pastoralism to crop farming and the eventual urban/rural divide drives home the point that a life dominated by animal husbandry is quite different from the lives of Varro's contemporary Romans. If we extend the logic of this sequence from the work to the workers, we see that Varro gives the impression that herdsmen are in some way backwards and even less civilized – at least by Roman standards – than farmers, who have followed and surpassed them.

The farmer in the Roman imagination

Farmers appear throughout the Roman imaginary as exempla of old-fashioned Roman morality, from Cincinnatus to Diocletian. Farmers – or at least the farmers of the past who tended their own fields – are portrayed by a variety of authors as not only innately moral, but also quintessentially Roman. In our surviving literary sources, this begins with Cato the Elder, who famously claims the following: 'when they would praise a good man, they would praise him thusly: he is a good farmer and a good yeoman' (*virum bonum quom laudabant, ita laudabant, bonum agricolam bonumque colonum*).[27] Pliny the Elder, in his introduction to book 18 of his *Historia Naturalis*, builds upon this with a lengthy discussion on the connection between Rome and agriculture.[28] An emphasis on the crop-oriented religious practices established under Romulus and Numa elevates farming beyond the mundane and illustrates its integral role in not only Roman life but also Roman identity.[29] While Pliny the Elder acknowledges that agriculture was held in high esteem 'even among foreigners' (*etiam apud exteros*), the focus remains on the relationship between farming and Rome.[30] While much changes between the times of Cato the Elder and Pliny the Elder, both maintain the centrality of farming to Roman identity.

Throughout book 1, Varro makes it clear that Italy is especially suited for farming and therefore closely connected to it. The beginning of the dialogue in book 1 serves as a *laus Italiae*, opening with Agrasius asking his companions: 'You all, who have wandered many lands, have you ever seen one better farmed than Italy?' (*Vos, qui multas perambulastis terras, ecquam cultiorem Italia vidistis?*).[31] Abundant examples are provided of the remarkable success of farming throughout Italy. In his analysis of references to specific locations in the *Rust.*, Nelsestuen determines that 77 out of 116 (or roughly 66 per cent) refer to either a specific region within Italy or the entire peninsula in general; he terms this a 'pattern of exemplification'.[32] A reliance on Roman sources over Greek demonstrates that this success is as much a matter of specialized knowledge and skill as the predisposition of the land; it is not simply Italy, but the Romans themselves that are such notable farmers.[33] This association, strengthened throughout book 1 as Varro's cast of characters discusses crop farming, is carried with the audience into the opening of book 2.

The herdsman in the Roman imagination

Prior to the practical information on animal husbandry in book 2, Varro himself – within the dialogue – gives a brief speech on the origin (*origo*) and dignity (*dignitas*) of animal husbandry, picking up on many of the same ideas from the opening of the book. This speech is filled with citations and references, creating a pedigree for animal husbandry and those who practise it. Animal husbandry is said to predate farming, being the first way in which people deliberately cultivated natural resources rather than relying on the natural abundance of the landscape. This matches the chronology from the opening of book 2 – 'the herdsmen taught their descendants the cultivation of the fields' (*culturam agri docuerunt pastores progeniem suam*) – although it refers to the development rather than the implementation of the two fields.[34] The dignity of animal husbandry is not so much explained as demonstrated, with Varro identifying ways in which livestock are honoured.

While the first portion of the passage on dignity includes both Greek and Roman examples – this is overt, as Varro states: 'Among the ancients every illustrious man was a herdsman, as the old poets point out in both the Greek and Latin language' (*de antiquis illustrissimus quisque pastor erat, ut ostendit et

Graeca et Latina lingua et veteres poetae)[35] – the later portion is almost emphatically Roman. This begins with the etymological claim that *Italia* is derived from *vituli*, followed by a rhetorical question: 'Who does not say that the Roman people truly arose from herdsmen?' (*Romanorum vero populum a pastoribus esse ortum quis non dicit?*).[36] This is further supported with references to Romulus and Remus as herdsmen, the founding of Rome on the Parilia, the literal and representational use of animals as currency, the practice of the *suovetaurilia*, and finally a list of *cognomina* derived from the names of livestock.[37] This integration of animal husbandry into Roman life – especially early Roman life – is used as key evidence of its dignity.

Despite this, book 2 is filled with indications that animal husbandry is less Roman than the passage suggests. Nelsestuen convincingly argues that book 2 demonstrates a greater preoccupation with the provinces than Italy itself.[38] I argue that book 2 – and as such, Varro's treatment of animal husbandry – is in fact oriented around Greek regions. While both the speakers and the setting are technically Roman – Epirus under Roman *imperium* and the speakers as Romans living in Greece – Varro stresses their Greek identity. When introducing Scrofa to his companions, the internal character Varro prefaces a Greek quote by saying, 'as I speak Greek to half-Greek herdsmen' (*ut semigraecis pastoribus dicam graece*); Scrofa picks up the same thread, addressing their companions as 'you, who are the champions of Epirote animal husbandry' (*vos, qui estis Epirotici pecuariae athletae*).[39]

Book 2's focus on Greece both relies on and reinforces pre-existing associations between Greece and animal husbandry in the Roman imagination. While animal husbandry was practised throughout Italy, much of it occurred in areas that had strong ties to Greece. Many of the regions where animal husbandry dominated – especially areas in the Apennines and throughout southern Italy – were still newly Roman, following the Social War. The setting of the dialogue in Epirus (the homeland of Pyrrhus) would likely remind the audience of the histories of these areas, calling to mind Roman expansion throughout Italy.[40] Varro's contemporaries may have considered these areas still as something between Roman and Greek – something between self and other. This sense of animal husbandry as non-Roman is strengthened by the fact that herdsmen themselves are typically portrayed throughout Roman literature as outsiders. They have stereotypical features that distinguish them from the general population such as their clothes, equipment, and speech.[41] They were often enslaved, taken from other parts of the Mediterranean. They were generally viewed as a threat, given their work kept them physically fit, armed, and away from the oversight of the

Roman elite.[42] Animal husbandry may take place in Italy, but the people doing it are not Romans.

As Varro reminds us, it is true that the Romans see themselves as born from herdsmen.[43] We see this confirmed in various sources outside of Varro, such as Livy, who begins book 2 of his *Ab Urbe Condita* with the reminder that the earliest Roman population were herdsmen.[44] However, in the world Varro describes, Romans are no longer herdsmen. Instead, they control the people who are, whether directly on their own estates or more generally through Roman dominion.[45] We see Varro's chronology of agricultural development enacted: the Romans have progressed past animal husbandry but must continue to integrate it into their lives.

Varro the political philosopher

As a treatise on agriculture, the *Rust.* is a complex work, the result of the author's considerable skill. Known to Quintilian as 'the most educated of the Romans' (vir Romanorum eruditissimus), Varro was knowledgeable on a wide variety of topics, a fact that is reflected in his diverse corpus.[46] Although read today primarily as a source on Roman agriculture, he was a soldier and a statesman during the tumultuous period of the late Republic. He saw first-hand the effects of the Social War and the conflicts that followed; he served at a high level in the military under Pompey the Great, Julius Caesar, and the young Octavian. It is certainly possible that, in writing the *Rust.* as an eighty-year-old man experiencing the ongoing chaos of the 30s BCE, Varro sought to distance himself from the fraught world of politics.[47] However, given the complexity of the work and the details of Varro's own life, it is more likely that Varro wrote the *Rust.* as a way of engaging in the political conversations of his day.

Over the past few decades, scholars have explored the complex literary and philosophical dimensions of Varro's *Rust.*, acknowledging its dual purposes as a philosophical dialogue and an agricultural handbook. This has had a profound impact on our understanding of Varro and the role he played in the late Republic. One of the most fruitful approaches has been analysis of the layers of metaphor present throughout the *Rust.*, especially those pertaining to politics. For example, focusing on book 3, Green characterizes the *Rust.* as a commentary 'on the social and political state of Rome … with farming as a Xenophontic, or Cincinnatan, metaphor for wise government'.[48] Kronenberg, interpreting the *Rust.* as a Menippean satire, has argued that it is 'a subversive work, which uses farming as a vehicle to expose the hypocrisy and pretensions of Roman morality, intellectual culture, and politics in the late Republic'.[49] Nelsestuen explores the metaphor of state as agricultural estate, developing a model in which each book of the *Rust.* – and its subject matter – maps onto a portion of the Roman empire: Italy is her fields, the provinces her pasture, and the city of Rome the villa at the heart of it all. These scholars have demonstrated that complex social and political arguments can and should be extracted through analysis of the layered metaphors of the *Rust.*

A look at Varro's contemporary and friend Cicero supports the idea that Varro wrote the *Rust.* as a way of influencing the political world around him. The eight surviving letters from Cicero to Varro (*Ad Familiares* 9.1–8) attest to the time when both men were in similar positions: recovering from supporting the losing side in the civil war, pushed to the margins of politics, and turned increasingly towards writing. One passage provides insight into this approach:

> If no one will take advantage of our works, nevertheless let us both write and read 'Republics', and let us govern the state and debate about customs and laws in letters and books – as the most educated men of the past did – if not in the Curia and the Forum.
>
> si nemo utetur opera, tamen et scribere et legere πολιτείας et, si minus in curia atque in foro, at in litteris et libris, ut doctissimi veteres fecerunt, gubernare rem publicam et de moribus ac legibus quaerere.[50]

Kronenberg convincingly argues that the *Rust.* is how Varro responds to this request, cloaking his arguments about the *res publica* in the metaphor of *res rustica*.[51] The use of metaphor enables Varro to build in complex layers of meaning that would not be possible in a more straightforward political work.

Agriculture as a metaphor for statecraft is not without precedent. In his *Republic*, Plato uses a pastoral metaphor to explain the structure of his envisioned society, dividing the population into herdsmen, working dogs, and livestock.[52] Within a Roman context, the metaphor operates in the same way as that of *familia* for *res publica*, with the *pater familias* – or, on the farm, the *dominus* and his representative the *vilicus* – as a stand-in for the *pater patriae*, or the governing class as a whole. An estate with different tasks productively coexisting may then be representative of different factions – however we may choose to identify them – within the Roman state existing in concord.

There are many tasks on the Roman farm, any of which could be used to create this metaphor. Vinedressers and reapers could act as the agricultural side of the metaphor, for example, without the need to include any reference to animal husbandry. Varro makes the deliberate choice to use the dichotomy of crop farming and animal husbandry. It could be argued that he does this because the dichotomy is a familiar one: the subject of the metaphor is less important than the image of concord that it presents. However, this approach engages with the metaphor on only the most superficial level. Treating the choice of objects within the metaphor as significant enables us to engage much more deeply with Varro's message. Herdsmen and farmers are not only familiar figures, but ones with deep, symbolic meaning within Roman thought. By exploring these layers of meaning, we gain greater insight into what this metaphor means for Varro's vision of Rome.

As we have seen, Varro draws significant attention to the ways in which these two parts of agricultural life interact, arguing for the integration of both into a productive Roman estate. We have also seen evidence of what these two industries may represent. Within both Varro and the Roman literary tradition more broadly, farming is associated with Roman identity and morality. Responsible Romans fight, farm, and govern. Animal husbandry, on the other hand, is more closely connected to people whom the Romans of Varro's time were likely to consider 'other'. By arguing for the integration of these different industries into a single estate, Varro argues for the controlled integration of those considered 'other' into the Roman state.

Through an agricultural metaphor, Varro affirms the complexity of this social problem. Throughout the *Rust.*, Varro has his speakers go to great lengths to explain the complexity of agriculture.[53] Like agriculture, integration is a practical necessity that must be carefully managed by the people in charge.

There is never any question in the *Rust.* that crop farming is integral to an agricultural estate. Within our metaphor, the Roman empire will always have the Romans themselves at its core. What is up for discussion is the role played by animal husbandry, or the non-Roman population of the empire. As the preface to book 2 makes clear, animal husbandry is not always a good thing, especially when done through ignorance. Greed (*avaritia*) motivates people to practise animal husbandry in unsuitable ways; this impulse must be moderated. Animal husbandry can be of great benefit to crop farming, but not when it is favoured to the detriment of valuable farmland. Crop farming must remain the focus, with animal husbandry performing a supportive role: providing oxen for ploughing and manure for fertilizer. Within our metaphor, while non-Roman people can offer significant benefits to Rome, they cannot be permitted to dominate or redefine the priorities of Rome. Others may be led by their greed towards foreign *luxuria*, Varro suggests, but this is unwise. The traditional needs of Rome – including cultural needs – must be prioritized over the temptations offered by the expanded Roman empire.

What does it mean for Rome if we say that animal husbandry represents not just the provinces in general but the Greek world in particular? We must first acknowledge that it is not inevitable that Varro would so closely associate animal husbandry with Greece. Plenty of other groups under Roman *imperium* were well known in Varro's time for their prominence in animal husbandry, such as people in parts of Gaul and northern Africa, where transhumance and large agricultural operations were more common. Just as Varro chooses animal husbandry deliberately, he chooses to emphasize its Greek associations deliberately. While some of these reasons are mentioned in the discussion above, it is also important to acknowledge how Varro's chronology of agriculture impacts the metaphor. Animal husbandry is an earlier stage in human development than crop farming, but parts of it can and should be retained in Varro's own time. Similarly, Greece was a dominant force in the Mediterranean earlier than Rome, parts of which have been retained into Varro's own time. The parts of Greek dominance that remain – such as literature, philosophy, and other arts – can and should be integrated responsibly into Roman culture.[54] As farmers must use the manure from livestock to fertilize their fields, the Romans musts take advantage of the foundation of Greek culture to enrich their own, even as they take care to not let it corrupt them.

Conclusion

In the preface to book 2 of the *Rust.*, we see Varro's model for the Roman empire. It is guided by a strong and highly knowledgeable ruling class, Varro and his peers; these people must utilize the structure and resources of the Roman government to improve Roman society by integrating its diverse components. According to this model, these leaders must prioritize the needs and traditions of the Romans, building and improving upon them with study and consideration. People who have in the past been considered 'other' but under Roman control must be integrated into the Roman empire as responsibly as possible; doing so is of great benefit both to Rome and to these people themselves. The Greek world in particular offers an invaluable contribution to an integrated Roman world, justifying its prominence in book 2. Greed and excess must be avoided, as they cancel out the benefits of integration on the creation of a prosperous empire. This model may not be highly refined – Varro does not lay out detailed guidelines for governance – but it is oddly optimistic for a product of its time. While Varro does criticize his contemporaries, he does not present these failures as inevitable;

even the people criticized for greedily turning crop lands into pastures do so out of ignorance. By providing a model, Varro seeks to correct that ignorance and provide a path towards a better future for the Roman world.

It is because agriculture is itself so complex and so important that it provides a uniquely profitable metaphor through which Varro may address the major issues of his day. There are endless ways in which one may adapt even the metaphor of state as estate. That Varro uses it as he does, to discuss how the 'other' should be integrated into Rome, demonstrates the importance he assigns to that issue. During Varro's lifetime, the Roman empire had reached its greatest extent yet, but Rome was still struggling to cope with how to integrate even other Italians into that picture. Varro's metaphor not only provides a model of integration, it also provides some assurance that it can and should be done. Just like the estate, the Roman state will thrive through well-managed cooperation and integration.

Notes

1 Varro, *Rust.* 2.pr.4. All translations are my own.

2 Varro, *Rust.* 2.pr.1. This same idea is expanded upon by Pliny the Elder, who provides additional examples to support the claim that this was the view of their ancestors (*HN* 18.3.13–14).

3 Varro, *Rust.* 2.pr.3.

4 Plin., *HN* 18.4.20; Columella, *Rust.* 1.pr.13–14.

5 Columella, *Rust.* 1.pr.15.

6 Varro, *Rust.* 2.pr.4–5.

7 This includes what may more correctly fall under the term horticulture: the growing of vegetables and flowers.

8 Note, however, that non-specialized does not mean unskilled; as discussed below, there is a clear awareness in the Roman agricultural treatises that all agricultural work requires both knowledge and skill, being a complex art and science (Varro, *Rust.* 1.3.1). Columella is perhaps even more insistent than Varro about this fact, comparing agriculture to oratory and philosophy in their having a nearly limitless scope (Columella, *Rust.* 11.1.9–12). The very existence of agricultural treatises – and the agricultural handbooks that, while not extant, are attested by our sources – is a testament to that fact. Varro makes numerous references to these technical handbooks, for the rhetorical purpose of which see Doody 2017: 182–202. On the use of these handbooks by herdsmen, see Varro, *Rust.* 2.1.23, 2.2.20, 2.3.8, 2.6.16, 2.10.10.

9 Varro, *Rust.* 2.10.1–4.
10 See in particular Columella, *Rust.* 1.9, which additionally references a force of unspecialized workers.
11 The techniques and benefits of well-integrated animal husbandry are discussed by Kron 2000: 277–87; 2004: 119–34, who makes a compelling case for the sustainable efficiency of this approach in Roman Italy.
12 We now know that composted animal manure is a rich source of nitrogen and other nutrients necessary for plant growth; the use of manure and other forms of compost are ubiquitous throughout global agriculture. The Romans were aware of the importance of manure for improving soil for agricultural purposes, whether crop farming or pasturage, and this is reflected in the abundance of references found in the literary record. Particularly illustrative of their knowledge are the passages in which our authors rank different varieties of manure for different purposes; Pliny the Elder provides a convenient summary of his predecessors' views (Plin. *HN* 17.50–54). For a thorough introduction to manuring and other fertilization practices known to the Romans, see White 1970: 125–45. Semple 1928: 129–56 provides a more literature-oriented approach, including evidence beyond the Roman canon. On the use of other agricultural byproducts such as chaff and compost, see Foxhall 1998: 35–40.
13 As an illustration of the scale of this issue, data available from the US Department of Agriculture indicate that a 100-lb lamb produces approximately 4 lb of solid excrement per day; this does not include additional waste such as soiled bedding, which is commonly added to composted manure (US Natural Resources Conservation Service 2012). On this basis, we can estimate that a single flock of 100 sheep – a rather small operation by the standards of the agronomists – would produce 73 tons (146,000 lb) of solid excrement each year. Conversion of this and other waste products into manure and compost is the safest and most effective way of handling these potentially hazardous waste materials, while benefitting crop farming.
14 For this argument, see esp. Kronenberg 2009: 95–9.
15 This is true of the agronomists in general, who exclusively describe multipurpose estates which integrate villas and diverse forms of agriculture. The exception to this rule is Varro, who includes a reference to an estate exclusively devoted to apiculture (Varro, *Rust.* 3.16.10–11). While Varro does present the most diverse image of Roman agricultural practices – notably being the only writer to overtly reference long-distance transhumance in Italy (Varro, *Rust.* 2.1.16, 1.2.9) – he does not ever endorse a model equivalent to ranching.
16 References to *latifundia* are primarily critical, with Pliny the Elder's critique most infamous: '*latifundia* ruined Italy, and truly even the provinces' (*latifundia perdidere Italiam, iam vero et provincias*) (Plin., *HN* 18.35). The existence of *latifundia* outside

of rhetorical contexts remains a subject of debate, with archaeological survey presenting a more diverse picture of small and medium-sized estates throughout Italy than Pliny's claim suggests; for two recent perspectives on the application of these surveys, see de Ligt 2012, esp. chapter 6, and Fracchia 2013: 181–97. On the origins of the modern debate and a catalogue of ancient references to *latifundia*, see White 1967: 62–79 and, in response, van Hooff 1982: 126–8.

17 Varro, *Rust.* 1.2.18. The participants in this portion of the dialogue reference, though with some disagreement, a law prohibiting the grazing of goats in certain areas for this reason.

18 For a recent and thorough discussion of this inscription, especially the socio-political forces at work behind its creation, see Bernard et al. 2014: 953–85, esp. 962–8.

19 While the event referenced may or may not have taken place in the area where the inscription was found, it clearly had relevance for the people living there. On both the findspot and the significance of Lucania, see Bernard et al. 2014: 963.

20 For the benefits of combined crop farming and animal husbandry to be felt, their interactions must be managed. Manure must be properly aged and applied; rotational grazing practices are necessary to ensure that animals fertilize land rather than damage vulnerable crops. Contracts were often used to facilitate this between private parties; see, for example, the recommendations Cato the Elder provides for a contract concerning winter pasturage (Cato, *Agr.* 149).

21 Varro, *Rust.* 2.1.4.

22 Varro, *Rust.* 2.1.4–5.

23 For a thorough consideration of this progression that incorporates book 3 and *pastio villatica*, see Brown 2019: 317–51.

24 Varro, *Rust.* 3.1.3.

25 While I usually translate *agri cultura* as crop farming, here the context makes it clear that the phrase refers to the broader concept of agriculture.

26 Varro, *Rust.* 3.1.7.

27 Cato, *Agr.* 1.2.

28 Plin., *HN* 18.1.5.

29 Plin., *HN* 18.2.

30 Plin., *HN* 18.5. An element of this association absent from Varro is the specific connection between farmers and soldiers, an idea prominent in other works (see, e.g. Cato, *Agr.* praef.; Columella, *Rust.* 1.pr.13–14; Plin., *HN* 18.19–20). While this is certainly significant, the topic is too large to be addressed in the present medium.

31 Varro, *Rust.* 1.2.3. Agrius provides the response in the affirmative before others pick up the praise in turn.

32 Grant Nelsestuen 2015: 93, appendix 4: 265–9. This may seem unremarkable given Varro's own background, but comparison with book 2 (in which just 72 out of 164 or roughly 44 per cent of references are Italian) suggests that this is significant.

33 Nelsestuen 2015: 87.

34 Varro, *Rust.* 2.pr.4. For more on the significance of this chronology, see below.

35 Varro, *Rust.* 2.1.6.

36 Varro, *Rust.* 2.1.9.

37 Varro, *Rust.* 2.2.9–10.

38 Nelsestuen 2015, with particular attention to 117–18.

39 Varro, *Rust.* 2.1.2.

40 Nelsestuen 2015: 121.

41 Many references to their distinct appearance are vague, as when Livy references 'herdsman garb' (*pastoralis habitus*) (Liv., *AUC* 9.2.2, 9.36.6, 10.4.10). Although set in a Greek context, one of the clearest examples of the appearance of a herdsman can be found in Theocritus, *Idyll* 7.13–19; Lycidas is said to be immediately recognizable as a herdsman, as a well-tanned man wearing a rough, belted tunic and a goatskin, carrying a crook, and smelling strongly of cheese. For discussion of these and other examples, see Frayn 1984: 66–93. Frayn suggests, primarily based on evidence found in Livy, that herding communities may have had a recognizable dialect as well, distinct from other rural speech.

42 This threat does manifest at various points in Roman history, such as the leading role enslaved herdsmen played in the Servile Wars.

43 Varro, *Rust.* 2.1.9.

44 Liv., *AUC* 2.1.4.

45 This aspect of control is explored by Nelsestuen 2015, esp. 148–55.

46 Quint., *Inst.* 10.1.95.

47 In the opening of book 1, Varro tells Fundania – and the rest of his audience – that he has written the *Rust.* as a way of wrapping up his final business before he dies an old man: 'For my eightieth year warns me that I should pack my bags, before I depart from life' (*annus enim octogesimus admonet me ut sarcinas conligam, antequam proficiscar e vita*) (Varro, *Rust.* 1.1.1). The pretense is that he must leave written instructions for his wife concerning how to manage her newly acquired agricultural estate profitably even after his inevitable death. The same logic may apply to the choice to leave written guidance on how to manage an empire well going forward.

48 Green 1997: 431.

49 Kronenberg 2009: 74.

50 Cic., *Ad Fam.* 9.2, written in late April of 46 BCE.

51 Kronenberg 2009: 31.

52 Plato, *Resp.* 343a–b, 440d.

53 Particularly notable is the discussion on the parameters of agriculture in book 1 (Varro, *Rust.* 1.2.11 ff.).

54 It is unfortunately beyond the scope of the present work to delve into what aspects of Greece Varro suggests should be retained, much less the vast history of thought and

scholarship on the Roman reaction to and integration of Greece. Within the *Rust.*, he demonstrates a willingness to use and build upon Greek knowledge of the natural sciences: see, for example, the list of Greek written sources mentioned in the opening to book 1 (Varro, *Rust.* 1.1.8–9). For a recent discussion of the scholarship on Roman reception of Greek science, see Fögen 2016: 1131–47. For a broader discussion of the Roman attitudes towards the integration of Greece into Rome, see Alcock 1996; Gruen 1984; Spawforth 2011. Dench's (1995, 2005) work offers insight into how Italian peoples may have fit into this complex dynamic; see also Roselaar 2012: 93–110.

Bibliography

Alcock, S. E. (1996), *Graecia Capta: The Landscapes of Roman Greece*, Cambridge: Cambridge University Press.

Bernard, S. G., C. Grey and C. Damon (2014), 'Rhetorics of Land and Power in the Polla Inscription (CIL I2 638)', *Mnemosyne*, 67 (6): 953–85.

Brown, N. (2019), 'A Res Rustica for All the People? Varro, Villatica Pastio, and the Villa Publica', *TAPA*, 149: 317–51.

Deman, A. (1988), 'Bergers transhumants et mouvements de résistance en Italie depuis les Gracques jusqu'à César', in T. Yuge and M. Doi (eds), *Forms of Control and Subordination in Antiquity*, 209–25, Leiden: Brill.

Dench, E. (1995), *From Barbarians to New Men: Greek, Roman, and Modern Perceptions of Peoples from the Central Apennines*, Oxford: Clarendon Press.

Dench, E. (2005), *Romulus' Asylum: Roman Identities from the Age of Alexander to the Age of Hadrian*, Oxford: Oxford University Press.

Doody, A. (2017), 'The Authority of Writing in Varro's *De re rustica*', in G. Woolf and J. König (eds), *Authority and Expertise in Ancient Scientific Culture*, 182–202, Cambridge: Cambridge University Press.

Fögen, T. (2016), 'Roman Responses to Greek Science and Scholarship as a Cultural and Political Phenomenon', in G. L. Irby (ed.), *A Companion to Science, Technology, and Medicine in Ancient Greece and Rome*, 1131–47, Hoboken, NJ: Wiley.

Foxhall, L. (1998), 'Snapping Up the Unconsidered Trifles: The Use of Agricultural Residues in Ancient Greek and Roman Farming', *Environmental Archaeology*, 1 (1): 35–40.

Fracchia, H. (2013), 'Survey, Settlement and Land Use in Republican Italy', in J. D. Evans (ed.), *A Companion to the Archaeology of the Roman Republic*, 181–97, Hoboken, NJ: Blackwell.

Frayn, J. M. (1984), *Sheep-Rearing and the Wool Trade in Italy during the Roman Period*, Liverpool: Francis Cairns.

Green, C. M. C. (1997), 'Free as a Bird: Varro *De Re Rustica* 3', *American Journal of Philology*, 118 (3): 427–48.

Green, C. M. C. (2012), 'The Shepherd of the People: Varro on Herding for the Villa Publica in *De re rustica* 2', in J. A. Becker and N. Terrenato (eds), *Roman Republican Villas: Architecture, Context, and Ideology*, 32–41, Ann Arbor, MI: University of Michigan Press.

Gruen, E. S. (1984), *The Hellenistic World and the Coming of Rome*, 2 vols, Berkeley, CA: University of California Press.

Kapteyn, J. (2015), 'All Italy an Orchard: Landscape and the State in Varro's *de Re Rustica*', PhD dissertation, University of Washington.

Kron, G. (2000), 'Roman Ley-Farming', *Journal of Roman Archaeology*, 13: 277–87.

Kron, G. (2004), 'Roman Livestock Farming in Southern Italy: The Case against Environmental Determinism', *Collection de l'Institut Des Sciences et Techniques de l'Antiquité*, 939 (1): 119–34.

Kronenberg, L. (2009), *Allegories of Farming from Greece and Rome: Philosophical Satire in Xenophon, Varro, and Virgil*, Cambridge: Cambridge University Press.

Nelsestuen, G. A. (2015), *Varro the Agronomist: Political Philosophy, Satire, and Agriculture in the Late Republic*, Columbus, OH: Ohio State University Press.

Nelsestuen, G. A. (2017), 'Varro, Dicaearchus, and the History of Roman Res Rusticae', *Bulletin of the Institute of Classical Studies*, 60 (2): 21–33.

Ridley, R. T. (2000), '*Leges agrariae*: Myths Ancient and Modern', *Classical Philology*, 95 (4): 459–67.

Roselaar, S. T. (2012), 'The Role of Italians in Local Economies of the Late Roman Republic', *Revue Belge de Philologie et d'Histoire*, 90 (1): 93–110.

Semple, E. C. (1928), 'Ancient Mediterranean Agriculture: Part II. Manuring and Seed Selection', *Agricultural History*, 2 (3): 129–56.

Spawforth, A. J. S. (2011), *Greece and the Augustan Cultural Revolution*, Cambridge: Cambridge University Press.

Tipps, G. K. (1989) 'The Generosity of Public Grazing Rights under the "Lex Sempronia Agraria" of 133 B.C.', *Classical Journal*, 84 (4): 334–42.

US Natural Resources Conservation Service (2012), *Agricultural Waste Management Field Handbook*, H_210_NEH_651, Washington, DC: US Department of Agriculture. Available online: https://directives.sc.egov.usda.gov/viewerFS.aspx?hid=21430 (accessed 30 August 2021).

van Hooff, A. J. L. (1982), 'Some More Latifundia', *Historia: Zeitschrift für Alte Geschichte*, 31 (1): 126–28.

White, K. D. (1967), 'Latifundia', *Bulletin of the Institute of Classical Studies*, 14 (1): 62–79.

White, K. D. (1970), *Roman Farming*, Ithaca, NY: Cornell University Press.

5

Pirate Alterity in Plutarch: The Roman Influence on the Construction of the *autre* Pirate in the *Moralia*

Francisco Martínez Sánchez

Approach

Plutarch of Chaeronea's oeuvre[1] is one of the most representative examples of cultural alterity as to pirate identity-building during the early empire. Besides being a very important historical source, the polymath's profound knowledge of Greek and Roman culture enabled him to write a series of works devoted to glossing and extolling the major figures and events of both worlds, but always from the moralistic, didactic, and personal perspective of a Greek living under Roman domination.

The treatment of piracy by diverse authors differs greatly depending on the social consideration of those involved, the socioeconomic repercussions, and the magnitude of the problem at each moment. In the time of Plutarch, there were still echoes[2] of the unceasing attacks on merchant ships and the abduction of people by Lycian, Pamphylian, Cilician and Cretan pirates, Pompey's war against the pirates, the sea blockades, the fratricidal conflicts during the final years of the Republic, and so forth. In his oeuvre, describing these fundamental events, it is possible to determine his stance on them, as well as that of the contemporary society to which he was catering.

Thus, a detailed analysis of the texts that have come down to us enables deeper insight into the broad and, in recent years, very much in vogue[3] pirate world in Antiquity. Although this would ideally call for a systematic study of his oeuvre, especially his *Lives* of Pompey, Caesar, Sertorius, and Lucullus in which the pirate theme is particularly prominent, owing to restrictions of space it is limited here to the most important fragments of the *Moralia*, analysing them systematically following the order of the books and traditional pagination.

References to pirates in the *Moralia*

Focusing on its content, this series of works, as with *Parallel Lives*, is capable of revealing Plutarch's main political, philosophical, ethical, and religious ideas, as well as many of the personal vicissitudes, relationships, and tastes that shaped his personality. Nevertheless, and despite the title imposed by the medieval tradition, it does not only address the moral realm, but is also very varied: the series includes ethical, philosophical, didactic, historical, and theological treatises, letters of consolation, plus banquet, amatory, political, literary, natural history, and physiological dialogues, and many others. Given this thematic scope, it would only be natural for the subject of piracy, so important for the Greeks and Romans, to appear in one or more of these treatises. Accordingly, the aim here is to trace and analyse some of the main references to piracy in order to identify the elements comprising its 'other' image, far removed from the initial perceptions of the phenomenon,[4] and the devices employed to introduce stereotypes into the general Roman discourse.

One of the first references to piracy, which should come as no surprise since Plutarch himself remarks (*Mor.* 984D) that the story 'is familiar to all and widely known', appears in *Mor.* 161A–162B, which recounts the nearly fatal adventure of Arion.[5] Having embarked on a Corinthian ship, Arion came to realize during the passage that the sailors were planning his murder, something that the pilot himself confirmed later on when confessing that they had intended to do the evil deed that same night. The story continues with the Methymnian, dressed for the occasion, proposing to sing the ode to Pythian Apollo for the salvation of all and, when halfway through it and night had still not fallen, seeing the sailors with their knives bared, he dived into the sea where, fortunately for him, a pod of dolphins rescued him. Once safe on dry land, he recounted his misfortunes to the authorities of Tenarus, giving them the names of the captain, the pilot, and the ship's emblem, and hiding to prevent them from making their escape. However, when arriving at the port, which was being watched by soldiers, he discovered that they had been arrested, as if by divine will.

Arion was a musician who, after amassing a fortune in Italy and wanting to return to Corinth, as confirmed by Herodotus (1.24.1–4), chartered a ship crewed by Corinthian ferrymen, who, once on the high seas, plotted to cast him overboard to steal his money. For his part, Arion, throwing himself at their mercy and offering them his possessions, unsuccessfully attempted to convince them to spare his life. In Plutarch's text, similarly to what occurs in the fragment from the work of Herodotus, most of the defining traits of the *autre* pirate, although not employing the term – a point to which we will return later – can be identified: plotting to commit robbery and murder on the high seas; impiety for depriving a Greek of funerary rites and a proper burial[6] and interrupting the ode to Pythian Apollo; the greed of the sailors who sought to steal Arion's riches, the use of weapons on board ship,[7] their penchant for violence, using the cover of night to commit their crimes, and so forth. In this sense, the author's views on acts of piracy are very similar to those held by Herodotus, which he obviously condemns, as evidenced by the intervention of divine providence in the arrest of the culprits.

When contrasting Plutarch's account with those narrated by authors closer to his time, like Strabo (13.2.4), one can see how his posture differs in one essential aspect, since, albeit without going into details, the geographer tells the story of the musician citing Herodotus, but describing how the pirates cast him into the sea and how he managed to reach the coast of Tenarus riding on the back of a dolphin. There is a similar account in Oppian (*Hal.* 5.448 ff.) who, when recalling the famous event, claims that Arion reached the Laconian coast on the back of a dolphin, thus escaping certain death at the hands of pirates. To offer a Latin example, Cicero (*Tusc.* 2.67) also refers to this legend and classifies the wrongdoers as pirates. In these three examples, the Corinthian sailors that appear in the story, who, one might say, pragmatically exemplify the Greeks as an eminently trading and maritime nation, are branded as pirates, which is no trivial issue, for it betrays the ideology underlying the Plutarchan narrative: as someone proud of being Greek, he does not intend to classify his compatriots[8] as pirates, even less so in view of the fact that Apollo himself plays such a conspicuous role in the legend.[9] However, bandits of that sort deserved to be punished, because that was what, by rights, the citizens of the empire expected and what should be done to people committing such crimes, especially when bearing in mind that Arion had set sail from the coast of Italy. Curiously, neither Strabo, who was born in the latter stages of the most dramatic moments of Cilician piracy, nor Oppian, who was Corycian, where one of the great pirate strongholds was located, had any qualms about calling Corinthian sailors pirates.

In *Mor.* 205F–206A, Plutarch highlights another of the most eloquent episodes of piracy and a faithful reflection of the narrative aimed at a Roman public eager to receive news in this respect. It describes the moment when still young and fleeing from Sulla, Caesar was captured by a band of pirates. When they demanded that a sum of money be paid for his ransom, he laughed at them and agreed to give them double the amount. While being kept under guard until the ransom money was raised, he told the bandits to be quiet when they disturbed his rest. He also wrote poems and speeches which he then read to them, calling those who did not praise them insensitive barbarians and threatening to have them all crucified. When the ransom money finally arrived and he was freed, he obtained men and ships from Asia, captured the pirates, and was good to his word.

This treatise, which would then be elaborated on in the respective *Life*, paints a practically complete picture of pirate alterity. On the one hand, it records one of the most serious problems facing the Romans, namely, the abduction of free people and their ransoming, and, on the other, in clear contrast with the might and *auctoritas* of Rome, personified by Caesar, a whole series of derogatory traits building the pirate identity. In sum, Plutarch depicts pirates as ignorant, despicable, submissive, lacking in leadership, and uncultured, even akin to robbers and barbarians, as does Seneca (*Contr.* 1.2.20) who draws the same parallel, without sufficient sensitivity to appreciate Roman culture. As in the previous treatise there is reference to punishment, which is described as necessary and consubstantial with the Roman *potestas* for those who dared to perturb it.

Unlike the previous case, there are many similarities between the fragment of the *Moralia* and, for instance, the work of the contemporary Latin historian Suetonius, who recounts how, during the winter months, he was captured[10] by some pirates close to Pharmacusa and, much to his indignation, held hostage by them for nearly forty days, in the company of a physician and two valets, for he had sent the rest of his servants to raise the money for the ransom. Yet again, the Chaeronean omits a fundamental detail, this time the place where it occurred, namely, the Greek island of Pharmacusa, located close to the coast of Asia Minor, to the north of Miletus. It is curious also that nor does he mention, as he indeed does in *The Life of Julius Caesar*,[11] the Cilician provenance of the pirates. Even though it comes from another source, the fact that Caesar remained in captivity for many days, until the ransom money was raised – although his living conditions do not seem to have been that bad, since, evidently, an important prisoner is more valuable alive than dead – is also striking to say the least.

In both texts, the propaganda element is blindingly evident, as to both the way in which Caesar handled the situation and administered justice, because, if Suetonius (*Caes.* 1.74) is to be believed, after he had captured the bandits, as he had promised to hang them from crosses, he ordered that they be crucified, but that their throats be slit beforehand. So, in this anecdote, Caesar – and Rome – remained firm, refusing to allow the audacity of the pirates to break his spirit and not only promising retribution, but also fulfilling his promise, although without falling prey to impiety or barbarism, for he displayed a certain degree of humanity when eliminating the sadism from a just punishment. Similarly, in Valerius Maximus (6.9.15) and Velleius Paterculus (2.42.1–3) there are novel – relating to the type of vessels, the piratical actions, and so forth – and propagandistic nuances extolling the figure of Caesar, but in the main and apart from the details as to the location, they hardly differ from Plutarch's account.

This persecution of piracy was not only characteristic of Rome, but can also be found in most of the works mentioning it. This is the case of *Mor.* 223D, which recounts how a pirate, who while roaming the country was captured by the Spartans, defended himself saying that his soldiers were starving, for which reason he seized food from whoever had any, regardless of whether they put up a fight or not. In view of this, Cleomenes replied that wickedness was concise. Beyond the evident relationship between piracy and undisciplined troops, this fragment can be contrasted, for example, with a passage in Titus Livy (37.13.12) describing how the Strait of Cephalenia was infested with Lacedaemonian pirates, thus preventing Roman shipping from passing through it. However, Plutarch goes a step further in the construction of pirate alterity, as, on this occasion, he offers, although by no means in reply to Livy, the testimony of a Greek king who had captured and mocked a pirate. Plutarch portrays this character as someone who robs by force – albeit alluding to the fact that he acts, in part, out of necessity – and as a villain, but this does not prevent him from stressing that, as part of his general discourse, the Greeks also suffer from acts of piracy and persecute them.

Following this guiding thread, there are two references to the same event in which the Hellenic people are depicted as victims of piracy, appearing in *Mor.* 247A and 296B, which this time will be presented together, ignoring this study's numerical order. The first tells the story of the abduction of the Athenian women of Brauron by the Tyrrhenians established on Lemnos and Imbros, who subsequently gave birth to children who were expelled by the Athenians for being considered as semi-barbaric, while the second states, practically in the same vein, that the daughters and women of the Athenians of Brauron were abducted.

In this case, although piracy is not expressly mentioned, it is indeed possible to observe a series of very interesting characteristics. As to the first fragment, the alleged natural superiority of the Greeks over other nations is recognizable, although in this specific case it might have been a way of justifying Athenian domination of the island of Lemnos. Similarly, the provenance of the assailants is identified so as to underscore that piracy was not a problem inherent to the

Greek world. Exactly the same occurs in the second fragment in which it is again clear that the assailants were Tyrrhenians, which further stresses the piratical character of the event, since in Antiquity[12] they were regarded as incorrigible pirates. On the other hand, the abduction of women in Roman mythology, as also occurs in its Greek counterpart, did not have such negative connotations – when restricted to the Heroic Age – as in the time of Plutarch, and can be explained as a relic of ancient exogamic matrimonial customs, as occurred with the Sabines in the foundational legend of Rome or the endless list of divine abductions. However, this episode cannot be classified in the same way, since when it is contrasted with other accounts of the same event, it is clear that it was a pirate attack. In Herodotus (6.138.1), the story goes that, driven by a desire for revenge, when the Pelasgians established on Lemnos learnt about the festivals of the Athenians, they obtained some penteconters so as to ambush the women while they were celebrating the festival in honour of Artemis in Brauron. After abducting quite a few of their number, they set sail to return to Lemnos with them, where they converted them into their concubines. The Halicarnassan's account, if we are to give credence to it, includes most of what would be expected of pirates: swift ships perfect for surprise attacks, a timely ambush and an abduction with criminal intent, among other aspects.

Obviously, there is a clear difference between the two, since Plutarch, as with Polyaenus (*Strategematon* 7.49), indicates that they were Tyrrhenians. In Dionysius of Halicarnassus (1.28.4), however, there is an explanation for this: he has Myrsilos say that the Tyrrhenians, after abandoning their territory, were called *pelargoi* – from the Greek Πελαργός, meaning storks – owing to their resemblance to those birds, for flocks of them migrated between Greece and the barbarian lands. In a rather veiled manner, therefore, the Chaeronean introduces the idea that the Etruscans were given to piracy, thus attempting to dispel the usual suspicions that it was a Greek practice.[13]

In this connection, it is no coincidence that Plutarch broaches the subject of mythical events that help to distance the pirate phenomenon from Rome and Greece, reinforcing the idea that both were involved in the struggle to eradicate it. Thus, notwithstanding its apparently mythical nature, *Mor.* 247F–248A includes the story of how Amisodarus arrived from the Lycian colony in the vicinity of Zeleia with pirate ships commanded by Chimarrhus, a warlike man, bloodthirsty and brutal. He sailed in a vessel which had a lion as its figurehead at the prow and a serpent at the stern, doing much evil to the Lycians and making it impossible to sail the sea or live in the coastal cities. Pursuing him with Pegasus as he was trying to escape, Bellerophon slew him.

Here, Plutarch digresses from the tradition, since in Hom. *Il.* 6.179–181 there is a similar description of the Chimera which Bellerophon also slew, for the purpose of offering a rationalized version of the myth – very similar to the account in Palaephatus (*Mythographi Graeci* 28 and 31) – which is demystified in the figure of an *archipirata*, whose flagship displayed the attributes of the mythical monster on its prow and stern so as to strike terror into the hearts of his enemies, and who devoted himself to plundering shipping and coastal settlements. This behaviour does not differ from the legend, which was still circulating in more recent times, like, for example, in Apollodorus (*Biblio.* 2.3), while even being echoed by Latin authors including Hyginus (*Fab.* 57.3–4), who specifies that 'the front, lion; the rear, snake; and the middle, the Chimera itself. He killed this one on the back of Pegasus, and it is said that he fell in the Aleian fields' still in the time of the Antonines. Similarly, Ovid (*Ibis* 257–258) recalls he who fell headlong from his horse in the Aleian fields. In any case, when analysing the fragment, there are new elements that give shape to the ideological frame characteristic of pirates and flesh out their image of alterity with attributes: bloodthirsty and brutal warriors, which can be regarded not only as a Hellenic literary *topos*, but also as a Latin borrowing; for instance, Cicero (*S. Rosc.* 50.146 and *Dom.* 140), concerning an injustice committed against his defendant, remarks that he was acting with heartless cruelty, a fierce and monstrous nature, like a wicked bandit and a barbarous pirate. Pirates also prove to be cowards when confronted, hinder shipping and pose a threat to coastal areas, moving about in bands under the command of charismatic individuals; they cease to be a despicable but anonymous collective from which emerge figures who display the character traits of the pirate archetype in Antiquity in their being and behaviour.

In the text, the Chaeronean distances himself completely from the orthodox version of the myth, which allows him to offer a story about the persecution and death of a cruel pirate at the hands of a Greek hero. Be that as it may, besides the interesting use to which Chimarrhus puts the attributes of the Chimera, this event can be placed in Lycia and, in the Latin narratives, there is also reference to Bellerophon's fall in the Aleian fields, located in Cilicia. Both places were inextricably linked to piracy[14] in the Roman mind-set owing to the campaigns launched against the Lycian, Pamphylian, and Cilician pirates by Marcus Antonius Orator in 101 BCE, P. Servilius in 77 BCE, and Pompey the Great in 67 BCE. So, from this it can be inferred that Greek and Roman heroes were practically placed on an equal footing in their relentless struggle against piracy.

Continuing this enquiry into the pirate phenomenon, in *Mor.* 298E–F there is yet another exceedingly useful and interesting fragment for identifying the mechanisms employed for building the pirate identity. According to Plutarch, on a pirate vessel anchored off the island of Ithaca there chanced to be an old man with earthenware jars containing pitch. Pyrrhias, a local ferryman, realized his situation accidently and rescued him without asking for any reward, only out of pity and because the old man had managed to persuade him. He only accepted some of the earthenware jars that the old man offered him. When the pirates had departed and it was now safe, he showed him that in the jars there was much gold and silver mixed with the pitch. So, Pyrrhias suddenly became rich and treated the old man very kindly, even going so far as to slay an ox for him. This is the reason why there is a saying that goes, 'No one but Pyrrhias has slain an ox for his benefactor.'

The main character who rescues the old man from the clutches of the pirates is yet again a Greek who receives a fabulous reward.[15] The story being set in the famous Ithaca, it would seem that the pirates had a safe port there for supplying their ships and selling their booty, but the vessel was anchored not moored, for which reason the action had to take place off the coast. Accordingly, the Ithacans did not necessarily have to be aware of the pirate vessel and, by chance, a ferryman who was fishing nearby had the opportunity to rescue the old man who had been abducted, moved by his situation and his appeals for help. By my reckoning, it is telling that stress is placed yet again on the modus operandi of pirates, to wit, abducting people, in this case an old man, which is no trivial issue, for the respectability and dignity of the aged was beyond doubt in Antiquity, especially in the Graeco-Roman world. It is also significant that it was not safe until the pirates had departed, for they posed one of the dangers at the time, above all around the islands, and that it was a truly profitable business, given the wealth that they accumulated, namely, another of their defining traits. In this respect, the story also brings to mind the comedies of Plautus (*Bac.* 2.3), like, for example, the one in which two brothers who had embarked on a ship with a large quantity of gold, spied a pirate vessel whose crew was watching them at a distance, for which reason they decided to unload the gold before their eyes in order to be able to set sail safely; or the one (*Men.* 2.2) in which there was a pirate ship in port. Lastly, it is just as interesting to observe how this episode had made its way into the collective memory, giving rise to a proverbial expression[16] which already had specific piratical connotations.

Further on, in this same treatise (*Mor.* 303D), there is reference to another very relevant event which allows for taking a different approach to the issue at hand. The Chaeronean wonders why among the Samians, when sacrifices are performed to Hermes, dispenser of happiness, it is permitted to rob and to steal clothing from anyone. He then explains that this is perhaps due to the fact that, according to an oracle, the Samians travelled there from the island to Mycale, where, after establishing themselves, they devoted themselves to piracy for the next ten years.

On this occasion, it can be seen how Plutarch interweaves a Hellenic tradition (not for nothing is this same formula of Hermes the dispenser found in the *h. Hom.* 18.12) with a festival easily recognizable to the Romans, while offering a feeble excuse for the Greeks' pirate activities, however ancient they may be, by linking them to religiosity: certainly, the Hermetic festival that it describes shares many similarities with the Saturnales – 'the best of days' in the words of Catullus (14.15) – during which the established social order was subverted.[17] For which reason, this equating of customs places the two peoples on the same social and cultural level. In addition, it establishes piratical acts in the past, given that the contemporary tradition that it attempts to explain derived from the memory of ancient events in which a cause/effect relationship is practically established between observing the prophesies of the oracle and devoting themselves to piracy,[18] as if they were complying with divine will, thus exonerating themselves. So, the thieving and piracy described in this fragment does not seem to have such negative undertones, as least in Plutarch's narrative, since it is understood as a consequence of a sacrifice performed to Hermes[19] or of devoutly obeying an oracle.

Until now, all the references to the pirate phenomenon have involved listing the outrages and character traits of this collective, identifying the victims of their pillaging and those responsible for bringing them to heal and for punishing them as they deserve. In his treatises, nevertheless, Plutarch also indicates the main causes and moral defects that compel them to become pirates, as in *Mor.* 498F–499A, in which there is talk about a hypothetical public contest of purpose for making a life wretched, and that Fortune and Vice come with different proposals for achieving this. To lead such a wretched and deplorable life, one of them draws after her terrible piracies, wars, bloody tyrannies, storms at sea, and lightning from the sky. She also mixes hemlock, brings in swords, hires slanderers, kindles fevers, jingles shackles, and builds prisons. Although, according to Plutarch, most of these things are rather the result of Vice than Fortune.

It is difficult to draw parallels between the woes to which Vice gives rise in the lives of men, but it is curious that the use of terms like bloody tyrannies, fevers, wars, and prisons, together with piracies, storms at sea, and lightening from the sky, which are understood as divine reprimands, is a matter of course. This passage recalls a controversy about the vices of Seneca the Elder (*Contr.* 1.2.8), in which the licentiousness and cruelty of pirates, who laugh off the notion of good and evil and, brandishing their weapons, plunder the land and the sea, is mentioned. To Plutarch's mind, vice violates the laws of gods and men and brings none other than misfortune. Or, in other words, the pirate and the tyrant are not virtuous, for they deprive people of their freedom and their assets, among other things. It is obvious that, by defending this posture, he intends to establish a moral behaviour encouraging man to tread the path of virtue, prudence, and moderation,[20] which should guide his steps and warn him about the dangers of straying from it, including a multitude of calamities whose prime example is piracy.

In this same treatise (*Mor.* 499B), there is yet another brief reference to the issue at hand. Here, Plutarch poses a rhetorical question about whether or not servitude, bonds, and being sold as a slave are acceptable practices. In his reply, he claims that, if you attacked it, Diogenes would despise you, since when being sold by some pirates, he cried out, 'Who will buy a master?' He is referring, of course, to the illustrious cynic philosopher of Sinope, as do Dio Chrysostom, Epictetus, Lucian, and Diogenes Laërtius, among many others. Curiously enough, Diogenes Laërtius describes (6.29) a similar situation when mentioning a 'Sale of Diogenes' by Menippus of Gadara, in which it is said that, after being taken prisoner and before being sold as a slave, Diogenes was asked what he could do, to which he responded that he knew how to govern men, for which reason he told the auctioneer to enquire if anyone wanted to purchase a master for himself. In essence, the two versions are identical, although in Plutarch's the Greek philosopher appears as a new victim of piracy and there is reference to one of its lucrative lines of business,[21] the abduction of people, whether they were free or not,[22] and their subsequent sale.

Continuing with the numerical review of the *Moralia*, there are a couple of fragments in the *Quaestiones convivales* in which, for other purposes, piracy is mentioned. In one of those fragments (*Mor.* 630E–F), it is observed how much some people enjoy talking about their own successes, for many, Plutarch contends, derive pleasure from being asked several times how they enjoyed being in the rostrum or when the king spoke to them or, while the rest succumbed in a storm or to pirates, they escaped from danger; thus getting the most out of the experiences, they never weary of recalling and expounding on them. In the Graeco-Roman sources, there are many references to misfortunes of this type, a paradigmatic Latin example of which being Plautus (*Mil.* 2.1) insofar as the action takes place in the Greek world and the misfortune is narrated in the first person singular: Palaestrio tells the story of how, when he was travelling from

Ephesus to Naupactus and already on the high seas, there appeared a pirate vessel which captured his ship and, as a result, he met his downfall. These examples underscore yet again the risks and dangers posed by pirates in the lives of people and how, remembering them as successes, they accept to relive those traumatic episodes – it warrants noting that the danger posed by pirates is equal to that of a storm, which is a big claim in an age when storms, waterspouts, and gales at sea were all but synonymous[23] with shipwreck.

The second reference (*Mor.* 661E–F) is a lot less evident than the rest and denotes the depth of Plutarch's knowledge. In this case, he cites some verses of Euripides (cf. Nauck, *Trag. Gr. Frag. fr.* 754) recalling the mythical events involving Hypsipyle. Broadly speaking, this fragment has to do with the Lemnian women and their neglect of the cult and sanctuaries of Aphrodite. Accordingly, the goddess punished them by making them smell particularly foul, which resulted in their menfolk repudiating them in favour of slave-girls; in revenge, the women decided to kill all the men. Only Hypsipyle forgave her father Thoas, the king of Lemnos, hiding him to save his life; so, she herself ended up being chosen as queen just before the Argonauts arrived on the island, with whom the Lemnian women slept. Later on, after their departure, the Lemnian women learned about her treachery and plotted to kill her, but Hypsipyle escaped one night and was captured by some pirates who subsequently sold her as a slave to Lycurgus, the king of Nemea, where she became the wet nurse to his son Opheltes. Sadly, while she was informing the army of the Seven where they could find water, she neglected the boy who was killed by a monstrous serpent.

As with many others, this is a story from the mythical Hellenic world in which piracy acted as a mere catalyst. Albeit veiled by poetic licence and, therefore, only accessible to those familiar with Greek culture, its moral lesson is clear to all: neglecting the gods leads to misfortunes, in this case a whole chain of events resulting in several tragedies, one of which was the abduction of Hypsipyle by pirates and her change from queen to slave.

Mor. 779A contains another of the most revealing fragments *vis-à-vis* Plutarch's stance on piracy. Here, he holds that an artisan would enjoy making a helm, if he knew that it would govern the flagship of Themistocles in his struggle to defend Hellas or that of Pompey in his victorious sea campaign against the pirates. The huge importance of this fragment in the construction of pirate alterity stands out a mile, while the alliance between Greece and Rome against their enemies is further developed: a naval carpenter would enjoy making the helm of Themistocles' or Pompey's flagship, namely, he would be overjoyed to participate, if only in a secondary role, in the deeds of any one of these leaders;

to help with his expertise he who had won at sea the freedom of Greece against the barbarians or he who had done away with the pirates infesting the *Mare Nostrum*. Evidently, neither are they similar situations, nor even remotely comparable naval campaigns, but that artisan represents any Greek or Roman citizen, equal in adversity, whose future, welfare and freedom – in the literal sense of the word – had been decided in a war against barbarians or pirates. In a brief sentence, the stance of the Chaeronean is thus summarized, while laying another brick in the construction of pirate alterity.

It is well known that the methods employed by Herodotus to cast doubt on some of the actions of the Greek *poleis* were not at all appreciated by Plutarch, as evidenced by his *De Herodoti malignitate*. And he maintains this posture in a particular fragment (*Mor.* 859B–C) describing some events that, in my view, have to do with the pirate phenomenon. The Chaeronean mentions Herodotus' account (3.47.1–2) of the expedition of the Lacedaemonians against the tyrant Polycrates, claiming that the Samians thought and said that the Spartans, to recompense them for their former assistance against the Messenians, both brought back the Samians who had been banished and made war on the tyrant. For their part, the Lacedaemonians denied this, contending that their aim was not to help or deliver the Samians, but to punish them for having stolen a cup sent by them to Croesus, as well as a breastplate sent them by Amasis.

In this case, it is again possible to observe the piratical attitudes of Greeks which are not classified as such. However, the references in Herodotus (1.70.2–3) in this respect are enlightening because the Spartans asserted that, when the cup, which was on its way to Sardis, arrived at Samos, the Samians, who had got wind of this, launched an attack with warships (literally, with long ships; unlike trading vessels that tended to be short and rounded) and seized it. The anecdotal meaning of Herodotus is proverbial and the variety of digressions in his oeuvre is no accident. Here, the references to the cup, which he surely had the chance to see personally in the Heraion during his stay on Samos, might seem like a debt that needed to be settled and the effective cause behind the Lacedaemonian expedition against the Samians. However, the real reason behind it was to put an end to the pirate activities[24] of Polycrates' fleet, which were affecting Aegina and Corinth, Sparta's trading partners. Either way, in Plutarch rapine on the high seas boils down to a brief reference to an ancient episode involving the mere robbery of a cup and a shield, thus distancing yet again and as much as possible anything that smacks of piracy from the Greek world.

There is another treatise in which it is possible to encounter new references to piracy with certain novel nuances, specifically in *Mor.* 985A–B. As the story goes,

Coeranus, a Parian by birth, bought a pod of dolphins at Byzantium, which had been caught in a net and were in danger of being slaughtered, and set them free. Sometime later, so they say, Coeranus was on a sea voyage in a penteconter, with fifty pirates on board, and in the strait between Naxos and Paros the ship capsized and all the others perished. Reportedly, a dolphin sped towards Coeranus and buoyed him up, putting him ashore at Sikinos, near a cave which is pointed out to this day and bears the name of Coeraneum. This text is curious because it offers details about the piratical life of Coeranus which are not included in the other versions of the story (for instance, in Ael., *NA* 8.3, Archil., *fr.* 192 West, and *Ath.* 13.606D–F who cites Philarcus) that have come down to us, although Athenaeum says that he was from Miletus and Aelianus confirms that he was sailing in a penteconter on which Milesians had embarked, a type of vessel that, as already noted, was used in the pirate attack against Brauron. In this case, and differing completely from all the aforementioned examples, the pirate life of a Greek is underscored, although as a way of exonerating him, the accent is also placed on how kindly he treated the dolphins, animals preferred by Apollo, while refraining from recounting any of the atrocities committed by the pirate band, but indeed mentioning their tragic comeuppance. A just and well-deserved punishment from which only Coeranus escaped thanks to his piety and the divine will of Apollo.

Another of the most eloquent references to the pirate phenomenon can be found in *Mor.* 1065E–1066A, in which Plutarch wonders what need had Zeus, the paternal, as master-craftsman who fashioned the universe as a town common to gods and men, who should live as lawful partners in right and virtue, concordantly and blissfully, of pirates, murderers, parricides, and tyrants to attain this most fair and majestic goal. He replies that, effectively, evil is not a clever interlude pleasant to the divinity. Beyond its philosophical posture on the Stoics, the interesting point about the fragment is the identification of pirates with murderers, parricides, and tyrants as the embodiment of evil, the dregs of society at the time. And this is nothing new, not even in the Latin world, for in Cicero (*Phil.* 13.8), for example, this same tendency to put them on the same level can be found. Even in the controversies of Seneca the Elder (*Contr.* 1.2.8) it can be observed that not even pirates believed that they had the right to harm tyrannicides, despite that fact that they were offered double the money to chop their hands off. This lays even more stress on Plutarch's comparison between tyranny and piracy, but that is not the only aspect that he highlights. For him, they remain beyond the pale of society and civilization, beyond peaceful coexistence, virtue, happiness, justice, and rationality. Therefore, from this it is inferred that pirates are also depraved, wretched, iniquitous, and irrational. From the point of view of morality and philosophy, it is an evil that exists in the world and poses a danger to the town common to gods and men.

In *Mor.* 1090E–F, there is one of the last explicit references to piracy in the *Moralia*. As before, Plutarch rhetorically wonders about the outrages of rabbles, the cruelty of pirates, the injustices of inheritors, the airborne plagues or the sea whipped up by Euros, which was on the point of swallowing Epicurus on his voyage to Lampsacus; he had to leave so hastily that he was obliged to embark during a season that was inadvisable for sailing and with the sea infested with pirate bands, thereby the specific references. In this regard, the fragment refers to the cruelty of pirates, who are lumped together with other dangers that the philosopher had to face: outrages, injustices, plagues, and so forth. On the other hand, as seen before, the risk posed by pirates on sea voyages becomes a platitude in accounts of this type, although in this case it seems that Plutarch limits himself to citing what Epicurus included in his 'Letter to the Philosophers of Mytilene', which must have been the direct source as he himself admits (*Mor.* 1101B). By and large, the text revolves around the figure and doctrine of the Samian philosopher, who is often treated with hostility, for which reason the piratical component or all the misfortunes that he suffered are perhaps a sort of consequence of his teachings with which he did not agree at all.[25] Thus, he avoids concealing that the waters of Lesbos were infested by pirates, probably Greek ones, in order to highlight the fact that it was the Hellenes who were the main victims of piracy.

Conclusions

In the time of Plutarch, Rome pragmatically strove to maintain its power, without disdaining the political structures of the Greek cities, but guaranteeing their loyalty and control through the elites and the support of the local aristocracy. The Chaeronean would have formed part of that nobility and, owing to his privileged position in Graeco-Roman society, accepted the Roman domination of Greece. Above all, when bearing in mind the advantages resulting from the *Pax Romana* and the relative freedom that the Greeks enjoyed. From this perspective, he allowed himself to assess the history of both nations without abandoning the dignity of the Hellenic tradition and his own convictions as a Greek, while leaving traces of his admiration for Rome.

At least in most of the references to piracy in the *Moralia*, the Chaeronean offers a narrative that, at all times, seems to minimize the relationship between

Greeks and piracy, as if he wanted to divert the attention of his Roman readership from the baleful Cilician precedent. Returning to the example of Arion, the term 'piracy' is not mentioned, as it is indeed in Strabo and Oppian. Exactly the same occurs in the squabble between the Samians and the Spartans, with everything boiling down to a robbery by rapacious sailors. Similarly, in the anecdote about Caesar, in which it is now impossible for him to pretend that his abductors were not pirates, while at the same time omitting the setting and their Cilician provenance, unlike Suetonius. Here, they are called barbarians, as occurs in the episode of the abduction of the women in Brauron, which not only accords them demeaning attributes, but also distances them from the Greek world, as being opposed to the Hellenic one, as least since Aeschylus.[26] In this connection, nor does it seem to be a coincidence that the great personalities of both worlds are honoured, recognizing their struggle against the barbarian/pirate enemy, be they real characters like Pompey and Themistocles or mythological, as in the case of Bellerophon and the rationalized legend of the Chimera.

In other fragments, in which there are geographical ambiguities, the Greeks are portrayed as avengers or victims in Plutarch's narrative. This is the case of the remark attributed to Cleomenes of Sparta, who captures a pirate who has been plundering the country, the abduction of the old man in Ithaca, the sale of Diogenes, and Epicurus' adversities at sea. And when it is impossible to conceal the relationship between the Greeks and piracy, an excuse is offered for explaining or toning down the events, more often than not of a religious nature and, therefore, unquestionable, as in the case of the Samians of Mycale, the fragment referring to Coeranus and the subtle reference to Hypsipyle.

In any case, Plutarch participates in the process of discrediting pirates, who initially emerged in ancient Greece, and to this end fleshes them out with real or imaginary attributes. This behaviour is evinced throughout his oeuvre, but specifically in the *Moralia* it has been possible to observe all kinds of qualifiers directly associated with this predatory activity or framed in similar situations: murderers, impious, abductors, thieves, violent, scheming, barbarians, uncultured, slavers, unjust, depraved, wretched, irrational, miserly, insensitive, wicked, cruel, malign, cowardly and dangerous, and their effects are analogous to war, storms or plagues; and pirates can be compared with nothing less than parricides and tyrants.

In conclusion, we can claim that in the different treatises making up the *Moralia* it is possible to identify the importance of the pirate phenomenon, its impact, and its persistence in culture through the centuries since its mythical origins, as well as the ferocious and malign image that they had when Plutarch was writing and which has prevailed down to the present day. In his accounts, he contributed to the development of the *other* image of pirates that had been taking shape, introducing many nuances and demeaning characteristics that reinforced this perception of those individuals who were already reviled by then. Nonetheless, it can also be observed how the Chaeronean strove to distance piracy from the Hellenic world, to play down, as far as possible, the pairing *Greek piracy* and to present a common Graeco-Roman objective of pursuing and punishing it.

In any Spanish dictionary, the term 'barbarian' does not only signify a foreigner, a sense in all likelihood stemming from its original meaning, but is also employed to describe a fierce, uncultured or uncouth person, as in English ones, in which it is defined as a less advanced but more violent foreign group. Likewise, in the case of the term 'pirate',[27] it is not only used to refer to people devoted to attacking and robbing ships on the high seas, as defined in English dictionaries, but also cruel and ruthless individuals by its definition in Spanish. As to other languages, in Italian pirates even pillage coasts and are described as grasping and unscrupulous individuals, while in French, the accent is placed on the term's romantic connotations, portraying them as adventurers who, together with their crews, ply the seas devoting themselves to brigandage. In this sense, the success of the construction of pirate alterity, which is due in part to Plutarch, is equivalent to that of the Persians, since most of the Graeco-Roman stereotypes about pirates remain valid.

Notes

1 Cf. Ziegler 1965; Barrow 1967; Lesky 1968; Jones 1971; Russell 1973; Halliday 1975; Pérez Jiménez 1985; Morales Otal 1992; Stadter 2015.

2 Plut., *Pomp.* 24.6.10–13, 25.1–2; *Caes.* 2.1–7. Cic., *Man.* 11, 12, 18; *Sest.* 31; *Agr.* 2.80; *Flac.* 14, 29, 31; *Pomp.* 56, 32, 33; *Post Red. in Sen.* 11; *Verr.* 2, 4, 23. App., *Mith.* 56, 93, 95; *B.C.* 2.23, 106. Oros., *Hist.* 6.4.1, 3.5. Flor., *Epit.* 1, 41.1, 6, 2, 18. Vell. Pat. 2.31.2, 42.3. Plaut., *Poen.* 4.2. Str. 14.6.6. Val. Max. 6.9.15. Suet., *Caes.* 4.1–2, 74.1. Eutrop., *Brev.* 6, 12. Caes., *bell. civ.* 3.104.3, 110.1–3, 112.1–4. *Res Gestae* 1.25. Liv., *Per.* 68.1, 93.1, 99.3, 123.1, 128.1. D.C. 36, 17.3, 21.1–3, 22.2–3, 38, 30.5. Sall., *Cat.* 39.1; *Hist. Fr.* 3.3, etc.

3 Cf. Souza 1999; Gabrielsen 2001; Wiemer 2002; Rauh 2003; Braccesi 2004; Grünewald 2004; Álvarez-Ossorio 2008; Tarwacka 2009; Álvarez-Ossorio et al. 2014; Sintes 2016; Mastrorosa 2018; Evans and De Marre 2019.

4 Since it was initially considered as an eminently prestigious activity (*Th.* 1.5.1), cf. Álvarez-Ossorio 2006: 35.
5 Cf. Stebbins 1929: 66 ff.; Bowra 1963: 121.
6 Cf. Burkert 2007: 257–63; Dubisch 1989: 190.
7 The presence of armed men on merchant ships would help to repel pirate attacks due to the danger of the mid-second century BCE, but this implies, in turn, the use of weapons by the piratical hosts. Cf. Philostr., *VA*. 3.35; Gianfrotta 1981: 240; Domínguez Monedero 2009: 138.
8 In this sense, as proposed in Silva (2010: 43), Plutarch aims to build a favourable image of the Greek past.
9 Corinth also housed one of the most important temples of Apollo (*Paus.* 2.3.6), and even a nearby oracle of mythical origin (*Paus.* 2.5.4).
10 Suet., *Caes.* 1.4.1–2, expression very similar to the one found in Cic., *Pomp.* 32 and 33.
11 Cf. Plut., *Caes.* 1.8–2.7; see Ward 1975: 268 and Günther 1999: 321–37 for a detailed analysis of the sources.
12 As we can see in the Homeric Hymns (*h. Bacch.* 7–13), Palaephatus (*Mythographi Graeci* 3.2, 20), Euripides (*Cyc.* 10–14), Dionysius of Halicarnassus (3.45.1–2), or Philostratus (*VA*. 1.19.1) to cite just a few examples from different eras. Cf. Gras 1976: 367; Sánchez Jiménez 1991: 20; Romizzi 2003: 352.
13 On the defence of the Greek past as a matter of cultural survival, cf. Barigazzi 1984: 264; Sierra 2014: 39.
14 Cf. Ormerod 1922: 40; Broughton 1946: 40; Seager 2002: 44–7; Arsian 2011: 198.
15 This type of behaviour will be the basis of many medieval legends and tales, as Halliday 1975: 149 argues.
16 That comes to swell a list that includes expressions such as doing the Corycian (Str. 14.1.32), lying like a Cretan (Alcm., *Fr.* 164 Page, Str. 10.4.17), or those that have to do with Tyrrhenian piracy. Cf. Mariño and García Romero 1999: 12; Lelli 2007: 141.
17 Cf. Guittard 2003: 227; Sharland 2005: 104.
18 As Álvarez-Ossorio 2008: 84 ff. argues, piracy has long been an alternative economic activity and whose practice was carried out according to the circumstances, in this way and in the face of precariousness, some communities would opt for looting to survive.
19 The god of travellers, thieves, merchants, and pirates, who unite a little of each guild and also, a Roman deity, therefore, not censorable. Cf. Álvarez-Ossorio 2010: 139.
20 Cf. *Mor.* 451C; Panagopoulos 1977: 223; Buganza 2012: 32.
21 As we saw with Caesar, the kidnapping of important people provided high ransoms, cf. Garlan 1978: 7.
22 In Str. 14.3.2 there is a moral distinction between slave merchants and pirates, although in their appearance and behaviour they should not be differentiated; cf. Fernández Vizcaíno 2015: 419.

23 Cf. Huxley 1952: 117–24; Throckmorton and Kapitän 1968: 182; Moreno Torres 2005: 787.

24 See Hdt. 3.39.3–4; Polyaenus, *Strat.* 1.23; Diod. Sic., 10.16.1; cf. Jeffery and Cartledge 1982: 256 or Haas 1985: 37.

25 Cf. Babut 1969; Opsomer 2014.

26 Cf. Miller 2006: 123; Hall 2007: 76–99; García Sánchez 2009: 37.

27 According to the Cambridge Dictionary, the Spanish Academy of Language, the Treccani Institute of the Italian Encyclopedia, and the Dictionary of the French Academy respectively.

Bibliography

Álvarez-Ossorio Rivas, A. (2006), 'Aspectos mercantilistas en el seno de una actividad genuinamente prestigiosa: el caso de la piratería cilicia en los siglos II y I a.C.', in G. Chic García (ed.), *Economía de prestigio 'versus' economía de mercado*, 33–48, Seville: Padilla.

Álvarez-Ossorio Rivas, A. (2008), *Los piratas contra Roma, Estudio socioeconómico y cultural de la piratería cilicia (143–36 a.C.)*, Écija: Gráficas Sol.

Álvarez-Ossorio Rivas, A. (2010), 'Algunas consideraciones sobre la religiosidad de los piratas de la Antigüedad', *Habis*, 41: 138–56.

Álvarez-Ossorio Rivas, A., E. Ferrer Albelda and E. García Vargas, cords (2014), *Piratería y seguridad marítima en el Mediterráneo Antiguo.* SPAL Monografías XVII, Seville: Universidad de Sevilla.

Arsian, M. (2011), 'Pirates' Havens in the Mediterranean: "Korykos"es in Cilicia, Pamphylia, Lycia and Ionia', *Adalya*, 14: 189–206.

Babut, D. (1969), *Plutarque et le stoïcisme*, Paris: Publications de l'Université de Lyon.

Barigazzi, A. (1984), 'Plutarco e il corso futuro della storia', *Prometheus*, 10 (3): 264–88.

Barrow, R. H. (1967), *Plutarch and His Time*, London: Chatto & Windus.

Bowra, C. M. (1963), 'Arion and the Dolphin', *Museum Helveticum*, 20 (3): 121–34.

Braccesi, L., ed. (2004), *La pirateria nell'Adriatico antico*, Rome: L'Erma di Bretschneider.

Broughton, T. S. R. (1946), 'Notes on Roman Magistrates: I. The Command of M. Antonius in Cilicia. II. Lucullus' Commission and Pompey's Acta', *TAPA*, 77: 35–43.

Buganza, J. (2012), 'Reflexiones éticas a partir de Plutarco', *Revista Filosofia*, 23: 17–35.

Burkert, W. (2007), *La religión griega: arcaica y clásica*, Madrid: Abada.

Domínguez Monedero, A. J. (2009), 'El final del Arcaísmo y la transformación de los mecanismos de intercambio en el Mediterráneo', *Gerión*, 27 (1): 127–46.

Dubisch, J. (1989), 'Death and Social Change in Greece', *Anthropological Quarterly*, 62 (4): 189–200.

Evans, R. and M. De Marre, eds (2019), *Piracy, Pillage and Plunder in Antiquity*, New York: Routledge.

Fernández Vizcaíno, B. (2015), 'La piratería en la Roma republicana: la *lex gabinia de piratis persequendis*', *RIDROM*, 14: 404–61.

Gabrielsen, V. (2001), 'Economic Activity, Maritime Trade and Piracy in the Hellenistic Aegean', *Revue des études anciennes*, 103: 219–40.

García Sánchez, M. (2009), 'Los bárbaros y el Bárbaro: identidad griega y alteridad persa', *Faventia*, 29 (1): 33–49.

Garlan, Y. (1978), 'Signification historique de la piraterie grecque', *DHA*, 4: 1–16.

Gianfrotta, P. (1981), 'Commerci e pirateria: prime testimanianze archeologiche sottomarine', *Mélanges de l'École française de Rome: Antiquité*, 93 (1): 227–42.

Gras, M. (1976), 'La piraterie tyrrhénienne en mer Egée: mythe ou réalité?', *Publications de l'École française de Rome*, 27: 341–70.

Grünewald, T. (2004), *Bandits in the Roman Empire: Myth and Reality*, London: Routledge.

Guittard, C. (2003), 'Les Saturnales à Rome: Du mythe de L'âge d'or au banquet de Décembre', *Pallas*, 61: 219–36.

Günther, L. M. (1999), 'Caesar und die Seerauber – eine Quellenanalyse', *Chiron*, 29: 321–37.

Haas, C. (1985), 'Athenian Naval Power before Themistocles', *Historia: Zeitschrift für Alte Geschichte*, 34 (1): 29–46.

Hall, E., ed. (2007), *Persians*, Oxford: Aris & Phillips.

Halliday, W. R. (1975), *The Greek Questions of Plutarch with a New Translation and Commentary*, New York: Arno Press.

Huxley, H. H. (1952), 'Storm and Shipwreck in Roman Literature', *G&R*, 21 (63): 117–24.

Jeffery, L. H. and P. Cartledge (1982), 'Sparta and Samos: A Special Relationship?', *Classical Quarterly*, 32 (2): 243–65.

Jones, C. P. (1971), *Plutarch and Rome*, Oxford: Clarendon Press.

Lelli, E. (2007), 'Towards a Classification of Greek Proverbs', *Paremia*, 16: 139–48.

Lesky, A. (1968), *Historia de la literatura griega*, Madrid: Gredos.

Mariño, R. and F. García Romero (1999), *Proverbios griegos. Menandro: Sentencias*, Madrid: Gredos.

Mastrorosa, I. G., ed. (2018), *Latrocinium maris: Fenomenologia e repressione della pirateria nell'esperienza romana e oltre*, Firenze: Aracne.

Miller, M. (2006), 'Persians in the Greek Imagination', *Mediterranean Archaeology*, 19/20: 109–23.

Morales Otal, C. (1992), *Obras morales y de Costumbre*, Madrid: Gredos.

Moreno Torres, S. (2005), 'Rutas de navegación en el Mediterráneo occidental: condicionantes atmosféricos y aspectos técnicos de la navegación en la antigüedad', *Mayurqa*, 30 (2): 781–99.

Opsomer, J. (2014), 'Plutarch and the Stoics', in M. Beck (ed.), *Companion to Plutarch*, 88–103, Hoboken, NJ: Wiley-Blackwell.

Ormerod, H. A. (1922), 'The Campaigns of Servilius Isauricus against the Pirates', *JRS*, 12: 35–56.

Panagopoulos, C. (1977), 'Vocabulaire et mentalité dans les Moralia de Plutarque', *DHA*, 3: 197–235.

Pérez Jiménez, A., trans. (1985), *Plutarco: Vidas paralelas*, Madrid: Gredos.

Rauh, N. K. (2003), *Merchants, Sailors and Pirates in the Roman World*, Stroud: Tempus.

Romizzi, L. (2003), 'Il mito di Dioniso e i Pirati Tirreni in epoca romana', *Latomus*, 62: 352–61.

Russell, D. A. (1973), *Plutarch*, London: Duckworth.

Sánchez Jiménez, F. (1991), 'Tirrenos en el Egeo. Problemática general y tendencias de la investigación', *Habis*, 22: 19–26.

Seager, R. (2002), *Pompey the Great: A Political Biography*, Oxford: Blackwell.

Sharland, S. (2005), 'Saturnalian Satire: Proto-Carnivalesque Reversals and Inversion in Horace, Satire 2.7', *Acta Classica*, 48: 103–20.

Sierra, C. (2014), 'Plutarco contra Heródoto: razones de una censura', *Talia Dixit*, 9: 23–46.

Silva, M. A. O. (2010), 'Da Malícia de Heródoto: Discurso e Resistencia cultural em Plutarco', *Mimesis*, 31: 33–52.

Sintes, C. (2016), *Les pirates contre Rome*, Paris: Les Belles Letres.

Souza, P. (1999), *Piracy in the Graeco-Roman World*, Cambridge: Cambridge University Press.

Stadter, P. A. (2015), *Plutarch and His Roman Readers*, Oxford: Oxford University Press.

Stebbins, E. B. (1929), 'The Dolphin in the Literature and Art of Greece and Rome', PhD dissertation, Johns Hopkins University.

Tarwacka, A. (2009), *Romans and Pirates: Legal Perspective*, Warsaw: Wydawnictwo Uniwersytetu Kardynała Stefana Wyszyńskiego.

Throckmorton, P. and G. Kapitän (1968), 'An Ancient Shipwreck at Pantano Longarini', *Archaeology*, 21 (3): 182–7.

Ward, A. M. (1975), 'Caesar and the Pirates', *CPh*, 70: 267–8.

Wiemer, H. U. (2002), *Krieg, Handel und Piraterie: Untersuchungen zur Geschichte des hellenistischen Rhodos*, Berlin: Akademie Verlag.

Ziegler, K. (1965), *Plutarco*, Brescia: Paideia.

6

Where Reason Could Not Prevail: Barbarian Othering and Diplomatic Double-Standards in Caesar's *Commentarii De Bello Gallico*

Ralph Moore

The ethics of war and diplomacy in the ancient world are inevitably far removed from our own and thus can be difficult to reconstruct comprehensively. A perspective favoured and articulated to varying degrees and formats by Harris, Eckstein, and Rosenstein is that of the 'Realist' position of international relations in the ancient Mediterranean.[1] According to this view, in the absence of an international authority to establish and enforce a common code of conduct, interstate relations in the late first millennium BCE were, by necessity, utterly ruthless, Machiavellian exercises in self-interest. Thucydides' infamous 'Melian Dialogue' (Thuc. 5.84–116) is a favoured point of illustration of this worldview, dividing the world into ethical interactions between equals and brutally amoral ones between the strong and weak. One of the issues with the application of such an approach to Rome, however, is explaining it in the light of Roman cultural attitudes towards the morality of war, conquest, and imperialism. The underlying brutality and militarism of Roman society cannot be ignored and, from a distant, etic perspective of the *longue durée*, violent, cynical self-interest would appear to be the primary animating force in Roman foreign policy. From a more emic perspective, however, Roman projections of morality in their international conduct had to be informed by concerns for their ethical appearance, even if not in the eyes of the gods or barbarians, then at least in the eyes of their highly observant and judgemental peers, as well as the Roman masses.[2] Indeed, in Caesar's case, according to Suetonius at least (*Iul.* 24), a senatorial commission was established during his campaigns to investigate his conduct, with the threatened possibility of him being sent back to his barbarian enemies as a captive if they were left unsatisfied. Rome was, unquestionably, the supreme authority and deserved the respect of all as such, but it derived that authority from the favour of gods granted in return for the *pietas* (piety/moral conduct) of its people. The crucial rite of *deditio in fidem* (roughly translatable as 'surrender into faith'), in which defeated enemies accepted Roman rule, underlines this dichotomy well, being a ritual of unconditional surrender that emphasized the good faith of the conqueror rather than the abjection of the conquered.[3] How, then, did Roman commanders in the field balance the concerns of cynical powerplays with those of just conduct? The potential missing ingredient from many of these conversations, that this chapter will explore, is a Roman view of moral particularism in international relations supported by norms of ethnocentrism and ethnic othering. Good faith and justice are of little use when faced with opponents too ignorant of etiquette and reality, too irrational and bellicose to be dealt in a spirit of mutual trust and honesty.

Three sections from Caesar's *Commentarii de Bello Gallico* illustrate the problems of Roman diplomatic conduct and the potential for double standards on the basis of ethnic othering that they could entail, two from book 1 of the text and the third from book 4. In all three episodes, when faced with a threatening barbarian foe, Caesar attempts to reach a diplomatic settlement but fails due to his opponents' intractability, arrogance, and refusal to recognize the authority he wields as representative of the Senate and people of Rome, underscored by reflections on their ethnic status. This failure of diplomacy invariably precipitates a conflict resulting not merely in the barbarians' defeat, but merciless slaughter. This tendency contrasts sharply with the behaviour displayed by Caesar towards his opponents in the Civil War, in which he habitually made a point of sparing even his bitterest foes from death or indignity, attempting to reconcile or at least de-escalate rather than punish. The contrast is evident not merely in Caesar's own commentaries, but in later biographies by Suetonius and Plutarch, the former in particular noting his much-vaunted *clementia* (mercy/clemency; *Iul.* 75.1). The distinction is not merely of differing turns of events, though the narrative of the conflicts is quite varied. Caesar, when faced with similar resistance to compromise and/or denial of his right to offer terms from Gallic or Germanic counterparts and Roman ones, treated the former with brutality and the latter with mercy.

Looking at two key incidents, and the language used to describe them, in greater detail while drawing comparisons with other related episodes will illuminate the matter further.

The crucial episode from the Gallic Wars under scrutiny here is Caesar's attempts to treat with Ariovistus, a Germanic warlord occupying lands in eastern Gaul under a title of 'king', previously with Roman sanction (provided by Caesar himself during his consulship in 59 BCE).[4] The initial attempt to arrange a meeting to discuss allegations of abuse and mistreatment made against him by Gallic allies of Rome, who painted him as the cruellest, most arbitrary tyrant imaginable, was hampered by Ariovistus' refusal to attend without an army and demands that Caesar instead travel to him (*BG* 1.34).[5] Turning to an exchange of letters, the Germanic king's response offers a good indication of the Roman worldview of moral and political superiority. He frames Caesar's overtures as hypocritical; just as the Romans have the right to treat those whom they have conquered as they wish, he has the right to treat the Gauls whom he has conquered as he sees fit. Not content to simply assert his rights, the king also backed up his words with a threatening boast of his undefeated status and the prowess of his warriors.[6]

Both sides having made military preparations and Caesar advanced towards Ariovistus' territory, the latter indicated through envoys his readiness to accept a face-to-face conference. This prompted Caesar to remark in text that perhaps Ariovistus had returned 'ad sanitatem' (to sanity; *BG* 1.42), implying that his earlier standpoint could be attributed to an emotional outburst or fit of irrationality. When their dialogue occurs, however, the situation does not improve (*BG* 1.43–45). The same demands from Caesar produce the same responses from Ariovistus, coupled with a threatened repudiation of his status as *rex et amicus populi Romani* (king and friend of the Roman People) if it does not begin to produce more tangible benefits for himself, a threat that he might seek to arrange Caesar's disgrace or even assassination through contacts in the Roman Senate, and another that he would otherwise make war against Rome itself unless left alone. The exchange of demands and threats is interrupted when alarms are sounded that Germanic horsemen were attacking the Roman army (*BG* 1.46). Despite Caesar expressing concerns that he should not immediately move to retaliate, lest it be thought he did so dishonestly under the guise of peace talks, talk around the camp of Ariovistus' *arrogantia* (arrogance/hubris) in treating with Caesar, his attempts to demand the obedience of Roman forces, and his own warriors' disrespect for the sanctity of the conference moved his soldiers to begin the inevitable battle.

The episode of the *Commentarii* offers an impressive laundry list of *faux pas* to make in dealing with representatives of the Roman Republic. We see here that an attempt by barbarians to treat Romans as peers, especially one entailing taking on the mantle of command and authority in dealings with them, warrants harsh reprisal. Rome, with Caesar as its representative, is the supreme power in Gaul and any challenge to that will be answered. Threats, even when made in the interests of warning off attempts at further conflict, merely invite it. Treating the *amicitia* (friendship/goodwill) of Rome as a negotiable ornament, rather than a generous gift and obligation further underlines the portrait of obscene temerity. If this was not enough, the *Commentarii* even recount that Ariovistus, after making a final call for the resumption of diplomacy, had Caesar's envoy seized on accusations of being a spy, imprisoned, and threatened with human sacrifice (*BG* 1.51). So damning is the text's characterization of Ariovistus that Caesar cannot be faulted for ultimately making war upon him despite his legal status as a friend and ally of the Roman people without apparent Senatorial consultation.[7] The text takes pains to establish that, as a man with no respect for the authority of Rome or his obligations to it as *socius,* no peace treaty would be worth establishing with him.[8]

While Ariovistus is one of the worst offenders in the text, he is not alone. Before clashing with him, Caesar had battled the Gallic Helvetii on behalf of the provincial dependents and allies they had threatened and raided.[9] While his primary conference with their representative Divico (*BG* 1.13–14) is marked by similar problems of a refusal to accept Caesar's authoritative position or the proffered peace terms in favour of making hubristic threats, what sets this encounter apart is the overshadowing memory of the Helvetii's prior interactions with Rome. They were responsible for inflicting a particularly humiliating defeat on an army of the Republic led by the consul L. Cassius Longinus roughly fifty years beforehand, forcing the survivors of an ambush to undergo the rite of *deditio* by passing under the yoke.[10] This fact creates problems for both parties. Caesar cites it as a reason to treat all negotiations undertaken with them in bad faith and pursue opportunistic attacks against them. Their first recorded interaction sees the proconsul deliberately fobbing off Helvetian envoys, playing for time in order to muster his forces for the inevitable battle. The author's stated reasons for this are remembrance of the group's historical misdeeds and that their status as *homines inimico animo* (people hostile in spirit; *BG* 1.7) means that their words are simply not to be trusted.[11] Divico, meanwhile, re-emphasizes the issue by using allusions to the earlier defeat as the thrust of his threats and insolence to Caesar. The narrative is framed to portray the massacres that Caesar's forces inflict upon the Helvetii as merely deserved punishments for their incorrigible violent tendencies rather than choices pursued at the expense of peace.[12]

Similarly, Caesar's interactions with the Usipetes and Tenchtheri (*BG* 4.7–13), Germani attempting to settle in northern Gaul after expulsion from their homelands by expansionistic neighbours, are fraught with bad faith predicated on ethnic othering. In contrast with Ariovistus' initial aversion to diplomatic negotiation, the Usipetes and Tenchtheri at first welcomed envoys from the proconsul, offering their own terms in the form of loyal military service to Rome in exchange for a grant of settlement on any Gallic land the Republic saw fit to assign them. Opposed to this idea, on the grounds of fearing further influxes of Germanic settlers and having already expelled Ariovistus' followers from the region on that basis, Caesar instead made the firm suggestion that they ally with another Germanic people, the Ubii, against their oppressors and reclaim their territory, thus vacating Gaul and returning east of the Rhine. Not unreasonably, representatives of the Usipetes and Tenchtheri requested at least three days to secure terms of alliance with the Ubii before proceeding with the plan. Caesar, however, ignored this request, suspecting it to be a ruse to play for time, gathering their forces to assault his own. Zeroing in on claims made in initial exchanges that it was the Germanic ancestral custom to resist aggression with force rather than entreaty (*BG* 4.7), the proconsul manoeuvred his forces into position and advanced on their encampment, despite repeated pleas to hold back and allow the Germani space, until an attack upon his vanguard appeared to confirm his suspicions and precipitated the usual battle and massacre.[13] It is on the basis of this incident, so Plutarch tells us, that Cato the Younger pushed for the inquiry into Caesar's conduct and the punishment of his misdeeds by remanding him to the custody of his foreign foes in the Senate (as Suetonius alluded), arguing that the massacre had in fact been a breach of diplomatic custom (*Vit. Cat. Min.* 51.1–4).[14] Caesar's own version of events can thus be read through the lens of attempting to put the controversy to bed once and for all, with ultimately mixed success.

Regardless of whether we side with Cato or not, the double standard in Caesar's behaviour here is evident. Caesar can use claims of diplomatic consideration to play for time and assemble forces, as he did against the Helvetii, but such an approach is improper and worthy of retribution when employed by barbarians. The contrast could be chalked up to the cynical Realist stance discussed earlier; Caesar is strong, his opponents are weak, and they will suffer what they must. However, his description of the Usipetes and Tenchtheri, stating that favouring war over diplomacy is an ancestral Germanic custom, emphasizes the ethnic character of the problem. Caesar was obligated to fight and slaughter the Germani because it was in their nature to be bellicose rather than peaceful.[15] At a macrocosmic level, Caesar's justifications for violence lie in the simple and effective matter of defence; harm done to allied Gallic peoples threatened the hegemony that Rome relied upon, and the Germani, if unchecked, could overrun

Gaul and threaten Italy (*BG* 4.16).[16] In order to make this argument, however, and make it persuasively, Caesar had to establish that there was no way to ameliorate the situation through discussion, the easiest way to do so being to appeal to stereotypes of barbarian irrationality and untrustworthiness.

Turning to the accounts of the Civil War, we see very different patterns of behaviour and explanation emerge. The key episode of comparison here is the treatment of the Pompeian lieutenants, Afranius and Petreius, at the conclusion of Caesar's campaign against them in Iberia *c.* 49 BCE (*BC* 1.84–85). After the former were reduced to submission by repeated skirmishes, retreats, and loss of supplies, Caesar lectured them on their refusal to accept earlier overtures and condemned their brutal attack on a peaceful exchange between the two armies looking for reconciliation. As in the case of Ariovistus, the term *arrogantia* is thrown around as a term of reproach and potential justification for harsher treatment. However, not only are the defeated enemy forces spared (as citizens forced to fight against their own), but Caesar makes it clear that he is not interested in making terms for his own benefit but merely for the establishment of peace, requesting that Petreius and Afranius leave the province and go unharmed. Similar protocol attends his accounts of the Siege of Corfinium (*BC* 1.22–23) and other victories over Pompeian forces throughout the text. Although it is notable that Caesar's Roman enemies do mostly offer terms of surrender after defeat, rather than hubristically fighting to the bitter end, they perform many similar actions to the barbarians of the earlier *Commentarii* who receive unreserved condemnation.

At a shallow reading, we might assume that the distinction between foreign and civil war would cover all variances in Caesar's behaviour; the citizenship and compatriot status held by his Roman opponents meriting mercies that his barbarian foes did not. It does, ultimately, indicate that Caesar the individual (as opposed to the more compartmentalized versions of Caesar the author or Caesar the character) was capable of mercy towards those who had fought against him. His ruthlessness towards foes in the Gallic Wars was not a matter of mere instinct or inflexible habit but a conscious choice. Placed in the broader context of attitudes towards war and diplomacy in late Republican Roman society, however, Caesar's rhetorical strategies to explain and defend his choices of behaviour become clearer.

Cicero's *De Officiis*, in its exposition of ideal Roman behaviour, sheds light on the ethical grey zones which Caesar exploits. The text's description of *bellum iustum* (just war; *Off.* 1.38) under Roman Fetial Law offers a relatively clear blueprint for military conduct, setting out the proper grounds on which war should be promulgated and the proper treatment of the defeated. Cicero here emphasizes the establishment of *pax* (whose non-cognate status with the contemporary English 'peace' is well established in a paper by Carlin Barton) as the primary purpose of war, and states that the dividing line between those who should be spared and those worthy of destruction is their behaviour.[17] The latter category belongs to those who are *crudeles in bello* (cruel in war) or *immanes* (inhumane) in their conduct, offering Carthage and Numantia as examples. A further distinction is made between wars for survival against ruthless enemies (*inimici*) and those meant to bring imperial glory to the Republic against competitors or disputants, the latter worthy of restraint and fair resolution, citing the honourable conduct of King Pyrrhus of Epirus as an example of the latter.[18] Carthaginian treachery and cruelty are cited as reasons for treating them as an exception, rendering them bitter enemies (entailing merciless total war) rather than as rivals for empire.[19] This illustrates the potential for ethnic othering on the basis of perceived behaviour and its impact on Roman moral considerations of diplomacy and warfare. Because it cannot be trusted to maintain *fides* (faith) in an honest, Roman manner, *Carthago delenda est.*

Cicero's words here can help to contextualize Caesar's actions and his account of them but can only do so somewhat equivocally. On one hand, the *De Officiis* was composed after Caesar's assassination, meaning that cannot be used as a standard against which the *Commentarii*'s accounts of conduct are to be judged. Similarly, it should be remembered that the text was also an exposition of an ideal form of morality, penned by an individual with very limited experience as a military commander in the field. On the other hand, Cicero's moral framework is not a radical one cut from whole cloth but a commitment of largely unwritten traditions of Roman practice to writing, meaning that it is, at least, reflective of the beliefs held by the audience Caesar was writing for. Furthermore, the text demonstrates a certain intertextuality with the *Commentarii* themselves, offering a rebuke to Caesar's invocation of the tradition that a battering ram's impact on enemy fortifications marked the point at which their surrender no longer had to be accepted (*Off.* 1.35), a relatively minor quibble but telling nonetheless. Caesar's conduct against foreign enemies in Gaul and beyond was thus not given a *carte blanche* on the basis of his opponents' non-Roman status. His portrayal of his Gallic and Germanic opponents as variously cruel, dangerous, and unreliable fitted into long-accepted traditions of ethnic othering that justified foregoing attempts at peaceful diplomacy in favour of ruthless devastation.

In order for his approach of ethnic othering to function as a viable defence of his conduct, Caesar had to be confident that his audience would be familiar enough with the stereotypes and tropes which he employed to engage with them. While the Germani of Caesar's narrative were exotic enough to warrant frequent asides explaining their behaviour, stereotyping of Gauls was a well-established practice at Rome by the time of the *Commentarii*'s dissemination in the mid-first century BCE.[20] Cicero himself made extensive use of similar, in some cases almost identical, stereotypes to those of Caesar in surviving orations.[21] The *Pro Fonteio*, a defence speech offered on behalf of a pro-praetorian governor accused of extortion and corruption by his Gallic subjects, frames the prosecution witnesses as greedy thugs driven by racial enmity towards Rome and incapable of being trusted to obey court proceedings (*Font.* 19–20).[22] *De Provinciis Consularibus*, a political speech partially made in support of Caesar's ongoing campaigns *c.* 56 BCE, offers references to Gallic belligerence and the threats it could pose to Italy if left unchecked as reasons to extend the proconsul's term of office and permit his continuation of war in the north (*Prov. Cons.* 13–14).[23] That Cicero could easily deploy such *topoi* effectively in his rhetoric is an indication that the audience Caesar hoped to reach with his writings were primed to accept the prejudices he invoked.

Looking further into related areas of Roman historiography, an account of the infamous Gallic Sack of Rome in the early fourth century BCE further adds to the notion of diplomacy as a locus of ethnic othering in Roman thought. In contrast with versions of events produced by Polybius, Dionysius of Halicarnassus, and Plutarch, Livy's description emphasizes the precipitating incident of the Gallo-Roman conflict as one of Roman fault. During a parlay with Roman ambassadors aimed at lifting the Gallic siege of Clusium, one of the envoys broke with accepted diplomatic conduct in taking up arms against the Gauls and killing at least one in his unprovoked attack (Liv., 5.36.7–10). When demands were made for the offender to be rendered to the Gauls for judgement and restitution the Senate refused. The historian's narrative not only frames these actions as almost karmically responsible for the humiliation of the Roman defeat at the River Allia and subsequent occupation and burning of the city itself but notes that such behaviour is expected of Gauls rather than Romans.[24] When the Gauls in question, particularly their leader Brennus, begin to behave in such a manner (with their massacre of Roman elders, looting of temples, and attempts to cheat the defeated out of more gold than is fair for their ransom) they are in store for divine retribution at the hands of the returning Roman general Camillus (Liv., 5.43.6–8). Even here, wherein Rome's code of Fetial conduct is turned against itself, the association between the Gauls and the kind of behaviour that warrants destruction through total war is writ large, further establishing the existence of a longstanding rich vein of stereotyping that Caesar could tap into for his own purposes.

In addition to self-representation through his own writings, Caesar appears as a historical figure in Sallust's account of the Catilinarian Conspiracy (*c.* 65–63 BCE), in a manner which potentially sheds further light on his conduct in the Civil War. Sallust had been a follower of Caesar, notably taking an active role in the African Campaign against Scipio and Cato the Younger in 46 BCE and took to writing in the years following his former general's assassination. Caesar's primary role in the *Bellum Catilinae* is to provide a counterweight to voices calling for the summary execution of convicted conspirators in the Senate (*Cat.* 51.1–43). His reported speech criticizes the killing of citizens as a response to internecine conflict, framing it as a slippery slope from the elimination of criminal or universally unpopular men to indiscriminate slaughter and a practice contrary to the hallowed wisdom of *mos maiorum* (ancestral custom), advocating for the conspirators' exile and stripping of assets instead. Although this might be argued to fit more into the realms of criminal justice and civil politics than of diplomacy, this portrait only serves to underline the contrast between the Caesar of *clementia* (mercy/leniency) towards his fellow citizens, even in war and civil strife, and the brutal, prejudicial Caesar of the Gallic commentaries.[25]

A highly useful point of comparison for how to deal diplomatically with non-Roman peoples, especially far-flung ones, also comes from Sallust's *Bellum Iugurthae*, a historical account of the Roman Republic's conflict with the Numidian ruler Iugurtha *c.* 112–106 BCE, in its discussion of the conduct of war against non-Romans and diplomatic relations arising therefrom. While a historical account composed at a distance of several decades rather than an autobiographical one, the work offers a potential insight into how the audience of Caesar's *Commentarii* might have looked to the actions of earlier generations for templates of expected conduct in times of foreign conflict.

The text elucidates much of the complex diplomatic manoeuvring of Iugurtha himself, his rival for power Adherbal, and King Bocchus of Mauretania (a frequently vacillating third party), in their dealings with both the Senate and with the Roman magistrates sent to prosecute the conflict, namely Q. Caecilius Metellus Numidicus and G. Marius. Adherbal, framed as the rightful heir to the throne of Numidia and a loyal ally of Rome, repeatedly makes overtures to the Senate for aid against Iugurtha's machinations (*Iug.* 14.1–25, 24.2–10), which, while unsuccessful in Sallust's narrative due to corruption and bribery, can perhaps be taken as a blueprint for how, ideally, a *peregrinus* (non-citizen/foreigner) should treat with Rome. A speech of his, as the text gives it, makes a point of acceding sovereignty of Numidia to the Roman people (under which he merely acts as a deputized administrator) instead of conducting himself as an independent peer. Its persuasive thrust focuses on two points: appealing to Roman *fides* on the basis of ancestral custom (the alliance had begun with Adherbal's grandfather Massinissa) and longstanding loyalty, along with emphasizing his moral position of filial piety, honesty, and duty (all prized traits of Roman culture) in contrast with Iugurtha's venal ambition and guile. The beleaguered Numidian king offers an appeal aimed neither at cynical common interest or an international code of conduct but specifically Roman morality and his place in it as a foreigner. The Senate's initial inaction on the matter, and the suspected corruption behind it, are lambasted in the text by Plebeian Tribune G. Memmius, who offers the biting aphorism that they were 'treating enemies as allies and allies as enemies'.[26]

Conversely, Bocchus, it is noted, was essentially uncontacted by Rome prior to the development of the conflict (though he was indirectly familiar with the Republic by reputation; *Iug.* 19.7) and his journey from alien to Roman *socius* (ally) is not a straightforward one. The sticking point of his participation in the conflict was his provision of sanctuary to Iugurtha and his guerrilla forces, after the latter's defeat on the field, allowing the war to drag on for several years. Presiding consuls Metellus and Marius, as successive prosecutors of the war, both sent envoys to Bocchus with the goal of persuading him to accept Roman *amicitia* at the price of handing over Iugurtha. In the final exchange before the war's conclusion, Bocchus is praised as a morally upstanding man deceived by a wicked one (i.e. Iugurtha) and allowed to defend his earlier military actions against Roman forces near the Numidian/Mauretanian border on the basis that he had feared for the safety of his kingdom without overt comment or modification of terms (*Iug.* 104.3–5). Despite repeated back and forth entreaties, attempts at negotiation (rather than unconditional acquiescence), and actual conflict with Roman forces, the goal of diplomatic overtures to the king remained consistent throughout. There is little, if any, discussion in Sallust's text of the possibility of making direct war on Bocchus with the aim of *deditio in fidem*, or of considering his kingdom as an equal with the power of the Republic. Indeed, despite asides from Sallust alluding to the inconstancy of either Bocchus himself (*Iug.* 108.3) or communities of North Africans in general (*Iug.* 18.1–2) in ways that are not too dissimilar from Caesar's comments on Gallic national character, all diplomatic dealings with him by Roman representatives are approached in good faith.

What the comparison with the *Commentarii* reveals is that Caesar's conduct was not, in fact, standard procedure for dealings with distant barbarians, nor was the potential for vacillation on the part of a non-Roman polity in diplomatic dealings an automatic warrant for their destruction. While Sallust's framing of Adherbal makes for a tragic ideal of diplomatic conduct on the part of barbarians, the fact that Bocchus' failures to match it do not in any way disqualify him from peaceful reception as a Roman ally throws Caesar's imposition of unusually exacting standards on his opponents into sharp relief. Unable to rely solely on attributing less than perfect behaviour to his opponents as a justification for inciting violence against them, he further had to frame said behaviour in the light of prejudicial attitudes that rendered it a threat rather than merely a failure.

The brutality that Caesar meted out against opponents in Gaul was not something his writings could excuse on bases of normative expected conduct as a commander at war but something that had to be justified on specific grounds of ethnic othering, as well as expedience, as applied to those he faced. While as non-citizen foreigners, adversaries such as Ariovistus' followers or the Helvetii had virtually no guaranteed rights under Roman Law, their treatment under the dictates of *fides* was a matter of ethical concern that Caesar's peers could pass judgement upon. Instead, Caesar's rhetoric of ethnic othering helped to portray what was, in fact, an unusually expansive and prejudicial approach to warfare as morally upright and in line with Roman ideals and allow its perpetrator to reap the benefits of social, political, and financial capital associated with victory rather than face criticism for it.

Notes

1 Eckstein 2006: 17–18; Rosenstein 2007: 228–9, 241; Harris 2016: 11–13.

2 Brunt 1978: 174–81; Mehl 2011: 24–5.

3 Barton 2016: 857–8.

4 Gardner 1983: 184.

5 Caesar is careful to frame himself as a heroic defender reacting to the pleas and abuses of others in this case (Kraus 2009: 169). For the rhetorical underpinnings of the sketch of Ariovistus, see Vasaly 2009: 248–51.

6 For Caesar's use of fear and threat as a literary theme in this section of the *Commentarii*, see Murphy 1977: 235–6.

7 Sherwin-White 1967: 14–18.

8 A contrasting narrative of events, that paints Caesar as a cynical agent provocateur in his dealings with the Germanic king, is preserved by Cassius Dio 38.34–35. Tarpin 2013: 672–4.

9 The precise circumstances under which the Helvetic War of *c.* 58 BCE began are perhaps the most contested aspect of Caesar's narrative. The stated goals of a mass migration on the part of the Helvetii to re-settle in new lands on the Atlantic coast as part of a larger plot to secure dominance over Gaul (*BG* 1.4) is widely regarded as a misrepresentation, if not fabrication, of events with more plausible alternatives suggested variously by Delbrück 1975: 459–70, Cunliffe 1998: 222–3, Thorne 2007: 32, and Raaflaub and Ramsey 2017: 2.

10 The incident, occurring at Burdigala (modern Bordeaux) in 107 BCE, is independently attested in Liv., *Ep.* 65 and Tac., *Germ.* 37. For the stereotyping of the Helvetii and their martial tendencies, see Schadee 2008: 161.

11 In tying his ethnic characterization of the Helvetii to their historical actions rather than blunt assertions, Caesar allows for a subtler, more effective form of propagandization. See Rankin 1987: 136.

12 For Caesar's propagandistic pictures of threatening Gauls, see Gardner 1983: 185–6. For the problems of framing the 'Celts' and other protohistoric peoples as 'warrior societies', eager for battle, in anthropological terms, see Webster 1996: 114–19.

13 In addition to textual descriptions of the fate of the Usipetes and Tenchtheri provided by Caesar et al., the material reality of the violence they suffered at Roman hands is increasingly evinced by available archaeological evidence. See Roymans 2018: 167–82.

14 Dimitrova 2018: 42.

15 Riggsby 2006: 69.

16 Riggsby 2006: 55; Woolf 2011: 73–4.

17 Barton 2007: 246–8.

18 Cicero's point here is linked to his quotation of Ennius (*Ann.* 6, Vahlen^2, 11.194–201) concerning Pyrrhus' supposed free return of Roman prisoners-of-war on the basis that it would be more honourable to defeat them fairly in battle once more than to ransom or mistreat them.

19 For further discussion on the trope of *punica fides* (Punic faith) and related stereotypes of Carthaginian treachery, see Isaac 2004: 328–32.

20 For the roles played by anti-Gallic stereotyping in late Republican Rome, see Williams 2001: 1–3, 46–67, 76–8, 171, and Woolf 2011: 23. For the exoticism of the Germani in Caesar's narrative, see Schadee 2008: 168 and Krebs 2011: 206.

21 Vasaly 1993: 191–2.

22 Vasaly 1993: 151–2. For a further discussion of Cicero's use of a trope of racial enmity towards Rome on the part of 'Gauls' as a broad ethnic category, see Moore 2019: 134–3.

23 Steel 2001: 158–9; Riggsby 2006: 21.

24 Liv., 5.36.1, *mitis legatio, ni praeferoces legatos Gallisque magis quam Romanis similes habuisset* (It would have been a peaceful embassy were it not for the violence of the ambassadors, who were more like Gauls than Romans).

25 It may also be noted that Suetonius (*Iul.* 14, 17) alleges that Caesar's calls for mercy on the Catilinarian Conspirators were motivated less by a concern for the rights of all citizens than by either his association with the conspiracy itself or at least sympathy for its populist goals.

26 *Iug.* 31.23–24, *postremo sociis nostris veluti hostibus, hostibus pro sociis utuntur.*

Bibliography

Barton, C. A. (2007), 'The Price of Peace in Ancient Rome', in K. A. Raaflaub (ed.), *War and Peace in the Ancient* World, 245–56, Oxford: Oxford University Press.

Brunt, P. A. (1978), 'Laus Imperii', in P. D. A. Garnsey and C. R. Whittaker (eds), *Imperialism in the Ancient* World, 159–92, Cambridge: Cambridge University Press.

Cunliffe, B. (1998), *The Ancient Celts*, Oxford: Oxford University Press.

Delbrück, H. (1975), *History of the Art of War within the Framework of Political History, vol. I: Antiquity*, trans. W. J. Renfroe, London: Greenwood Press.

Dimitrova, M. (2018), *Julius Caesar's Self-Created Image and Its Dramatic Afterlife*, London: Bloomsbury.

Eckstein, A. M. (2006), *Mediterranean Anarchy, Interstate War, and the Rise of Rome*, Berkeley, CA: University of California Press.

Gardner, J. F. (1983), 'The "Gallic Menace" in Caesar's Propaganda', *Greece & Rome*, 30: 181–9.

Harris, W. V. (2016), *Roman Power: A Thousand Years of Empire*, Cambridge: Cambridge University Press.

Isaac, B. (2004), *The Invention of Racism in Classical Antiquity*, Princeton, NJ: Princeton University Press.

Kraus, C. S. (2009), 'Bellum Gallicum', in M. Griffin (ed.), *A Companion to Julius Caesar*, 159–74, Chichester: Wiley-Blackwell.

Krebs, C. (2011), 'Borealism: Caesar, Seneca, Tacitus, and the Roman Discourse about the Germanic North', in E. S. Gruen (ed.), *Cultural Identity in the Ancient Mediterranean*, 202–21, Los Angeles, CA: Getty.

Mehl, A. (2011), *Roman Historiography: An Introduction to its Basic Aspects and Development*, trans. H. F. Mueller, Chichester: Wiley-Blackwell.

Moore, R. (2019), 'Blame it on the Barbarians: Ethnic Categorisation and Jingoism in the Cultural Memory of the Sack of Rome *c.* 390 BCE', *Trinity Postgraduate Review*, 18: 132–54.

Murphy, P. R. (1977), 'Themes of Caesar's "Gallic War"', *CJ*, 72: 234–43.

Omrani, B. (2017), *Caesar's Footprints: Journeys to Roman Gaul*, London: Pegasus.

Raaflaub, K. A. and J. T. Ramsey (2017), 'Reconstructing the Chronology of Caesar's Gallic Wars', *Histos*, 11: 1–74.

Rankin, D. (1987), *Celts and the Classical World*, London: Routledge.

Riggsby, A. M. (2006), *Caesar in Gaul and Rome: War in Words*, Austin, TX: University of Texas Press.

Rosenstein, N. (2007), 'War and Peace, Fear and Reconciliation at Rome', in K. Raaflaub (ed.), *War and Peace in the Ancient World*, 226–44, Oxford: Oxford University Press.

Roymans, N. (2018), 'A Roman Massacre in the Far North: Caesar's Annihilation of the Usipetes and Tenchtheri in the Dutch River Area', in M. Fernández-Götz and N. Roymans (eds), *Conflict Archaeology: Materialities of Collective Violence from Prehistory to Late Antiquity*, 167–82, New York: Routledge.

Schadee, H. (2008), 'Caesar's Construction of Northern Europe: Inquiry, Contact and Corruption in *De Bello Gallico*', *CQ*, 58: 158–80.

Sherwin-White, A. N. (1967), *Racial Prejudice in Ancient Rome*, Cambridge: Cambridge University Press.

Steel, C. E. W. (2001), *Cicero, Rhetoric, and Empire*, Oxford: Oxford University Press.

Tarpin, M. (2013), 'Arioviste et César: 61–58 a.C.', in S. Krausz, A. Colin, K. Gruel, I. Ralston, and T. Dechezleprêtre (eds), *L'Âge du Fer en Europe: mélanges offerts à Olivier Buchsenschutz*, 671–9, Bordeaux: Ausonius.

Thorne, J. (2007), 'The Chronology of the Campaign against the Helvetii: A Clue to Caesar's Intentions', *Historia*, 56: 27–36.

Vasaly, A. (1993), *Representations: Images of the World in Ciceronian Oratory*, Berkeley, CA: University of California Press.

Vasaly, A. (2009), 'Characterization and Complexity: Caesar, Sallust, and Livy', in A. Feldherr (ed.), *The Cambridge Companion to the Roman Historians*, 245–61, Cambridge: Cambridge University Press.

Webster, J. (1996), 'Ethnographic Barbarity: Colonial Discourse and "Celtic Warrior Societies"', in J. Webster and N. Cooper (eds), *Roman Imperialism: Postcolonial Perspectives*, 111–24, Leicester: Leicester University Press.

Williams, J. H. C. (2001), *Beyond the Rubicon: Romans and Gauls in Republican Italy*, Oxford: Oxford University Press.

Woolf, G. (2011), *Tales of the Barbarians: Ethnography and Empire in the Roman West*, Chichester: Wiley-Blackwell.

Wyke, M. (2007), *Caesar: A Life in Western Culture*, Chicago, IL: Chicago University Press.

7

Contra mores maiorum: Barbarian Women Prisoners during the Principate and the High Empire[1]

Denis Álvarez Pérez-Sostoa

Vero novum genus obsidum

A well-known passage of Suetonius records some of Augustus' foreign policy achievements in *Germania*. The episode runs as follows:[2]

> ut quorundam barbarorum principes in aede Martis Ultoris iurare coegerit mansuros se in fide ac pace quam peterent, a quibusdam vero novum genus obsidum, feminas, exigere temptaverit, quod neglegere marum pignora sentiebat.

> He forced the chiefs of certain barbarians to take oath in the temple of Mars the Avenger that they would faithfully keep the peace for which they asked; in some cases, indeed, he tried to exact a new kind of hostages, namely women, realizing that the barbarians disregarded pledges secured by males.

At first reading, the text suggests a certain change in Roman practice. Two ideas stand out in Suetonius' testimony. In the first, the expression *vero novum genus obsidum* (a new kind of hostages) underlines the fact that women would be taken as a new type of hostage. The second, the fact that Augustus had to choose this kind of guarantee because of the particular circumstances inherent to the Germanic tribes. Women as *pignora* (pledges), it seems, were more valuable than men to some peoples. Given this, the need to accommodate Rome's interests prevailed over traditional customs. Nevertheless, it also provided an ideological point of view, wherein Romans and barbarians had different perspectives on the matter.

Obviously, modern scholars have studied this fact, though without placing much emphasis on it. For some even, Suetonius' claim was far from reality, and they have argued that the practice was not alien at all to the Roman world.[3] At the same time, it is striking that no allusion to this episode is included in the *Res Gestae*. Indeed, as Braund has pointed out,[4] in the Latin and Greek versions of Augustus' political will there is no direct mention of the terms *obses* or *homeros* (hostage). Aside from this, throughout the document and among Augustus' achievements, the only mention related to *Germania* is that Augustus himself had pacified that region, without entering into further details.[5]

A passage from Tacitus has been used as the best argument to validate the testimony of his contemporary Suetonius. In his *Germania*, when talking about the possibility of becoming prisoners, Tacitus explains that the Germanic peoples feared more than anything that this fate would fall upon their women. The evidence recorded by Tacitus is this:[6]

> monstrata comminus captivitate, quam longe inpatientius feminarum suarum nomine timent, adeo ut efficacius obligentur animi civitatum, quibus inter obsides puellae quoque nobiles imperantur.
>
> For so is it brought home to men that the slavery, which they dread much more keenly on their women's account, is close at hand: it follows that the loyalty of those tribes is more effectually guaranteed from whom, among other hostages, maids of high birth have been exacted.

This explanation by Tacitus is of great interest, in that once again it reflects the value placed on women by the Germanic tribes and, in this way, a practice that in theory was not performed by the Romans is highlighted as a new element. However, to some extent, the above two quotations are no more than two isolated testimonies in the wide corpus that during the Roman period details the delivery or demand of hostages. In fact, Tacitus himself quotes that the German peoples had also carried out another different custom. The historian argues that nephews were held in high esteem both by their fathers and their uncles and, as potential targets, they were preferred as hostages among any other choice. Once again, family ties were of great value, but the difference lies in the option of selecting not their sons or daughters, but their sisters.[7]

However, quotes as specific as these two are not common in the conserved literary production. This does not imply that women as hostages were not an option or that, at any other moment throughout Roman history, the presence of women in a larger group of captives was not mentioned. It is the latter concept, 'captive', that can likely shed some light on this issue.

The plurals *captivi* in Latin and *aichmalotoi* in Greek refer to persons who have been captured, meaning those who have been deprived of their freedom because of a defeat. In other words, everything that belonged to the loser would fall into the hands of the victor who, following the *ius belli* (law of war), could make whatever use he deemed appropriate of the loot, including the detainees. Although the legal status of hostages and prisoners is clearly defined, if we consider the idea of the prisoner in its broadest sense, the possibilities limited only to the concept of a hostage-woman are greatly expanded. Initially, the *captivi* could form a homogeneous group as long as the actual legal status of each individual was identified as such. Subsequently, appropriate decisions could be made regarding the fate of each one of them. On the other hand, as Gueye affirms, overall the Latin term *captivus* is linked to warfare and, consequently, is linked to the male sphere. In this case, if mentioned, 'la prisonnière de guerre était plutôt désignée par son ancienne fonction dans la société et son état civil antérieur'.[8]

Of course, another problem arises when the same individual is differently catalogued by the author. For example, after the conquest of Carthago Nova by Scipio in 209 BCE, the Roman soldiers brought a young maiden to their general. This is one of those scarce occasions in which the feminine *captiva* is attested. Whilst Livy, followed by Florus, talks precisely about a *captiva*, Valerius Maximus states that an adult maiden was found among the *obsides* (hostages) captured in the city.[9] Perhaps the changing of this status after a subjugation lies at the core of this matter. In this sense, Scardigli notes that if the terms of an agreement guaranteed by the handover of hostages were not respected, they could be used as slaves.[10] Alvar, on his side, pointed out that the captured hostages directly became hostages of the conqueror.[11] Nevertheless, the standing classical sources do not seem to support any of these options. On the contrary, the presence of hostages is often hidden because it is not possible to track them after their delivery, or because they are included in a larger group identified as *captivi*.

Evidence of this can be seen in some examples during the Republic. Scipio Nasica received hostages from the Boii as recorded by Livy.[12] Later on in his account, when Nasica celebrated his triumph in Rome, no mention of those hostages is attested. Instead, Livy uses the expression *cum captivis nobilibus* (alongside with noble captives).[13] A similar instance occurred when Publius Cornelius Scipio paraded in triumph some ten years before Nasica. No source describes the presence of hostages during Scipio's triumphal procession, but the Carthaginian hostages taken after Zama or even some taken during his previous campaigns in Spain could have been among the prisoners displayed in Rome. Certainly, the Numidian king Syphax was at the centre of the triumph, the most important figure 'among the prisoners led through the town'.[14]

Terminology can constrain and limit a more accurate analysis. There is no doubt that *obses* and *homeros* were the Latin and Greek terms for hostage, as were *captivus/captiva* and *aichmalotos* for prisoner. However, Greek and Roman authors very often use another series of nouns with the same purpose. Thus, the concept of *pignora* mentioned by Suetonius is linked with *pignus* (pledge), while its closest Greek equivalent would be *pistis*.[15] Because of this and according to Moscovich, '*Pignus*, or *pignus fidei*, is the terminology often employed by the sources to describe the function of hostages'.[16] And, of course, none of these concepts takes into account the gender of the prisoner or the hostage except if specifically mentioned. Equally, when ancient authors talk about *liberi* or *tekna* (sons and/or daughters), it is difficult to know if those groups might have been composed of both young boys and girls.[17]

In addition to this, anonymity is one of the most common features for both hostages and prisoners of war. Usually, agreements were secured with a variable number of hostages whose identity we know little or nothing about. Thus, beyond the fact that they might be members of the most representative families of the peoples from which they were taken, except in rare and notorious instances, identity is not that relevant for the classic authors.[18] The context of prisoners of war is similar. Therefore, in general only in high-profile cases, such as that of Syphax, do we know the identity of one of them. The representativeness and symbolic value of the defeat and, by contrast, of the Roman victory, are very influential in the identification of the captives. Not forgetting the emotional element of both the triumph's viewers and of the potential readers of the historians' works. As Benario suggested, 'the reader is compelled to imagine the human suffering embraced by the single word *captivi*'.[19]

Three questions

The claims of Suetonius and Tacitus open the way to different interpretations. Overall, however, the issues that might arise could be as follows. First, are we presented with a real change in pattern or are Suetonius' and Tacitus' statements pure rhetoric instead? In other words, is this a part of the effort to establish a clear distinction between Romans and non-Romans? That is, we Romans do not demand female hostages while you the barbarians, 'the others', actually do? The answer to these two questions can only be found by analysing former episodes and examining traditional Roman customs on the matter with those followed, for example, by Greeks, Carthaginians or any other enemy that the Romans confronted during the Republic and at the beginning of the empire.

Thus, the first concern is linked directly with the second. If we conclude that both testimonies are real facts, a not-to-be crossed line by which Rome's and others' actions could be differentiated, are they pointing to a custom among the barbarians or just a single episode related to the Germanic peoples? If we expand the research to later periods and Rome's policy in the East or at the northern boundaries during the high empire, would the outcome still be the same?

Finally, a third question can also be posed. Both passages describe the German tribes, those northern barbarians far from the civilization represented by Rome. So, could it be that our sources are describing one more of those particular examples interpreted from a Roman point of view? A way by which the Romans themselves added a new element to reinforce their superiority?

In fact, according to various sources, the presence of women as part of a group of hostages or prisoners of war does not seem to be alien to Roman knowledge. It is true that in all cases the enemies of Rome did not hesitate to demand women or girls, and make use of them as one of the elements with which they could guarantee a treaty or an alliance. Athenaeus, quoting Duris of Samos' third book of his *History of Agathocles*, said that 'Cleonymus the Spartan was the first man to take such hostages as he took from the Metapontines, namely, two hundred of their most respectable and beautiful virgins'.[20] The episode, dated to the years 303–302 BCE, recalls Cleonymus' expedition in southern Italy to help Taranto in his fight against the Lucanians. If Duris' fragment is to be believed, the end of the fourth century BCE would be the starting point for this custom, at least for the Greeks, which is quite far from Augustus' first movement in the same direction.

In any case, because of the conflicts they had with the Romans, and thanks to the greater abundance of information, it seems that the Carthaginians chose this measure more broadly. Although the most well-known episodes belong to the Second Punic War, the background of their policy demonstrates how widespread this practice was among them.

Therefore, after the end of the First Punic War in 241 BCE, Carthage had to resolve the problem caused by their mercenary troops, who were located near the capital. The lack of pay and the confinement in Carthage only heightened tensions, so the Carthaginians decided to move them to the nearby town of Sicca. The mercenaries' demands did not quell, so once they had gathered an army of more than 20,000 men they went back and camped once again outside the capital. Polybius criticized the Carthaginian policy and, anticipating the revolt, blamed them for not taking precautions in advance.[21] The Carthaginians themselves were quite soon aware of the mistake they had made. Polybius speaks clearly:[22]

> τούτου δὲ μεῖζον ἔτι, προέμενοι τὰ τέκνα καὶ τὰς γυναῖκας καὶ σὺν τούτοις τὰς ἀποσκευάς· οἷς ἐξῆν ὁμήροις χρησαμένους ἀσφαλέστερον μὲν αὐτοὺς βουλεύσασθαι περὶ τῶν ὑποπιπτόντων, εὐπειθεστέροις δ᾽ ἐκείνοις χρῆσθαι πρὸς τὸ παρακαλούμενον.
>
> Their second error was even more serious, to let out of their hands the women and children of the mercenaries as well as their movables, all which would have served as hostages, giving themselves greater security in their deliberations about the circumstances and ensuring a more favourable reception for their demands.

Ultimately, had the women and children of the mercenaries been in custody, that is, if they had been held as hostages, the security of the city would not have been compromised. However, by not doing so, Carthage ran the risk of suffering a war at the gates of the city. It is possible that the subsequent policy of the Barca family in Spain could be understood in part because of these events.

First in Sagunto and then in Carthago Nova, in two similar episodes and with a similar end, the Roman generals eventually took control over all the hostages that the Carthaginians had secured in these cities. These belonged to the Hispanic peoples that the Carthaginians had subjected during the last decades of the third century BCE.

First, with the help of an indigenous person that supported the Romans, Publius and Gnaeus Cornelius Scipio, father and uncle of Scipio Africanus, managed to secure the Hispanic hostages held in Sagunto. Both Polybius and Livy indicate that the alliance between the Hispanic peoples and Hannibal was essentially based on the presence of the hostages in Sagunto, so once they were returned to their homes the support of the Carthaginians would be considerably weakened.[23]

It appears that the decision to hold all Hispanic hostages together in one location was not considered by the Carthaginians to be a danger to their interests. In fact, they did it again, as evidenced by the account of Carthago Nova's capture by Scipio in 209 BCE. Obviously, the parallels to the Sagunto episode are clear, though in this case, as Walbank pointed out, the importance of the capture of Carthago Nova was a military success with few precedents and the first on a list that would raise the reputation of the Roman general, making him little less than a legend.[24]

Beyond the adornment of the story by the classic authors, starting with Polybius and Livy, followed by Valerius Maximus, Florus, and Plutarch, among the achievements of Scipio his management of victory and, especially, the decisions he made regarding the prisoners who had fallen into his power were highlighted above all else.

The image transmitted by the literary sources is diametrically opposed to the performance of the Carthaginians, once again establishing a clear line between the behaviour of a Roman general and that of his opponents. The first measure by Scipio was to bring before him all the prisoners captured, which, according to Polybius, numbered close to 10,000. They were formed into two groups: on the one side the inhabitants of the city together with their women and children, the artisans on the other.[25]

He then summoned the Hispanic hostages that the Carthaginians had entrusted there. Again, according to Polybius, the number of hostages was more than 300. The group included several women, such as the wife of Mandonius and the daughters of Indibilis, who had been demanded by Hasdrubal,[26] and several children.[27] Scipio attended the complaints of the Ilergetes regarding the treatment of their relatives. The story of the historian of Megalopolis indicates that

> μεταλαβὼν ὁ Πόπλιος καὶ τοῖς ὑπ᾽ ἐκείνων εἰρημένοις ἔφη πιστεύειν, μάλιστα δὲ γινώσκειν τὴν Καρχηδονίων ὕβριν ἔκ τε τῆς εἰς τοὺς ἄλλους Ἴβηρας καὶ μάλιστα τῆς εἰς τὰς ἐκείνων γυναῖκας καὶ θυγατέρας ἀσελγείας,

> Scipio had the clearest evidence of the tyrannical conduct of the Carthaginians in their licentious treatment of the wives and daughters of the speaker [Indibilis] and his friends, whom he himself had found in the position not so much of hostages as of prisoners and slaves.[28]

Scipio's criticisms of the humiliations that he had personally witnessed are once again framed in a speech that aims to distance the two sides. Moreover, the hypothetical mistreatment of the hostages would have done nothing but harm Carthaginian interests in Spain. Instead, their proper care, and in conditions quite far from those that Scipio is said to witness, would be more beneficial. The climax of the Roman performance arrived thanks to the unilateral decision of Scipio to choose to return the captives without ransom. The general only asked two conditions: they had to claim for their relatives, and they had to accept the friendship of the Romans.

Previously, in order to encourage the departure of the hostages and prove that he was not like the Carthaginians, Scipio had tried to approach the captives who had fallen into his power. In requesting that the hostages be carried to him, he paid special attention to the boys and girls who were among them, addressing them with kind words, with close treatment and with the surrender of presents to give emphasis to his intentions:[29]

> Καὶ τοὺς μὲν παῖδας καθ᾽ ἕνα προσαγαγόμενος καὶ καταψήσας θαρρεῖν ἐκέλευε, διότι μετ᾽ ὀλίγας ἡμέρας ἐπόψονται τοὺς αὑτῶν γονεῖ . . . Ταῦτα δ᾽ εἰπών, καὶ

> παρεσκευακὼς πρότερον ἐκ τῶν λαφύρων τὰ λυσιτελέστερα πρὸς τὴν ἐπίνοιαν, τότε κατὰ γένη καὶ καθ' ἡλικίαν ἑκάστοις ἐδωρεῖτο τὰ πρέποντα, ταῖς μὲν παισὶ κόνους καὶ ψέλλια, τοῖς δὲ νεανίσκοις ῥαμφὰς καὶ μαχαίρας.
>
> calling the children to him one by one and caressing them bade them be of good cheer, as in a few days they would see their parents. . . . After speaking thus, having reserved from the booty the most suitable objects for this purpose, he gave them such gifts as became their sex and age, presenting the girls with earrings and bracelets and the young men with poniards and swords.

The consequences of these provisions were immediate. He had in his hands the mechanism to reverse the situation on the peninsula in favour of Rome. Those prisoners or hostages who were not claimed at the time were taken to the winter camps to Tarraco where those who wanted to recover them had to head from that moment on. According to Polybius and Livy, the first chief who appreciated the change in the situation was 'Edeco, prince of the Edetani, who on receiving news of the capture of New Carthage and learning that his wife and sons were in Scipio's power'[30] made his way to Scipio's camp. Polybius added that Edeco 'begged that his wife and children might be restored to him and that before returning to his home he should be pronounces to be a friend'.[31]

Though risky, Scipio's gamble proved beneficial both to his interests and to the evolution of the war in Spain. The voluntary return of the captives to their respective peoples was renewed by the commitment of almost all the Hispanic peoples to the Roman cause,[32] and served further to enhance Scipio's standing as one of the best military generals in history. Certainly, the entire campaign concerning Carthago Nova proved to be a milestone in the personal interests of the Roman general and, by contrast, to the detriment of the Carthaginians disrespect in regarding the *ius belli*.

In spite of this, it was not an *uniquum* (unique testimony). For example, during his Eastern campaigns in Armenia in 69 BCE, Lucullus acted in exactly the same way. After the siege and the capture of Tigranocerta, thanks to the help of foreigners living there, Lucullus saved 'from outrage many of the wives of the principal men, when they had been captured . . . won over their husbands also'.[33] Pompey also followed an analogous policy after Mithridates' concubines were brought to him. According to Plutarch, 'most of them were daughters and wives of generals and princes' and by returning them safe to their parents Pompey could expect to profit.[34] In both cases, despite capturing women, being merciful reaped more benefits for the Romans than doing the opposite.

One example that serves to bridge the two matters, that is, the reception of female hostages and their return to their homelands, comes in the aftermath of the civil war between Mark Antony and Augustus. Dio Cassius writes:[35]

> ἐπειδή τε συχνοὶ παρ᾽ αὐτῷ καὶ δυναστῶν καὶ βασιλέων παῖδες οἱ μὲν ἐφ᾽ ὁμηρείᾳ οἱ δὲ καὶ ἐφ᾽ ὕβρει τρεφόμενοι εὑρέθησαν, τοὺς μὲν οἴκαδε αὐτῶν ἀπέστειλε, τοὺς δὲ ἀλλήλοις συνῴκισεν, ἑτέρους τε κατέσχεν.

> And since there were found at the court many children of princes and kings who were being kept there, some as hostages and others out of a spirit of arrogance, he sent some back to their homes, joined others in marriage with one another, and retained still others.

The passage of Dio Cassius could be ambiguous when using the plural *paides* with which we cannot identify whether he was referring to boys or girls. However, since Augustus promoted marriages between these prisoners, it is clear that both genders were a part of the group. Therefore, in Alexandria's court, ruled by Cleopatra and Mark Antony, the presence of female hostages or prisoners was not surprising.

Public display of prisoners in Rome

Indeed, the arrival of Augustus in Alexandria could have carried with it the capture of Cleopatra and her subsequent dispatch to Rome to be displayed at the triumphal parade. According to the classic authors, beyond the defeat suffered at Actium, the ultimate reason why the queen of Egypt decided to take her own life was precisely to avoid the disgrace of being paraded on the streets of Rome as a trophy, humiliated on her way to her final destination.[36] Indeed, she had direct knowledge of what the loss of freedom entailed and the chances of being treated as an object that served, at the same time, as a decorative element and as reminder of the Roman victory, for her sister Arsinoë had been one of the most prominent elements of Caesar's quadruple triumph in the year 46 BC. In fact, Dio Cassius highlighted the parading of Arsinoë in chains during the triumph of Caesar as being the first instance of such a thing.[37] Since Cleopatra could not be taken on the parade, Augustus decided to show an image of the queen lying down upon a couch in her death. Alongside this picture were the other prisoners and Cleopatra's children Alexander Helios and Cleopatra Selene.[38]

It is true that the importance from the viewers' perspective varied, since the empathy they might feel towards the prisoners was obviously not the same when they were representations than when they were real people who could not hide their passions and feelings. That was the case, among others, of Aemilius Paulus' triumph in 167 BCE. Paulus brought in front of him King Perseus of Macedonia, who could not hide his dismay, while the king's own children were not aware of their fate due to their young age. The most important prisoner was no doubt the king, but the pity and the sorrow the spectators felt at seeing his young sons was more of an issue than the triumph itself.[39]

Yet there was still an impact, as the achievements of the generals were highlighted and, as Ferris said, 'a triumph at which both real barbarians and images of barbarians were paraded would have created in their viewers' minds a perception of the world in which the power of Rome held sway over the bodies of other peoples'.[40] The arrival of the triumphator represented the most important moment of the celebration, but also symbolized the two sides of the victory, 'dividing the exhibits into two main groups. Spoils, captive, and representations, forming the group of others'[41] as they were paraded before his chariot. This impact also had a second effect, since the victorious commander who returned to the capital together with his men achieved a clear benefit of his own in showing off these large and varied spoils, including prisoners and hostages, men and women alike. As Nabel pointed out, 'success in the battlefield led to a strengthened domestic position'.[42]

The triumph would be remembered by the Romans and by the families of the triumphant general. Because of this, the more important the spoils, the prisoners or hostages, the better. One of the examples that perhaps most effectively showed the pursuit of grandeur and that included all the elements to make it memorable over the centuries was Pompey's triumph in 61 BCE. Pompey the Great celebrated his campaigns in the East against the pirates and Mithridates, king of Pontus. Plutarch's and Appian's accounts provide all the details of that parade. When they both relate information about the prisoners and hostages Pompey paraded in front of him, both men and women are described with their titles, origins, and family ties. Plutarch's account includes several women, most notably the relatives of Tigranes, king of Armenia and some Scythian women. In addition, alongside them an indefinite group of hostages:[43]

> αἰχμάλωτοι δ᾽ ἐπομπεύθησαν, ἄνευ τῶν ἀρχιπειρατῶν, υἱὸς Τιγράνου τοῦ Ἀρμενίου μετὰ γυναικὸς καὶ θυγατρός, αὐτοῦ τε Τιγράνου τοῦ βασιλέως γυνὴ Ζωσίμη, καὶ βασιλεὺς Ἰουδαίων Ἀριστόβουλος, Μιθριδάτου δὲ ἀδελφὴ καὶ πέντε τέκνα, καὶ Σκυθίδες γυναῖκες, Ἀλβανῶν δὲ καὶ Ἰβήρων ὅμηροι καὶ τοῦ Κομμαγηνῶν βασιλέως.

> The captives led in triumph, besides the chief pirates, were the son of Tigranes the Armenian with his wife and daughter, Zosime, a wife of king Tigranes

> himself, Aristobulus, king of the Jews, a sister and five children of Mithridates, Scythian women, and hostages given by the Iberians, by the Albanians, and by the king of Commagene.

Appian, in turn, writes two different passages regarding Pompey's triumph. The first, which focused more on the presence of women that were supposed to be Amazons, is interesting, because prisoners and hostages are not easy to distinguish as they are reported together:[44]

> καὶ ἐθριάμβευσεν ἐς Ῥώμην καὶ ἀπὸ τῶνδε. πολλαὶ δὲ ἔν τε τοῖς ὁμήροις καὶ τοῖς αἰχμαλώτοις ηὑρέθησαν γυναῖκες, οὐ μείονα τῶν ἀνδρῶν τραύματα ἔχουσαι: καὶ ἐδόκουν Ἀμαζόνες εἶναι,

> Pompey was afterward awarded one of his triumphs at Rome for these exploits. Among the hostages and prisoners many women were found, who had suffered wounds no less than the men. These were supposed to be Amazons.

The second passage is close to Plutarch's account. More exhaustive than his first mention, Appian says that the prisoners and hostages numbered up to 324 and, among them, the only women reported in detail are Orsabaris and Eupatra, Mithridates' daughters, and the Scythian women.[45]

Obviously, all of the events cited so far correspond to a period when Roman expansion had yet to reach German lands. Thus, direct precedents to Augustus' politics do not occur until Caesar's campaigns during the Gallic Wars. Specifically, the adoptive father of the *princeps* (first citizen) includes two episodes in his account of the war that could be used as an advance to later periods. In the first book, Caesar recounts the Roman victory in the Battle of Vosges in 58 BCE and the defeat of the Suebi commanded by Ariovistus. While the king fled crossing the Rhine, Caesar states that the relatives of Ariovistus were taken prisoner. Caesar's text is not very clear because it only details that the chief of the Suebi had two wives and two daughters. One was killed while the others were placed in custody. Orosius, in contrast, adds that all four were captured.[46]

Later, in response to an embassy that Caesar sent to the peoples across the Rhine, only the Ubii responded positively. Caesar insists that they were the only people that sent ambassadors and accepted the giving of hostages as a guarantee. In this particular case, Caesar does not provide any further details about the gender of these hostages.[47] Although nothing is said about the fate of Ariovistus' relatives, the chance of them being part of Caesar's triumphal parade in Rome exists, and equally for the hostages received from the Ubii. However, the wives and daughters of Ariovistus were less important than Vercingetorix, the chieftain of the Arverni, the central figure of that triumph.

In contrast, a woman occupied this position in Germanicus' triumph in 17 CE.[48] After avenging, to some extent, Varus' defeat against the coalition of the Germanic tribes commanded by Arminius, Germanicus was able to capture Thusnelda, Arminius' wife. Although with some differences, Strabo and Tacitus have transmitted similar versions of Thusnelda's fate. Strabo says that Germanicus paraded in public the most illustrious captives, both men and women:[49]

> ἐν ᾧ ἐθριαμβεύθη τῶν ἐπιφανεστάτων ἀνδρῶν σώματα καὶ γυναικῶν, Σεγιμοῦντός τε Σεγέστου υἱός, Χηρούσκων ἡγεμών, καὶ ἀδελφὴ αὐτοῦ, γυνὴ δ' Ἀρμενίου . . . ὄνομα Θουσνέλδα, καὶ υἱὸς τριετὴς Θουμέλικος·

> He leading publicly as his captives the most illustrious persons, both men and women, amongst whom were Segimuntus, the son of Segestes, the chief of the Cherusci, and his sister, named Thusnelda, the wife of Arminius . . . likewise his son Thumelicus, a boy three years old.

Other important Germanic figures are also in Strabo's list, including Rhamis, daughter of Ucromiros, chieftain of the Chatti, but none as relevant as Thusnelda. Tacitus adds other details, but the most important is that he insists on the presence of female prisoners:[50]

> inerant feminae nobiles, inter quas uxor Arminii eademque filia Segestis, mariti magis quam parentis animo, neque victa in lacrimas neque voce supplex; compressis intra sinum manibus gravidum uterum intuens.

> In the number were some women of rank; among them, the wife of Arminius, who was also the daughter of Segestes, but who exhibited the spirit of her husband rather than of her father, subdued neither to tears nor to the tones of a suppliant, her hands tightly clasped within her bosom, and eyes which dwelt on her hope of offspring.

In contrast to Strabo, Tacitus says that Arminius' son was still not born. Whatever the case, his story differs greatly from that quoted above about Aemilius Paulus' triumph and the desperation that Perseus showed in his misfortune. Generally, we know little about the destiny of the prisoners after being displayed in Rome. Nevertheless, the story of Thusnelda continues in Tacitus' other chapters. Of course, she was captured, but her husband remained at large and was still a target for the Romans. That is why on at least two other occasions, Tacitus mentions Thusnelda's destiny in Rome.[51] First, in a conversation that took place between Arminius and Germanicus, when the Roman commander explained to the chieftain that his wife and child were being well treated in Rome and, unlike his father, not as enemies.[52] In the second, criticizing Arminius' attack on Varus and his legions, Tacitus changes his tone and underlines that 'his wife and his son were still enduring slavery'.[53] Segestes, Thusnelda's father, represents the last element in this equation. Unlike Arminius and his own daughter Thusnelda, Segestes remained loyal to the Romans. Like Cleopatra some sixty years earlier, he was a guest in Rome during Germanicus' procession and an eyewitness to his own daughter's fate.

Other examples during the high empire can be taken into account, including the capture of the wife and daughter of Arpus, the chief of the Chatti, by Gaius Silius in Tiberius' reign.[54] However, one of the few triumphs to achieve almost equal status to that of Pompey or Germanicus was Claudius' after capturing Caratacus, chieftain of the Catuvellauni. As Tacitus writes, the victory carried with it the capture of Caratacus' wife and daughter, alongside his brother's surrender.[55] The news of this victory was highly celebrated in Rome and when the emperor paraded in triumph, the crowd was eager to watch the barbarian and his relatives being paraded through the streets.[56]

Conclusions: *exigere et imperare*

The episodes mentioned above demonstrate that women hostages and prisoners of war were not as strange as might be expected in Roman society. It is true that the classical sources create a quite clear distinction between Roman policy and that of other peoples. Since the Middle Republic, Rome had come into contact with Greeks and Carthaginians, to whom demanding females as hostages seemed to be common or, at the very least, not an unknown phenomenon. Moreover, Polybius, one of the most important sources for the Roman Republic, states that trust and respect could only be achieved 'after receiving adequate pledges, such pledges being oaths, wives and children held as hostages'.[57] This short assertion belongs to a fragment of book 8 of the historian of Megalopolis, but it is surprising that it is not frequently used in relation to hostage-taking, precisely when it underlines that women and children were more valuable as sureties. So, if Polybius himself details that those pledges were the best one could hope for, how is it that Romans did not follow this custom until Augustus' time?

As mentioned above, no mention of hostages was included in Augustus' *Res Gestae*. Nevertheless, a later section of the same document, the one dealing with Augustus' diplomatic exchanges with the Parthian Empire and the arrival of

King Phraates' sons to Rome, has been under discussion for quite some time.[58] The relevant passage is the following one:[59]

> ad me rex Parthorum Phrates, Orodis filius, filios suos nepotesque omnes misit in Italiam non bello superatus, sed amicitiam nostram per liberorum suorum pignora petens.
>
> Phraates, son of Orodes, king of the Parthians, sent all his sons and grandsons into Italy to me, even though he had not been conquered in war, but asking for our friendship through pledging his children.

Once again, with the word *obses* missing, the choice of describing the young Parthians as *pignora* – *enechurois* in the Greek version – opened up debate about their actual juridical status.[60] Hence, Dabrowa insisted that they were not hostages *stricto sensu* and that the Romans didn't treat them as such.[61] Following an identical point of view, Lee said that 'the term hostages is hardly appropriate, because the Persian king Phraates certainly did not send his four sons in response to Roman demands, but on his own initiative'.[62]

The main problem arises when comparing this testimony with other written sources. For example, Suetonius states that the Parthians 'offered him hostages' for the first time;[63] and later, when Augustus led the Parthians through the arena, he insists that they were 'the first Parthian hostages that had ever been sent to Rome'.[64] So does Eutropius, highlighting that they were certainly the first Persian hostages to arrive in Rome.[65] Still, neither of these provides further information about who those hostages were. Instead, Strabo's evidence is more relevant:[66]

> καὶ καλέσας εἰς σύλλογον Τίτιον τὸν ἐπιστατοῦντα τότε τῆς Συρίας, τέτταρας παῖδας γνησίους ἐνεχείρισεν ὅμηρα αὐτῷ, Σερασπαδάνην καὶ Ῥωδάσπην καὶ Φραάτην καὶ Βονώνην, καὶ γυναῖκας τούτων δύο καὶ υἱεῖς τέτταρας, δεδιὼς τὰς στάσεις καὶ τοὺς ἐπιτιθεμένους αὐτῷ.
>
> And, having called Titius to a conference, who was at that time praefect of Syria, he put in his hands as hostages four of his legitimate sons, Seraspadanes and Rhodaspes and Phraates and Bonones, and two wives and four sons of these, for fear of seditions and attempts upon his life.

Strabo's text is interesting. On the one hand, he does not hesitate to define Phraates' children as *homera*. Unlike the *Res Gestae*, it does not use an equivalent term, but identifies them directly as what they were. In addition, the stay of Phraates' children in Rome is attested by an inscription that includes the names of two of the children mentioned by Strabo.[67]

The contrast between the classic authors and the testimony of the *Res Gestae* can be read in a diplomatic context. Augustus' intended propaganda would be the main reason behind the use of both the recovery of the standards lost by Crassus in Carrhae in 53 BCE and the arrival of Phraates' family members. This could motivate the choice of *pignora* instead of another term such as *obsides* or *homera*. Not in vain, by receiving what Sheldon has defined as 'political hostages', Augustus was putting under his direct control the succession of the Parthian realm.[68] Similarly, according to Nabel, 'the Arsacids of Rome were showpieces, a way for the emperors to proclaim Rome's supremacy over the Parthian empire in absence of the military success that had fueled the imperialism of the late Republic'.[69] This situation gave the impression of some control over the feared enemies of the East, although the arrival of the royal hostages was motivated more by a personal interest of Phraates than by a real need of submission to Rome.[70] In addition, Strabo adds that together with his sons the Parthian ruler sent two of his daughters-in-law (*gynaikas duo*), thus preceding the arrival of the Germanic hostages.

The reception of female hostages, if not often, is documented in the Imperial period. For example, Tacitus records that in 63 CE Tiridates of Armenia went on a trip to Rome to visit his mother and his brothers. Before departing, Tiridates gave up his daughter as a hostage to Domitius Corbulo.[71] We also know from the *Historia Augusta*, that King Osroes of Parthia sent his daughter as a hostage to Emperor Hadrian.[72]

Obviously, modern scholars have debated this issue. For Phillipson, it was possible that during the Archaic Republic this might have been a common practice within Rome itself,[73] although the truth is that there is no surviving record of any similar episodes. Meanwhile, for Elbern, the exceptions were due to relations with the eastern monarchies and in cases where there were no male descendants. Thus, the search for a guarantee would be more important than the application of custom, in a situation similar to that detailed by Suetonius in relation to Augustus' policy with the Germanic tribes.[74]

When comparing the Carthaginian policy in Spain with that of Scipio, who after the conquest of Carthago Nova decided to return all prisoners and hostages and, in addition, refused to take more hostages for his own security, Alvar highlights two main ideas. The first, 'la idea de la *humanitas*' (the *humanitas* concept), that is, not to ask for women or children as hostages while his enemies actually had done; the second, 'más práctica, estaría relacionada con la percepción de la inutilidad de la mujer a propósito de los restantes postulados' (more practical, would be linked to the idea of the uselessness of women).[75] According to these suggestions, the value of women and children as hostages was less than that of men.

Yet, probably the most well-known hostage in the Roman world was a woman, the maiden Cloelia, who was handed over along with other young men and women to the Etruscan king Lars Porsenna at the beginning of the Republic.[76] Many classical sources talk about Cloelia's episode[77] and, although what lies at the core of the story is the surrender of the Romans to a foreign king, tradition changed the event into an *exemplum* (example).[78] As Mustakallio quotes, the 'story achieved lasting fame because it tells about an unmarried girl' that 'acts bravely in a situation of danger'.[79] Although, as Forsythe states, the episode was probably a product of Roman folklore and was possibly generated around 300 BCE.[80]

The debate over the legend of Cloelia is not limited to the possible veracity of the facts. Another element that has caused great controversy is the presence of an equestrian statue of the Roman heroin near the *Via Sacra*.[81] Regardless of whether it was Cloelia or some feminine goddess, the Romans identified her as one of their most relevant myths, as one of the *exempla* to follow, and that despite her being a hostage. The defeat against Porsenna thus becomes a moral victory represented by a young woman embodying the more traditional Roman values.

This depiction is another of the ways by which Rome symbolized its sense of superiority. The manifestation of this supremacy was therefore not limited to the *pompa triumphalis* (triumphal procession). Various commemorative urban elements such as statues, triumphal arches, and bas-reliefs immortalized the greatness of Rome by representing the peoples they had defeated or taken under their rule by other means. One of those examples is the *Ara Pacis* where, according to an excellent analysis by Rose, the representation of Eastern barbarian children would have been included.[82] Similarly, the Parthians were incorporated in the Parthian Arch. Rose notes that 'although the Parthians' lower position and smaller size *vis-à-vis* Augustus would have made their subordinate status clear, there is nothing inherently negative about their imagery'.[83] However, under this semblance of respect, actually there is always 'an exercise in the manipulation of the image of the barbarians as was their appearance in static works of art'.[84] Marcus Aurelius' column, in turn, includes images of some barbarian women taken as prisoners.[85]

As can be seen, the demand for women or girls as hostages is not a strange phenomenon. Although not frequent, we do have significant examples to show that it did occasionally happen. It is true that it did not seem to be a problem for the Greeks or Carthaginians, whilst in Rome it is not witnessed, even though the

Romans themselves made the Cloelia episode one of their most significant *exempla*.

Further, the presence of certain women in the triumphs of the Roman generals did not come as a surprise. From the point of view of the viewer, the Roman or the foreigner who attends one of the greatest displays of Roman power, the feeling of pity, surprise or affinity is not so much because they were women or children, but because it was clear what their fate would be.

In effect, the passage of Suetonius, which states that Augustus had decided to take barbarian women as hostages for the first time and as a result of specific circumstances, should be analysed from another perspective. Unlike the other examples of both prisoners of war and hostages, the verbal construction used by Suetonius is *exigere temptaverit* (he tried to exact) and that of Tacitus *imperantur* (have been exacted). Both *exigere* and *imperantur* implicitly carry a component of violence, a meaning close to an obligation that could well be translated to command, oblige, force or even urge. Close parallels can be traced in other authors, such as Caesar or Livy, always respecting the same idea of command.[86] On the other hand, both Appian, in the triumph of Pompey, and Strabo, when reporting the arrival of Phraates' children, used the verb *didomi* (to give), whereas in Latin, mainly in relation to the capture of prisoners, the forms of *capio* (to take) dominate.[87]

In this sense, it should be noted that there is not a single time in Roman history when women were commanded as hostages. They were made prisoners, they were sent willingly by their relatives as hostages, and quite probably, they were even summoned as such by the Greeks and Carthaginians, but not by Rome. The choice of using *exigere* and *imperare* by Suetonius and Tacitus was not random, but deliberate. Rome's dominion, if not through diplomacy, had to be achieved by force, and in certain circumstances, there was no shame in choosing opportunity over tradition.

Notes

1 This work is part of the project *Amigas y aliadas de Roma II: La intermediación femenina en la práctica política y diplomática romana*, PID2019-108811GB-I00 led by Prof. Elena Torregaray Pagola. It is also part of Research Group GIU19/064 *Sociedad, poder y cultura en la antigua Roma (ss. III a.e – III d.e.) SCPU* led by Prof. Antonio Duplá Ansuategui.

2 Suet., *Aug.* 21.2. Except where indicated, all English translations are taken from Loeb's editions.

3 For example, Aymard 1961: 137–9; Elbern 1990: 108–9; Ricci 1996: 562; Allen 2006: 180–8.

4 Braund 1984: 12–13.

5 *RGDA* 26.2. For the *Res Gestae*, I have used the 2009 edition of A. E. Cooley.

6 Tac., *Ger.* 8.1.

7 Tac., *Ger.* 20.4.

8 Gueye 2013: 39–40.

9 Liv. 26.50.1; Flor. 1.22.40; Val. Max. 4.3.1. For this particular case, see Gueye 2013: 165–6.

10 Scardigli 1994: 122.

11 Alvar 2000: 374.

12 Liv. 36.39.3, 36.40.3.

13 Liv. 36.40.12.

14 Plb. 16.23.6. Rather, Livy pointed out that the king had died before the parade, Liv. 30.45.4.

15 On *pistis*, cf. Álvarez Pérez-Sostoa 2014: 131–2.

16 Moscovich 1979–80: 126.

17 Cf. Álvarez Pérez-Sostoa 2012: 9–12.

18 Examples include Demetrius of Macedonia, the son of Philip V, and Armenas, the son of Nabis of Sparta: Pol. 21.3; Eutr. 4.2.2.

19 Benario 2005: 178.

20 Duris, *Fr.* 18 (36) = Athen. 13.84 605DE. See also D. S. 20.14. Livy, instead, when describing Cleonymus' actions in book 10.2.1–15 does not tell the story.

21 Plb. 1.65.7.

22 Plb. 1.68.3.

23 Plb. 3.98–99; Liv. 22.22; Zonar. 9.1.

24 Walbank 1967: 68. In addition, Gabba 1975; Torregaray Pagola 1998: 56–66.

25 Plb. 10.17.6.

26 Plb. 9.11.3, 10.35.6.

27 Plb. 10.18.3–14; Liv. 26.49.11–13. Also, Val. Max. 4.3.1.

28 Plb. 10.38.1–2.

29 Plb. 10.18.3–6. Also, Flor. 1.22.40: *Quippe qui captivos pueros puellasque praecipuae pulchritudinis barbaris restituit.*

30 Plb. 10.34.2; Liv. 27.17.1–2.

31 Plb. 10.34.10.

32 Eutr. 3.15.3.

33 D.C. 36.2.4.

34 Plut., *Pomp.* 36.3.

35 D.C. 51.16.1.

36 Liv., *Per.* 133.2; Suet., *Aug.* 17.4; Flor. 2.21.10–11; D.C. 51.11.3, 13.1–2; Oros. 6.19.18.

37 Flor. 2.13.88–89; D.C. 43.19.3.
38 D.C. 51.21.7–8. See Östenberg 2009: 142–44.
39 Liv., *Per.* 45.6; Plut., *Aem.* 33.6–34.4; Flor. 1.28.13.
40 Ferris 2000: 149.
41 Östenberg 2009: 263.
42 Nabel 2017: 30. See also, Pittia 2009: 117.
43 Plut., *Pomp.* 45.4.
44 App., *Mith.* 103.
45 App., *Mith.* 117.
46 Caes., *BG* 1.53.4; Oros. 6.7.7.
47 Caes., *BG* 4.16.5.
48 Among others, Benario 2005: 176–7; Östenberg 2009: 138–9.
49 Str. 7.1.4.
50 Tac., *Ann.* 1.57.4.
51 The destiny of the hostages and prisoners is analysed by Scardigli 1994: 135–7.
52 Tac., *Ann.* 2.10.1.
53 Tac., *Ann.* 2.46.1.
54 Tac., *Ann.* 2.7.2.
55 Tac., *Ann.* 12.35.3.
56 Tac., *Ann.* 12.36. See Östenberg 2009: 135.
57 Plb. 8.36.2.
58 In general, for the diplomacy with the Parthians, cf. Campbell 1993: 220–8.
59 *RGDA* 32.2.
60 For the use of *enechuron* (pledge) as a possible substitute for *homeros*, see Álvarez Pérez-Sostoa 2014: 132–3.
61 Dabrowa 1987: 63.
62 Lee 1991.
63 Suet., *Aug.* 21.3.
64 Suet., *Aug.* 43.4.
65 Eutr. 7.9.
66 Str. 16.1.28.
67 *CIL* 6.1799 = *ILS* 842. The sons of Phraates mentioned in the inscription are Seraspadanes and Rhodaspes. On this matter, see Ricci 1996: 568; Álvarez Pérez-Sostoa 2010: 176–8.
68 Sheldon 2010: 85. See also Gowing 1990: 329–30.
69 Nabel 2017: 30. Likewise Rich 2009: 144–7 and 164.
70 Cf., for example, Rich 2009: 146.
71 Tac., *Ann.* 15.30.2; D.C. 62.23.2.
72 SHA, *Hadr.* 13.8.
73 Phillipson 1911: 402.

74 Elbern 1990: 109.
75 Alvar 2000: 375.
76 Among many others, Gagé 1988.
77 The most important being Livy 2.13.10; D.H. 5.31.4, 32.3; Plin., *HN* 34.13.28; Plut., *Publ.* 18.2, 19.4; *De mul. vir.* 250.
78 An excellent analysis in Roller 2018: 66–94.
79 Mustakallio 1999: 59.
80 Forsythe 1994: 253.
81 Cf. Flory 1993.
82 Rose 1990: 455–7.
83 Rose 2005: 33.
84 Ferris 2000: 19.
85 Cf. Pirson 1996.
86 *Obsides exigere*: Caes., *BG* 3.12.1; *obsides imperare*: Caes., *BG* 4.27.5–6, 5.1.8, 6.4.4–5; Liv. 9.16.1. In general, see Álvarez Pérez-Sostoa 2010: 180–2.
87 App., *Mith.* 117; Str. 16.1.28.

Bibliography

Allen, J. (2006), *Hostages and Hostage-Taking in the Roman Empire*. Cambridge: Cambridge University Press.

Alvar, J. (2000), 'El sexo y la edad en la derrota: los romanos en Hispania', in M. M. Myro, J. M. Casillas, J. Alvar, and D. Plácido (eds), *Las edades de la dependencia*, 363–84. Madrid: Ediciones Clásicas.

Álvarez Pérez-Sostoa, D. (2010), '*Opsides abdoucit*: la toma de rehenes en la epigrafía latina', *Epigraphica*, 72: 169–89.

Álvarez Pérez-Sostoa, D. (2012), 'Traduttore traditore: a propósito de Polibio 21.42.22', *REA*, 114 (1): 3–15.

Álvarez Pérez-Sostoa, D. (2014), '*Homeroi* y *obsides* en los autores clásicos', *Athenaeum*, 102 (1): 120–49.

Aymard, A. (1961), 'Les otages barbares au début de l'empire', *JRS*, 51: 129–47.

Benario, H. W. (2005), 'Females in Germanicus' Triumph', *AHB*, 19 (3–4): 176–80.

Braund, D. C. (1984), *Rome and the Friendly King*, London: Croom Helm.

Campbell, B. (1993), 'War and Diplomacy: Rome and Parthia, 31 BC–AD 235', in J. Rich and G. Shipley (eds), *War and Society in the Roman World*, 214–40, London: Routledge.

Cooley, A. E. (2009), *Res Gestae Divi Augusti: Text, Translation and Commentary*, Cambridge: Cambridge University Press.

Dabrowa, E. (1987), 'Les premiers "otages" parthes à Rome', *Folia Orientalia*, 24: 65–71.

Elbern, S. (1990), 'Geiseln in Rom', *Athenaeum*, 78: 97–140.

Ferris, I. M. (2000), *Enemies of Rome: Barbarians through Roman Eyes*, Stroud: Sutton Publishing.

Flory, M. B. (1993), 'Livia and the History of Public Honorific Statues for Women in Rome', *TAPhA*, 123: 287–308.

Flory, M. B. (1998), 'The Integration of Women into the Roman Triumph', *Historia*, 47: 489–94.

Forsythe, G. (1994), *The Historian L. Calpurnius Piso Frugi and the Roman Annalistic Tradition*, New York: University Press of America.

Gabba, E. (1975), 'P. Cornelio Scipione Africano e la leggenda', *Athenaeum*, 53: 3–17.

Gagé, J. (1988), 'Les otages de Porsenna', in D. Porte and J. Néraudau (eds), *Hommages à Henri Le Bonniec. Res Sacrae*, 236–45, Brussels: Latomus.

Gowing, A. M. (1990), 'Tacitus and the Client Kings', *TAPhA*, 120: 315–31.

Gueye, M. (2013), *Captifs et captivité dans le monde romain. Discours litteraire et iconographique (IIIe siècle av. J.-C. – IIe siècle ap. J.-C.)*, Paris: L'Harmattan.

Isayev, E. (2017), *Migration, Mobility and Place in Ancient Italy*, Cambridge: Cambridge University Press.

Lee, A. D. (1991), 'The Role of Hostages in Roman Diplomacy with Sasanian Persia', *Historia*, 40: 366–74.

Moscovich, M. J. (1979–80), '*Obsidibus traditis*: Hostages in Caesar's *De Bello Gallico*', *CJ*, 75: 122–8.

Mustakallio, K. (1999), 'Legendary Women and Female Groups in Livy', in P. Setälä and L. Savunen (eds), *Female Networks and the Public Sphere in Roman Society*, 53–64, Rome: Acta Instituti Romani Finlandiae.

Nabel, J. (2017), 'The Seleucids Imprisoned: Arsacid-Roman Hostage Submission and Its Hellenistic Precedents', in J. M. Schlude and B. B. Rubin (eds), *Arsacid, Romans and Local Elites*, 25–50, Oxford: Oxbow.

Nedergaard, E. (1988), 'The Four Sons of Phraates IV in Rome', in T. Fischer-Hansen and T. Mette Moltesen (eds), *East and West: Cultural Relations in the Ancient World*, 102–15, Copenhagen: Museum Tusculanum Press.

Östenberg, I. (2009), *Staging the World: Spoils, Captives, and Representations in the Roman Triumphal Procession*, Oxford: Oxford University Press.

Phillipson, C. (1911), *The International Law and Custom of Ancient Greece and Rome*, 2 vols, London: Macmillan.

Pirson, F. (1996), 'Style and Message on the Column of Marcus Aurelius', *PBSR*, 64: 139–79.

Pittia, S. (2009), 'L'arrivée de Persée au camp de Paul-Emile: mise en scène d'une capitulation', *Veleia*, 26: 103–25.

Ricci, C. (1996), 'Principes et reges externi (e loro schiavi e liberti) a Roma e in Italia. Testimonianze epigrafiche di età imperiale', *RAL*, 9 (7): 561–92.

Rich, J. W. (2009), 'Augustus, War and Peace', in J. Edmondson (ed.), *Augustus*, 137–64, Edinburgh: Edinburgh University Press.

Roller, M. B. (2018), *Models from the Past in Roman Culture: A World of Exempla*, Cambridge: Cambridge University Press.

Rose, C. B. (1990), '"Princes" and Barbarians on the *Ara Pacis*', *AJA*, 94: 453–67.

Rose, C. B. (2005), 'The Parthians in Augustan Rome', *AJA*, 109: 21–75.

Scardigli, B. (1994), 'Germanische Gefangene und Geiseln in Italien (von Marius bis Konstantin)', in B. Scardigli and P. Scardigli (eds), *Germania in Italia*, 117–50, Rome: Consiglio Nazionale delle ricerche.

Sheldon, R. M. (2010), *Rome's Wars in Parthia: Blood in the Sand*, London: Valentin Mitchell.

Torregaray Pagola, E. (1998), *La elaboración de la tradición sobre los 'Cornelii Scipiones': pasado histórico y conformación simbólica*, Zaragoza: Institución Fernando el Católico.

Walbank, F. W. (1967), 'The Scipionic Legend', *PCPhS*, 13: 54–69.

8

The Use of Wet-Nurses in Ancient Rome as a Way of Rupturing the *mores maiorum*[1]

Pedro David Conesa Navarro and Sara Casamayor Mancisidor

Introduction

Infant breastfeeding in the ancient world is a subject that has only been studied in detail in recent years. The lack of previous work is partly due to the fact that it is a silent, domestic activity, which supposedly has no significant social repercussions. In iconography in particular, it was treated in a superficial or allegorical way, linked to certain divinities such as *deae nutrices* (goddesses of the wet-nurses). The images were concentrated in the tombs of wet-nurses, where the latter appear breastfeeding, in a smaller proportion than those of the mothers themselves and with a more complex elaboration in the sarcophagi.[2] Other issues such as the relationship between milk and maternal blood, especially menstrual blood, whose imbalance could cause diseases, were widely discussed by ancient authors, creating a whole series of theories and medical precepts that permeated Graeco-Roman society. The quality of milk or the selection of a good wet-nurse, as we shall see, appear in medical texts because, despite being feminine in nature, they were considered of great importance since the survival of society itself largely depended on this care. A whole series of stereotypes of folk medicine were established, most of which were limited to observation, where magical practices, superstitions, and speculations played a major role.[3] The same could be said of childcare, reduced to several precepts related to specific pathologies or the treatment and care of children after birth.[4]

It was believed that mother's milk was derived from blood and that the foetus was nourished by it from the moment of conception. It was thought that the 'boiling process' and the volatility of the womb could affect the configuration of individuals.[5] Males, for example, had the particularity of being fully formed, a partial justification for them being superior to females. The latter, viscous, cold, wet, and soft, were the direct consequence of not having acquired enough vital warmth during gestation. However, the formation and viability of the foetus was an issue that transcended the medical to affect the social and legislative spheres. It was important to know the moment of conception to determine if a posthumous heir was legitimate, or the fruit of an extramarital relationship the mother entered into. It was agreed that the time from conception to birth was between nine and ten months, although there was no strict time limit.[6] For example, Oribasius fixed on a period of approximately six months, except for those born in Egypt, since the influence of the Nile – together with other reasons that he did not specify – allowed for it to be extended to eight months.[7]

Ancient physicians claimed that breastmilk was the best food a newborn could have.[8] However, Soranus advised waiting two days before breastfeeding. In addition to the trauma of birth, the baby's body was satiated, and it was considered necessary to first digest the nourishment passed on by its mother during pregnancy and then to gradually incorporate mother's milk. During these days, to check appetite, the lips were to be rubbed with warm water and honey. On the third day, it was considered that the mother's milk was of sufficient quality for breastfeeding to commence. Still, it was advised a wet-nurse be employed for twenty days, owing in part to what the mother had gone through during childbirth, where fever, pallor, and the expulsion of a large amount of blood made the milk thick.[9] Most of these recommendations could only be adhered to by wealthy women. Hiring a *nutrix* or having domestic slaves was not within the reach of all Romans. However, sources seem to confirm that a few poor families were also able to use wet-nurses, if not to the same extent.[10] Many questions arise in relation to breastfeeding in the classical world. Here, we will focus our analysis on how its use was perceived by much of society, which considered it an external practice that disturbed the *mores maiorum* that marked Roman tradition and identity.

Constraints to the use of *nutrices*: beyond the family

As noted earlier, there were cases in which the assistance of these women was necessary. Soranus indicated that, although it was advisable for newborns to be fed by the mother herself from the beginning, breastfeeding could accelerate the mother's ageing in the process of nourishing her child.[11] It was during the period of the mother's physical recovery, then, that feeding of newborns was entrusted to a *nutrix*. There were other circumstances in which a *nutrix* was employed, the most common being the death of the mother in childbirth,[12] as well as the inability to breastfeed as a result of illness or lack of milk; regarding the latter, Soranus himself recommended a wet-nurse so that the newborn could receive breastmilk the biological mother could not produce, especially during the first few days.[13] It is also known that, due to the high prevalence of premature deaths, some mothers refrained from breastfeeding their own offspring to avoid establishing bonds of affection until they were older and out of danger. There were also moral issues, such as the refusal of some *matronae* (married women) to bare certain parts of their bodies, which women of more humble status were unable to contemplate for economic reasons. Some women considered it a painful or boring activity, something that was censured by the classical authors; others felt that were social and economic connotations of having wet-nurses among the enslaved staff.[14] Finally, it was believed that while a woman was breastfeeding, she could not become pregnant again. This led to *nutrices* being used by wealthy families with the purpose of enabling the *matronae* to produce new offspring, a practice also applied to the slave population.[15] Forced by their *dominus* (slave master), a *nutrix* was used so that slaves could have more children and thus increase the servile population of the household, or directly, so that they could continue to carry out their work. The desire to increase the number of servants born in the family (*uernae*) was particularly evident from the end of the Republic onwards, as epigraphy and papyri show. By this time, the battles fought by Rome in the Mediterranean, which had become the main source of slaves, had come to an end. This meant that new strategies had to be devised to avoid a shortage of domestic staff. Also, like the free women who refrained from bonding with their offspring until they were old enough to survive, the cohabitation of female slaves with their offspring was avoided – not only because it could disrupt the order and work of the house, but also because these newborns were often separated from their mothers and sold.[16]

In Rome, as in other pre-industrial societies, the abandonment of newborns was a common practice, and became more prevalent in imperial times. Legislation did not consider penalties for such practices until the fourth century CE.[17] The *expositio* (infant exposure) was an effective method of birth control, especially if the economic conditions of the family did not extend to a new member. It was also justified by the rich, to allow a single heir to inherit an estate, or even to conceal an extramarital affair. More traumatic were the separations of slaves and their children, as mentioned above. Keeping them was a financial burden for the *dominus*, which he was often unwilling to bear. All of this shows that the reasons for infant exposure were very varied.[18]

There were also other social, personal, and religious motivations. The malformation of a child was considered a divine punishment and a rupture of the *pax deorum* (peace of the gods); thus individuals born with disabilities or deformities were more likely to be abandoned.[19] However, in the hope that they might recover, or simply because the mothers were interested in their fate, some of these infants survived. In Rome there was the *columna lactaria* in the Forum Holitorium, located near the Temple of Pietas, where *nutrices* were to be found. This became a regular place where children were fed for the various reasons described above, as can be seen from Festus' expression: 'lactaria columna in foro oliotiro dicta, quod ibi infantes lacte alendos deferebant' (the *columna lactaria* in the Forum Holitorum, so-called because they would bring babies there to be fed with milk).[20]

Unwanted infants were often left outside cities and towns (the *Urbs*), in places such as the *spurci lacus* (dirty cisterns). In Egypt, they were commonly found abandoned on rubbish dumps, the *kopriai*, as specified in sections 41 and 105 of the *Gnomon* of the *Idios Logos*. However, as in Rome, some parents took care to leave them in busy places so that they could be taken in by someone.[21] This was because if it could be proved that they were free-born, even if after their abandonment they had been raised as slaves, they could immediately regain their original status and revert to their biological family. Therefore, as Grubbs pointed out, the concepts of *expositio* and infanticide cannot be linked.[22] An example of the restoration of rights to an individual can be seen in Plautus' *Rudens*. Palaestra is recognized by her biological father, Démones, when carrying a golden *bulla* the girl had been given at birth. Palaestra was kidnapped in Athens and thanks to an argument over a suitcase, her identity was established.[23] Although this is fiction, it helps to understand what some infants experienced and how, thanks to the *nutrices* who breastfed them, they were able to survive. It is true that the happy ending of the comedy rarely matched the reality; nevertheless, it is interesting to know the many scenarios in which *nutrices* carried out their activities, a direct consequence of the different realities in the Roman world, some of which were very cruel.

Characteristics of wet-nurses: social status, physical and moral qualities

Economic and social circumstances were a determining factor in whether individuals had to leave their homes and enter the labour force, regardless of their sex or age. Activities linked to motherhood, such as *obstetrics* (midwifes) or *nutrices*, were mostly carried out by humble women, whether enslaved, freed or *ingenuae* (free-born). Sometimes social prestige was demanded of them, especially if they offered their services in the homes of respectable families.[24] These practices were permitted if they did not intrude on male domains, in accordance with the public-male/private-female division that remained unchanged until the nineteenth century. Since these women carried out a task linked to motherhood, some of them enjoyed a certain recognition and respect.[25] At times, they took on responsibilities that went beyond breastfeeding, taking charge of education, as well as looking after those entrusted to their care.[26] Most women who had a protracted relationship of this sort were slaves, as free women left the *domus* when their contract ended. The presence of *nutrices assae*, elderly women who did not breastfeed, is a sign of this tendency to remain in the household, creating bonds of affection and very strong feelings between them and the children; bonds, in some cases, stronger than those established with their relatives.[27] From this we can understand the praise for these women frequently mentioned in epitaphs or in literature, including some epigrams of Callimachus.[28] Furthermore, it is known from the *Digest*[29] that they sometimes received inheritances; they were therefore considered to be members of the family, as was the case with the milk siblings, the *conlactei*.[30]

Permanence in the household and the presence of a large servile population are issues that have allowed historiography to avoid considering this work as a job under the classical conception of labour.[31] However, although it is true that if a *nutrix* was a slave she did not receive economic remuneration if she performed her services in her owner's house, sometimes the *dominus* would offer his servants up to breastfeed the children of other families. In these cases, economic exchange did take place, and it was possible to speak of labour as there was remuneration involved, regardless of who received it. Moreover, it should be noted that this activity involved a specialization, which would allow us to classify it as a profession.[32] Epigraphic testimonies are fundamental for this last assessment, where the fact that several women appear with the word *nutrix* indicates that this activity became part of their identity and that their heirs took care to leave a record of it for posterity.[33]

Apart from inscriptions, there is also clear evidence of contracts from Roman Egypt. Around forty of them have been preserved; they are written on papyrus and come mostly from heavily hellenized territories such as Alexandria or Oxyrhynchus.[34] Most of these *nutrices* were obliged to breastfeed children who were born in their master's family home or directly abandoned and who were taken in as slaves, since from the age of twelve they began to become profitable for their owner and, therefore, the collecting of individuals from the dunghills was frequent, as can be seen in different lawsuits. However, there are also examples of free individuals as nurses. As far as the social status of these women is concerned, in addition to slaves who worked in the service of their *dominus*, there are also documents of free women of humble status, although a very small number. Therefore, broadly speaking, the pattern in this area was similar to other places in the empire. As for the length of these contracts, the vast majority were for two years, the minimum being six months, although in some cases they were extended to three years.[35] Finally, it is important to note that recent research in 113 non-industrial populations has confirmed that the weaning process began at around five or six months; however, it was not an abrupt process, with other foods being gradually introduced in the form of porridge that could be combined with breast milk until the age of three, which is supported by Egyptian documentation.[36] According to Laes, we cannot know how widespread a practice the use of wet-nurses was in Egypt. To this end, the author gives as an example a text from the third century BCE written by a concerned father who urged his son-in-law not to force his daughter to breastfeed her newborn, recommending the use of a *nutrix* instead, which, apart from the problem of generalization, could indicate that these women also breastfed a free population and that this was not an unusual practice.[37]

The selection of wet-nurses was an important issue, as it was thought that certain values or vices were transmitted through milk. Therefore, we find in the medical treatises a series of recommendations, as well as different tests that were to be carried out on the candidate. Although there was no single standard, medical treatises established a series of physical and moral qualities that *nutrices* had to meet, including being of good health and sound mind.[38] Soranus indicated that the milk should be of a certain temperature and for this purpose, in addition to undertaking a series of physical exercises, it was recommended to avoid a sedentary lifestyle. This would prevent the milk from becoming thick and indigestible.[39] The diet to be followed by the *nutrix* was very strict, with the consumption of certain foods, such as garlic and leeks, being prohibited.[40] These women had to be well cared for, as their good health was essential for the child, as well as for producing the right quality and quantity of milk. Their routine was regulated from the moment they woke up, and Soranus established a daily schedule according to which the *nutrix* had to lie down for a while before getting up in the morning, walk and exercise so that all of her limbs would receive the necessary nutrients.[41] This is why we think that slaves or freed women related to the main families were used, as this would significantly reduce costs. For a *serua* (slave) to be able to breastfeed the children of the family on which she depended, her biological child would often be taken away from her. Upon separation she was given a child that she was obliged to care for.[42] We also must take into account the high infant mortality rate, as the *ingenuae* were often able to obtain an income from an activity only they, because of their sex, could perform.

If there were no slaves available, it was recommended that the *nutrix* should be similar in physical appearance to the mother, as genetic features could be transmitted through milk. She had to be between twenty and forty years old, and it was recommended that she should not be a first-time mother, as this not only ensured the care of the children, but also that she was experienced. In addition, she should not have breastfed in the previous three months. As for physical characteristics, the breasts had to be of medium size and the nipples had to be thin, with no stretch marks or wrinkles, to ensure an abundance of milk. Keeping in mind that these women would spend long periods with the child, sometimes even beyond their infancy, and that they were also in charge of teaching a series of precepts, they should have a good character, as well as manners, and a soft language.[43]

The survival of the children depended in part on the *nutrix*'s knowledge. She had to know, for example, the best positions for breastfeeding and cradling and had to have basic medicinal knowledge.[44] She was to be temperate and self-controlled and to avoid inappropriate impulses such as sex and the drinking of wine.[45] Such faultless behaviour was important both because the *nutrices* were expected to be an example for the children and because it was believed that their corrupt morals could be transmitted through milk. Similarly, if they were distracted by drinking or spending time with men, their attention to the baby would be diminished, with possible fatal consequences.

As part of their tasks as educators, *nutrices* were part of the first stages of socialization of the children through the songs, stories, and games they shared with them.[46] Ausonius believed that children should grow up accompanied by stories and lullabies from their wet-nurses, because they would be entertained and learn at the same time.[47] Although *nutrices* had to show affection for the children they cared for, they also had to be strict so that the children would grow up properly, although affection often made them indulgent.[48] In fact, the children spent so much time with their *nutrix* that there was a danger they would prefer them to their mothers.[49] In this regard, it has been suggested that elite families may have sent their newborns with their *nutrices* to their estates in the countryside, where the environment was healthier than in urban centres, and if the mother did not accompany them, the influence of the wet-nurse would likely increase.[50] For this reason, Soranus recommended that a child should have not one but several *nutrices*, because if the infant became accustomed to one woman, who died and was replaced by a new one, the baby could reject the new *nutrix* and starve to death.[51]

Finally, another important consideration when choosing a good *nutrix* was her origin. Egyptians and Thracians were valued for their natural affection for children, Gauls for being vigorous, faithful, and fertile.[52] In contrast, Syrians were to be avoided, as they behaved rudely towards babies, even causing them sores.[53] Finally, Greek *nutrices* were preferred, especially because speaking in their mother tongue would make the child bilingual.[54] In fact, promoting correct speech was an important concern when choosing a *nutrix* because of the importance of orality in Roman public life.[55] This preference for Greek *nutrices* may be responsible for the fact that most names that have come down to us through epigraphy are Greek.[56] However, we should bear in mind here the Roman practice of giving Greek names to slaves regardless of their origin; a practice which is ideal in this regard, since if the *nutrix* was not Greek, by choosing a Greek name it could be pretended she was. The use of the name Sophona for theatrical *nutrices* should be interpreted in the same way, as it meant 'she of good judgement', thus indicating the character's suitability for the job.

The use of wet-nurses among Rome's elite: a danger to social stability

As Cid López has stated, the insistence on the importance of breastfeeding in medical treatises, as well as Graeco-Latin literature praising women who decided to breastfeed their children, would confirm that the female population, especially the upper class, used the services of these wet-nurses.[57] Mentioned in the works of Plautus and Terence,[58] *nutrices* were already present in the early Republic. In the second half of the first century BCE, Publilius Syrus writes: 'secundus est a matre nutricis dolor' (the pain of a *nutrix* is close to the pain of a mother),[59] which indicates the importance of these women in the Roman Republican family.[60] However, it is generally interpreted that their use became widespread in the Imperial period. It is then that the use of *nutrices* appears in literature as a symptom of the decline of Roman culture due to foreign values.

In Roman literature, allusion to the decadence of the times became a way of indicating dissatisfaction with the political and social situation, with the Republic being depicted as the ideal to be recovered. In order to explain this social decadence, which may seem abstract, its advocates drew attention to various stereotypical characters, both foreigners who imported evil behaviours and Romans who had been influenced by orientalism. The Thessalian witch, the treacherous political ally, the chatty and unmanly Greek, and the nouveau riche obsessed with ostentation are just a few examples.[61] The danger of Greek slaves is also noteworthy, a fact that Tacitus highlighted precisely through a *nutrix*.[62]

An effective way of creating anxiety about the dangers of abandoning traditional Roman life was to allude to the disintegration of the family, the fundamental foundation of society and the main socializing axis. Thus, external influences caused loss of respect for the elderly, women to adopt male behaviour, men to disengage from public affairs, and houses to be filled with unnecessary luxuries. In addition, the use of *nutrices* meant, in cases where the mother was alive, that she was neglecting her duties as a woman, another sign of moral decadence. Therefore, it was recommended to use the services of a *nutrix* only when the biological mother was unable to breastfeed.[63] To follow Soranus' instructions and have not one but several *nutrices* would not be in the reach of the majority families, and is therefore another indication of luxury and ostentation. According to Aulus Gellius, the philosopher Favorinus was of the opinion that mothers of the senatorial elite should not use *nutrices*, as it was an unnatural practice, hindering the formation of an affective bond between mother and child, calling these women half-mothers, accusing them of being too concerned with frivolities, such as the fact that breastfeeding could change the shape of their breasts, and saying that a child entrusted to a *nutrix* was the same as a dead child.[64] Furthermore, he considered that foreign *nutrices* passed on their degenerated and lustful manners to children. It is remarkable to note that in this episode Favorinus was talking with the husband and mother of a woman who had just given birth, and that when the grandmother asked for calm for the new mother and that her daughter ought to proceed as she thinks best, the philosopher accused her of being ignorant, although unlike him this woman had given birth and raised children. For Plutarch, mothers who left their children in the hands of *nutrices* and spent little time with them took them not as their offspring, but as mere pets to be frivolously put on display.[65] In his sixth satire, Juvenal presents Ogulnia, a paradigm of female decadence, who uses the services of a wet-nurse, among other luxuries, to be able to attend the circus.[66] In the same way, Tacitus praised Germanic women, who breastfed their children, in contrast to the wealthy Romans of his time, who delegated this task to *nutrices*.[67] This comparison served the author to highlight the moral decadence of Roman women and how they had abandoned one of their main civic tasks, breastfeeding, pointing out that their behaviour was worse than that of 'primitive' people. At the opposite extreme, and alluding to a supposedly idyllic Republic, would be Cato's family, whose wife Licinia not only took care of their child, but even breastfed the children of her slaves.[68]

Considering the role *nutrices* played in the early years of infancy, the concern about the training of these women is understandable. For the critics of this practice, the danger of *nutrices* was not only that they gave children bad milk or were negligent in their care, but also the moral implications of their relationship. We have already shown that these women were an important part of early socialization and education through songs and stories, even being the main adult reference when baby and *nutrix* were sent to the countryside and parents remained in the city. These methods of entertainment and education, generically called 'old wives' tales' (*aniles fabulae*), could be used to transmit knowledge contrary to the *mores maiorum* if their content was not properly supervised by the *paterfamilias*, since they were considered to be typical of illiterate people and close to superstition as they lacked an instructive objective and only aimed to entertain; entertainment based on lies, as they narrated fictional stories.[69] A description that matches the characterization of female ways of expression from the patriarchal point of view, and of women as chatty and of unable to partake in substantial conversation.[70] Philostratus, in considering the value of myths and fables and describing the latter as insubstantial stories without credibility, defined them as 'charlatanry fit to be devoured by old women and children'.[71] In this vein, when Philinion's old *nutrix* came to her masters to tell them her deceased daughter appeared in the form of a ghost, they thought she was lying because of the reputation of old women and *nutrices* for inventing stories and believing in supernatural phenomena.[72] The old woman did not regain credibility until Philinion appeared before her parents.

However, and despite the effort of some authors to dismiss the knowledge of the *nutrices* as insubstantial, we know that stories and songs are a means of socialization through the reproduction of stereotyped stories through which the audience acquires basic social values and concepts, while internalizing behavioural patterns and learning how to cope in various circumstances.[73] As such, they can be subversive and transmit knowledge contrary to the cultural norm, with consequent moral corruption and disastrous consequences for the survival of the social order. This is especially dangerous if we consider that *nutrices* could continue to influence nurslings after having reached adulthood. For example, according to Suetonius, Augustus enjoyed *aniles fabulae* so much that he used them as an adult to combat insomnia, and Nero was advised by his *nutrix* as an emperor.[74] In fact, *nutrices* appear in the sources as the only ones who remain faithful to those they raised even if they had committed an execrable act. Thus, Nero's *nutrices* seem to have been the ones who took charge of depositing his mortal remains in the tomb, something that can also be interpreted as an attempt by Suetonius to show how Nero's acts were so execrable that only those who raised him could remain faithful to him until the end.[75] The same scene is repeated in the case of another emperor considered morally corrupt, Domitian, with the *nutrix* Phyllis being responsible for paying him his last respects and secretly taking his remains to the temple of the Flavian family and mixing them with the ashes of Julia, daughter of Titus, whom she had also raised.[76] This perverse influence of *nutrices* was strongest in the case of women. This is both because women were considered morally weaker and therefore more easily corruptible, and also because they probably spent more time at the side of the wet-nurses, especially in the case of unmarried girls, sharing female domestic spaces and times. The slave who accompanies the poetic *puella* everywhere, the one who watches over and advises her and whom the lover must bribe to gain access to his beloved, may well be her former *nutrix*.[77] On the mythical side, an illustrative example in this respect is that of Myrrha's old *nutrix*, who helps her to commit incest.[78]

Thus, the influence of a *nutrix* can drive women to transgress the established order and seek their own benefit over the interests of the *paterfamilias*, which are ultimately the interests of the Roman state. *Nutrices* are not only dangerous because they are part of the process of degradation of Roman culture as the empire expands its borders and imports corrupt customs, but also because they are linked to affection, to primordial socialization, and to an eminently feminine and infantile everyday life that is alien to and to some extent uncontrollable by adult men. Therefore, and as is common in Roman literature, the perverse model has an ideal opposite, which is adapted to the schema of *romanitas* (Romanness). Thus, from being the instigator of transgression, the *nutrix* is re-elaborated as the guarantor of the *mos maiorum* (the unwritten code from which Romans derived social norms), especially in the case of the slave *nutrices*, those who remain for many years in the same family and have therefore been integrated. In theatre, the saviour *nutrix* is used as a form of control of slave women by showing them that if they behave according to social norms – that is, as expected of them by free men – they will be rewarded with the satisfaction of serving the system.[79] In four of Terence's surviving plays, the *nutrices* Sophrona, Sostrata, and Mysis play a major role in reuniting lost daughters with their families.[80] They are the only ones able to recognize certain particulars of the girls or their relatives that allow for their identification; a detail that highlights how little time some Roman fathers spent with their offspring, especially their daughters, if they could not recognize them.

The wet-nurse who favours civic peace does so not only out of a sense of duty, but also a strong affection for the person in her charge. So, there is a real possibility of genuine affection between wet-nurses and the children they breastfed or cared for, arising from their daily contact and the innocence of the babies, who were not yet aware of the slave system or that some women who raised them did so purely for economic gain. However, highlighting this affection between a slave and her *dominus/a* serves the ruling ideology to oppose the resentment, fear, and hatred that enslaved people must have felt towards those who denied them their freedom, and to make invisible the fact that few *nutrices* would exercise their labour freely or willingly. Perhaps in this respect epigraphic sources are more realistic, since in them most of the affectionate adjectives addressed to *nutrices* come from their partners or descendants, while *nutritus/ae* (the person who was cared for by the *nutrix*) or *domini/ae* are more succinct.[81] A class-based pattern also seems to emerge, as the relationship would have been closer in the case of *nutrix* and nursling sharing a servile status.[82]

In short, we see how the *nutrix* is constructed as an ambiguous character, since on the one hand she enjoys a certain power over the children in her care and is supposed to have great influence over them, but on the other hand her body and personality must be totally controlled so that she can perform her work according to her master's wishes.

Conclusions

In this chapter, we have tried to reflect how an issue that was part of everyday life in Roman families, that of owning or hiring women to breastfeed and care for their children, became an object of regulation and debate because of the importance of motherhood for the survival of the Roman state. For centuries, thousands of free and enslaved women nursed other women's children, singing lullabies, telling stories, and performing tasks related to their survival. Some of these children were orphans, others had mothers who could not or would not breastfeed.

While this is a task that may seem trivial or natural in principle, it is of the utmost importance to ensure that as many babies as possible reach adulthood, are able to take up their proper roles and occupations, and in turn have their own children. We could thus say that *nutrices* were responsible for the survival of Rome.

From the point of view of the male Roman slaveholder, the anxiety provoked by the fact that a woman, probably a slave and a foreigner, could exert such influence on his offspring as to lead them to commit acts contrary to the *mores maiorum* in adulthood is evident. A very close bond with the wet-nurse could lead to disaffection towards the parents and put an end to the necessary *pietas*. To reduce possible risks, Roman men tried to control women's bodies and their life choices. This control was exercised both over mothers, who were required by critics of the *nutrices* to devote their bodies to breastfeeding and were considered immoral not to do so, and over wet-nurses, whose physical appearance, education, personality, and behaviour were evaluated down to the smallest detail. In an environment of hypervigilance such as that suggested by the sources, it is hard to imagine that *nutrices* had much freedom to impose an agenda contrary to the *mos maiorum*.

Having to produce healthy milk for the infants and being able to care for them as was needed, *nutrices* were provided with good food and plenty of rest, privileges not common in the enslaved population.[83] In addition, and due to the crucial role they played in the survival of the family, they could be rewarded with manumission or with an economic contribution that guaranteed them a peaceful old age. Thus, for example, Pliny the Younger gave a property as a gift to his former *nutrix* in a reversal of the roles of caregiver and cared-for, and the *Digest* refers to how *nutrices* received inheritances and could enjoy the property of those in their care.[84] That some women or their relatives chose to name themselves as *nutrices* in the inscriptions they commissioned for themselves or for those they cared for may be indicative of the social importance of the work, as well as the pleasure with which they performed it, but we must not forget, especially for slaves, that their employment would have been an important part of their identity and, in the case of free-women, that although it was a job considered honourable,[85] it was done out of economic need.

Finally, we have shown how the figure of the *nutrix* embodies various anxieties about the other – the foreigner, the slave, the woman – and the way in which they could alter the established social order.

Notes

1 This chapter is part of the R+D+I project *Vulnerabilidad intrafamiliar y política en el mundo antiguo* (PID2020-116349GB-100/AEI/10.13039/501100011033), whose principal researchers are Susana Reboreda Morillo (University of Vigo) and Rosa María Cid López (University of Oviedo).

2 Carroll 2014: 164–8, 173–4; Pedrucci 2019: 21.

3 Rawson 1991: 13; López Pérez 2004–5: 227; Dasen 2016: 3.

4 On this issue, with a selection of texts and bibliography, cf. Dasen 2021: 107.

5 Sor. 2.126; Orib., *Col. Med.* 22.3.2, 22.3.8; López Pérez 2006: 901 and 2010: 115–17, 158–9.

6 Macrob., *Sat.* 7.2–7; Conesa Navarro and González Fernández 2015: 103; Pedrucci 2019: 21. Sexual differentiation can also be seen in the position in which they were placed in the mother's womb; cf. Orib., *Col. Med.* 22.3.18. The same could be said about childbirth, with girls' births being slower than boys'. Cf. Orib., *Col. Med.* 22.3.22; López Pérez 2010: 161.

7 Orib., *Col. Med.* 22.3.28, 22.5.1–7; López Pérez 2010: 161–2.

8 Dasen 2010: 704; Cid López 2016: 132.

9 Sor. 2.7.35–69, 76–84. On why on the third day breastmilk was of high quality, cf. Sor. 2.7.60–69.

10 Bradley 1986: 214; Dasen 2012: 42 and 2021: 107.

11 Sor. 2.7.87–110.

12 Dasen 2010: 704.

13 Sor. 2.7.

14 Dasen 2012: 42; Cid López 2016: 133; Laes 2017: 64; Pedrucci 2018: 93; Rubiera Cancelas 2014: 232–3; Carroll 2014: 160.

15 Dasen 2010: 704.

16 *Dig.* 50.16.210; Dasen 2012: 43; Rubiera Cancelas 2014: 232 and 2015: 155; Cid López 2019b: 161.

17 Grubbs 2010: 297. Cf. this page n. 4 with classical references.

18 Harris 1994: 11–15; Corbier 2001: 61; Rubiera Cancelas 2018: 212.

19 Allély 2018: 198.

20 Festo 105. See also Corbier 2001: 62–3; Rubiera Cancelas 2014: 150; Cid López 2019b: 149–50, 152–4, 156–7, 160–1.

21 Juv. VI.602–603; Biezunska-Malowist 1973: 84; Harris 1994: 9; Corbier 2001: 62–3; Rubiera Cancelas 2014: 150–1. On the *Gonomon of the Idios Logos*, cf. Speidel 2013: 3390–1.

22 Grubbs 2010: 297, 305.

23 Plaut., *Rud.* 1080–1180.

24 Dasen 2012: 41 and 2021: 107; Cid López 2016: 161; Casamayor Mancisidor 2019: 186.

25 Medina Quintana 2010: 147, 203 and 2019: 199; Cid López 2019a: 173–4.

26 Cid López 2016: 130.

27 Dasen 2012: 44.

28 Callim., *Anth. Pal.* 7.458.

29 *Dig.* 33.2.34.1. Thanks to Ulpian we know that there were certain requirements, such as age, to be able to be manumitted, being *nutrices* and pedagogues or *conlactei* who were often granted freedom: *Dig.* 49.2.18.

30 Conesa Navarro 2019: 171–92.
31 For example, Crespo Ortiz de Zárate 2006: 19 defines it as a personal service. This issue is dealt with in Conesa Navarro 2018: 150.
32 Harders 2012: 14; Medina Quintana 2017: 163–4.
33 Dasen 2010: 703 and n. 20.
34 Rowlandson 1998: 245, 275–6.
35 Biezunska-Malowist 1973: 84; Bradley 1980: 321–2; Rowlandson 1998: 245, 275–6; Dasen 2010: 705 and 2012: 42; Rubiera Cancelas 2014: 150–1; Goñi Zabalegui 2018: 216; Cid López 2019b: 161–2; Nifosi 2019: 27.
36 Laes 2018: 183.
37 Laes 2011: 69–70; Rubiera Cancelas 2014: 147.
38 Rubiera Cancelas 2014: 147–8; Pedrucci 2018: 92.
39 Sor. 2.6–13.
40 López Pérez 2004–5: 230–1; Conesa Navarro 2018: 151.
41 Sor. 2.13–20.
42 Rubiera Cancelas 2015: 164.
43 Cid López 2001: 27–8.
44 Gal., *De san. tuenda* 1.8; Ov., *Fast.* 6.130–168; Sor. 2.37.
45 Gell. 12.1.17; Sor. 2.19.
46 Lucil., *Fr.* 955; Philostr., *Imag.* 1.15; Tib. 1.3.85–90.
47 Auson., *Ep.* 10.2.90.
48 Auson., *Protrept. ad nep.* 2.69; Cic., *Am.* 74; Tac., *Dial.* 28.5–6.
49 Auson., *Protrept. ad nep.* 2.18–20.
50 Gell. 12.1; Sen., *Contr.* 4.6; Sparreboom 2009: 26.
51 Sor. 2.20.
52 Strab. 4.1.2, 4.4.3, 17.2.53; Orib., *Lib. Incert.* 15; Sor. 2.21.
53 Sor. 2.51.
54 Sor. 2.12; Tac., *Dial.* 28.
55 Quint., *Inst.* 1.1.3–4, 1.12.12.
56 On the names of *nutrices*, see Crespo Ortiz de Zárate 2006.
57 Cid López 2016: 132.
58 On *nutrices* and theatre, see Feltovich 2021.
59 Pub. Syr., *Sent.* 600.
60 Pedrucci 2020: 130.
61 Cic., *Att.* 6.1.15; Hor., *Epod.* 5; Juv. 3.58–113, 6.295–300; Liv. 12.22; Luc., *Dial. Meret.* 4; Mart. 10.65–76.
62 Tac., *Dial.* 29.
63 Sor. 2.18.
64 Gell. 12.1.
65 Plut., *Cons.* 5.6.1.

66 Juv. 6.352–354, 6.592–593.

67 Tac., *Germ.* 20.1.

68 Plut., *Cat. Maior* 20.2–3.

69 Apul., *Met.* 4.27.8; Arn., *Adv. Nat.* 5.14; Auson., *Protrept. ad nep.* 2.69; Hor., *Sat.* 2.6.76–77; Pers. 2.30–34; Philostr., *Her.* 7; Quint., *Inst.* 1.8.19; Sen., *Ben.* 1.4.5–6; SHA, *Clod.* 12.12.

70 Juliano Corregido 2005: 15. A stereotype that Roman authors applied to all women: Apul., *Met.* 9.17.3; Juv., 6.435–455; Plaut., *Aul.* 123–126, *Cist.* 149, and *Trin.* 800; Val. Max. 7.2.

71 Philostr., *V. A.* 5.14.1.

72 Phl., *Mir.* 1.

73 Ros García 2016: 10.

74 Suet., *Aug.* 78, *Ner.* 42.

75 Suet., *Ner.* 50.

76 Suet., *Dom.* 17.

77 Plaut., *Curc.* 96–140; Tib. 1.5.60.

78 Ov., *Met.* 10.382-464.

79 Feltovich 2021: 90.

80 Ter., *An.*, *Eun.*, *Hec.*, and *Phorm.*

81 Crespo Ortiz de Zárate 2006.

82 Joshel 1986: 19–21.

83 Sor. 2.10; Ter., *Hec.* 768–771.

84 *Dig.* 33.2.34; Plin., *Ep.* 6.3.

85 Dio Chrys. 7.114.

Bibliography

Allély, A. (2018), 'Les enfants handicapés, infirmes et malformés à Rome et dans l´Empire romain pendant l´Antiquité tardive', *Pallas*, 106: 197–211.

Biezunska-Malowist, I. (1973), 'L'esclavage dans l´égypte gréco-romaine', in *Actes du colloque 1971 sur l'esclavage: Besançon 10–11 mai 1971*, 81–92, Besançon: Presses universitaires de Franche-Comté.

Bradley, K. R. (1980), 'Sexual Regulations in Wet-Nursing Contracts from Roman Egypt', *Klio* 62 (2): 321–25.

Bradley, K. R. (1986), 'Wet-Nursing at Rome: A Study in Social Relations', in B. Rawson (ed.), *The Family in Ancient Rome: New Perspectives*, 201–29, London: Cornell University Press.

Carroll, M. (2014), 'Mother and Infant in Roman Funerary Commemoration', *Journal of Roman Archaeology: Supplementary Series*, 96: 159–78.

Casamayor Mancisidor, S. (2019), *La vejez femenina en la antigua Roma: cuerpos, roles y sentimientos*, Oviedo: Ediciones Universidad de Oviedo.

Cid López, R. M. (2001), 'La educación de la niña romana: de *puella* a *matrona docta*', in V. Alfaro Bech and R. Francia Somalo (eds), *Bien enseñada: la formación femenina en Roma y en el occidente romanizado*, 19–44, Málaga: Universidad de Málaga.

Cid López, R. M. (2016), 'Madres sustitutas y oficios femeninos: Nodrizas y niñeras en la Roma antigua', in A. Delgado Hervás and M. Picazo Gurina (eds), *Los trabajos de las mujeres en el mundo antiguo: Cuidado y mantenimiento de la vida*, 129–38, Tarragona: ICAC.

Cid López, R. M. (2019a), '*Domus*, mujeres y género. Imágenes y espacios de la dependencia femenina', in M. García Sánchez and R. S. Garraffoni (eds), *Mujeres, género y estudios clásicos: un diálogo entre España y Brasil / Mulheres, gênero e estudios clássicos: um diálogo entre Espanha e Brasil*, 173–91, Barcelona: Universitat de Barcelona.

Cid López, R. M. (2019b), 'La *Columna Lactaria*, las *mutrices* y la *expositio* infantil: Lactantes y *pietas* en la ciudad de Roma', *Dialogues d'Histoire Ancienne: Supplément*, 19: 149–69.

Conesa Navarro, P. D. (2018), 'Madres sustitutas: Una perspectiva comparada de las nodrizas en la antigua Roma y en la sociedad contemporánea', in M. J. Bravo Bosch, A. Valmacha Ochaíta. and R. Rodríguez López (eds), *No tan lejano: Una visión de la mujer romana a través de temas de actualidad*, 145–69, Valencia: Tirant Humanidades.

Conesa Navarro, P. D. (2019), 'Los *conlactei* en la Roma Antigua: Imágenes epigráficas, iconográficas y literarias', *Dialogues d'Histoire Ancienne: Supplément*, 19: 171–92.

Conesa Navarro, P. D. and R. González Fernández (2015), 'De salvajes a domesticadas: aproximación a un ensayo sobre la justificación de la condición femenina en el mundo romano', *Revue des Études Anciennes*, 117 (1): 87–108.

Corbier, M. (2001), 'Child Exposure and Abandonment', in S. Dixon (ed.), *Childhood, Class and Kin in the Roman World*, 52–73, London: Routledge.

Crespo Ortiz de Zárate, S. (2006), *Nutrices en el Imperio romano. II: Estudio social*, Valladolid: Universidad de Valladolid.

Dasen, V. (1997), 'A propos de deux fragments de Deae nutrices à Aveches: Deéesses-mères et jumeaux dans le monde italique et gallo-romain', *Bulletin de l'Association Pro Aventico*, 39: 125–40.

Dasen, V. (2010), 'Des nourrices grecques à Rome?', *Paedagogica Historica*, 46 (6): 699–713.

Dasen, V. (2012), 'Construire sa parenté par la nourriture à Rome', in V. Dasen and M.-C. Gérard-Zai (eds), *Art de manger, arte de vivre: Nourriture et société de l'Antiquité à nos jours*, 40–59, Gollion: Infolio.

Dasen, V. (2013), 'Normal, anormal? Aux forntières de la différence dans le monde classique', in S. Reyff, M. Viegnes, and J. Rime (eds), *Les frontières de la tolérance:*

Colloques interdisciplinaires sur les valeurs-Premier volumen-Université de Freiburg, 19–20 mars 2009, 77–103, Neuchâtel: Éditions Alphil – Presses universitaires suisses.

Dasen, V. (2015), *Le sourire d´Omphale: Maternité et petite enfance dans l'Antiquité*, Rennes: Presses universitaires de Rennes.

Dasen, V. (2016), 'L'*ars medica* au féminin', *EuGeStA*, 6: 1–40.

Dasen, V. (2021), 'Roman Childhood Revisted', in L. A. Beaumont, M. Dillon, and N. Harrington (eds), *Children in Antiquity: Perspectives and Experiences of Childhood in the Ancient Mediterranean*, 105–20, London: Routledge.

Dupont, F. (2002), 'La lait du père romains', in P. Moreau (ed.), *Corps romains*, 115–38, Grenoble: Jérôme Millon.

Feltovich, A. (2021), 'Controlling Images: Enslaved Women in Greek and Roman Comedy', *Arethusa*, 5: 73–92.

Goñi Zabalegui, A. (2018), *Género y sociedad en el Egipto romano: Una mirada desde las cartas de mujeres*, Oviedo: Trabe.

Grubbs, J. E. (2010), 'Hidden in Plain Sight: *Expositi* in the Community', in V. Dasen and T. Späth (eds), *Children, Memory, and Family Identity in Roman Culture*, 293–310, Oxford: Oxford University Press.

Harders, A.-C. (2012), 'Beyond Oikos and Domnus: Modern Kinship Studies and the Ancient Family', in R. Laurence and A. Strömberg (eds), *Families in the Greco-Roman World*, 10–26, London: Continuum.

Harris, W. V. (1994), 'Child-Exposure in the Roman Empire', *Journal of Roman Studies*, 84: 1–22.

Joshel, S. R. (1986), 'Nurturing the Master's Child: Slavery and the Roman Child-Nurse', *Signs*, 12: 3–22.

Juliano Corregido, M. D. (2005), 'El saber de las mujeres', in A. Freixás Farré (ed.), *Abuelas, madres, hijas: La transmisión sociocultural del arte de envejecer*, 15–32, Barcelona: Icaria.

Laes, C. (2011), *Children in the Roman Empire: Outsiders Within*, Cambridge: Cambridge University Press.

Laes, C. (2017), 'Touching Children in Roman Antiquity: The Sentimental Discourse and the Family', in C. Laes and V. Vuolanto (eds), *Children and Everyday Life in the Roman and Late Antique World*, 60–78, London: Routledge.

Laes, C. (2018), 'Women, Children and Food', in P. Erdkamp and C. Holleran (eds), *The Routledge Handbook of Diet and Nutrition in the Roman World*, 177–88, London: Routledge.

López Pérez, M. (2004–5), 'La alimentación del lactante: la nodriza y el examen probatorio de la leche en la obra de Oribasio', *Espacio, Tiempo y Forma. Serie II: Historia Antigua*, 17/18: 225–36.

López Pérez, M. (2006), 'La transmisión a la Edad Media de la ciencia médica clásica', *Antigüedad y Cristianismo*, 23: 899–911.

López Pérez, M. (2010), *Ginecología y patología sexual femenina en las* Colecciones Médicas *de Oribasio*, Oxford: BAR Publishing.

Medina Quintana, S. (2010), 'Las nodrizas: una maternidad comprada', in R. M. Cid López (ed.), *Maternidad/es: representaciones y realidad social: Edades Antigua y Media*, 203–14, Madrid: Al-Mudayna.
Medina Quintana, S. (2014), *Mujeres y economía en la Hispania romana: Oficios, riqueza y promoción social*, Oviedo: Trabe.
Medina Quintana, S. (2017), 'El trabajo de las mujeres en la Roma antigua: Reflexiones sobre género y economía', *Dialogues d'histoire ancienne*, 43 (2): 153–76.
Medina Quintana, S. (2019), 'Oficios maternales: la imagen de las nodrizas en la literatura latina', *Dialogues d'Histoire Ancienne: Supplément*, 19: 193–203.
Nifosi, A. (2019), *Becoming a Woman and Mother in Graeco-Roman Egypt: Women's Bodies, Society and Domestic Spaces*, London: Routledge.
Pedrucci, G. (2018), *Maternità e allattamenti nel mondo greco e romano: Un percorso fra scienza delle religioni e studi sulla maternità*, Roma: Scienze e lettere.
Pedrucci, G. (2019), 'Allattamento e co-allattamento nel mondo greco e romano', in C. Lambrugo (ed.), *Una favola breve: Archeologia e antropologia per la storia dell'infanzia*, 21–27, Firenze: All'insegna del Giglio.
Pedrucci, G. (2020), 'Mothers for Sale: The Case of the Wet-Nurse in the Ancient Greek and Roman World: An Overview', *Arenal*, 27: 127–40.
Rawson, B. (1991), 'Adult–Child Relationships in Roman Society', in B. Rawson (ed.), *Marriage, Divorce, and Children in Ancient Rome*, 7–30, Canberra/Oxford: Humanities Research Centre/Clarendon Press.
Riess, W. (2012), '*Rari exempli femina*: Female Virtues on Roman Funerary Inscription', in S. L. James and S. H. Dillón (eds), *A Companion to Women in the Ancient World*, 491–501, Malden, MA: Wiley-Blackwell.
Ros García, E. (2016), 'Socialización del género a través del cuento infantil en la Comunidad Autónoma de Andalucía', PhD dissertation, Universidad de Sevilla.
Rowlandson, J. (1998), *Women and Society in Greek and Roman Egypt: A Sourcebook*, Cambridge: Cambridge University Press.
Rubiera Cancelas, C. (2014), *La esclavitud femenina en la Roma antigua: Famulae, ancillae et seruae*, Oviedo: Trabe.
Rubiera Cancelas, C. (2015), 'Esclavitud femenina en la Roma antigua: Entre la reproducción biológica y la maternidad', *Dialogues d'histoire anciennes*, 41 (2): 151–70.
Rubiera Cancelas, C. (2018), 'Seruae, Mothers and the Mother–Child Bond in Roman Italy: The Analysis of the Epigraphic Evidence', in M. Sánchez Romero and R. M. Cid López (eds), *Motherhood and Infancies in the Mediterranean in Antiquity*, 211–22, Oxford: Oxbow.
Sparreboom, A. (2009), 'Wet-Nursing in the Roman Empire: Indifference, Efficiency and Affection', MA dissertation, Vrije Universiteit Amsterdam.
Speidel, M. (2013), 'Idios logos, Gnomon of in the-Law', in R. S. Bagnall, K. Brodersen, C. B. Champion, A. Erskine, and S. R. Huebner (eds), *The Encyclopaedia of Ancient History*, 3390–1, Malden, MA: Wiley-Blackwell.

9

The Geography of Otherness in the Roman Empire: Exile and Belonging

Eleni Bozia

Introduction

The political landscape of the high empire is multi-ethnic and culturally polyvalent. So, autochthony, Romanness, and alterity are constantly rethought. Aelius Aristides argues for global citizenry under the Roman Empire: 'Neither the sea nor any distance on land shuts a man out from citizenship. Asia and Europe are, in this respect, not separate. Everything lies open to everybody; and no one fit for office or responsibility is an alien' (*Or.* 14. 213.26–30).[1] Similarly, Rutilius Namatianus praises Romans for '[making] from distinct and separate nations a single fatherland' (*Red.* 1.63–66). And Favorinus redefines exile, making a case for *paideutic* origins and cultural belonging: 'That a fatherland is not the country in which we ourselves were born is clear from the following: Many people, though born in one place, regard another land as their fatherland' (*De ex.* 10.1). This chapter suggests a different appreciation of nativeness and otherness and argues for a redefined sense of identity within the empire formulated as a notional space, a *lieu littéraire* if you will.

More specifically, the first section discusses the geography of being through the eyes of Ovid and his exilic experiences and Juvenal's multi-racial Rome. How is geography set? How does Ovid remember Rome, and how does Umbricius in Juvenal's *Satire* 3 paint it in comparison? Who is the impostor, and is it the physical emplacement or the cultural reconsiderations that render one a native or an interloper, respectively? The second section then considers the transcendence of physical geography through a rereading of Aelius Aristides' *Encomium on Rome*, where the topography assumes a global perspective. Against this backdrop, Hadrian's establishment of the *panhellenion* also prompts us to rethink people's locality or lack thereof. Finally, the chapter makes a case for a post-geographic world as Favorinus, Plutarch, and Musonius Rufus rethink their identity through their exilic fate and opt for a more inclusive literary belongingness that reappreciates physical barriers and concepts of otherness.

The geography of belongingness or lack thereof

There have been lengthy discussions of Ovid's exile,[2] the possibility that it was a literary *topos*[3] – more of a politically motivated literary scheme – and generally, the poetics behind the *Tristia* and *Ex Ponto*.[4] Moving beyond the above debates, I wish to explore the geography of belonging, the concepts of the fatherland, and how they bear in the *psyche* and socio-cultural positioning of the individual against the backdrop of ethnic foreignness. I then consider this alongside the actual topography of Rome as it was delineated by Umbricius, who is deserting Rome because of 'the others' that have infiltrated the eternal city. Where does one draw the line between being and belonging? And how do we account for the same places and perhaps even monuments becoming the signals of both 'us' and 'the others' and simultaneously the reason for nostalgia or for abandoning the very same place?

In *Tristia* 3.10, Ovid maps the barbarian land he inhabits, a harsh land with an unforgiving climate. With one stroke of his pen, he gives us the geography of his physical presence, a place among the Sarmatians, the Bessi, and the Getae, and before one could form an opinion about them, Ovid has already classified them as barbarians. The winter is cold, the land cannot be cultivated, there is no peace of mind, and the wine is not to speak of. He also confirms that not only does he not belong politically (with the Aristotelian meaning of the word) but intellectually as well, as these races are not worthy of his wit.

> suppositum stellis numquam tangentibus aequor
> me sciat in media uiuere barbaria.
> Sauromatae cingunt, fera gens, Bessique Getaeque,
> quam non ingenio nomina digna meo! . . .
> Pellibus et sutis arcent mala frigora bracis,
> oraque de toto corpore sola patent.
> Saepe sonant moti glacie pendente capilli,
> et nitet inducto candida barba gelu;
> nudaque consistunt, formam seruantia testae,
> uina, nec hausta meri, sed data frusta bibunt.
>
> *Tr.* 3.10.3–6, 19–24

> Let him know that beneath the stars which never touch the sea I am living in the midst of the barbarian world. About me are the Sauromatae, a cruel race, the Bessi, and the Getae, names how unworthy of my talent! ... With skins and stitched breeches they keep out the evils of the cold; of the whole body only the face is exposed. Often their hair tinkles with hanging ice and their beards glisten white with the mantle of frost. Exposed wine stands upright, retaining the shape of the jar, and they drink, not draughts of wine, but fragments served them![5]

Later, Ovid mentions the unfriendly coast of Pontus mirroring his inability to communicate verbally with the locals. Whether he implies that he does not speak their language or that his literacy is lost to them and his talent is wasted (*nulla mihi cum gente fera commercia linguae*; 'no interchange of speech have I with the wild people'; *Tr.* 3.11.9), the physical geography of foreign nations is compared t o and contrasted with the typology of culture that he wishes to establish for himself and the Romans.[6] In a culturally charged geographical vignette of those far-flung places, Ovid echoes Euripides' *Iphigeneia in Tauris*, Caesar's vignettes of uncouth nations, Tacitus' historico-ethnographic *Germania*, and in general, panoramas the Graeco-Roman world paints when it wishes to define what it is in contrast to what it is not. Ovid's structured and overly defined sense of ethnicity and self becomes more conspicuous when in 3.12, he hopes to converse even in Greek or, of course, more preferably in Latin. He also longs to hear of the Germanic defeat to the Romans as he proclaims that this place is not to be considered his home but rather a temporary lodging, punitive in spirit. Again, the actual landscape geography collides with his emotional one, and Ovid finds the need to define himself in terms of language and wishful locale.

> usus equi nunc est, leuibus nunc luditur armis,
> nunc pila, nunc celeri uoluitur orbe trochus;
> nunc ubi perfusa est oleo labente iuuentus,
> defessos artus Virgine tingit aqua.
> Scaena uiget studiisque fauor distantibus ardet,
> proque tribus resonant terna theatra foris . . .
> Siue tamen Graeca scierit, siue ille Latina
> uoce loqui (certe gratior huius erit;) . . .
> Is, precor, auditos possit narrare triumphos
> Caesaris et Latio reddita uota Ioui,
> teque, rebellatrix, tandem, Germania, magni
> triste caput pedibus supposuisse ducis.
>
> *Tr.* 3.12.19–24, 39–40, 45–48

> Now there is exercise on horse, now there is play with light arms, with the ball or the swift circling hoop; now the young men, reeking of slippery oil, are bathing wearied limbs in Virgin water. The stage is full of life, and partizanship ablaze with warring passions, and three theatres roar in the place of three forums. ... Yet if he knows how to speak with the voice of Greek or Roman (this last will surely be the sweeter) ... May he, I pray, have power to tell of Caesar's triumphs and vows paid to Jupiter of the Latins; that thou, rebellious Germany, at length hast lowered thy sorrowing head beneath the foot of our leader.

Of particular interest for the purposes of the current study is *Tristia* 5.7, in which the poet granulates further the character of the place and gives a panoramic view of the people, their lifestyle, and customs, as well as of language being set as the litmus test not only of communication but of being, too. Ovid describes the people as a mixture of Greeks and Getae, with the preponderant element being the barely civilized Getic. People walk around with bow and arrow in hand; they wear untrimmed beards and carry themselves uncouthly. *Au contraire*, Ovid dedicates himself to his studies, hoping to attain everlasting memory, yet another sign of a cultured individual who looks forward to a more meaningful existence and presence that does not necessarily assume an in-person physical residence.[7] The point, though, that dramatically contrasts the perception of the revisionist idea of the self as developed at the time of the high empire and was mainly achieved through *paideia* and multilingualism is the very issue of language use. Ovid expresses a fear – whether disingenuously as *captatio benevolentiae* or in earnest does not alter the perception at this point – regarding potential barbarisms that he might commit.

> Ille ego Romanus uates (ignoscite, Musae)
> Sarmatico cogor plurima more loqui.
> En pudet et fateor, iam desuetudine longa
> uix subeunt ipsi uerba Latina mihi.
> Nec dubito quin sint et in hoc non pauca libello
> barbara: non hominis culpa, sed ista loci.
> Ne tamen Ausoniae perdam commercia linguae,
> et fiat patrio uox mea muta sono,
> ipse loquor mecum desuetaque uerba retracto,
> et studii repeto signa sinistra mei.
>
> *Tr.* 5.7.55–64

> I, the Roman bard—pardon, ye Muses!—am forced to utter most things in Sarmatian fashion. I admit it, though it shames me: now from long disuse Latin words with difficulty occur even to me! And I doubt not there are even in this

> book not a few barbarisms, not the fault of the man but of the place. Yet for fear of losing the use of the Ausonian tongue and lest my own voice grow dumb in its native sound, I talk to myself, dealing again with disused words and seeking again the ill-omened currency of my art.

So, loss of language would also signify the loss of self, which Ovid attempts to avoid. Both Stevens and Williams argue that any lament for the deterioration of his linguistic abilities is simply a literary *topos*.[8] At this point, I intend to emplace Ovid's alleged linguistic displacement within a more practical scope of examining self and otherness that continues through the empire and seeks to emplace 'us' and 'the others' with respect to language use. Writing in Latin signifies his persistence against the dissolution of his geographical and physical bonds with his native land. Language has always borne the weight of establishing one ethnically but, more importantly, socially and politically.[9] In *Scholia Londinensia*, we get a glimpse of the significance of proper speaking through the story of Solon and his compatriots who went to Cilicia to establish a colony. Upon their repatriation to Athens, the group is said to have been unable to safeguard their native speech, with reference not only to grammar and syntax but, interestingly enough, to pronunciation as well. Hence, this type of mistake was named 'solecism' after them.

> ὠνόμασται δὲ ἀπὸ Σόλωνος καὶ τῶν μετ᾽ἐκείνου εἰς Κιλικίαν ἐλθόντων καὶ κτισάντων τοὺς Σόλους, οἵ χρόνῳ ὕστερον Ἀθήναζε οὐκέτι τὸ πατρῷον τῆς ὁμιλίας ἐφύλασσον. Οἱ δέ φασι σολοικισμὸν προφορὰν σεσαλευμένην τοῦ οἰκείου σώου λόγου αἰκισμόν.
>
> *GG* 1.1/3: 446.36–447.2

> It was named after Solon and those who came with him into Cilicia and founded Soloi, who later on after their repatriation to Athens no longer kept their native conversational language. And, by solecism, they mean a distorted pronunciation, a shock to proper intact speech.[10]

Similarly, Strabo comprehensively describes the history of the term *barbarizo* in one paragraph about the Carians, clarifying its linguistic aspect and subsequent evolvement into a social term. In so doing, Strabo sheds light on the politicization of this particular lemma and the role of language and society, each reflecting the other (Str. 14.2.28).

The issue of language and belonging appears even more often as we go through the Imperial authors' *oeuvre*. In those cases, the known and the unknown, and the foreign and the familiar are being inverted, thus creating a space for interloper citizens and speakers and allowing for a more inclusive appreciation of the world.[11] For instance, this is the world of Lucian of Samosata, who in *Scytha* presents Anacharsis as a foreigner who tries to get his bearings in a new city. Language, of course, is the medium of communication *par excellence* and the first instance through which one considers a place as familiar or not. Initially, Anacharsis is described as lacking confidence in his new surroundings.

> οἷα δὴ ξένος καὶ βάρβαρος οὐ μετρίως τεταραγμένος ἔτι τὴν γνώμη, πάντα ἀγνοῶν, ψοφοδεὴς πρὸς τὰ πολλά, οὐκ ἔχων ὅ τι χρήσαιτο ἑαυτῷ.
>
> Luc., *Scyth.* 3

> In no small perturbation of spirit; a foreigner and a barbarian, everything was strange to him, and many things caused him uneasiness; he knew not what to do with himself.

Then Lucian stresses that Anacharsis cannot find someone who speaks his native language until he encounters his long-lost compatriot, Toxaris. So, he redefines otherness and has Anacharsis converse with Toxaris in Scythian in the middle of Athens (Ἀλλὰ Τόξαρις Σκυθιστὶ προσειπὼν αὐτόν; 'But Toxaris addressing him in the Scythian language', Luc., *Scyth.* 4).[12]

And now, I would like to turn the reader's attention to *Ex Ponto* 1.8, where the poet relates some memories from his native Rome. The point is to establish the city's topography and then consider it alongside Umbricius' topography in Juvenal's *Satire* 3.[13] In the *Letter to Severus*, Ovid reminisces about Rome and the surrounding areas in a soliloquy worthy of being considered a *syntaktikon*, a farewell speech.[14] The poem's first half is devoted to his current locale and resounds with words of warfare. After he has set the mood and the reader's expectations, he continues with the actual geography of the place. He mentions the Danube and the Getae, and the reader is immediately situated in the land of the barbarians. The wording then takes a complete turn when Ovid starts with words of pleasure that invoke warm feelings, such as *dulces* (delightful) (*Pont.* 1.8.31) and *pulchrae* (lovely) (*Pont.*1.8.32, 37), and proceeds with the topography of the city of Rome, notionally revisiting places such as the Campus Martius, the fora, Aqua Virgo, the temples, and the theatres. Then, taking the way out of Rome through via Flaminia and via Clodia, he paints the canvas of the countryside, the Paelignian rural area, and the pine-bearing hills.[15] The poem closes symmetrically as Ovid reminds the reader that he wishes to leave the war-ridden space he now inhabits.

> aque domo rursus pulchrae loca uertor ad Vrbis

cunctaque mens oculis peruidet illa suis.
nunc fora, nunc aedes, nunc marmore tecta theatra,
nunc subit aequata porticus omnis humo.
gramina nunc Campi pulchros spectantis in hortos
stagnaque et euripi Virgineusque liquor.

Pont. 1.8.33–38

And from my own house I am once again visiting the localities of the beautiful town, my mind surveying everything with eyes of its own. Now the fora, now the temples, now the theatres sheathed in marble, now every portico with its levelled ground comes before me; now the greensward of the Campus that looks towards the lovely gardens, the pools, the canals, and the water of the Virgo.

Ovid gives us the view of an exile's notional and reminiscing geography. Areas and places around his native city of Rome bear the stamp of being and belonging for the Roman citizen and are strikingly contrasted against the host nation's physical and cultural roughness. For Ovid, 'being' assumes the comfort and familiarity of the place and the socio-cultural parameters that mark what 'to be Roman' is, namely, to stroll the porticoes, recite poetry, attend the theatre, and imbue oneself with the tranquil pleasures of the countryside. Suppose we were to bring Juvenal to the forefront of the discussion, particularly *Satire* 3, where Umbricius complains that he feels displaced in the middle of Rome. Are we able to account for what being and belonging mean as the empire opens up, as people travel and migrate, and as geography is being rethought and reappraised?

Umbricius' topography of Rome delineates a city of socio-cultural exile or of (be)longing for native Romans.[16] The Satire is a dystopic geography of cultural miscegenation that challenges the sense of belonging of native Romans to the point that departure from the city is a requirement for the preservation of one's sense of being. Umbricius mentions the Subura, the Aqua Marcia, the Porta Capena, and the Valley of Egeria, setting more the outer boundaries of the city as he prepares to leave as if native Roman life has been pushed to the edges. The remaining of the city's topical references are heavy with cultural and political alienation as the poet and his mouthpiece sketch a native's cultural exile within the boundaries of his city. Starting with Egeria, albeit a thoroughly Roman spot visited by Numa and the Nymph, the place is now used by the Jewish, and the Muses have been displaced.

Sed dum tota domus raeda componitur una,
substitit ad veteres arcus madidamque Capenam ...
hic, ubi nocturnae Numa constituebat amicae
(nunc sacri fontis nemus et delubra locantur
Iudaeis, quorum cophinus fenumque supellex.

Juv. 3.10–14

But while his entire house was being loaded onto a single wagon, he halted under the ancient arch of dripping Capena ... Here, where Numa used to date his nighttime girlfriend, the grove and shrine of the sacred spring are rented out to Jews, with their equipment, a hay-lined chest.[17]

The Satire teems with words of departure, such as *cedamus* (3.29), and proclamations that feature the locative *Romae* (3.41, 137, 183) but are instead imbued with a sense of loss of place rather than with one of belonging.[18] Displacement becomes even more pronounced as Rome is called a 'Greek city' in a question that Umbricius addresses to Quirites, thus pointing to and contrasting the nativeness of the place with the alienation of the socio-cultural circumstances that now condition life there.[19] What is more, in the following line, the Tiber, the very heart of the city, is flooded by the Syrian Orontes both figuratively, as in the Eastern immigrants who are now living in Rome, and positionally, as *Tiberim* is in the middle of the verse surrounded by *Syrus* and *Orontes*.

non possum ferre, Quirites,
Graecam urbem. quamvis quota portio faecis Achaei?
iam pridem Syrus in Tiberim defluxit Orontes
et linguam et mores et cum tibicine chordas
obliquas nec non gentilia tympana secum
vexit et ad circum iussas prostare puellas.

Juv. 3.60–65

My fellow-citizens, I cannot stand a Greekified Rome. Yet how few of our dregs are Achaeans? The Syrian Orontes has for a long time now been polluting the Tiber, bringing with it its language and customs, its slanting strings along with pipers, its native tom-toms too, and the girls who are told to offer themselves for sale at the Circus.

Another part of the out-of-place topographical vignette is addressed to Quirinus. It lists a barrage of Greek places, overpowering the ancestral toponymics and alienating the very sense of belongingness.

> hic alta Sicyone, ast hic Amydone relicta,
> hic Andro, ille Samo, hic Trallibus aut Alabandis.
>
> Juv. 3.69–70

> This one leaving the heights of Sicyon, this other from Amydon, this one from Andros, that one from Samos, this one from Tralles or Alabanda.

In sum, Ovid and Juvenal define identity and belonging against the backdrop of geography. They frame their sense of being in terms of the city of Rome. For Ovid, being physically distanced, challenges and enhances his idea of Romanness. Conversely, Juvenal manipulates the established sense of physical being and stresses the impact the foreign citizenry living in Rome has on belongingness. In both cases, though, it is evident that a physical location determines the authors' socio-cultural identity.

Transcending physical geography

Thus far, we have examined Ovid's and Juvenal's topographic substantiations of 'being' against the backdrop of actual geographies. Whether politically or culturally exiled, the two authors use the city of Rome as their point of reference for their definition of the self. And the map of belongingness coincides with the geography of the city and its surroundings. Thus, even when Juvenal chastises the hellenization of Rome, he addresses the Quirites, making it clear that this locality should ground them. Whatever other elements are to be found there, they only pollute, infiltrate, and trespass the Roman nativeness.

However, this delineation of space becomes infinitely more complex when we reach the time of the high empire and read the voices of those dregs speaking for themselves. So, what does the map look like when an interloper native draws it? It is the unique case of Aelius Aristides and his portrait of Rome that I wish to examine next and compare it with those of Ovid and Juvenal. *To Rome* begins as is customary for a *periegesis*. The author promises to deliver a speech as a sign of gratitude worthy of the city's magnitude (*Or*. 14.197–199).[20] Aristides continues in a seemingly traditional manner mentioning the hills, the bordering with the sea, and the size and height of the city. The somewhat point-by-point description, though, stops here, and then Aristides relates Rome's political and cultural expanse, extrapolating from the city to the whole empire and its reach.[21] More importantly, what Juvenal describes as a polis of miscegenation, mis- and displacement, Aristides defines as a cosmopolis that hosts people from everywhere and features products from all ends of the world.

> ἄγεται δὲ ἐκ πάσης γῆς καὶ θαλάττη ὅσα ὧραι φύουσι καὶ χῶραι ἕκασται φέρουσι καὶ ποταμοὶ καὶ λίμναι καὶ τέχναι Ἑλλήνων καὶ βαρβάρων.
>
> *Or.*, 14.200.19–22
>
> From everywhere, land and sea come all that the seasons bring forth, all that is produced by each country, by rivers, lakes, and the skills of Greeks and foreigners.

And instead of a multitude of individuals as lone units that are out of place, Aristides considers immigration and movement as creating one country and one race, concluding that:

> καὶ τὸ Ῥωμαῖον εἶναι ποιήσατε οὐ πόλεως, ἀλλὰ γένους ὄνομα κοινοῦ τινος, καὶ τούτου οὐχ ἑνὸς τῶν πάντων, ἀλλ᾽ ἀντιρρόπου πᾶσι τοῖς λοιποῖς.
>
> *Or.*, 14.214.19–22
>
> You have made the word 'Roman' apply not to a city but to a whole nationality, – and at that, not one of all the nationalities there are but equal to all the rest.

Towards the end of the speech, he erases borders in a statement that can be considered a universal apprehension and a before-his-times sense of cosmopolitanism and globality or a veiled accusation against Roman imperialism. The arguments in favour of either of the above, as well as the implications, are countless. However, my focus is rather on how Aristides uses this literary vignette to re-present physical location and ultimately expand its borders. To this end, I believe, he argues the following:

> καὶ μὴν τό γε ὑπὸ πάντων λεγόμενον, ὅτι γῆ πάντων μήτηρ καὶ πατρὶς κοινὴ πάντων, ἄριστα ὑμεῖς ἀπεδείξατε.
>
> *Or.*, 14.214.19–22
>
> You have most effectively proved what all people merely said – that the earth is the mother of all and the common fatherland of all.

So, taking this at face value, the Smyrnaean has deleted Ovid's and Juvenal's sense of geography and being, replacing it with a revised geography accommodating culture, *paideia*, and socio-political mobility.[22] Clearly, the circumstances are ripe for such reconsiderations of individual and social positionalities. Within this context, we should also consider Hadrian's *panhellenion* and his take on *paideia*, being, becoming, and ultimately one's sense of belonging.[23] One might argue that the *panhellenion* recurred the world to the time of Erechtheus' autochthony, distancing itself from Isocrates' *paideutic* Hellenicity and, of course, the Imperial age's inclusive citizenship. However, the membership of Asian cities, including Aizanoi of Phrygia and Sardis, can actually claim the opposite.[24] Hadrian's attempt to re-establish Greekness led to its reconstituted conceptualization that produced a *milieu* of so-called pure Greek blood, colonized elements (with, of course, the negatives of colonization alongside the openness to aspects of a newly received Hellenicity), and Roman citizenship, which was the status quo for several individual members of the *panhellenion*.

Additionally, cases such as that of Corinth that involve the *paideutic* and culturally constituted reidentification of an entire city can only strengthen the argument in favour of rethinking the world's geography.[25] Within this context, in *Oration* 37, Favorinus addresses Corinth as a Hellenic city by blood but thoroughly Romanized as well. So, he entreats her citizens to preserve his statue, as he primarily sees and presents himself against the backdrop of re-evaluation of provenance and *paideia*.[26]

To sum up, what for Ovid and Juvenal was a geography of distress and displacement, Aelius Aristides turns into a reconsidered trans-locality that does not necessarily transgress so much as transcends people's physical emplacement. Whether implicitly criticizing Roman imperialism or marvelling at their expanse, he still showcases their open-border, socio-cultural openness.

Orating a post-geographic world

This section looks at the topic of geography and belonging through the lens of exile and argues that even the concept of forceful relocation was reconsidered by Imperial authors, attributing new meaning to one's personal attributes and the power of culture and *paideia* in the formation of the self. Socrates opts for death instead of exile and the loss of his citizenship. Euripides' Polynices declares that the loss of one's country is a great ill. In addition to the other evils that have been incurred upon her, Medea laments her exile in a foreign land where she has no family. *Au contraire*, at the time of the high empire, Dio argues that 'If I narrate the time of my exile, someone will say, not that I am lamenting, but far rather that I am bragging' (*Or.* 45.2). Literature has always been the mediator and conveyor of socio-cultural patterns. So, how can we explain the perspectival shift from the former literary and historical figures to the literature of exile that appears in these later times? Imperial authors reinterpret exile as a cultural space that mediates nativeness, otherness, and different levels of belonging. All concepts are modulated into unique lifestyles against the backdrop of the empire's post-ethnographic, post-geographic, and post-cultural world.

Plutarch's *On Exile*, Musonius Rufus' *That Exile is not an Evil*, and Favorinus' *On Exile*, all seek to redefine space and belonging and end up also reconsidering the empire and the self. Plutarch and Musonius agree that departure from one's native land guarantees a respite from public affairs, politics, service, and cosying up to influential individuals. As a matter of fact, Plutarch's vignette of city life resembles Umbricius' condemnation of life in Rome with the informers and busybodies very closely (*Mor.* 603D9–F6). Plutarch brings forward famous individuals who have made a case for more inclusive belongingness, such as Socrates, who declared himself a citizen of the world (*Mor.* 600F7–8). Throughout the work, he rethinks space when he says that not all Athenians live in Attica. Thus, he enlists science to his side to argue that astronomers teach that the universe is one. He contests the traditional concept of autochthony and nativism, claiming that any place can become one's native land (*Mor.* 601B7–C4). Towards the end, in a Plutarchian *coup de grâce*, he eloquently summarizes his idea of belonging in a statement that could very easily become a motto for the modern world as well. He proclaims that exile is a term of reproach only to fools – those who also use words such as 'pauper', 'bald', 'short', 'foreigner' or 'immigrant' derogatorily.

> Ἀλλ' ἐπονείδιστον ὁ φυγάς ἐστι. παρά γε τοῖς ἄφροσιν, οἳ καὶ 'τὸν πτωχὸν' λοιδόρημα ποιοῦνται καὶ 'τὸν φαλακρὸν' καὶ 'τὸν μικρὸν' καὶ νὴ Δία 'τὸν ξένον' καὶ 'τὸν μέτοικον.' ἀλλὰ μὴν οἱ μὴ τούτοις ὑποφερόμενοι θαυμάζουσι τοὺς ἀγαθούς, κἂν πένητες ὦσι, κἂν ξένοι, κἂν φυγάδες.
>
> *Mor.* 607A4–9

> But 'exile' is a term of reproach. Yes, among fools who make terms of abuse of 'pauper', 'bald,' 'short,' and indeed 'foreigner' and 'immigrant.' But those not carried away by such considerations admire good men, even if they are poor, foreigners, or exiles.[27]

Similarly, Musonius Rufus argues for a cosmopolitan and somewhat scientific and Socratic appreciation of the world and a re-conception of one's space and locality, thus contesting the stereotypical pains of exile.

> Φυγὴν γάρ, ἔφη, πῶς ἄν τις μὴ ἀνόητος ὢν βαρύνοιτο; ἥτις ὕδατος μὲν καὶ γῆς καὶ ἀέρος, ἔτι δὲ ἡλίου καὶ τῶν ἄλλων ἄστρων οὐκ ἀπείργει ἡμᾶς οὐδαμῶς, ἀλλ' οὐδὲ ἀνθρώπων ὁμιλίας, ἁπανταχοῦ γὰρ καὶ πάντῃ τούτων

μετουσία ἐστίν. εἰ δὲ μέρους τινὸς τῆς γῆς ἀφαιρούμεθα καὶ τινῶν ἀνθρώπων συνουσίας, τί τοῦτο δεινόν; οὐδὲ γὰρ οἴκοι ὄντες ἁπάσῃ τῇ γῇ ἐχρώμεθα, οὐδὲ ἀνθρώποις ἅπασι συνῆμεν.

Ep. 9.2–8

Why, he asked, should anyone who was not devoid of understanding be oppressed by exile? It does not in any way deprive us of water, earth, air, or the sun and the other planets, or indeed, even of the society of men, for everywhere and in every way there is opportunity for association with them. What if we are kept from a certain part of the earth and from association with certain men, what is so dreadful about that? Why, when we were at home, we did not enjoy the whole earth, nor did we have contact with all men.[28]

He welcomes the relief from civic and familial responsibilities, thus diminishing the essence of exile's pain traditionally focused on the loss of family and social belonging (*Ep.* 9.32–35). He also demolishes other stereotypical motifs about exile by arguing that men lead a more respectable lifestyle (*Ep.* 9.40–50) and lists several famous exiles to make his case (*Ep.* 9.62–85). Finally, in the same vein as Plutarch, he refutes the claim that exile deprives one of their freedom of speech (*Ep.* 9.110–116), thus essentially reinforcing his positionality. Dio's entire oration on his banishment can support this last argument as he uses the literary and physical space to philosophize openly and teach the Romans how to lead a more decorous life.

Finally, Favorinus creates the meta-narrative of the exile narratives above, reversing the discussion about nativeness and belonging. So, not only does he proclaim in *Oration* 37 that he wishes to not only seem Greek but be Greek, but in *On Exile,* he questions the very meaning of native land.[29]

εἰ δέ τις οὐ Λευκανὸς ὤν, ἀλλὰ Ῥωμαῖος, οὐδὲ τοῦ πλήθους, ἀλλὰ τῶν ἱπποτρόφων, οὐδὲ τὴν φωνὴν μόνον ἀλλὰ καὶ τὴν γνώμην καὶ τὴν δίαιταν καὶ τὸ σχῆμα τῶν Ἑλλήνων ἐζηλωκώς ἵν' αὐτῷ περιῇ ἓν ἀντὶ πάντων Ἕλληνι δοκεῖν τε καὶ εἶναι.

Or. 37.25

Well, if someone who is not a Lucanian but a Roman, not one of the masses but of the equestrian order, one who has affected, not merely the language, but also the thought and manners and dress of the Greeks. Aiming to achieve one thing at the cost of all else, namely, not only to seem Greek but to be Greek too.[30]

ε[ἰ] δέ [τι]νες ὀλίγοι αὐ|τόχθονες ẹἶν[αι ἡγούμε]νοι ἐπὶ τούτῳ μ[έγα φρον] οὖσ̣ιν, οὗτοι ὄν|ṭ[ω]ṣ ἀλαζον[εύονται· ἦ]ν γάρ τοι καὶ μυῶ̣ν κα̣ὶ ἄ̣[λλων ε] ὑτελεστέ|ρ[ων] ζῴ̣ων [χθονογέ]νεια, ἀνθρώπῳ δὲ ὄντι οὐ κ̣α̣λ̣ὸ̣ν μὴ | ἐξ ἀ̣νθρώπο[υ γενέσθαι]. εἰ δ' αὖ διὰ τοῦτο πρ̣ὸ̣ς τὴν γῆ̣ν ο̣ἰκειότε|ρον ἑτέρων [ἁπά]ντ[ων ὁμο]ιοῦνται, ἀλλ' οὐχ ὥσπερ ἐκ τρυμαλιᾶς | ἐξαναδύντα χρὴ [. . . . ἐκ]εῖνο τὸ καθ' αὑτὸν μέρος μόνον περι|έπειν, ἀλλὰ πᾶσαν τὴν γῆν οἰκεῖν ὡς πάντων μητέρα καὶ |τροφὸν τὴν αὐτὴν οὖσαν.

De Ex. 96.10[31]

If, however, a few certain people considering themselves native-born, think big of themselves for that reason, they truly become arrogant. For, let me tell you, there is earth nativeness both in mice and other less important animals, but, being a man, it is not fine not to be born from a man. But if again, for this reason, they liken themselves more closely with the earth than all the others, at least, they must not treat that very place only as someone who has emerged from a hole but must rather inhabit the entire earth as she is the same mother and nurturer of all.[32]

And in a strong statement that comprehensively encapsulates the high empire's debates on Greekness, Romanness, foreignness, and belonging, Favorinus not only redefines but manages to reinstitute his very roots. He deracinates autochthony and establishes himself as a citizen, not of the world but one particular city by his own choice.

Τὴν δὲ πατρίδα | φιλῶ μὲν [καὶ αὐ]τὸς οὐδενὸς δεύτερος καὶ | ἑκὼν αὐτῆς οὐκ ἄν ποτε ἀπελείφθην· λο|γιζόμενος δὲ εὑρίσκω οὐδὲν ἕτερον οὖ|σαν ἢ ἐν ᾗ οἱ πρόγονοι ἡμῶν κατῴκη|σαν ἢ διέτριψαν. ὅτι γὰρ οὐκ ἐν ᾗ αὐτοὶ | ἐγενόμεθα, δῆλον ἐκ τούτου· πολλοὶ γὰρ | ἑτέρωθι γεννηθέντες ἑτέραν πατρίδα |νομίζουσιν. εἰ δὲ τοῦτό ἐστιν πατρίς, τὸ | σύνηθες τοῖς προγόνοις χωρίον, τί δὴ |οὐχὶ τῇ αὐτῇ γνώμῃ καὶ ταύτην φιλη|τέον, ἐν [ᾗ] τὰ νῦν διατρίβομεν; πο⊠λὺ γὰρ ἑκά[στῳ ἐγγυτέ]ρω ἐν ᾗ αὐτός τις οἰκεῖ ἢν ᾗ οἱ πρόγονοι | αὐτοῦ ᾤκ[ησαν, τοῖς δ]ὲ̣ ἐξ ἐμοῦ γενησομένοις ἡ αὐτὴ αἰτία καὶ |πολὺ δικα[ιοτέρα τὴν] ἐμὴν ἀναγκαίαν ἐνδιαίτησιν πατρίδα | ποιεῖν.

Favorin., *De ex.* 96.10.1–2

And I too love my fatherland; my love is second to no one's, and I should never have left it willingly. On reflection, however, I discover that it is nothing other than the place in which my forebears settled or resided. That a fatherland is not the country in which we ourselves were born is clear from the following: many people, though born in one place, regard another land as their fatherland. If our fatherland is this, the territory to which our ancestors have become accustomed, why by the same token should we not also love the country in which we currently reside? After all, the land in which one dwells is much closer than that in which one's ancestors dwelled, and my future descendants will have the same reason (or even more just cause) to make my enforced dwelling-place their fatherland.[33]

Conclusion

To sum up, should one attempt to define belonging in terms of geography and provenance? This brief survey of Ovid, Juvenal, Aristides, Plutarch, Musonius Rufus, and Favorinus shows that geography could and was manipulated. Space was described and defined in socio-cultural terms and was nuanced to appear familiar or foreign regardless of whether the land was the author's native land. So, as boundaries become malleable and *paideia* builds a culturally conditioned world, native lands, exilic lands, and belonging become the spheres of influence for socio-political and *paideutic* dynamics. We could call these works geographies of exile or apprehend a more 'corinthicized' space accommodating to support post-native inclusiveness.

Notes

1 All translations of Aelius Aristides' *To Rome* are by Levin 1950.

2 Thibault 2018 examines all the hypotheses regarding the reasons behind Ovid's exile and concludes that there is not enough evidence available to determine what the actual reasons were. Claassen 2016 discusses the political underlayer of the exilic poetry and the Ovidian 'voice' of Augustus. See also Hutchinson 2017.

3 Van der Velden 2020 discusses Hartman's argument that Ovid's exile was fictional. Williams 1994: 3–8 presents the debate in a section titled 'The "unreality" of Ovid's exile poetry'.

4 See McGowan 2009 who studies both the exilic collections against the backdrop of poetry, religion, and law. Gaertner 2007: 172 suggests about Ovid's exilic work that: '... exilic literature is neither a collection of psychograms nor a literary "genre" or "mode", but rather a stock of literary roles that keep being re-enacted'. For a thorough analyses of the exilic poetry, see also Claassen 2008; Williams 1994.

5 All translations of Ovid are by Gould and Wheeler 1924.

6 Grebe 2010 suggests that Ovid associates exile with an expulsion from the known world that is represented by Rome to the unknown that is Tomis in a similar manner to the unknown of death.

7 Ingleheart 2015 discusses *Tristia* 3.3 and Ovid's attempts towards and hopes for immortality through his poetry.

8 Stevens 2009; Williams 1994: 102. Conversely, Nagle suggests that Ovid is turning into a Getic poet (Nagle 1980: 139).

9 Language bore *gravitas* in the archaic and classical Greek world as the denominator *par excellence* of Greekness, and dialectal variety played a role in determining geographic and/or literary belonging. Numerous studies have been dedicated to the study of the Greek language. For a thorough study, see Horrocks 2010. Similarly, the

development of Latin from its origins to its development into classical Latin and then its expanded use throughout the empire have been studied extensively. For a comprehensive overview, see Clackson and Horrocks 2007. For Latin within the context of bilingualism, see Adams et al. 2002; Adams 2003; Biville 2002; Dubuisson 1983; Mullen 2013. For multilingualism at the time of the empire, see Biville 2018; Bozia and Mullen 2021; Kaimio 1979.

10 My translation.

11 Extensive studies have been written on the topic of language and belonging either with a focus on Greek and Latin bilingualism, as indicated above, or with respect to new forms of Latin and Greek as spoken by non-native speakers. Some general bibliography includes Clackson 2015, Swain 1996, Whitmarsh 2001a. For specific case studies, see Bozia 2018 on Lucian and Favorinus; Lee et al. 2014 on Apuleius; and Swain 2004 on Apuleius, Fronto, and Gellius.

12 Lucian's translations are by Kilburn 1959. For a detailed discussion of this work from the perspective of otherness and belonging, see Bozia 2015: 67–8, 73–8.

13 See Moodie 2014 for a close reading of *Satire* 3 and Juvenal's representation of the city and its corruption.

14 On the topic of the traditional *syntaktikon* in comparison to Umbricius' inverted presentation, see Braund 1996: 230–1; Cairns 1972: 48.

15 Philbrick 2016 discusses Ovid's idyllic and utopian description of Rome and its contrast with the dystopic reality of Tomis. He emphasizes the dismantling of the traditional clash of urban and rural and the idealized portrayal that the exile paints. Curtis 2015 offers an interesting reading of space and Ovid's relationship with Rome and Tomis.

16 Edwards 1996: 110–33 provides a very interesting discussion on the view of exiles from and visitors to Rome and their respective views of the city.

17 All translations of Juvenal are by Braund 2004.

18 Geue 2015 presents the comedic-farcical aspect of Umbricius' self-inflicted departure as a hackneyed literary *topos* that originates in Stoic philosophy and exile as a literary *topos* that is developed in Vergil's *Eclogue* 1.

19 On foreigners and prejudice in Juvenal, see Gallia 2016; Gellérfi 2019; Moore 1976; Watts 1976.

20 The edition consulted is Dindorf 1964.

21 For a discussion, see Pernot 1997: 91.

22 Pernot 2008 makes a very interesting case for the dubious intentions of Aristides' so-called encomium on Rome and questions its honesty.

23 On the *panhellenion*, see Willers 1996.

24 Spawforth and Walker 1985 discuss particular member case studies and the dynamics of power and belonging in the *panhellenion*.

25 See Engels 1990: 67–74. Goldhill 2010: 60–8 has an illuminating discussion on the fate of Patrae, its rebuilding by Augustus, and the role of Artemis Laphria against the

backdrop of Pausanias and his personal sense of identity and belonging. Ajootian 2014 studies the building programme of Roman Corinth.

26 Whitmarsh 2001b: 294–303 discusses this speech as an example of mimetic artificiality, as it is seemingly delivered by the statue. Gleason 1995: 3–20 analyses the speech as the strongest proclamation of a gendered promotion.

27 Translation by De Lacy and Einarson 1959.

28 Translation by Lutz 2020.

29 See also Whitmarsh 2001a: 134–41. For an analysis of Favorinus' exile as a display of the rhetorical figure of impersonation, see Gleason 1995: 145–58. See also Nesselrath 2007, who discusses Favorinus' use of traditional literary and philosophical tropes. Bozia 2018 discusses Favorinus' *paideutic* approach to identity and belonging.

30 Translation by Cohoon and Crosby 1940.

31 The edition consulted is Barigazzi 1966.

32 My translation.

33 Translation by Whitmarsh 2001a: 299.

Bibliography

Adams, J., M. Janse and S. Swain (2002), *Bilingualism in Ancient Society: Language Contact and the Written Text*, Oxford: Oxford University Press.

Adams, J. N. (2003), *Bilingualism and the Latin Language*, Cambridge: Cambridge University Press.

Aelius Aristides, R. (1950), *ΕΙΣ ΡΩΜΗΝ To Rome*, trans. Saul Levin, Glencoe, IL: The Free Press.

Ajootian, A. (2014), 'Simulacra Civitatum at Roman Corinth', *Hesperia: Journal of the American School of Classical Studies at Athens*, 83 (2): 315–77.

Barigazzi, A. (1966), *Favorino di Arelate: Opere*, Florence: Monnier.

Biville, F. (2002), 'The Graeco-Romans and Graeco-Latin: A Terminological Framework for Cases of Bilingualism', in J. Adams, M. Janse, and S. Swain (eds), *Bilingualism in Ancient Society*, 77–102, Oxford: Oxford University Press.

Biville, F. (2018), *Multilingualism in the Roman World*, Oxford: Oxford University Press. Available online: https://www.oxfordhandbooks.com/view/10.1093/oxfordhb/9780199935390.001.0001/oxfordhb-9780199935390-e-101 (accessed 16 January 2020).

Bozia, E. (2015), *Lucian and His Roman Voices: Cultural Exchanges and Conflicts in the Late Roman Empire*, New York: Routledge.

Bozia, E. (2018), 'Immigration as Acculturation: Voluntary Displacement in the Roman Empire', in D. Arroyo (ed.), *Displacement in Language, Literature and Culture*, 2016 CMLL Symposium, 49–82, Selected Proceedings, Benalmádena, Málaga, Spain.

Bozia, E. and A. Mullen (2021), 'Verbal and Social Translingualism in the Greek and Roman Worlds', in S. G. Kellman and N. Lvovich (eds), *Routledge Handbook of Literary Translingualism*, 45–59, London: Routledge.

Braund, S. M. (1996), *Juvenal: Satires, Book 1*, Cambridge: Cambridge University Press.

Braund, S. M., ed. and trans. (2004), *Juvenal and Persius*, Loeb Classical Library #91, Cambridge, MA: Harvard University Press.

Cairns, F. (1972), *Generic Composition in Greek and Roman Poetry*, Edinburgh: Edinburgh University Press.

Claassen, J. M. (2008), *Ovid Revisited: The Poet in Exile*, London: Duckworth.

Claassen J. M. (2016), 'Seizing the Zeitgeist: Ovid in Exile and Augustan Political Discourse', *Acta Classica*, 59: 52–79.

Clackson, J. (2015), *Language and Society in the Greek and Roman Worlds*, Cambridge: Cambridge University Press.

Clackson, J. and G. C. Horrocks (2007), *The Blackwell History of the Latin Language*, Oxford: Blackwell.

Cohoon, J. W. and H. Lamar Crosby, trans. (1940), *Dio Chrysostom. Discourses 31–36*, Loeb Classical Library #358, Cambridge, MA: Harvard University Press.

Curtis, L. (2015), 'Explaining Exile: The Aetiological Poetics of Ovid, Tristia 3', *TAPA*, 145 (2): 411–44.

De Lacy, P. H. and B. Einarson, trans. (1959), *Plutarch. Moralia, vol. VII: On Love of Wealth. On Compliancy. On Envy and Hate. On Praising Oneself Inoffensively. On the Delays of the Divine Vengeance. On Fate. On the Sign of Socrates. On Exile. Consolation to His Wife*, Loeb Classical Library #405, Cambridge, MA: Harvard University Press.

Dindorf, W. (1964), *Aristides*, vol. 1, 321–70, Leipzig: Reimer (reprint Hildesheim: Olms).

Dubuisson, M. (1983), 'Recherches sur la Terminologie Antique du Bilinguisme', *Revue de philology, de literature et d'histoire ancienne*, 57: 203–25.

Edwards, C. (1996), *Writing Rome: Textual Approaches to the City*, Cambridge: Cambridge University Press.

Engels, D. W. (1990), *Roman Corinth: An Alternative Model for the Classical City*, Chicago, IL: University of Chicago Press.

Gaertner, J. F. (2007), 'Ovid and the "Poetics of Exile": How Exilic Is Ovid's Exile Poetry', in J. F. Gaertner (ed.), *Writing Exile: The Discourse of Displacement in Greco-Roman Antiquity and Beyond*, 155–72, Leiden: Brill.

Gallia, A. (2016), '"Some of my Best Friends . . ." Reading Prejudice in Juvenal's Third Satire', *Classical Journal*, 111 (3): 319–46.

Gellérfi, G. (2019), 'Xenophobic Utterances in Juvenal's Satires', *Graeco-Latina Brunensia*, 24 (1): 81–91.

Geue, T. (2015), 'The Loser Leaves (Rome's Loss): Umbricius' Wishful Exile in Juvenal *Satire* 3', *Classical Quarterly, NS*, 65 (2): 773–87.

Gleason, M. W. (1995), *Making Men*, Princeton, NJ: Princeton University Press.

Goldhill, S. (2010), 'What Is Local Identity? The Politics of Cultural Mapping', in T. Whitmarsh (ed.), *Local Identities and Microidentities in the Imperial Greek World*, 46–68, Cambridge: Cambridge University Press.
Gould, G. P. and A. L. Wheeler, trans. (1924), *Ovid: Tristia. Ex Ponto*, Loeb Classical Library #151, Cambridge, MA: Harvard University Press.
Grebe, S. (2010), 'Why Did Ovid Associate His Exile with a Living Death?', *The Classical World*, 103 (4): 491–509.
Horrocks, G. (2010), *Greek: A History of the Language and Its Speakers*, 2nd edition, Chichester: Wiley-Blackwell.
Hutchinson, G. O. (2017), 'Some New and Old Light on the Reasons for Ovid's Exile', *Zeitschrift für Papyrologie und Epigraphik*, 203: 76–84.
Ingleheart, J. (2015), '"Exegi Monumentum": Exile, Death, Immortality and Monumentality in Ovid *Tristia* 3.3', *Classical Quarterly*, 65 (1): 286–300.
Jones, H. L., trans. (1917), *Strabo. Geography*, vol. I: books 1–2, Loeb Classical Library #49, Cambridge, MA: Harvard University Press.
Kaimio, J. (1979), *The Romans and the Greek Language*, Helsinki: Societas Scientiarum Fennica.
Kilburn, K., trans. (1959), *Lucian VI*, Loeb Classical Library #430, Cambridge, MA: Harvard University Press.
Lee, B. T., E. Finkelpearl and L. Graverini (2014), *Apuleius and Africa*, London: Routledge.
Lutz, C. E., ed. (2020), *Musonius Rufus. That One should Disdain Hardships: The Teachings of a Roman Stoic*, New Haven, CT: Yale University Press.
McGowan, M. M. (2009). *Ovid in Exile: Power and Poetic Redress in the Tristia and Epistulae ex Ponto*, Leiden: Brill.
Moodie, E. (2014), 'Umbricius' Farewell Tour', *Classical World*, 108 (1): 27–44.
Moore, P. (1976), 'Juvenal and the Orontes', *Classical World*, 69 (6): 376–7.
Mullen, A. (2013), 'The Bilingualism of Material Culture? Thoughts from a Linguistic Perspective', *Journal on Hellenic and Roman Material Culture*, 2: 21–43.
Nagle, B. R. (1980), *The Poetics of Exile: Program and Polemic in the Tristia and Epistulae ex Ponto of Ovid*, Bruxelles: Latomus.
Nesselrath, H. G. (2007), 'Later Greek Voices on the Predicaments of Exile from Teles to Plutarch and Favorinus', in J. F. Gaertner (ed.), *Writing Exile: The Discourse of Displacement in Greco-Roman Antiquity and Beyond*, 87–108, Leiden: Brill.
Pernot, L. (1997), *Éloges grecs de Rome*, Paris: Les Belles Lettres.
Pernot, L. (2008), 'Aelius Aristides and Rome', in W. V. Harris and B. Holmes (eds), *Aelius Aristides between Greece, Rome, and the Gods*, 175–201, Leiden: Brill.
Philbrick, R. (2016), 'Utopian Rome in Ovid's Externalized View from Exile', *Classical Outlook*, 91 (2): 42–5.
Romeo, I. (2002), 'The Panhellenion and Ethnic Identity in Hadrianic Greece', *Classical Philology*, 97 (1): 21–40.

Sabine, G. (2010), 'Why Did Ovid Associate His Exile with a Living Death?', *Classical World*, 103 (4): 491–509.

Spawforth, A. J. and S. Walker (1985), 'The World of Panhellenion. I. Athens and Eleusis', *Journal of Roman Studies*, 75: 78–104.

Stevens, B. (2009), '*Per gestum res est significanda mihi*: Ovid and Language in Exile', *Classical Philology*, 104 (2): 162–83.

Swain, S. (1996), *Hellenism and Empire*, Oxford: Clarendon Press.

Swain, S. (2004), 'Bilingualism and Biculturalism in Antonine Rome: Apuleius, Fronto, and Gellius', in L. Holford-Strevens and A. D. Vardi (eds), *The Worlds of Aulus Gellius*, 3–40, Oxford: Oxford University Press.

Thibault, J. C. (2018), *The Mystery of Ovid's Exile*, Berkeley, CA: University of California Press (orig. pub. 1964).

van der Velden, B. (2020), 'J. J. Hartman on Ovid's (Non-)Exile', *Mnemosyne*, 73 (2): 336–42.

Watts, W. J. (1976), 'Race Prejudice in the Satires of Juvenal', *Acta Classica*, 19: 83–104.

Whitmarsh, T. (2001a), *Greek Literature and the Roman Empire*, Oxford: Clarendon Press.

Whitmarsh, T. (2001b), '"Greece is the World": Exile and Identity in the Second Sophistic', in S. Goldhill (ed.), *Being Greek under Rome*, 269–305, Cambridge: Cambridge University Press.

Willers, D. (1996), 'Die neugestaltung Athens durch Hadrian: Hadrians panhellenisches Programm', *Antike Welt*, 27 (1): 3–17.

Williams, G. D. (1994), *Banished Voices: Readings in Ovid's Exile Poetry*, Cambridge: Cambridge University Press.

10

Dio of Prusa's Γετικά in the Context of the Ethnographic Production of His Age

Paolo Desideri

In the long preface of his *Olympic* speech, the philosophically-minded Bithynian sophist Dio recalls, among other things, that he has arrived at Olympia – the seat of the great Olympian games, where he is delivering his speech – having come from far away – that is, from a Roman military camp, presumably located in Moesia, to which he had moved 'desiring to see strong men contending for empire and power, and their opponents for freedom and native land'.[1] Although the date of this visit is not certain, it seems to me extremely reasonable to think that we are here at the beginning of Trajan's second Dacian campaign (105 CE)[2] – which coincides, more or less, with the Olympiads of 105 CE – and that, in delivering these words, Dio is strongly criticizing Trajan's imperialist politics against the Dacians. A number of arguments may be put forward to support this idea. First of all, it is true that Dio had a very good, perhaps even friendly, relationship with Trajan: but this does not mean that he felt committed to sharing all the political choices of the emperor. On the contrary, more than once he states that his duty, as a loyal adviser, is to speak to the emperor himself frankly, and without any complacency or flattery.[3] Thus, Dio could freely express his disapproval for a war which the Romans were apparently waging without any good reason. In fact, there is no doubt that the whole conceptual framework of Dio's *Olympic* is aimed at promoting an anti-militaristic idea, which is not just connected with the traditional pacifistic ideal of the Olympiads, but even goes so far as to push its author to embark, with the help of Phidias, the creator of the celebrated statue of the god in the Zeus temple of Olympia, on a harsh controversy with Homer on the best way of interpreting the religious meaning of Zeus, the 'father of men and gods'. In Dio's (and Phidias') opinion, Zeus' most genuine significance was the promotion of peace and concord among men, both Greeks (and Romans, of course) and barbarians.[4] Finally – and most importantly – Dio may have had a powerful personal reason for disagreeing with Trajan's war-like attitude against the Dacians, in particular. From Dio himself we know that after being exiled (or, if one prefers, marginalized by the upper echelons of the Roman political and intellectual elite),[5] he had decided to visit that people, which he preferred to call Getans,[6] passing from the city of Borysthenes, located in the north-western corner of Pontus Euxinus, via the Scythians, who lived in between;[7] and according to Philostratus' *Life*, Dio had not only travelled, during his exile, across the Dacian territory, but had also dedicated to them what Philostratus calls ἱστορία (*historia*) – which in fact more properly ought to be regarded as an ethnographical essay – Τά Γετικά.[8] This work is now lost, but its few fragments, preserved in Iordanes' *De origine actibusque Getarum* (written in 551 CE),[9] clearly reveal the author's strong admiration for and sympathy towards this proud and noble population, which had warmly welcomed him in a difficult period of his life.

We do not know exactly when Dio wrote his *Getica* or – even more importantly – when this work was published, but it can be reasonably assumed it was published after the end of Dio's exile, that is, when the once-famous intellectual had recovered his prestige and social status. It is difficult to imagine, nonetheless, that the spirit of this text differed significantly from that of his *Olympic* speech, in which the author expressed his belief that, 'concerning the nature of the gods in general, and especially that of the ruler of the universe', there is 'an idea regarding him and a conception of him common to the whole human race, to the Greeks and to the barbarians alike, a conception that is inevitable and innate in every creature endowed with reason';[10] in other words, the idea of a substantial unity of the human race, as far as such an important aspect of human civilization as religion is concerned, at least. Indeed, the scant remains of the *Getica* only confirm this idea, as I trust I convincingly explained a few years ago.[11] However, what must be underlined first is the connection that in the *Olympic* Dio *de facto* establishes between this general principle – which, in the same way as that of the affinity (*syngeneia*) between men and gods (77), is a well-known feature of Stoic thought[12] – and the idea that the religious feeling, precisely because of its universality, ought to become an instrument for the promotion of a general peace among men. From this point of view, two passages in the final part of Phidias' speech are particularly significant. Speaking of the correspondence that can be found between the irenic character of his Zeus and the traditional appellatives (*eponymiai*) of the god, Phidias insists, in the first passage, both on Φίλιος καὶ Ἑταιρεῖος – because, the artist says, 'the god brings all men together and wills that they be friends of one another and never enemy or foe' – and on that of Ξένιος, 'because we should not be unmindful even of strangers, nor regard any human being as an alien'.[13] Even more meaningful is the second passage, where Phidias speaks of the warlike elements of the representation of the god, which can be found in Homer together with, and actually more often than, the irenic ones. Here is his final comment on the Homeric sections where 'the god who sends grievous strife upon Greeks and barbarians so as to inspire tired and despairing men with unceasing love for war and battle' is represented: 'that god, I say, it was not possible to represent by my art, nor assuredly should I have ever desired to do so even had it been possible'.[14] The last sentence, in particular, is clear proof of the anti-militaristic spirit of Dio's speech, and implicitly confirms his criticism of Trajan's imperialistic aggression of the Dacians, as we have noted in the beginning of his speech.

The main lines of Dio's *Getica* can be retrieved from the already mentioned work by Iordanes on the Getae: meaning from the three passages where Dio – who in 9.58 is styled *storicus et antiquitatum diligentissimus inquisitor* (the historian and diligent investigator of ancient times) – is explicitly quoted, as well as those which, according to Jacoby, may plausibly be attributed to his work, even though Dio's name is not mentioned. To these passages another may possibly be added, as I endeavoured to argue in my above-mentioned essay on Dio's *Getica*: the one, also from the *Preface* of the *Olympicus*, in which Dio incidentally tells his audience that the region from which he has come is inhabited by the Getae or Mysi, 'as Homer, using the modern designation of the race, calls them'.[15] It seems likely that this reference to Homer was also present in the *Getica*, where we know that Dio, basing himself first of all on the ancient poet, traced the remote history of the inhabitants of the Danubian region (including the southern bank of the river), where in his own times the Getae (Dacians) were settled. Aiming at ennobling their origins, Dio laid claim to tracking down their ancestors in Homer's Mysi, who during the war of Troy were supposed to be settled in the westernmost part of Asia Minor, from where they evidently would afterwards migrate to Europe. It is easy to guess that this Homeric mention could be a good starting point on which to base the following statement, which Iordanes explicitly attributed to Dio: 'the Goths (sc. *Getae*) have always been wiser (*sapientiores*) than the other barbarians and were nearly like the Greeks, as Dio relates, who wrote their history and annals with a Greek pen'.[16] A statement like this can be considered a sort of general comment on the fundamental characteristics of Getan society, as Iordanes saw it, based mainly on Dio's portrayal. What I can say, limiting myself to a summary of the main elements of the analysis in my above-mentioned article, is that in reconstructing the history of the Getan people Dio underlined the managerial role which had been exercised by a number of great intellectual personalities (*eruditi*, in Iordanes' Latin): Zeuta, Zalmoxes, and finally Dicineus, who, in his capacity as an adviser to the king, succeeded in providing the Getan people with their characteristic philosophical temperament.[17] Thanks to the education received by these intellectuals, and especially by Dicineus, who lived from Sulla's times on, the Getae had been able to preserve their freedom from the Romans until Domitian's times – Caesar himself 'could not prevail against them, despite his frequent attempts'.[18] But Dicineus' activity as philosophical educator of his people was not just limited to the political level. As Iordanes points out, it included many other elements, such as ethics ('he restrained their barbarous customs'), physics ('[he] made them live naturally under laws of their own'), logic ('[he] made them skilled in reasoning beyond all other races'), practical knowledge (*practicen*),[19] 'persuading them to abound in good works', and especially theoretical knowledge (*theoreticen*); in fact, 'he urged them to contemplate the twelve signs and the courses of the planets passing through them, and the whole of astronomy'.[20]

A very gratifying picture of Dacian society before the Trajanic conquest, indeed! 'Think, I pray you – this is Iordanes'/Dio's comment – what pleasure it was for these brave men, when for a little space they had leisure from warfare, to be instructed in the teachings of philosophy! You might have seen one scanning the position of the heavens and another investigating the nature of plants and bushes. Here stood one who studied the waxing and waning of the moon, while still another regarded the labours of the sun and observed how those bodies, which were hastening to go toward the east, are whirled around and borne back to the west by the rotation of the heavens. When they had learned the reason, they were at rest.'[21] To this idyllic picture other elements may be added, like the importance in this society of the *Telebosteses*, the aristocratic elite of the population, which the same Dicineus reorganized, converting them into a sort of priestly order. In fact, 'he taught them theology, bidding them worship certain divinities and holy places, and he gave the name of *Pilleati* to the priests he ordained, I suppose because they offered sacrifice having their heads covered with tiaras, which we otherwise call *pillei*'.[22] In this way, Dicineus wanted to strengthen the role of religion in Getan society, while at the same time affirming his own role as a 'philosopher in politics' of Platonic memory.[23] In fact, Dicineus, Dio underlines, 'gained marvellous repute among the Goths, so that he ruled not only the common men but their kings';[24] exactly the role that Dio himself, after the end of his exile, would aspire to play with the Roman emperor – and the same that, according to one of Dio's speeches, the Persians associated with the

Mages, the Egyptians with their priests, the Indians with the Brahmans, or the Celts with the Druids.[25] Barbarian peoples, one could say: yes, but Dio evidently believed that even some of the barbarians could give the Greeks (and Romans) useful suggestions, not just the other way round. As far as political organization is concerned, these peoples – and in particular the Dacians, of whom Dio had personal experience – could teach the leading Graeco-Roman imperial elite the best way to keep tabs, thanks to a sort of alliance between philosophy and religion, on an autocratic regime, of which otherwise they risked to become, as Dio knew even too well, innocent victims. We have no way of ascertaining whether Trajan was somehow informed about Dio's *Getica*, or ever had any conversation with him on this subject – although a passage from Philostratus' Dio's *Vita*,[26] besides two at least of the Περὶ βασιλείας speeches, and many passages of the *Bithynians*, suggest a strong personal relationship between the two men.[27] What we know for sure is that at the conclusion of two subsequent campaigns the Roman emperor succeeded in killing the Dacian king Decebalus, in destroying the independence of the Dacians, and in transforming the region into a Roman province – not the best way, indeed, of following Dio's advice, if there had been any!

However, it is not absurd to think that Dio's evident sympathy for the Dacians and their social and political organization may have had some influence on the way one of the most important still extant Roman public monuments, Trajan's Column (dedicated in 113 CE), was conceived and achieved. It has long been observed that the 'Maestro delle Imprese di Traiano' (that is, the 'Master of Trajan's Deeds') – as Ranuccio Bianchi Bandinelli called the author of the celebrated helical frieze which, covering the entire column, tells the story of the Roman conquest of Dacia – 'is characterized by lively sympathy for the figures of the barbarians, which was not only respect for the defeated enemy, but perhaps "the expression of personal feelings of the artist, who as a provincial directly knew the misery of subjection to Rome" as well; and therefore went so far as "the glorification of the proud and unfortunate fighter for the independence of his people", Decebalus the king of the Dacians'.[28] Salvatore Settis is right, when saying that it is impossible to think that Dio's sympathy for the Dacians might come at the expense of his admiration for Trajan, an emperor whom – as we have just recalled – he considered a friend, and to whom he believed he could dare to make suggestions as to the best way to interpret his high role as governor of the entire ecumene – as Dio does in his Περὶ βασιλείας speeches. What I am not sure of, on the other hand, is that Dio was really convinced that a universal empire was the best possible solution to the problems of a peaceful coexistence of men on earth. Trajan's good governance was not enough to make one forget Domitian's quite recent arbitrariness and despotism: nor in any case, was an individual's or even the people's desire for empire and power a good reason to destroy another people's freedom – just to recall the terms in which the war between Romans and Dacians had to be considered, according to the emblematic formula used by Dio at the beginning of his *Olympic*. Was it not possible to conceive a world where different peoples could coexist on friendly terms, each of them preserving its political and social system, as well as its freedom? Perhaps the 'Maestro delle Imprese di Traiano' was of the same idea as Dio, and the only way he could express it in his imposing monument – which, after all, had to be approved and financed by the Roman government (or better said, by the emperor) – was to represent the losers, and in particular their king, with the most sympathetic and gratifying features; while, of course, retaining for the Romans and their chief commander, the Emperor Trajan, their superior formal status as brave fighters and glorious winners. What Dio could add, and did in fact, was to give, through his Γετικά, a picture of the Dacians' social, political, and religious organization that he had carefully observed during the years of his exile, preserving its memory, after the Romans had destroyed it, for better times to come.

In this way, Dio renewed the ancient interest for 'ethnography' mixed with history (as we might say, following Philostratus' definition of this work),[29] which had originally inspired Herodotus in his *Histories*, and in the subsequent centuries accompanied, first, the Greek-Macedonian expansion to the East, and at the end the Roman penetration among the barbarian peoples of the West. It is nowadays established, after more or less thirty years of fresh research in this field, that what we are used to calling 'ancient ethnography' does not really exist; or rather, that it does not exist in the scientific sense we now give to the term 'ethnography', and (more important) that the interests we consider to be associated with it have changed over time, in the long course of Greek and Roman history.[30] As for Dio's work, I believe that – to the extent we are prepared to accept his paternity of Iordanes' passages examined above – the Bithynian author, who considered the Getae *pene omnibus barbaris sapientiores ... Grecisque pene consimiles*,[31] was not interested at all (as Herodotus was[32]) in finding in a foreign people elements that might serve to better define, by contrast, his Greek identity. Rather, what Dio – as a real or presumed exile – was looking for, in visiting a people that lived outside of the empire's borders, was a more authentic society than the political one from which he had so inexplicably and arbitrarily been expelled, and which appeared to him now as an unnatural world, dominated by false values: the message – easily recognizable above all in his *Diogenics* – that in his thirteenth speech (*In Athens, about his banishment*) he tells of having proclaimed in that period.[33] In other words, confronting foreign, so-called barbarian, people and customs meant to him finding a way to realize how worthless the lifestyle he had until then shared was, and possibly experiencing a meaningful alternative to it: a more radical and long-lasting experience – but not so different from the one Dio imagines (in his *Euboicus, or Hunter*) having lived in one of the most remote areas of Euboea, when saved from a shipwreck by a generous shepherd, a complete stranger to the city's life, and to the indifferent and egoistic frame of mind of its inhabitants.[34] These real or imagined experiences – like others, of which we can find traces in other speeches – give a clear indication of the way the ancient ethnographic discourse could be adapted, according to Dio, to the needs of his times. While proposing an alternative model of social, political, and cultural organization, it served to denounce by contrast the deficiencies of the Roman autocratic system, in which abuses and violence from an uncontrollable power, introducing false values and expectations into men's minds, corrupted the natural sociability among them.[35] In fact, what the Getan society revealed was basically a system in which the kings were assisted by great intellectuals, who not only controlled the exercise of their power, but were able to suggest to the people the expected religious and moral behaviour as well: so that the people respected the kings, while preserving their own freedom and independence.

From Dio's *Getica* to Tacitus' *Agricola* and *Germania*

At more or less the same time that Dio conceived his *Getica* – that is, at the beginning of Trajan's era – the much better known Roman senator and writer Cornelius Tacitus began his historiographical career with the two 'minor' works *De vita et moribus Iulii Agricolae* and *De origine et situ Germanorum*, in both of which what can be called an ethnographic interest plays an important role.[36] We do not know with certainty which of the two was composed first, but it seems highly probable that it was the *Agricola*, not least because of the more complicated structure in which the ethnographic interest itself is inserted in this work – what might depend on its being situated in a preceding stage of the development of Tacitus' intellectual laboratory.[37] Of course, our job now is not to analyse the *Agricola*'s structure as a whole, but simply to examine the role the ethnographic element itself plays in its context. Therefore, it will be sufficient to recall that

Tacitus' primary interest in this work – which is in principle a postponed, as it were, funeral oration – was to ensure the memory of one of the most important characters of the previous generation, the author's father-in-law Iulius Agricola, who had died in the last years of Domitian's rule, the emperor himself being suspected of having caused his death. In the *Agricola*'s introductory section, Tacitus declares that in those years, due to the dark, oppressive atmosphere imposed by a political regime which had banished, together with the philosophers, 'every noble pursuit', it had become dangerous even to praise the virtues of the great men: so that – the author underlines – 'we witnessed the extremes of slavery (*servitus*), wherein our "inquisitors" have deprived us even of the give and take of conversation'.[38] 'But now at last [i.e. with the new emperors Nerva and Traian, who are explicitly mentioned] *redit animus* (heart is coming back to us)' – Tacitus says, that is he has now, after Domitian's death, the impression that the possibility of uniting 'things long incompatible, Empire and freedom (*principatum ac libertatem*)' is becoming a reality (3.1). That is why he has finally decided to write a proper memoir of his wife's deceased father. It is immediately evident that the familiar piety, which gives the cue to the commemoration of a kinsman, is closely intertwined with the political intent to denounce the prevarications of the imperial power, as is confirmed soon after, when the historian begins his eulogy recalling that Agricola's father, Iulius Graecinus, member of the senatorial order, had been put to death by Caligula for refusing to impeach Marcus Silanus (4.1). From the very beginning of his work, at any rate, Tacitus makes clear that one of Agricola's qualities had been to be able to moderate (*ex sapientia modus*: 4.3) his intense desire for glory (first of all, military glory), in order to avoid any possible jealousy from the emperor – Nero, at that time (5.3). Agricola's self-restraint becomes increasingly clear in Tacitus' story of the years when the young officer covered the long series of military and administrative assignments, in Britannia and Aquitania, that eventually culminated in his appointment as governor of Britannia itself in 78 CE (9.6): a governorship which was to last ten years, during which he performed his most glorious feats. Yet, this quality was not enough to save Agricola from Domitian's envy: which is, as we will see, the leitmotiv of the final section of this work.

Moving forward, Tacitus declares his intention to describe *Britanniae situm populosque* (the geographical position of Britain and the races which inhabit it) (10.1): but what follows is not actually a geographic and/or ethnographic picture, designed to offer the readers the frame of reference for the subsequent narration of Agricola's military campaigns (18–38). Tacitus himself says that he absolutely does not want to compete with previous authors in this field, regardless of the fact that he will profit, of course, from the new knowledge that has been acquired precisely thanks to those campaigns.[39] Rather, what we have is a set of political and ideological reflections, whose main objective is to demonstrate the general principles that peace enervates a people, and that military courage goes hand in hand with freedom.[40] The history of the Roman conquest of Britannia – whose final and decisive steps were due to Agricola – was, according to Tacitus, a perfect illustration of these principles, as far as the behaviour of the Britons is concerned. The historian observes, in fact, that at the beginning, the Britons were similar to the Gauls, but prouder than them, 'not having been emasculated by long years of peace':[41] or, in other words, thanks to their quite recent entrance into the Roman world. In fact, Agricola (in Tacitus' account) had been particularly able, just at the beginning of his administration of the newly established province (43 CE), to turn the so-called advantages of peace into a superior instrument of permanent enslavement. The previous *legati* – including the excellent commander Petilius Cerialis, under whom Agricola himself had militated – had often conducted successful military operations (Tacitus says) but could not curb the greed and violence of their subordinates and troops, which inevitably had fuelled the impatience and the desire for revenge of the populations won on the battlefield: bloody riots and continued military upheavals had been the consequences. On the contrary, in the first two years of his appointment the new commander-in-chief Julius Agricola, holding back his victorious army and strengthening its discipline, and at the same time improving the Roman system of provincial administration, succeeded in showing the Britons that the Roman victory could produce a better standard of life: in this way, he 'cast a halo over such days of peace as the carelessness or harshness of previous governors had made not less dreadful than war'.[42] Then we have the famous passage (21), in which Tacitus summarizes this 'strategy of peace', which was in fact an acculturation, or assimilation, strategy towards the local populations. In particular, Agricola promoted the dissemination of an urban model, and recommended a liberal education for the children of the leaders, so that the Britons, 'who used to reject the Latin language began to aspire to rhetoric'. And finally, 'the wearing of our dress became a distinction, and a toga came into fashion, and little by little the Britons were seduced into alluring vices: to the lounge, the bath, the well-appointed dinner table'.[43] Tacitus' well-known comment – 'the simple natives gave the name of "civilization" (*humanitas*) to this factor of their slavery' – ends this crucial passage.

In what follows (22–38), we have a detailed description of Agricola's military activities from the third year of his governorship until his final victory at *mons*

Graupius, in the northernmost part of Britain. From our point of view, particularly interesting is the Briton commander's famous speech before the battle (30–32), where we find again the idea that remoteness is the most powerful protection against servitude – in Calgacus' words, 'we (sc. the Caledonians), the noblest souls in all Britain, the dwellers in its inner shrine, had never seen the shores of slavery and had preserved our very eyes from the desecration and contamination of tyranny'[44] – and the famous anti-Roman formula: 'To plunder, butcher, steal, these things they misname empire: they make a desolation and they call it peace' (a renewed denunciation of the falsehood of the term 'peace', as well as of 'empire').[45] More conventional is Agricola's speech (33–34), which reminds his soldiers of their loyalty and energy in fighting for seven years *auspiciis imperii Romani* (under the auspices of the Roman Empire) and finally subduing the Britons; and proclaims before them how glorious it would be even to perish, if necessary, 'at the world's edge and nature's end'.[46] The juxtaposition of the two speeches, in any case, can be considered the best commentary of the above-mentioned synthetic definition of the Romano-Dacian confrontation: 'strong men contending for empire and power, and their opponents for freedom and native land'. But, as I have mentioned previously, it is in the final part of his work (39 ff.) that one can find the real key to Tacitus' interest in the relationship *libertas/servitus* (freedom/servitude), such as is evidenced in his representation of what I called Agricola's 'strategy of peace' towards the barbarian Britons.[47] Agricola's fate after coming back to Rome, that is Domitian's envy and masked hostility towards him, his marginalization, and at the end his death (in 93 CE) – supposedly due to poisoning by the emperor's emissaries – proves according to Tacitus that a people's freedom is at risk if military virtues are not properly appreciated and honoured. At this point an individual course of life like Agricola's becomes a mirror of Roman society, and retracing it a way to remind the new *principes* of the need not to allow their power to go to the detriment of the people's, and above all the most prominent men's, freedom. But the parallelism between the *servitus* of the peoples subjugated by the Romans, including the Britons, and that of the Romans themselves submitted to Domitian's arbitrary rule – a parallelism which has so well been evidenced by Myles Lavan as a prominent characteristic of the *Agricola*[48] – must be further specified. Tacitus does not say that abuse of power and political arbitrariness are inevitable consequences of a militaristic and imperialistic policy, nor does he condemn Agricola's 'strategy of peace'. On the contrary, in his opinion this is instead the right way to confront barbarian peoples who must, willingly or not, be civilized. It is true that this means for them to be enslaved to the victorious people; but *regere imperio populos* (to rule the nations) is still, for Agricola (and Tacitus), the Romans' god-inspired mission (and, on this point, the difference from Dio's way of thinking is absolute).[49] What must be avoided, on the part of the heads of state – in our case the emperors – is weakening the strength of this commitment through disavowing or disregarding the virtues of the men who are engaged in this difficult task.

Tacitus, in any case, does not share the idea that one ought to frontally oppose an unjust power, or a tyranny. For him, Agricola, with his more than once recalled modesty, had been a role model from this point of view too, as he refused to adopt any behaviour that would expose him to the risk of becoming a victim of the regime. 'Let those whose way it is to admire only things forbidden learn from him that great men can live even under bad rulers; and that submission and moderation, if animation and energy go with them, reach the same pinnacle of fame, whither more often men have climbed, with no profit to the State, by the steep path of a pretentious death' (42.4).[50] This final comment – which is, incidentally, extremely ungenerous towards some of those same great characters of whose deaths Tacitus regrets having been co-responsible as a senator[51] – reaffirms conclusively the principle that a great Roman's primary duty was to ensure the Roman Empire's integrity. Conquering the barbarians meant not only spreading civilization through the world, but, in many border areas inhabited by hostile peoples, protecting the empire's security as well. The main reason for Domitian's hostility towards Agricola was in fact that he envied the general who had been able to report in Britannia the successes he had vainly tried to achieve himself in Moesia, Dacia, Germania, and Pannonia – that is, along the Rhine-Danubian frontier (41.2). And it cannot be excluded that, reviving his father-in-law's military greatness, as opposed to Domitian's inadequacy, Tacitus also intended to propose a pattern of behaviour to Trajan himself, indirectly suggesting to him the opportunity of strengthening his prestige through military accomplishments – a suggestion that, as is well-known, the new emperor, who was after all a great general, was only too ready to accept (although not, as we will see, on the German frontier)! In conclusion, it is evident that between Tacitus' interest in the Britons and Dio's in the Getans (or Dacians) there is a great difference, due perhaps to the fact that Tacitus had not experienced first-hand the brutality of the emperor's power: *dignitatem nostram . . . a Domitiano longius provectam non abnuerim* ('I cannot deny that my political career . . . has been carried further by Domitian'), he honestly recognizes when starting his first 'great' work, the *Histories* (1.1). In Tacitus' representation of the Britons there is a very small trace of Dio's sympathy for a people whom, although barbarian, the latter does not hesitate to define 'almost Greek'; whose intellectual interests he highly appreciates, as well as their military prowess; whose political organization – in particular the importance of the role of the kings' advisors – he even considers exemplary. It is easy to believe, as we have said above, that Dio, who spent many years among the Getans as an exile, would never have wished them to be attacked and subdued by the Roman imperial power, and even less for their culture to be assimilated to the Roman, or even Greek, culture – as implied clearly in the *Olympicus* passage quoted at the beginning. Tacitus, on the other hand, would not have accepted the idea that the Britons would have escaped the expansion of the empire, which in his opinion was after all the best fate they could expect, even at the cost of losing their freedom: so, the historian's ethnographic interest in the *Agricola* was *de facto* stifled by his imperialistic perspective.

But this way of thinking was destined to undergo a dramatic change in the *Germania*, where clearly ethnography is not, as in the *Agricola*, just one of the elements serving to connote the personality of a hero, the writer's father-in-law, who is the real protagonist of the story. In the new work, on the contrary, what can be called an ethnographic description constitutes the very centre of the author's interest.[52] Tacitus does not explain, explicitly, his reason(s) for writing it,[53] but at least one point is certain: the Germans, in his opinion, are a real problem for Rome, as is easily detectable in the famous phrase *maneat, quaeso, duretque gentibus, si non amor nostri, at certe odium sui* (long may it last, I pray, and persist among the nations, this – if not love of us – at least hatred for each other), which opens Tacitus' final comment on a bloody battle between the Germans themselves, which the Roman historian mentions with a sort of sadistic complacency (33.2).[54] Tacitus does not dare to say here that the Roman policy with the Germans ought to be to conquer and pacify them, as Agricola had done with the Britons (with the phrase *amor nostri* possibly the Britons' attitude towards the Romans, after they had been subdued, is defined). The writer openly reveals what can be called real anxiety for a possible military threat from those populations: 'for that length of time has the conquest of Germany been in process!' he says, recalling the first Romano-German (Cimbrian) battle, in Marius' times, 'two hundred and ten years ago' (37.2); before giving, immediately afterwards, a short summary of the countless, bloody, and indecisive clashes that had taken place between the two peoples, both in Italy and in Germany (37.4). It is probably correct to assume that in writing the *Germania* Tacitus intended to reinforce the suggestion to Trajan to take more decisive military action against the Germans,[55] which is implied in the already mentioned anodyne passage of the *Agricola* (41.2). But the impression is that now such a suggestion is aimed at a military policy of effective containment, not at a grandiose action of conquest. Not by chance, Tacitus' main concern is with the fundamental role the German society assigns to war – the very centre of that people's interests and way of life, in his opinion – which seems like an invitation not to embark on a risky attempt at global submission of what, in reality, is not a people, but a system of countless and pugnacious peoples. That is why Tacitus underlines the severe sanctions the Germans impose on the warriors who abandon their shields (6.4); the social importance of the generals (7.1); the military aspects of family ties, as regards women, too (7.2; 8.1; 18.2f.); the symbolic value of giving weapons to the young (13.1); the unbearable shame for surviving one's commander in battle (14.1); the military character of their ludic shows (24.1). Furthermore, in more general terms, the reader is constantly reminded that it is just the pervasiveness of this militaristic dimension – which also includes the special role of religion and of its officers, the priests (7.1; 10.1; 11.2; 40.3, regarding the Longobards) – that ensures the personal and collective freedom of the Germans. The fact, anyway, is that Trajan, in spite of his well-known propensity for war, accurately avoided any major military involvement in Germany!

Tacitus, on the other hand, is also fascinated by a large number of positive aspects of German society, which corroborate its military strength. The historian strongly appreciates, in general terms, the *boni mores* (good habits) of the Germans, as opposed to the Romans' *bonae leges* (good laws),[56] which have no chance of effectively stopping the growing corruption of the social body's customs .[57] We can find here some affinity with Dio's description of Getan society, as traceable in Iordanes. This is not to say that Tacitus has the same liking for the Germans as Dio has for the Getans (Dacians)[58] – a people that Dio loves, as we have seen, for their intellectual interests and socio-political organization rather than for their military performances. What the two authors apparently have in common is the idea that, outside of the 'civilized' world in which they live – the Roman Empire, the world of παιδεία or *humanitas*, but of autocracy and arbitrariness as well – different worlds exist, governed by different, more natural, laws and/or customs. Although the reason(s) why they are interested in such foreign worlds are diverse, they are equally stimulated to depict their features, highlighting similarities and differences with their own world: the general common element to emerge is that both the Getan and the German worlds are configured as less artificial than that which the two authors are accustomed to. Dio's perspective on the Getans, on the other hand, is strongly influenced not only – as we have already observed – by the circumstances which gave occasion to his stay among that people; one also has to consider his marked philosophical temper, strengthened perhaps by these same circumstances. From this point of view, it is evident that an important role in his appreciation of the Getans is played by the stoic philosophy, which, in the exasperated version of a cynic way of life, he adopted during his period of exile. One of the prominent elements of that philosophy, in fact, was cosmopolitanism – that is, the idea of a natural affinity of all the men, and of the secondariness of the political bodies, whose fundamental objective is to fragment the human world community into different states and social groups. From this general principle, the aversion to any form of conflict among peoples necessarily follows, as well as a way of conceiving the supreme God as something which brings them together, and does not divide: the idea that, as we have seen, is at the very centre of Dio's *Olympicus*. An ideology like this is clearly inconsistent with any state whatsoever's imperialistic perspectives: peaceful coexistence of all men and human groups, in full mutual respect for different customs and laws, ought to be the general law of human life on the earth; close observation of 'others' could even be useful for improving every single one's – individual or group – behaviour and political structure.

Tacitus apparently shares a completely different ideology in the *Agricola*, where he openly declares his sincere belief in the imperial mission of the Romans; whereas in the *Germania*, resigned as he is to acknowledging the impossibility of subduing that people – or complex of peoples – he is concentrated on describing their customs and values, which in the end serves only to explain the causes of this impossibility. What can be said conclusively is, perhaps, that for both authors the ethnographic research and writing was, in different ways, an instrument for grasping one of the great historical problems of their age: that of the prospected exhaustion of the Roman imperial push, which would finally take place under Hadrian. Hadrian's military police would try to ensure the empire's security through the strengthening of the *limes*, conceived as a line of defence against attempts of penetration into its territory by external peoples. Trajan's conquest of Dacia, in the preceding generation – which was Dio's and Tacitus' generation – was the last episode of the Roman conquest, and durable occupation, of a barbarian land. Dio's ethnographic work, as we have seen, was a way of strongly criticizing this military enterprise. As for Tacitus, we do not know what he may have thought about it; but the fact that he did not keep his promise, made at the beginning of the *Historiae*, to write, in his old age, the story of Nerva's and Trajan's times, may have been, at least in part, due to his disappointment for Trajan's renouncing any attempt to provide a final solution to the problem of Germany.

Notes

1 Dio 12.20, ἐπιθυμῶν ἰδεῖν ἄνδρας ἀγωνιζομένους ὑπὲρ ἀρχῆς καὶ δυνάμεως, τοὺς δὲ ὑπὲρ ἐλευθερίας τε καὶ πατρίδος·. Unless stated otherwise, all translations are from the Loeb Classical Library editions.

2 Desideri 1978: 207 and 279, n. 49; 2019: 46, n. 16.

3 E.g. 3.2, 13; 4.15.

4 See Desideri 2019 (2013): chapter 12. Regarding Dio's anti-militaristic approach – which can also be retrieved in a few other of his speeches – see Gangloff 2006: 294–9; 2009: 25–6.

5 On Dio's 'exile', see Desideri 2019.

6 Which is how 'some Greek writers' called the Dacians: see Dio Cass. (Xiphil.) 67.6.2.

7 Dio 36.1: Ἐτύγχανον μὲν ἐπιδημῶν ἐν Βορυσθένει τὸ θέρος, ὡς τότε εἰσέπλευσα μετὰ τὴν φυγήν, βουλόμενος ἐλθεῖν, ἐὰν δύνωμαι, διὰ Σκυθῶν εἰς Γέτας, ὅπως θεάσωμαι τἀκεῖ πράγματα ὁποῖά ἐστι (I happened to be visiting in Borysthenes during the summer, for I had sailed there then, after my exile, with the purpose of making my way, if possible, through Scythia to the Getan country, in order to observe conditions there). On the circumstances of this journey, see Desideri 2019: 188, n. 17 and n. 18.

8 Philostr., *VS* 1.7, ὡς δὲ καὶ ἱστορίαν ἱκανὸς ἦν ξυγγράφειν, δηλοῖ τὰ Γετικά, καὶ γὰρ δὴ καὶ ἐς Γέτας ἦλθεν, ὁπότε ἠλᾶτο (that he had also a talent for writing history is proved by his Treaty on the Getae; he did in fact travel as far as the Getae during his wandering as an exile). Judging by the few extant fragments, the work mixed the story of the events with the description of the costumes.

9 Not necessarily through Cassiodorus' lost *Historia Gothorum*. Dio's fragments were collected by Felix Jacoby 1958 in his *FGrHist*, III C *Ethnographie*. IX *Geten und Goten* (707 Dion von Prusa); but the main work had already been carried out by H. von Arnim in the *Preface* of the second volume of his Dio's edition (Arnim 1896: IV ff.). For a recent edition of Iordanes' *Getica*, see Grillone 2017. Iordanes' translations come from Mierow 1908.

10 Dio 12.27, Περὶ δὴ θεῶν τῆς τε καθόλου φύσεως καὶ μάλιστα τοῦ πάντων ἡγεμόνος πρῶτον μὲν καὶ ἐν πρώτοις δόξα καὶ ἐπίνοια κοινὴ τοῦ ξύμπαντος ἀνθρωπίνου γένους, ὁμοίως μὲν Ἑλλήνων, ὁμοίως δὲ βαρβάρων, ἀναγκαία καὶ ἔμφυτος ἐν παντὶ τῷ λογικῷ γινομένη (the expression ἀνθρωπίνου γένους appears again in 65). Dio (12.39) confirms this belief at the end of this section of his speech, where he defines the original δόξα καὶ ὑπόληψις about deity οὐ κατὰ πλάνην συστᾶσαν οὐδὲ ὡς ἔτυχεν, ἀλλὰ πάνυ ἰσχυρὰν καὶ ἀέναον ἐκ τοῦ παντὸς χρόνου καὶ παρὰ πᾶσι τοῖς ἔθνεσιν ἀρξαμένην καὶ διαμένουσαν, σχεδόν τι κοινὴν καὶ δημοσίαν τοῦ λογικοῦ γένους ([an idea] that was not framed confusedly nor yet at random, but has been exceedingly potent and persistent since the beginning of time, and has arisen among

all nations and still remains, being, one may almost say, a common and general endowment of rational beings).

11 Desideri 2019 (2016): chapter 10.

12 See Cic., *Fin.* 3.64 (= *SVF* III 333); *Leg.* 1.23; Sen., *Ot.* 4.1; etc.

13 Dio 12.76, Φίλιος δὲ καὶ Ἑταιρεῖος, ὅτι πάντας ἀνθρώποις ξυνάγει καὶ βούλεται φίλους εἶναι ἀλλήλοις, ἐχθρὸν δὲ ἢ πολέμιον οὐδένα οὐδενός, Ἱκέσιος δέ, ὡς ἂν ἐπήκοός τε καὶ ἵλεως τοῖς δεομένοις, Φύξιος δὲ διὰ τὴν τῶν κακῶν ἀπόφυξιν, Ξένιος δέ, ὅτι δεῖ μηδὲ τῶν ξένων ἀμελεῖν μηδὲ ἀλλότριον ἡγεῖσθαι ἀνθρώπων μηδένα.

14 Dio 12.78, (τὸν θεὸν) ἐπιπέμποντα ἔριν ἀργαλέαν Ἕλλησι καὶ βαρβάροις, <ὥστε> ἔρωτα ἐμβάλλειν πολέμου καὶ μάχης ἄπαυστον κάμνουσιν ἀνθρώποις καὶ ἀπειρηκόσιν· . . . οὐκ ἦν διὰ τῆς τέχνης μιμεῖσθαι· οὐ μὴν οὐδὲ παρὸν ἠθέλησά γ᾽ ἄν ποτε.

15 Dio 12.16, τῆς Γετῶν χώρας ἢ Μυσῶν, ὥς φησιν Ὅμηρος κατὰ τὴν νῦν ἐπίκλησιν τοῦ ἔθνους (it is evident that Dio identifies the Homeric Mysi with the modern Moesi). The Homeric passage is *Il.* 2.858; cf. 14.4–5.

16 Iord., *Get.* 5.40 (= *FGrHist*, n. 707 F1), *pene omnibus barbaris Gothi sapientiores semper extiterunt Grecisque pene consimiles, ut refert Dio, qui historias eorum annalesque Greco stilo composuit*; Iordanes himself says (9.58) that the Getae and Gothi are the same people (regarding this confusion, which after all Iordanes shares with many other writers in Late Antiquity, see Iordache 1983: 324–8).

17 The best known of these characters is Zalmoxes (or Zalmoxis), whom many other ancient sources mention; see Dana 2011.

18 Iord., *Get.* 5.68 (= *FGrHist*, n. 707 F4, Anhang), *Caesar vero, qui sibi primus omnium Romanum vindicavit imperium et pene omnem mundum suae dicioni subegit omniaque regna perdomuit, adeo ut extra nostro urbe in oceani sinu repositas insulas occuparet, et nec nomen Romanorum auditu qui noverant, eos Romanis tributarios faceret, Gothos tamen crebro pertemptans nequivit subicere* (then came Caesar, the first of all the Romans to assume imperial power and to subdue almost the whole world, who conquered all kingdoms and even seized islands lying beyond our world, reposing in the bosom of Ocean. He made tributary to the Romans those that knew not the Roman name even by hearsay, and yet was unable to prevail against the Goths, despite his frequent attempts).

19 This term, as well as the preceding *ethicam*, *fysicam*, *logicam*, and *theoreticen* which follows, are clearly original calques from (Dio's?) Greek (*TLL*, vol. 10.2.1 [1980–95], *c.* 371, s.v. *practicus*, 1a, ll.68 ff., speaks of *partes philosophiae more insolito explicatas* (parts of philosophy explained in an unusual way)).

20 Iord., *Get.* 5.69 (= *FGrHist*, n. 707 F4 Anhang), *Nam ethicam eos erudiens barbaricos mores conpescuit; fysicam tradens naturaliter propriis legibus vivere fecit . . .; logicam instruens rationis eos supra ceteras gentes fecit expertes; practicen ostendens in bonis actibus conversare suasit; theoreticen demonstrans signorum duodecem et per ea*

planetarum cursus omnemque astronomiam contemplari edocuit, etc. On the method of retrieving Dio's materials from Iordanes' complicated texts, see Desideri 2019 (2016): 192 ff.

21 Iord., *Get.* 5.70, *Qualis erat, rogo, voluptas, ut viri fortissimi, quando ab armis quantolumcumque vacassent, doctrinis philosophicis inbuebantur? Videris unum caeli positionem, alium herbarum fruticumque explorare naturas, istum lunae commoda incommodaque, illum solis labores adtendere et quomodo rotatu caeli raptos retro reduci ad partem occiduam, qui ad orientalem plagam ire festinant, ratione accepta quiescere* (Jacoby brackets this passage, considering it a comment by Iordanes rather than a fragment of Dio's).

22 Iord., *Get.* 5.71 (= *FGrHist*, n. 707 F4 Anhang), *Elegit namque ex eis tunc nobilissimos prudentioresque viros, quos theologiam instruens, numina quaedam et sacella venerare suasit fecitque sacerdotes, nomen illis pilleatorum contradens, ut reor, quia opertis capitibus tyaris, quos pilleos alio nomine nuncupamus, litabant*; on *Pilleati*, see Iordache 1983: 332–3.

23 On Dacian religion, see Carbó García 2013.

24 Ibid., *mirabilis apud eos [*sc. *Gothos] enituit, ut non solum mediocribus, immo et regibus imperaret*; on the Platonic ascendancy of such an idea, see Desideri 2019 (2018): 302–4.

25 Dio 49.7 ff. (see Desideri 1978: 286 ff.).

26 See Desideri 2019 (1991): 45.

27 See Desideri 1978: 264, 376, 382–7; 2019 (1991): 54 ff.; 2019 (2013): 220; 2019 (2017): 151.

28 Settis 1988: 100 (and 230), quoting Bianchi Bandinelli 1969: 242 and 249; on the artist's sympathy for the Dacians, see also Mandruzzato 2010.

29 See Philostratus' passage *supra*, n. 8, and the sections of historical relevance which can be found among the Dionean fragments of Jordanes (see *FGrHist* n. 707 *cit., passim*).

30 For a recent survey of the set of problems related to the (dubious) concept of 'ancient ethnography', see Woolf 2011: 13–17 ('ethnography was never regarded in antiquity as an autonomous discipline': 15); Almagor and Skinner 2013: 1–12; Tufano 2014 (a review of Skinner 2012, which provides a very useful expanded overview of the most recent literature on the subject).

31 *Supra*, n. 16.

32 Hartog 1992 (1980).

33 Dio 13.13 ff.

34 See also Dio's tale (1.50) of his wanderings (still during his exile) in the Peloponnesian country, 'among shepherds and hunters'; for Dio's polemic against the town, in general terms, see Desideri 2019 (2000): chapter 9. One could also think of a 'utopian' nuance of such Dionean passages: see Bost-Pouderon 2008.

35 For the *Borysthenitic* (36), which cannot be fully examined now, see Desideri 1978: 318–23 and 2019 (2018): 299–302.

36 Both works have been quite recently edited by Sergio Audano, with very rich introductory essays and commentary (in addition to an Italian translation): Audano 2017 (*Agricola*) and 2020 (*Germania*).

37 For the use of this term I am indebted to Devillers 2014; for the complexity of the *Agricola*'s structure, see Audano 2017: XVI–XXX.

38 Tac., *Agr.* 2.3; on the situation in Rome in Domitian's last years (in particular as regards the 'philosophical opposition'), see Desideri 2019 (2017): 149–54.

39 Ibid. 10.1, *rerum fide tradentur* (there will be found only a faithful representation of facts); see also 10.6 *naturam Oceani atque aestus neque quaerere huius operis est, ac multi rettulere* (the characters and tides of the Ocean it is beyond the function of this work to investigate, and many have recorded them). Concerning this passage (and more generally the *Agricola*'s ethnographic section), see Woolf 2011: 89–92.

40 Ibid.11.4, *amissa virtute pariter ac libertate* (about the Gauls).

41 Ibid. *plus tamen ferociae Britanni praeferunt, ut quos nondum longa pax emollierit.*

42 Ibid., 20.1, *egregiam famam paci circumdedit, quae vel incuria vel intolerantia priorum haud minus quam bellum timebatur*; see also 20.2, *invitamenta pacis ostentare* (referred to Agricola).

43 To this new attitude of the Britons towards Rome possibly Tacitus alludes when speaking, in *Germ.* 33.2, of *amor nostri* (love for us – evidently, as a consequence of assimilation): see *supra*, 202, with Audano 2020: LI.

44 *Agr.* 30.2, *nobilissimi totius Britanniae eoque in ipsis penetralibus siti nec ulla servientium litora aspicientes, oculos quoque a contactu dominationis inviolatos habebamus.*

45 Ibid. 30.5, *auferre trucidare rapere falsis nominibus imperium, atque ubi solitudinem faciunt, pacem appellant.*

46 Ibid. 33.6, *nec inglorium fuerit in ipso terrarum ac naturae fine cecidisse.*

47 The term appears in *Agr.* 11.1, 16.1 and 3, 33.1.

48 Lavan 2011.

49 On Tacitus' sharing this traditional Roman ideology, see Audano 2017: XXXI–XXXV, 106.

50 This passage is notoriously paralleled by the comment on Thrasea Paetus' behaviour in *Ann.* 14.12.2, *sibi causam periculi fecit, ceteris libertatis initium non praebuit* (creating a source of danger for himself, but implanting no germ of independence in his colleagues).

51 45.2, *mox nostrae duxere Helvidium in carcerem manus; nos Mauricum Rusticumque divisimus; nos innocenti sanguine Senecio perfudit* ('a little while and our hands it was which dragged Helvidius to his dungeon; we it was who put asunder Mauricus and

Rusticus; we it was who were bathed in Senecio's innocent blood'). See also 2.1; on this (and other) dramatic inconsistencies in Tacitus' political thought, see Giua 2016.

52 Always within the limits (see *supra*, 196) in which it is possible to speak of ethnography in ancient literature; see Woolf 2013: 133 ('There was no ethnography [of religion] in antiquity'), 136. On Tacitus' *Germania*, see Rives 1999; Woolf 2011: 99–105.

53 For a review of the various hypotheses which have been formulated, see Rives 1999: 48–58; Audano 2020: LXVII–LXXVI.

54 *Germ.* 33.2; the phrase ends with *quando vergentibus imperii fatis nihil iam praestare fortuna maius potest quam hostium discordiam* (since now that the destinies of the Empire have passed their zenith, Fortune can guarantee us nothing better than discord among our foes), which, not only in my opinion, is a sort of confession of the extreme difficulty of the military situation of the northern sector of the empire at that time, as Tacitus saw them (for the different interpretations of this passage, see Yavetz 1999: 108–10; and also Audano 2020: LXXII–LXXIV).

55 Audano 2020 gets to the point of titling his introductory essay *La Germania: una proposta geopolitica per Traiano*; but if the *Germania* is to be considered as 'una sorta di *suasoria* in veste geo-etnografica' (a sort of suasoria in a geo-ethnographic guise; ibid., LXXVIII), it must be admitted that it would have been better to define more clearly the content of that *suasio*.

56 *Germ.* 19.2 (closing a section where the German wives' modesty is considered); in the *Annals* Tacitus will speak of 'the infinite number and variety of (Roman) laws' (*multitudinem infinitam ac varietatem legum*, 3.25.2), which had been not only useless, but even harmful for public and private morality; see Hammer 2014: 325–31 for a penetrating analysis of the political aspects of this criticism, which resolves itself in a denunciation of the perverse effects of despotism on the mechanisms of individual psychology.

57 For a complete review of the elements of Tacitus' 'moralism' in the *Germania* (in the context of a much longer tradition, which can be traced in other Tacitean works too), see Audano 2020: XXXIII–L.

58 On the limits of Tacitus' appreciation, see Audano 2020: XVI.

Bibliography

Almagor, E. and J. Skinner, eds (2013), *Ancient Ethnography: New Approaches*, London: Bloomsbury Academic.

Arnim, H. von, ed. (1893 and 1896), *Dionis Prusaensis quem vocant Chrysostomum quae extant omnia*, vols I and II, Berlin: Weidmann.

Audano, S., trans. (2017), *Tacito, Agricola*, Ariccia: RL.

Audano, S., trans. (2020), *Tacito, Germania*, Cles: RL.
Bianchi Bandinelli, R. (1969), *Roma: L'arte romana nel centro del potere*, Milano: Rizzoli.
Bost-Pouderon, C. (2008), 'Ethnographie et utopie chez Dion Chrysostome (*Or.* 35, 18–22 et *Or.* 7, 1–80), *Kentron*, 24: 105–21.
Carbó García, J. R. (2013), 'Dii romani vs. Dii daci: La disolución de la religión dacia en la conquista romana', *Arys*, 11: 227–38.
Dana, D. (2011), *Fontes ad Zalmoxin pertinentes – Izvoare privitoare la Zalmoxis*, Iași: Editura Universității 'Alexandru Ioan Cuza'.
Desideri, P. (1978), *Dione di Prusa: Un intellettuale greco nell'impero romano*, Messina-Firenze: D'Anna.
Desideri, P. (1991), 'Dione di Prusa fra ellenismo e romanità', *ANRW II*, 33 (5): 3882–902 [= Desideri 2019: chapter 3].
Desideri, P. (2000), 'City and Country in Dio's Thought', in S. Swain (ed.), *Dio Chrysostom: Politics, Letters, and Philosophy*, 93–107, Oxford: Oxford University Press [= Desideri 2019: chapter 9].
Desideri, P. (2007), 'Dio's Exile: Politics, Philosophy, Literature', in I. F. Gaertner (ed.), *Writing Exile: The Discourse of Displacement in Greco-Roman Antiquity and Beyond*, 193–207, Leiden: Brill [= Desideri 2019: chapter 8].
Desideri, P. (2013), 'Lo Zeus di Olimpia emblema di pace secondo Dione di Prusa', *Arys*, 11: 239–47 [= Desideri 2019: chapter 12].
Desideri, P. (2016), 'I *Getica* di Dione fra etnografia e ideologia', in B. Virgilio (ed.), *Studi Ellenistici 30*, 331–44, Pisa: Serra [= Desideri 2019: chapter 10].
Desideri, P. (2017), 'Cultura e politica fra i Flavi e Traiano', in D. Pérez Sánchez, M. J. Rodríguez Gervás, J. R. Carbó García and I. Pérez Miranda (eds), *Poder y heterodoxia en el mundo greco-romano: Estudios en homenaje a la profesora Maria José Hidalgo de la Vega*, 167–88, Salamanca: Ediciones Universidad de Salamanca [= Desideri 2019: chapter 7].
Desideri, P. (2018), 'Platonismo di Dione', *Antiquorum Philosophia*, 12: 51–68 [= Desideri 2019: chapter 17].
Desideri, P. (2019), *Ellenismo romano: Nuovi studi su Dione di Prusa*, Pisa: Serra.
Devillers, O. (2014), 'Les *opera minora* "laboratoire" des *opera maiora*', in *Les* opera minora *et le développement de l'historiographie tacitéenne*, Bordeaux: Ausonius.
Gangloff, A. (2006), *Dion Chrysostome et les mythes: Hellénisme, communication et philosophie politique*, Grenoble: Millon.
Gangloff, A. (2009), 'Le sophiste Dion de Pruse, le bon roi et l'empereur', *RH*, 311: 1–38.
Giua, M. A. (2016), 'Tacito e il principato: fra pace e libertà', in G. Reggi (ed.), *Tacito storico e scrittore: Atti del corso d'aggiornamento per docenti di latino e greco del Canton Ticino (Lugano, 30–31 gennaio 2013)*, 37–58, Lugano: Casagrande.
Grillone, A., trans. (2017), *Iordanes,* Getica, Paris: Les Belles Lettres.
Hammer, D. (2014), *Roman Political Thought: From Cicero to Augustine*, Cambridge: Cambridge University Press.

Hartog, F. (1992), *Lo specchio di Erodoto*, Italian translation of *Le miroir d'Herodote*, Paris (1980), Milano: Il Saggiatore.

Iordache, R. (1983), 'La confusion "Gètes – Goths" dans la "Getica" de Jordanes', *Helmantica*, 34: 317–37.

Jacoby, F. (1958), *Die Fragmente der griechischen Historiker (FGrHist)*, III C *Ethnographie*. IX *Geten und Goten*, Leiden: Brill.

Lavan, M. (2011), 'Slavishness in Britain and Rome in Tacitus' *Agricola*', *CQ*, 61: 294–305.

Mandruzzato, A. (2010), '"Dalla parte degli infedeli". I Daci, Decebalo e la Colonna Traiana', *Hormos. Ricerche di storia antica*, 2: 164–74.

Mierow, C. C. (1908), 'Jordanes: The Origin and Deeds of the Goths', PhD thesis, Princeton University Press.

Rives, J. B., trans. (1999), *Tacitus:* Germania, Oxford: Oxford University Press.

Settis, S., ed. (1988), *La Colonna Traiana*, Torino: Einaudi.

Skinner, J. E. (2012), *The Invention of Greek Ethnography: From Homer to Herodotus*, New York: Oxford University Press.

Tufano, G. (2014), 'Rev. of Skinner 2012', *Mediterraneo Antico: Economie Società Culture*, 17 (2): 671–82.

Woolf, G. (2011), *Tales of the Barbarians: Ethnography and Empire in the Roman West*, Hoboken, NJ: Wiley.

Woolf, G. (2013), 'Ethnography and the Gods in Tacitus' *Germania*', in E. Almagor and J. Skinner (eds), *Ancient Ethnography: New Approaches*, 133–52. London: Bloomsbury Academic.

Yavetz, Z. (1999), *Tiberio dalla finzione alla pazzia, con un'appendice su Tacito: Il trauma della tirannia*, Bari: Edipuglia.

11

News from a *mundus senescens*: Romans, Visigoths and Saxons in a Letter by Sidonius Apollinaris (8.6)

Filomena Giannotti

The *ep.* 8.6 not only has the distinction of being, with its eighteen paragraphs, the longest of Sidonius Apollinaris' 146 letters, but, in its great detail, it also presents the peculiarity of offering a particular cross-section of the world of the 'other', outlining the most comprehensive 'portrait' that we have of the Saxons, depicted as having marked connotations of ferocity and barbarism, as opposed to the Roman values of a *mundus iam senescens* (world which is growing old[1]).

Before analysing these topics, it is first necessary to address some preliminary issues, starting with the complex structure of the letter, and then consider the identity of the addressee and the letter's debated dating.

The content and structure of *ep.* 8.6

In order to understand the structure of the letter, it would first of all be appropriate to draw up, for the benefit of the reader, a schematic summary of the content:

§§ 1–9. Sidonius tells Namatius he feels honoured by the praise of Nicetius, as happened to Julius Caesar, exalted by Cicero for his military and oratorical arts. Sidonius reciprocates the praise: memories of Nicetius.

§§ 10–12. Back to Namatius: is he dealing with agriculture, architecture or both? Some funny scenes demonstrate his lack of skill in hunting.

§§ 13–15. News from a messenger: Namatius is in command of a fleet keeping the Saxons under surveillance. Description of the reckless boldness of the Saxons and the tortures they inflict on their prisoners.

§§ 16–17. Plea to Namatius to let Sidonius have positive news.

§18. Dispatch of the books requested by Namatius, the *Logistorici* of Varro and the *Chronicon* of Eusebius.

Although a clear division into two parts is recognizable in the structure of this letter, with the conspicuous insertion of paragraphs 13–17 between the initial block of paragraphs 1–12 and the concluding one, its overall organization tends to confuse the reader, at first sight not appearing very linear. One wonders in particular why the author has chosen to complicate everything by including the scene of the arrival of the messenger in order to update the reader on Namatius' situation. In fact, as Hanaghan noted, 'this seemingly disorganised arrangement reveals a clear structure when the arrival of the messenger is read as a narratological device'.[2] According to the scholar, the arrival of the messenger would create a *Ringkomposition*, linking the end of the letter to its premise about Caesar's military and oratorical glory. If the example of Nicetius in fact offers Namatius a model of oratorical art and commitment to the public service rather than to the military one, it is the news unexpectedly brought by the messenger about the patrolling against the Saxons now carried out by Namatius to recall how important Caesar's example is also from the other point of view. Namatius should draw inspiration from him, more than from Nicetius or Sidonius himself. Through this development, the author achieves the double result of connecting the two main threads of the discourse, Nicetius' oratorical ability and the danger of military action against the Saxons, and of emphasizing the importance of *paideia* for Namatius.

The addressee

The *peregrinans amicus* (friend abroad: *ep.* 8.6.17) to whom the letter is addressed is Namatius and some of his few biographical data known to us can be obtained from these same Sidonian pages. Namatius owned land on the island of Oléron in the Gallic province of *Novempopulana*, where he lived with his father, while it is not clear whether he also had a house in the *Santones*, that is, around Santona, today Saintes,[3] where he had recently been put in charge of the fleet of the king of the Visigoths, Euricus, to defend the coast from attacks by Saxon pirates. From the letter one can also deduce that he had literary interests, given his request to Sidonius to send him the two books. According to Mathisen, Namatius could be the same person who appears among the correspondents of Ruricius of Limoges (*ep.* 2.1–5 and 2.62): if that were true, we would also know that he had a wife named Ceraunia and a daughter who had married one of the sons of Ruricius.[4] For Martindale, they are, instead, two different people.[5]

In the letter in question there is another figure known to us only through Sidonius, namely Flavius Nicetius. Also in this case, there is no agreement as to whether or not it is the same Nicetius whose inheritance is mentioned in *ep.* 3.1.3.[6] *Assessor* of the *praefectus praetorio Galliarum*, Nicetius was given the title of *vir spectabilis*. From among his memories, Sidonius recalls the panegyric that Nicetius had pronounced for the Consul Astyrius in Arles in 449, when Sidonius' father was prefect of the praetorium, and the *lex de praescriptione tricennii* which Nicetius had introduced in Gaul.

The dating

The dating to 478 hypothesized by Stroheker[7] was considered unacceptable by Loyen.[8] On the basis of some references in the letter, and in particular the expression *aevo viridis* (in the prime of life: *ep.* 8.6.2) relating to Sidonius' age, the French scholar anticipates its dating to a period between the advent of Euricus (466) and the episcopate of Sidonius, proposing 469. Loyen also applies the expression *praesentis opusculi volumina* (the various books of the present little work: *ep.* 8.6.2) to the first book of the correspondence. However, Stroheker's lower dating has found confirmation in subsequent studies: Martindale considers the letter 'perhaps written shortly before *c.* 478, when Sidonius published Book VIII of the letters'.[9] Kaufmann places it 'etwa 477/478', after disputing Loyen's arguments also regarding the interpretation of *praesentis opusculi volumina*.[10] Piacente dates it to 478 in all probability, after having made a detailed reconstruction of the exegeses of Stroheker and Loyen, and reinforced the former's hypothesis with further arguments.[11] More recently, while Fascione[12] and Mascoli[13] are still aligned with Loyen's positions, considering the letter datable to 469 and seeing the reference to *praesentis opuscoli volumina* as an allusion to the publication of the first book of letters rather than to the block constituted by the first seven, Kelly has reiterated that 'the plural *volumina* is sufficient here to show that this is not, as Loyen thought, a reference to Book 1, and in fact the letter clearly belongs to 477 or later, since Sidonius at its close affects just to have heard the news that Namatius has joined Euricus' navy. We are implicitly in a period after the end of Roman rule'.[14]

Therefore, the most probable dating appears to be no earlier than 477/478. Sidonius is forced to recognize as the victors the people under which Namatius is fighting against the Saxons (*victoris populi signa comitaris*, you follow the standard of a victorious people: *ep.* 8.6.16). And the people who subdued the

Romans of that area of Gaul are undoubtedly the Visigoths,[15] to whom in 475 the imperial power had ceded Arvernia in exchange for Provence, and whose Romano-barbarian reign was being consolidated after the collapse of the sovereignty of Rome in 476.[16]

The 'other' according to Sidonius: the Visigoths

Returning to the main issues addressed in this letter, one wonders, in the first place: after the important historical-political turning point that took place between 475 and 476, how did this aristocratic Gallo-Roman bishop define and describe the 'other'?

Among the barbarian populations, the Visigoths are, as is known, the most prevalent in the Sidonian correspondence.[17]

If, in *ep*. 1.2, there is a flattering portrait of King Theodoricus II,[18] which confirms the image of a devoted and friendly sovereign in *carm*. 7 to Avitus,[19] instead, several letters reveal, towards his killer and successor, Euricus, an attitude of hostility, or at least of contempt, attributable as much to his Arian creed as to his oppression of Arvernia. A particular case is that of the poem included in *ep*. 8.9 to Lampridius, apparently aimed at celebrating Euricus, but actually aimed at portraying him as a wicked tyrant and above all a crude barbarian.[20] This poem continually reaffirms the negative judgement already expressed in the long beginning of *ep*. 7.6, where the image of Euricus, accused of having broken the ancient *foedus* with the Romans, appears immediately after that of a wolf in the act of threatening sheep (an implicit reference to his anti-Catholic attitude).[21] And even in the accompanying verses to be engraved on a silver basin, written at the request of his friend Evodius for Euricus' wife, Queen Ragnahilda, Sidonius sarcastically comments: *in foro tali sive Athenaeo plus charta vestra quam nostra scriptura laudabitur* (in that sort of forum or Athenaeum your writing-material will get more praise than my writing: *ep*. 4.8.5). Even in the courtly dimension of the poetic homage, it is another sign of contempt for the ignorance of the Visigothic court, presented ironically and through antiphrasis as a sort of temple of culture.[22]

There should be a separate discussion regarding other passages in which Sidonius conveys his disgust for the Visigoths by means of particularly 'strong' lexical choices. The metaphorical fabric of an expression such as *Gothis credite, qui saepenumero etiam Septimaniam suam fastidiunt vel refundunt, modo invidiosi huius anguli etiam desolata proprietate potiantur* (you may learn even from the Goths, for they often feel constrained to despise or renounce their own Septimania for the prospect of gaining possession of this coveted corner: *ep.* 3.1.4) seems to insist on the act of vomiting: the 'migrating' of the barbarians would therefore be aligned, through images, with the vomit of someone who has gorged himself on something ad nauseam.[23] Similarly, the recollection of the suffering during the period of imprisonment spent within the *moenia Liviana* is linked to two *Getides*[24] *anus, quibus nil umquam litigiosius, bibacius, vomacius erit* (two old Gothic women, the most quarrelsome, drunken, vomiting creatures the world will ever see: *ep.* 8.3.2), and therefore once again to something nauseating. Instead, in the expression *siquidem quos humari nox succincta prohibuerat decervicatis liquere cadaveribus, tamquam minoris indicii foret quam villis agnosci crinitum dimisisse truncatum* (that is to say, they decapitated the bodies of all the men whose burial was prevented by the shortness of the night, and left them thus, imagining that less would be revealed if one abandoned a man in a headless state than if he were to be recognized by the tufts of hair on his head: *ep.* 3.3.7), the author employs the term *villus*, normally used to indicate the fur of some animals, to express his disgust for the outward appearance of the barbarians, in this case their 'mane'.

The letter to Ecdicius from which this last expression is taken presents, among other things, one of the most significant examples of the cruelty and fanaticism attributed to the Visigoths by Sidonius. Probably for celebratory reasons, namely to underline further the exceptional importance of the military enterprise of Ecdicius, the hero of the Arvernia resistance against the Visigoths, the author seems here to argue that the Visigoths would have proceeded to this decapitation of the corpses in order to make it less obvious how great their losses had been.[25]

Instead, with the above mentioned words from *ep.* 8.6.16, *victoris populi signa comitaris*, the author seems to accept as a matter of fact not only the victory of the Visigoths over the Gallo-Romans, but also the collaboration that some of his aristocratic fellow citizens like Namatius had begun with Euricus' court, sometimes even managing to carve out for themselves successful careers.[26] This is the case, for example, of the Victorius mentioned in *ep.* 7.17.1, who had entered the Visigothic administration.[27] Or the two figures who, like Victorius himself, played a role when Euricus granted Sidonius his forgiveness. The first one is his friend Leo of Narbonne, who interceded with the Visigothic king and was at that time one of his advisors: *cotidie namque per potentissimi consilia regis totius sollicitus orbis pariter* [*eius*] *negotia et iura, foedera et bella, loca spatia merita cognoscis* (for every day in the councils of a most powerful king you meticolously gather information about the whole world's affairs and rights, treaties and wars, localities, distances, and merits alike: *ep.* 4.22.3); *sepone pauxillulum conclamatissimas declamationes, quas oris regii vice conficis* (put aside for an instant those much-acclaimed declamations which you compose as the royal spokesman: *ep.* 8.3.3).[28] The second, Lampridius, to whom Sidonius sent, for reading, the poem for the above-mentioned Euricus, was in turn an official who fully enjoyed the rights of Visigoth citizens: *tu munificentia regia satis abutens* (when you are in full enjoyment of the King's munificence: *ep.* 8.9.1); *ago adhuc exulem, agis ipse iam civem* (I still in exile, you are now a citizen: *ep.* 8.9.3).[29] And even Sidonius' son, Apollinaris the Younger, a few years later, in 507, would have fought for the Visigoths against the Franks in the battle of Vouillé.[30]

However, it is significant that, in the same book 8, there is another letter, which can be considered more or less contemporary with the one sent to Namatius, as it is dated at 478, in which Sidonius defines the Visigoths a victorious *gens*, but *aliena* (*ep.* 8.2.2).[31] It is a sign that Sidonius' attitude would always remain critical towards them and that, as will be seen better later, the fight against the militarily undefeated barbarians had by then been transferred to the cultural level, taking the form of a struggle to maintain a Roman identity.

The very adjective *alienus* – of central importance in my opinion for the purposes of this discourse on how the 'other' is seen – occurs in two other letters of book 5 with this same meaning. In *ep.* 5.5, expressing to the noble Syagrius, descended from illustrious Roman ancestors, his amazement at the ease with which he had learned the language of the Burgundians (*sermo Germanicus*), Sidonius asks him: *velim dicas, unde subito hauserunt pectora tua euphoniam gentis alienae* (I should like you to tell me how you have managed to absorb so swiftly into your inner being the exact sounds of an alien race: *ep.* 5.5.2). That *alienus* is used here with the meaning of foreigner also finds confirmation in the following words: *aestimari minime potest, quanto mihi ceterisque sit risui, quotiens audio, quod te praesente formidet linguae suae facere barbarus barbarismum* (you have no idea what amusement it gives me, and others too, when I hear that in your presence the barbarian is afraid to perpetrate a barbarism in his own language: *ep.* 5.5.3). The concept of linguistic and broadly cultural extraneousness, introduced by *alienus* and reaffirmed immediately afterwards by *barbarus* (with the play on *barbarismus*), could not be expressed more clearly.[32] In a completely different but equally interesting context, *alienus* returns twice: in the *ep.* 5.12 to Calminius, a friend of Sidonius who fell into the hands of the Visigoths, who forced him to fight against his fellow citizens of Clermont. The letter therefore presents itself as a historical testimony not only of the treatment that the Visigoths reserved for their prisoners and of the changes that their advance imposed on

Gallo-Roman territory, but also of their brutality (in *pendant*, according to Loyen, with what emerges in the macabre description, mentioned above, of the beheading carried out by the Visigoths on the corpses of their army).[33] Even the justification that Sidonius gives of the fact that Calminius rarely received his letters provides a significant insight into the difficulties of communication, aggravated in those times by the risk of letters being intercepted. This could be the reason for the double use of the adjective *alienus*, which would have allowed the sender to call into question the Visigoths without explicitly naming them: *quod rarius ad vos a nobis pagina meat, non nostra superbia sed aliena impotentia facit . . . ad arbitrium terroris alienis vos loricae, nos propugnacula tegunt* (if a line from me comes to you all too seldom, it is not superciliousness in me but the violence in others that is to blame . . . at the dictate of a menacing foreign power you have donned your armour and we are covered by our fortifications: *ep.* 5.12.1). Also noteworthy is the fact that in both cases the adjective in question accompanies a term with a negative meaning: *impotentia*, which is widely used also in the metaphorical sense of '*intemperantia, nimia licentia, animi efferatio*', pertaining to the sphere of ethics,[34] and, in a syntactically inverted order, *terror*, which recalls how the climate imposed by the Visigoths conditioned the possibilities of contact between the prisoner and his former fellow citizens, the former protected by the armour of the attacker, the latter defended by the fortifications of the attacked.

The letter to Namatius, despite the brevity of the implicit and fleeting reference *victoris populi signa comitaris*, therefore constitutes an important stage in the evolution of Sidonius' attitude towards the Visigoths: from the propagandistic positive presentation of Theodoricus II to the aversion towards Euricus after the breaking of the *foedus* and the consequent misobarbarism; then from the acceptance of their victory and the collaborationism of friends and fellow citizens to the persistence of the feeling of the Visigoths' extraneousness, at least linguistic and cultural – a factor, destined, as will be seen later, to influence the perception and representation of the self.

But the importance of this letter in the Sidonian context (and beyond) is linked above all to the fact that it contains 'the best original account of the Saxon pirates'.[35]

The 'other' according to Sidonius: the Saxons

Before this letter, Sidonius had already had occasion to mention the Saxons in the panegyric to Avitus (*carm.* 7.88–92, 369–371, 388–390):

Victricia Caesar
signa Caledonios transvexit ad usque Britannos;
fuderit et quamquam Scotum et cum Saxone Pictum,
hostes quaesivit, quem iam natura vetabat
quaerere plus homines . . . .
Quin et Aremoricus piratam Saxona tractus
sperabat, cui pelle salum sulcare Britannum
ludus et assuto glaucum mare findere lembo.[36] . . .
'Ut primum ingesti pondus suscepit honoris,
legas qui veniam poscant, Alamanne, furori,
Saxonis incursus cessat.' . . .

Caesar took his victorious legions over even to the Caledonian Britons, and although he routed the Scot, the Pict and the Saxon, he still looked for foes where nature forbade him to look any more for men. . . . The Aremorican region too expected the Saxon pirate, who deems it but sport to furrow the British waters with hides, cleaving the blue sea in a stitched boat. . . . 'No sooner had he taken up the burden of the office thrust upon him than the Alaman sent envoys to crave pardon for their frenzy, the Saxon's raiding abated.' . . .

However, these references are believed to lack historical reliability. In the first case, relating to the predecessors of Avitus, because Caesar in his campaign in Britain had not actually had anything to do with the Saxons: the poet would therefore be projecting on to the first century BCE later ethnic data of the fifth century CE.[37] Later, the Saxons appear twice among the multitude of barbarians reduced to obedience by Avitus, but according to Kaufmann these statements are panegyristic *flosculi*, without any historical content:[38] it is not only the propagandistic tone which is striking here, but also Sidonius' debt to the analogous treatment reserved for the Saxons, according to Claudian, by Theodosius, Honorius' grandfather, and Stilicho, for how they are respectively praised in *Panegyricus de quarto consulatus Honorii Augusti* and *De consulatu Stilichonis*.[39] In common with Claudian there is also the fact that the Saxons were associated with the ideas of piracy and attacks from the sea.

The encomiastic dimension with regard to an honoured person also dominates in the subsequent mention of the Saxons present in the eulogy of Euricus included in *ep.* 8.9.5 (= *carm.* 34.21–27):

istic Saxona caerulum videmus
assuetum ante salo solum timere;
cuius verticis extimas per oras

non contenta suos tenere morsus
alta lammina marginem comarum,
et sic crinibus ad cutem recisis
decrescit caput additurque vultus.

Here in Bordeaux we see the blue-eyed Saxon afraid of the land, accustomed as he is to the sea; along the extreme edges of his pate the razor, refusing to restrain its bite, pushes back the frontier of his hair and, with the growth thus clipped to the skin, his head is reduced and his face enlarged.

The *caerulus Saxo* opens the catalogue of the peoples who parade in an act of submission to Euricus.[40] With respect to the mention in *carm*. 7 here there is no reference to piracy, but the detail of the Saxons' familiarity with the dangers of the sea is repeated, to which Sidonius adds two physical details, namely the blue eyes and the cut of their hair, of which he had probably had direct experience at the court of Euricus in Bordeaux.[41]

Finally, not a mere mention but an accurate description is what takes up three paragraphs in *ep*. 8.6 and which seems to be built on a sort of crescendo. In fact, the first comment presents the Saxons as *archipiratae* (pirate-captain)[42] who, aboard their *pandi myoparones* (curving sloops),[43] are all capable at the same time of commanding and obeying, of teaching and learning robbery (*ep*. 8.6.13). A little further on, the author goes so far as to define these people *hostis* [...] *omni hoste truculentior* (that enemy surpasses all other enemies in brutality: *ep*. 8.6.14), adding an explanation of the ruthlessness with which they face not only enemies but also storms and shipwrecks. The passage culminates with the description of the *superstitiosus ritus* (rite due to superstition: *ep*. 8.6.15) with which, when they are about to leave for their lands, the Saxons usually inflict drowning or crucifixion on one prisoner out of ten.[44]

A first question posed by this passage is whether it can be considered reliable or not. Although some details are reflected in other more or less contemporary sources,[45] it is probable, as Kaufmann believes, that Sidonius had mixed news he had learned about while in Bordeaux with other rumours.[46] It would not seem to be first-person knowledge like perhaps that of the physical traits of the Saxon group that the author must have had the opportunity of seeing at Euricus' court, but rather 'second-hand' knowledge, a hypothesis that could in some way undermine the veracity of its reconstruction.[47] The question is probably destined not to have a definitive answer, but, as Flierman himself points out, 'this description is the first of its kind to survive in the late antique record'.[48]

Another question is related to this, as to why Sidonius describes the Saxons in such detail to Namatius, who, as the commander of the fleet, should have been better informed than anyone about the enemies and the treatment they reserved for their prisoners. But since the author himself later confesses that he feels reassured, among other things, by his friend's wisdom (*in sapientes viros, quos inter iure censeris, minus annuo licere fortuitis*, with provident men, among whom you are rightly classed, there is less opportunity for accidents to happen: *ep.* 8.6.16:), it seems more probable that 'Sidonius might well have just seized the opportunity to present an educated fellow Roman with some interesting bits of hearsay on the coarse superstitions of an uncivilized people, duly wrapped up in stylized prose'.[49] And even if there were news of which the author had come to know personally from others and which he had felt duty-bound to transmit to Namatius,[50] the literary aspect – deducible among other things from the lexical references to Cicero's *Verrinae* – may have superceded reality, acting as a filter on contemporary facts.[51]

Actually, the description of the Saxons, together with the praise of Nicetius (*ep.* 8.6.6–7), presents the letter's greatest stylistic development, judging by the high concentration of rhetorical devices in paragraphs 14–15:

> – *hostis est omni hoste truculentior* (that enemy surpasses all other enemies in brutality)
>
> – *inprovisus aggreditur, praevisus elabitur; spernit obiectos, sternit incautos; si sequatur, intercipit, si fugiat, evadit* (he attacks unforeseen, and when foreseen he slips away; he despises those who bar his way, and he destroys those whom he catches unawares; if he pursues, he intercepts; if he flees, he escapes);
>
> – *ad hoc exercent illos naufragia, non terrent. Est eis quaedam cum discriminibus pelagi non notitia solum, sed familiaritas* (moreover, shipwreck, far from terrifying them, is their training. With the perils of the sea they are not merely acquainted – they are familiarly acquainted);
>
> – *ipsa si qua tempestas est huc securos efficit occupandos, huc prospici vetat occupaturos* (a storm whenever it occurs lulls into security the object of their attack and prevents the coming attack from being observed by victims);
>
> – *mortis iniquitatem, sortis aequitate* (the iniquity of death by the equity of the lot);
>
> – *talibus se ligant votis, victimis solvunt; et per huiusmodi non tam sacrificia purgati, quam sacrilegia polluti . . .* (such are the obligations of their vows, and such the victims with which they pay their obligations. Polluting themselves by such sacrilege rather than purifying themselves by such sacrifices . . .).

Such a formalized prose could be a way to emphasize, through rethorical expressions, all the brutality the Saxons showed in the exercise of piracy and of their religious practices.

Sidonius' representation of the self and self-perception

A second question posed by the letter to Namatius is how did his Gallo-Roman 'othering' impact Sidonius' representation of the self and self-perception?

To answer this question, it would be appropriate to start from the observation that what is most striking in this letter is perhaps its being permeated with a staggering sense of the end of time: *per aetatem mundi iam senescentis* (in an era when the world is growing old: *ep.* 8.6.3).[52]

At least two distinct literary traditions converge in this evocative expression. On one hand, the words *per aetatem mundi* refer to Florus' *Epitome*, with the division of Roman history into four ages, like those of human life, according to a biological conception of history for which Florus is in turn indebted to Seneca the Elder.[53] On the other hand, the idea of the *mundus senescens* fits into the well-codified *topos* of *Roma senescens*, as opposed to that of *Roma aeterna*.[54] Moreover, here, Sidonius seems to have mixed Christian and pagan traditions. In fact, the expression appears close to a couple of passages from Cyprian's *Ad Demetrianum*: *illud in primo loco scire debes, senuisse iam saeculum* and *mundo senescente* (you must in the first place know this, that the world has now grown old),[55] and very close to a page from Prudentius' *Hamartigenia*: *mundum* [. . .] *iam senescentem* (*Praef.* 17–18). In addition to this quotation from Prudentius, Mratschek points out a passage from Pliny, where Titinius Capito is praised as *litterarum iam senescentium reductor ac reformator* (the restorer and reformer of literature in its decline: *ep.* 8.2.1)[56] and which was certainly familiar to Sidonius.[57]

In effect, put back into its context – from which it has been briefly extrapolated by this short analysis of the literary background – the expression *per aetatem mundi iam senescentis* confirms that Sidonius' reflection on the decadence of the world around him is strictly cultural in nature: since his land is now definitively under the political dominion of the Visigoths, his attention turns to the situation in which the arts find themselves (*ep.* 8.6.3): *namque virtutes artium istarum saeculis potius priscis saeculorum rector ingenuit, quae per aetatem mundi iam senescentis lassatis veluti seminibus emedullatae parum aliquid hoc tempore in quibuscumque, atque id in paucis, mirandum ac memorabile ostentant* (for it was in the men of bygone ages that the Ruler of all the ages preferred to implant the talents for such arts; but now, in an era when the world is growing old, these arts have lost the power of germinating, they are exhausted, they produce little that is remarkable or memorable in anyone, and even that only in a few).

This is one of the culminating moments of the Sidonian reflection on the topic of cultural decadence that runs through his entire correspondence:[58] there are few men still able to excel in the arts with which the *saeculorum rector* endowed past generations; an equally small number of men are still able to create something admirable and memorable. Among these, the author undoubtedly includes himself, as evidenced by the fact that the foregoing and the following in the letter report the words of praise that Nicetius had for Sidonius' works. Moreover, even when it is Sidonius who praises the cultural work of others, he tends to bring out the awareness of his being at the forefront of a similar battle, with that sort of false modesty that is often found in his epistles.[59]

The *ep.* 8.6, although permeated with a sense of the end of time, is significantly involved in this struggle, with the perception and representation of Sidonius himself as the one who, with his literary and cultural activity, tries to prevent the Roman identity from being overwhelmed and erased.

Manifestations of Roman identity

This last point is the best introduction to a further question posed by this letter: what were the manifestations of Roman identity in this area of the Roman Empire? On the basis of the advice that Sidonius gives directly or indirectly to Namatius, it is evident that at least two other aspects of Roman identity must be added to the literary and cultural one that has already been partially mentioned: the first pertains to the linguistic sphere and the other is of a material nature and more broadly related to lifestyles.

Starting with the latter, a question that the author poses to the addressee at a certain point cannot go unnoticed: *venaris, aedificas, rusticarisne?* (do you hunt? do you build? do you live the life of a countryman?: *ep.* 8.6.10). Also from a stylistic point of view, the care with which the question has been constructed is evident – with three increasing *cola* of three, four, and five syllables respectively – perhaps precisely to emphasize that this is a crucial question, which marks, among other things, one of the hubs in the structure of the letter, with the end of Nicetius' praise. Hunting, building, and farming were three typical activities of a Roman citizen, in particular the third – in opposition, as is known, to the nomadism of the barbarians.

Curiously, Sidonius chooses to focus his attention on hunting, which was one of the favourite pastimes of the late antique aristocracy.[60] Curiously, because two entire paragaphs make fun of Namatius' poor success in this sport, with some particularly humorous passages, about the inefficiency of Namatius' dogs, and his consequent inability to catch wild boars and reach *lepusculi Olarionenses* (the hares of Oléron),[61] vainly solicited, except to be kept in training waiting for Sidonius' son to visit Namatius and his father and show them how to work best (*ep.* 8.6.11–12).

According to Harland, 'we have ... an illustration of Roman identity in crisis. Hunting was a traditional Roman aristocratic pastime: why would a Roman be bad at it?'[62] Personally, I do not believe that Sidonius here wanted to allude to a crisis of Roman identity, by stigmatizing that of hunting as a sort of crisis of one of its symbols. Otherwise, he might not have concluded the passage by envisaging the arrival of Apollinaris, almost certainly his son,[63] in aid of Namatius and his father: *dum tibi ac patri noster Apollinaris intervenit* (when our friend Apollinaris drops in on you and your father). I would therefore be inclined to believe that with these two paragraphs the author wants to counter the sustained tone of the letter, turning to a comic element, between the committed praise of Nicetius first and the later description of the brutality of the Saxons. The two sentences that open and close the account of his friend's clumsy hunts would seem to confirm this intention, respectively with the play on words, with an evidently ironic tone, *ut tibi de venatoris officio quam minimum blandiaris, maxume iniungo* (as regards the hunter's business I do most strongly urge you not to flatter yourself unduly: *ep.* 8.6.11) and with the explicit reference, once the digression is closed, to the fact that so far he has been joking: *exceptis iocis fac sciam tandem, quid te, quid domum circa* (joking apart, let me know at last the news of yourself and family: *ep.* 8.6.13).

In asking Namatius that question about his current occupation, Sidonius adds an interesting compliment: *sed de Vitruvio sive Columella, seu alterutrum ambosve sectere, decentissime facis* (as regards Vitruvius or Columella, whether you are a devotee of one of them, or of both together, you are acting splendidly: *ep.* 8.6.10). After mentioning Caesar and Cicero, at the beginning of the letter, there is a further reference to Latin literary production, which anticipates what in the last paragraph will present itself as the second of the manifestations of Roman identity, namely the insistence on classical studies. The final purpose of this letter is in fact to accompany the dispatch to Namatius of the two literary works he had requested from Sidonius: *Varronem logistoricum, sicut poposceras, et Eusebium chronographum misi* (I send you Varro logistoricus and Eusebius the chronographer, as you requested: *ep.* 8.6.18). In the first case, it was the entire Varronian collection and not just a single book of the *Logistorici*.[64] In the case of Eusebius, it is assumed that it is the second book of the *Chronicon* translated by Jerome.[65] A pagan writer and a Christian one, therefore, to allow Namatius to cover the two different spheres of knowledge, or rather 'to help him refine both his philosophical and Christian lifestyle'.[66] According to Overwien, Varro should be interpreted 'als Symbol für ein starkes Römisches Reich, Eusebios als Symbol für das katholische Christentum bzw. die Gefahr des Arianismus' (as a symbol of a stronger Roman Empire, Eusebius as a symbol of the Catholic Christianity or of the danger of Arianism).[67] What is surprising, in this passage, is not only Namatius' request for a work lost to us like the *Logistorici*, but also Sidonius' ability to fulfil it without difficulty. This reveals another aspect that, together with the defence of classical culture, was a sign of distinction for the Gallo-Roman senatorial aristocracy, namely the possession of rich libraries – in this case the library of Sidonius, which even included a Varronian text, whose total loss had already occurred, about the second half of the second century, in those cultural areas, such as Italy and Greece, where Gellius used to move while editing his notes.[68]

Sidonius' recommendation to his friend is to devote himself to Varro and Eusebius *inter excubiales curas* (amid the duties of the watch), and the reason for this is not insignificant, but opens up a new *pointe*: just as he will apply himself to cleaning his weapons, so Namatius will also be able to remove from his mouth the *loquendi robigo* (linguistic rust) thanks to their *lima* (refining tool), to be understood above all as the beneficial formative action in the field of expressive education and adequate linguistic expression (*ep.* 8.6.18).[69] Latin as a language of culture, pure, proper, elegant, and refined in its polished smoothness, or rather in its absence of 'rust', thus constitutes the third and last of the manifestations of the Roman identity. At the same time, the *loquendi robigo*, in its metaphorical allusion to the disfigured, if not exactly repellent aspect, which a Latin, stained by the negligence of the Romans and/or by interference or at least contacts with different languages and perceived as barbaric, must have had for a purist like Sidonius, also presents itself as a metaphor of the perception that the author must have had of the 'other', this time from the linguistic point of view. A confirmation of this type of perception by Sidonius emerges from the comparison with a passage in which the term *robigo* also occurs, namely the letter to Hesperius, a rhetorician of his circle, as well as the teacher of one of Ruricius' sons, and particularly esteemed for his battle in defence of Latinity: *tantum increbruit multitudo desidiosorum ut, nisi vel paucissimi quique meram linguae Latiaris proprietatem de trivialium barbarismorum robigine vindicaveretis, eam brevi abolitam defleamus interemptamque* (the mob of the sluggards has so grown in numbers that unless there are at least a modest few like yourself to defend the exact use of the language of Latium from the rust of vulgar barbarisms, we shall in a short time be lamenting its extinction and annihilation: *ep.* 2.10.1).

The passage is doubly interesting: here the noun *robigo* is in fact unequivocally accompanied by the specification *barbarismorum* and is in contrast with *mera linguae Latiaris proprietas*.[70]

As has recently been stressed by Wolff, for Sidonius 'the survival of ancient culture is conditional upon the preservation of proper Latin usage. It should be noted that Sidonius' opposition to the barbarians had far more to do with cultural issues than with problems of ethnicity, and he associated the empire's loss of influence with the precarious state of culture'.[71] Furthermore, the usual extremely elaborate style of this and in general of all Sidonius' other letters aims to provide, indirectly, a shining example of Latin eloquence, devoid of any possible residual linguistic barbarism, rust or scaliness. And it can therefore be considered another way in which Roman 'othering' impacts the self-perception, in this case the linguistic self-perception.

Conclusion

The letter to Namatius is thus a significant literary page on the theme of the 'other' in a precise historical and geographical context, that of the Gallic area of the Roman Empire in the fifth century CE. Its numerous points of reflection concern both the Visigoths and, above all, the Saxons, and their being negatively perceived by a member of the cultured senatorial aristocracy such as Sidonius Apollinaris. At the same time, the opposite tendency of the author emerges: to perceive and present, albeit indirectly, himself as one of the last defenders of the Latin language and literature, in contrast to the rampant barbarism. In making affectionate and at times even humorous suggestions to his friend, Sidonius also ends up wanting to prevent a sort of barbarizing process in Namatius, insisting on some of the main manifestations of the material, cultural, and even linguistic identity of the Gallo-Romans, such as agriculture, hunting (in which his friend still has to make progress), *paideia* and the survival of Latin as a language of culture in a *mundus iam senescens*.

Notes

1 All the English translations of Sidonius are by Anderson 1936 and 1965.
2 Hanaghan 2019: 84.
3 Martindale 1980: 771, *Namatius 1* and Kaufmann 1995: 325–6, n. 70 *Namatius*.

4 Mathisen 2020: 109, *Namatius* and Neri 2009: 247 and 413.

5 Martindale 1980: 772, *Namatius 2.*

6 Stroheker 1948: 194–5, Nr. 257 *Nicetius* and Nr. 258 *Flavius Nicetius*; Martindale 1980: 782, *Nicetius 1* and *Fl. Nicetius 2*; Mathisen 2020: 109, *Nicetius* and *Fl. Nicetius.* In the wake of Anderson 1965: 6, n. 1, Loyen 1970, vol. 2: 221–2, n. 4, identifies the person referred to here, who died in 471, as Flavius Nicetius whom Sidonius eulogizes in 8.6.2.

7 Stroheker 1948: 194, Nr. 253 *Namatius.*

8 Loyen 1970, vol. 3: 216

9 Martindale 1980: 771 *Namatius 1.*

10 Kaufmann 1995: 165–6, n. 459 and 325–6, Nr. 70 *Namatius.*

11 Piacente 1998: 191–4.

12 Fascione 2019: 29, n.126.

13 Mascoli 2021: 279–80, n. 15 and n. 18.

14 Kelly 2020: 187. Cf. Piacente 1998: 192.

15 Mascoli 2021: 284, n. 25.

16 For a detailed summary of these events, see Harries 1994: 54–81, 125–40, 222–42; also Kulikowski 2020: 206–13.

17 For the Visigoths in general, see Heather 1996. For the Visigoths in Gaul, see Luiselli 1992: 566–78; in Sidonius, see Kaufmann 1995: 106–39.

18 For this letter, see Köhler 1995, 1998, and 2014: 5–9.

19 For an analysis of these Sidonian pages, of the chronological relationship between *ep.* 1.2 and *carm.* 7, and the attempt, at this stage, to present Theodoricus' people in a positive light to make the alliance with the Visigoths acceptable to the Romans, see Gualandri 2000: 112–14. See also Consolino 2011 and Fascione 2019: 53–62.

20 See Fo 1999 (expanded in Fo 2002) and Overwien 2009.

21 For this letter, see van Waarden 2010. See also Fo 2002: 158–63; Fascione 2019: 38; 62–72.

22 Becht-Jördens 2017, in particular, insists on this aspect. For this letter, see Giannotti 2021, with further bibliography.

23 Giannotti 2016: 119. Also elsewhere, after all, Sidonius takes pleasure in describing coarse scenes not dissimilar about the barbarians' crapulences: cf. *carm.* 12, 13 ff. about the Burgundians: *felicemque libet vocare nasum,/ cui non allia sordidumque cepe/ ructant mane novo decem apparatus* (I am fain to call . . . happy too your nose, for you don't have a reek of garlic and foul onions discharged upon you at early morn from ten breakfasts); and *carm.* 5, 339 ff. regarding the Vandal sovereign Gaiseric: *ipsi autem color exsanguis, quem crapula vexat/ et pallens pinguedo tenet, ganeaque perenni/ pressus acescentem stomachus non explicat auram* (his cheeks are bloodless; a drunkard's heaviness afflicts him, pallid flabbiness possesses him, and his stomach, loaded with continual gluttony, cannot rid itself of the sour wind). For the use of the verb *ructare* in connection with the world of barbarism, see Fascione 2019: 23.

24 Cf. Harland 2019: 47.

25 Ecdicius' undertaking referred to here is that he managed to force the Visigoths' blockade and reach his besieged fellow citizens in Clermont-Ferrand: the letter referring to it (3.3) is of an uncertain date, oscillating between 472 and 474; for this passage and the following one, see Giannotti 2000–2 and 2016: 133 and 151–5.

26 For the Gallo-Romans in barbarian service, see Luiselli 1992: 576–8 and Mathisen 1993: 125–9. According to Overwien 2009: 104–5, Sidonius shows concern for Namatius' fighting against the Saxon pirates, but behind this concern lies a reproach for the fact that his friend is in the service of the Visigoths. The same reference to Caesar at the beginning of the letter would demonstrate Namatius' distance from an ideal model of the coexistence of the military and literary. For Caesar and Cicero as biographical and political parallels, see Meurer 2019, esp. 215–32.

27 On Victorius like *comes civitatis Arvernensis* and *dux septem civitatum*, cf. van Waarden 2016: 205–9 and Mathisen 2020: 126–7. On the possible role played by Victorius in Sidonius' release, see Loyen 1970, vol. 2: 134, n. 38.

28 Cf. Mathisen 2020: 104, *Leo*.

29 Cf. Mathisen 2020: 104.

30 Greg. Tur., *Hist.* 2.37. Cf. Mathisen 2020: 81.

31 Regarding this letter and its dating, see Giannotti 2020b. On *alienus*, see also Giannotti 2022: 74.

32 Regarding this letter and in particular the terms *euphonia* and *barbarismus*, see Condorelli 2001: 105–7. See also below, n. 70. For the word *barbarus* and its complexity in Sidonius, see Egetenmeyr 2021.

33 Loyen 1970, vol. 2: XLI–XLII.

34 *ThLL* t. VII 1, coll. 672–673, s.v. *impotentia*.

35 Gibbon 1776–1788, II.xxv.995, n. 105. For the Saxons in the Roman Empire between *c.* 150 and 500, see Flierman 2017: 23–51; in late antique Gaul, see Harland 2019. For the Saxons in Sidonius, see Kaufmann 1995: 163–8.

36 In underlining the detail that the fifth-century Saxons would have used skin boats, Wooding points out how Sidonius may have had in mind a passage from the *De ora maritima* by Rufus Festus Avienus (ll. 106–107: *navigia iunctis semper aptant pellibus/ corioque vastum saepe percurrunt salum*, they always fashion vessels from skins joined together and often run through the vast salt sea on hides, trans. Roller 2021), with which there is in common the use of the terms *pellis* and *salum* (Wooding 1988: 34–5).

37 See Flierman 2017: 44. Cf. also Fascione 2019: 31–2, according to which Sidonius would, here, be mistaking the Saxons for Britons.

38 'Eine Floskel aus dem Munde des Panegyrikers, die wohl des historischen Gehalts entbehrt' (a catchphrase from the mouth of the panegyricist, which probably lacks historical content: Kaufmann 1995: 164, n. 454).

39 *IV Cons.* 24–40 (esp. 31–32; cf. also *Nupt.* 219); *Stil.* II 246–255.

40 On the use of the adjective *caerulus* and on the topical image of blue-eyed barbarians (also in connection with the privileged link between the Saxons and the sea), see Fascione 2019: 28, 33–4.

41 See Kaufmann 1995: 165 and Flierman 2017: 45, who also discuss the possibility that this particular Saxon hairstyle is to be considered a sign of ethnic distinction. The discussion was taken up again by Harland 2019: 48.

42 The words *archipirata*, like, soon afterwards, *myoparon*, recur several times in the section *de suppliciis* of Cicero's *Verrinae* (5.64–136) about a group of pirates whose ship (*myoparo*: §§ 73, 89, 97, 100) Verres captured, sparing the leader (*archipirata*) and appropriating both the booty and the best pirates, whom he replaced with Roman citizens then killed in their stead. As has been pointed out by Wolff 2020: 400, 'there is an analogy between the two situations described; in both cases, we have pirates and gratuitous cruelty'. Wolff (ibid.) has observed that also another rare word in this letter, *lepusculus* (hare: *ep.* 8.6.12), recurs in *Verrinae* (4.47): see below, n. 61.

43 According to Wooding 1988: 33, the *myoparones*, regarding which also see the preceding note, were 'skin boats (presumably of the *curragh* type: i.e. a skin-covered vessel, of boat rather than *coracle* form)'. The scholar also indicates that, although '*myoparones* is selected for its romantic piratical associations, rather than use a more prosaic description of a Saxon ship', the word 'is consistent with the definition of a skin boat . . ., though there might be some debate as to whether a skin boat would be described as "curving" (*pandos*)' (Wooding 1988: 34). *Pandus* is in fact an adjective 'di colore nettamente poetico e di tradizione antica' (Gualandri 1979: 92, n. 58, who lists other matching passages from Sidonius). Regarding the *myoparones*, also see Fascione 2019: 30–1.

44 On the concept of *superstitio* which emerges in this letter, Squillante 2016 shows how, despite his Christian beliefs, Sidonius here resorts to a rational vision of religion of Lucretian structure as a possible instrument of power in the hands of the wicked who impose punishments at will, making the excuse that it is to appease the gods.

45 This is the case, for example, of the Saxons' ability to surprise their enemies (*inprovisus aggreditur*, he attacks unforeseen: *ep.* 8.6.14), which finds confirmation in Ammian. Marc. 28.2.12 and 30.7.8, or their practice of having human sacrifices (*ep.* 8.6.15), also documented in Ennodius with regard to the Franks, the Heruli, and the Saxons (*Vita Antoni* 13 = 240 Vogel 1885: 187).

46 Kaufmann 1995: 168.

47 Both Flierman 2017: 46 ('its author appears to have drawn on first- and second-hand experience with Saxons. This is, of course, no guarantee for truthfulness'), and, more categorically, Harland 2019: 46 ('not reliable ethnographic description. Namatius' Saxons existed, but Sidonius' observations on them need not be taken as fact').

48 Flierman 2017: 46.

49 Flierman 2017: 48. A different view is expressed by Wooding 1988: 34: 'It would not have been out of the ordinary for a literary man, such as Sidonius, to have offered advice (in the manner of Shakespeare's Polonius) about a practical concern, such as defence against the Saxons. Nonetheless, Sidonius was undoubtedly a well-travelled man and there is every reason to believe that he had both travelled to regions which had been directly affected by Saxon raiding and was, further, in regular receipt of information regarding their raids – just as the arrival of a messenger from Saintes was the occasion of his writing to Namatius. He provides substantial detail regarding their method of attack; noting that they often will attack under cover of a storm and brave the dangers of rocks and surf to achieve surprise (sailing practices for which a skin boat might be argued to be most appropriate . . .). Certainly these might simply be embellishments to heighten the 'slippery' image of the Saxons; there is however a quantity of detail in his comments which argues against an excessively fictionalised picture'.

50 See Kaufmann 1995: 168.

51 Cf. Gualandri 1979: 43.

52 On the theme of the end of the world in Sidonius' panegyrics and their *praefationes*, see Stoehr-Monjou 2009.

53 Condorelli 2020: 361, with reference to Ficca 2018.

54 Schwitter 2015: 230–1, with additional bibliography in n. 437.

55 Respectively § 3 (where *saeculum* is the reading of *S* – the most ancient manuscript, dating back to the sixth–seventh century, while other manuscripts present *mundum*: see the critical apparatus of von Hartel's edition for 'Corpus Scriptorum Ecclesiasticorum Latinorum', 3.1, Vindobonae 1868: 2, 352) and § 4; see also, at § 20, the sentence *inter ipsas saeculi labentis ruinas* (among these very ruins of a decaying world, trans. Wallis 1996). Cf. Gualandri 1979: 20–1, n. 71 and van Waarden 2018: 196, n. 39.

56 Translated by Mratschek 2020: 257.

57 Cf. Sidon. *ep.* 8.2.1, *aboleri tu litteras distulisti, quarum quodammodo iam sepultarum suscitator, fautor, assertor concelebraris* (if I delayed the tribute of praise due to you for delaying the extinction of literary culture, for you are acclaimed as its reviver, promoter, and champion). See Giannotti 2020b.

58 See Schwitter 2015: 229, who, in addition to 8.6.3, recalls in this regard *ep.* 2.10.1, 4.17.2, 5.10.4, 8.2.1, 9.7.2, 9.9.16. Cf. also the bibliography he cited in n. 431.

59 To limit to book 8, see Giannotti 2020b on *ep.* 8.2 and Giannotti 2020a on *ep.* 8.5.

60 See, for example, Aymard 1964.

61 See above, n. 42.

62 Harland 2019: 47.

63 See above, n. 30.

64 Piacente 1998: 197, with a reference to Zucchelli 1981.

65 Mratschek 2020: 243, n. 43. Cf. also Piacente 1998: 194 regarding Jerome's translation.

66 Mratschek 2020: 243.

67 Overwien 2009: 105.

68 Piacente 1998: 198, with reference to the fact that Gellius mentions the *Logistorici* in *Noctes Atticae* 20.11.

69 According to Gualandri 1979: 128, n. 75, in this case it is clear – and the parallel with the weapons proves it – that the term *lima* ('file') is not confined to generically evoking the idea of adding finishing touches, but vividly maintains the reference to the manual instrument.

70 For other examples of the metaphorical use of *robigo* in Sidonius and other authors, see Gualandri 1979: 129, n. 78. Regarding *barbarismus*, see Condorelli 2001 (cited above in n. 32) and Squillante 2018. For a different metaphor, the *sermonis Celtici squama* (*ep.* 3.3.2), see Giannotti 2016: 138–41, with bibliographic discussion.

71 Wolff 2020: 395–6. For literary studies as a unifying element for the Roman aristocrats in Barbarian Gaul, see Mathisen 1993: 105–18.

Bibliography

Amherdt, D. (2001), *Sidoine Apollinaire: Le quatrième livre de la correspondance: introduction et commentaire*, Bern: Lang.

Anderson, W. B., ed. (1936 and 1965), *Sidonius*, vol. 1, *Poems and Letters* [books 1–2], vol. 2 (completed by W. H. Semple and E. H. Warmington), *Letters* [books 3–9], London: Heinemann.

Aymard, J. (1964), 'Sidoine Apollinaire et la chasse', in M. Renard and R. Schilling (eds), *Hommages à Jean Bayet*, 47–53, Brussels: Latomus.

Becht-Jördens, G. (2017), 'Ein Waschbecken mit Versinschrift des Sidonius als Danaergeschenk für die Gotenkönigin Ragnahild: Zur Bedeutung von Materialität, Handwerks- und Dichtkunst im Diskurs der Ohnmächtigen (Sidon. *epist.* IV 8)', *A&A*, 63: 125–53.

Cameron, A. (2011), *The Last Pagans of Rome*, New York: Oxford University Press.

Condorelli, S. (2001), 'Una particolare accezione di *barbarismus* in Sidonio Apollinare', in U. Criscuolo (ed.), *Mnemosynon: Studi di letteratura e di umanità in memoria di D. Gagliardi*, 101–9, Napoli: La buona stampa.

Condorelli, S. (2020), 'Sidonio e Venanzio Fortunato', in A. Di Stefano and M. Onorato (eds), *Lo specchio del modello: Orizzonti intertestuali e* Fortleben *di Sidonio Apollinare*, 361–406, Napoli: Loffredo.

Consolino, F. E. (2011), 'Panegiristi e creazione del consenso nell'occidente latino', in G. Urso (ed.), *Dicere laudes: Elogio, comunicazione, creazione del consenso*, 299–336, Pisa: ETS.

Consolino, F. E. (2020), 'Sidonius' Shorter Poems', in G. Kelly and J. van Waarden (eds), *Edinburgh Companion to Sidonius Apollinaris*, 341–72, Edinburgh: Edinburgh University Press.

Egetenmeyr, V. (2021), 'Sidonius Apollinaris's Use of the Term *Barbarus*: An Introduction', in M. Friedrich and J. M. Harland (eds), *Interrogating the 'Germanic': A Category and its Use in Late Antiquity and the Early Middle Ages*. Supplement to *Reallexikon der Germanischen Altertumskunde*, 123: 145–66, Berlin: De Gruyter.

Fascione, S. (2019), *Gli 'altri' al potere: Romani e barbari nella Gallia di Sidonio Apollinare*, Bari: Edipuglia.

Ficca, F. (2018), 'Echi senecani nel proemio di Floro', *BSL*, 48: 596–604.

Flierman, R. (2017), *Saxon Identities, AD 150–900*, London: Bloomsbury.

Fo, A. (1999), 'Sidonio nelle mani di Eurico (*Ep.* VII 9): Spazi della tradizione culturale in un nuovo contesto romanobarbarico', in M. Rotili (ed.), *Memoria del passato e urgenza del futuro: Il mondo romano fra V e VII secolo. Atti delle VI giornate di studio sull'età romanobarbarica (18–20 giugno 1998)*, 17–37, Napoli: Arte tipografica.

Fo, A. (2002), 'Arginare la decadenza da "minore": Sidonio Apollinare', in S. Ronchey (ed.), *La decadenza: Un seminario*, 154–90, Palermo: Sellerio.

Giannotti, F. (2000–2), 'L'epistola III 3 di Sidonio Apollinare fra encomio di Ecdicio e misobarbarismo', *RomBarb*, 17: 161–82.

Giannotti, F. (2016), Sperare meliora. *Il terzo libro delle* Epistulae *di Sidonio Apollinare. Introduzione, traduzione e commento*, Pisa: ETS.

Giannotti, F. (2020a), '*Vivet in posterum nominis tui gloria*: La lettera di Sidonio a Fortunale (VIII 5)', *Maia*, 72: 139–48.

Giannotti, F. (2020b), '*Litteras nosse*: l'*ep.* 8, 2 di Sidonio Apollinare e l'importanza della cultura sotto i barbari', *Pan*, 9: 143–53.

Giannotti, F. (2021), 'Je suis le miroir à la fin de la décadence: Mirror-Games between Sidonius Apollinaris and Jean Marcel', *CC*, 7: 146–56.

Giannotti, F. (2022), '*Maxumam solitudinem appello*: the Presence of Tacitus in Sidonius Apollinaris', *Pan*, 11: 67–77.

Gibbon, E. (1776–88), *The History of the Decline and Fall of the Roman Empire*, London: Strahan & Cadell.

Gualandri, I. (1979), Furtiva lectio: *Studi su Sidonio Apollinare*, Milano: Cisalpino-Goliardica.

Gualandri, I. (2000), 'Figure di barbari in Sidonio Apollinare', in G. Lanata (ed.), *Il tardoantico alle soglie del Duemila: Diritto, religione, società*, 105–29, Pisa: ETS.

Hanaghan, M. P. (2019), *Reading Sidonius' Epistles*, Cambridge: Cambridge University Press.

Harland, J. M. (2019), 'Imagining the Saxons in Late Antique Gaul', in M. Augstein and M. Hardt (eds), *Sächsische Leute und Länder Benennung und Lokalisierung von Gruppenidentitäten im ersten Jahrtausend*, 45–56, Wendeburg: Uwe Krebs.

Harries, J. (1994), *Sidonius Apollinaris and the Fall of Rome AD 407–485*, Oxford: Clarendon Press.

Heather, P. J. (1996), *The Goths*, Oxford: Blackwell.

Kaufmann, F.-M. (1995), *Studien zu Sidonius Apollinaris*, Frankfurt am Main: Lang.

Kelly, G. (2020), 'Dating the Works of Sidonius', in G. Kelly and J. van Waarden (eds), *Edinburgh Companion to Sidonius Apollinaris*, 166–94, Edinburgh: Edinburgh University Press.

Kelly, G. and J. van Waarden, eds (2020), *Edinburgh Companion to Sidonius Apollinaris*, Edinburgh: Edinburgh University Press.

Köhler, H. (1995), *C. Sollius Apollinaris Sidonius Briefe Buch I: Einleitung, Text, Übersetzung, Kommentar*, Heidelberg: Winter.

Köhler, H. (1998), '"Der Geist ist offenbar im Buch wie das Antlitz im Spiegel": Zu Sidonius *epist.* I 2, III 13, VII 1', in M. Baumbach, H. Köhler, and A. M. Ritter (eds), *Mousopolos Stephanos: Festschrift für Herwig Görgemanns*, 333–45, Heidelberg: Winter.

Köhler, H. (2014), *C. Sollius Apollinaris Sidonius, Die Briefe, eingelaitet, übersetzt und erläutert*, Stuttgart: Hiersemann.

Kulikowski, M. E. (2020), 'Sidonius' Political World', in G. Kelly and J. van Waarden (eds), *Edinburgh Companion to Sidonius Apollinaris*, 197–213, Edinburgh: Edinburgh University Press.

Loyen, A., ed. (1960 and 1970), *Sidoine Apollinaire, texte établi et traduit par, vol. 1, Poèmes, vols. 2–3, Lettres*, Paris: Les Belles Lettres.

Luiselli, B. (1992), *Storia culturale dei rapporti fra mondo romano e mondo germanico*, Roma: Herder.

Martindale, J. R. (1980), *The Prosopography of the Late Roman Empire, vol. 2, A.D. 395–527*, Cambridge: Cambridge University Press.

Mascoli, P., ed. (2021), *Sidonio Apollinare. Epistolario: Introduzione, traduzione e note a cura di*, Roma: Città Nuova.

Mathisen, R. W. (1993), *Roman Aristocrats in Barbarian Gaul: Strategies for Survival in an Age of Transition*, Austin, TX: University of Texas Press.

Mathisen, R. W. (2020), 'A Prosopography of Sidonius: Persons Mentioned in the Works of Sidonius (Fourth and Fifth Centuries)', in G. Kelly and J. van Waarden (eds), *Edinburgh Companion to Sidonius Apollinaris*, 76–154, Edinburgh: Edinburgh University Press.

Meurer, T. L. (2019), *Vergangenes verhandeln: Spätantike Statusdiskurse senatorischer Eliten in Gallien und Italien*, Berlin: De Gruyter.

Mratschek, S. (2020), 'Creating Culture and Presenting the Self in Sidonius', in G. Kelly and J. van Waarden (eds), *Edinburgh Companion to Sidonius Apollinaris*, 237–60, Edinburgh: Edinburgh University Press.

Neri, M., ed. (2009), *Ruricio di Limoges, Lettere*, Pisa: ETS.

Overwien, O. (2009), 'Kampf um Gallien: die Briefe des Sidonius Apollinaris zwischen Literatur und Politik', *Hermes*, 137 (1): 93–117.

Piacente, L. (1998), 'Sopravvivenze dei classici: i *Logistorici* di Varrone', *InvLuc*, 20: 191–9.

Roller, D.W. (2021), *Three Ancient Geographical Treatises in Translation: Hanno, the King Nikomedes Periodos, and Avienus*, London: Routledge.

Schwitter, R. (2015), *Umbrosa lux: Obscuritas in der lateinischen Epistolographie der Spätantike*, Stuttgart: Steiner.

Squillante, M. (2016), 'Modello lucreziano e *superstitio* nell'epistolario sidoniano', in L. Cristante and V. Veronesi (eds), *Forme di accesso al sapere in età tardoantica e altomedievale*, vol. 6, 179–88, Trieste: Università degli Studi di Trieste.

Squillante, M. (2018), '*Vanescentium litterarum vestigia* . . .', *InvLuc*, 40: 125–34.

Stevens, C. E. (1933), *Sidonius Apollinaris and His Age*, Oxford: Clarendon Press.

Stoehr-Monjou, A. (2009), 'Sidoine Apollinaire et la fin d'un monde: Poétique de l'éclat dans les panégyriques et leurs Préfaces', *REL*, 87: 207–30.

Stroheker, K. F. (1948) *Der senatorische Adel im spätantiken Gallien*, Tübingen: Alma Mater.

van Waarden, J. (2010 and 2016), *Writing to Survive: A Commentary on Sidonius Apollinaris, Letters Book 7, vol. 1: The Episcopal Letters 1–11, vol. 2: The Ascetic Letters 12–18*, Leuven: Peeters.

van Waarden, J. (2018), '"Il tempo invecchia in fretta": la biografia di Sidonio Apollinare nella sua corrispondenza', *InvLuc*, 40: 187–98.

Vogel, F., ed. (1885), *Magni Felicis Ennodii Opera omnia recensuit F. Vogel. 'Monumenta Germaniae Historica, Auctores Antiquissimi' 7*, Berolini: apud Weidmannos.

Wallis, E., trans. (1996), *Cyprian of Carthage, An Address To Demetrianus*. Available online: https://www.ewtn.com/catholicism/library/address-to-demtrianus--ad-demetrianum-11410.

Wolff, É. (2020), 'Sidonius' Vocabulary, Syntax, and Style', in G. Kelly and J. van Waarden (eds), *Edinburgh Companion to Sidonius Apollinaris*, 395–417, Edinburgh: Edinburgh University Press.

Wooding, J. M. (1988), 'Saxons Who Furrow the British Sea with Hides', *The Great Circle*, 10 (1): 33–36.

Zucchelli, B. (1981), *Varro logistoricus: Studio letterario e prosopografico*, Parma: Università degli Studi di Parma.

Part Two

Confronting Identities: Othering Individuals

12

A Greek Lawgiver in the *Epitome* of Pompeius Trogus: Justin's Account of Lycurgus

Martina Gatto

In the third book of Justin's *Epitome* of Pompeius Trogus, two paragraphs are dedicated to Sparta's early history. Justin provides a biographical sketch of Lycurgus and a detailed account of the traditional Spartan laws despite the brevity. To explore Sparta's perception in Latin historiography and the Roman narratives about the 'otherness', this chapter endeavours to examine how Justin, following Trogus, portrayed Lycurgus and how his biographical and political tradition could be relevant for the Roman public during the Imperial Age. Moreover, a closer look at Justin's exposition shall reveal significant differences and aspects in common with Plutarch, Ephorus, and other Greek sources.

First, it is necessary to clarify the relationship between Trogus and Justin and the third book's content. Justin's chronology continues to be debated; chronological proposals range from the second to the fourth century.[1] He epitomizes the forty-four books of Pompeius Trogus' work, the first universal history known in Latin historiography, probably composed during the early years of Augustus' empire.[2] Apart from some fragments, most of the extant material of Pompeius derives primarily from Justin's *Epitome* and the so-called *prologi*, brief summaries of each book probably not written by Justin.[3]

According to the *prologus* of the third book, the first section focuses on Persia's events, such as the death of Xerxes, the conspiracy of Artabanus, and the Persian reconquest of Egypt. Next, Trogus deals with the emergence of conflicts between the Greeks following the Peace of Callias. The contrast between Athens and Sparta provides a pretext for Trogus to introduce an *excursus* on the origins of the Peloponnese and the Doric foundation of Sparta:

> ut Graecis cum rege pacificatis bella inter ipsos orta sint. Inde repetitae Peloponnensium origines: ut ab Herculis posteris Dorico populo sit occupata . . .

> How the Greeks, after the peace with the king of Persia, waged wars among themselves. There are recalled the origins of the Peloponnesians: how they were occupied by the descendants of Hercules, a Dorian people.

Furthermore, the prologue preserves the references to Sparta's wars against the Argives and the Messenians, the Isthmus' tyrannies, and the First Sacred War.[4]

Justin only includes some of these themes, omitting important episodes mentioned in Prologue III. However, at this time we shall consider the elements related to Spartan history exclusively: comparing the *prologus* with the *Epitome*, one immediately notices that the only surviving element of Trogus' *Origines Peloponnensium* is the account of Lycurgus and his constitution, while the Return of the Heraclids is absent.[5]

As Justin stated in his *praefatio*, the writer eliminated what was not pleasant to read or did not set a learning example. Thus, since the original account of Sparta had a moral value, the epitomizer considered Lycurgus' passage noteworthy enough to be included.[6] Still, Justin's omissions (partial or complete) of Trogus' digressions are not unusual, and we can distinguish several cases of complete suppression involving *excursus* on the origins of peoples – for instance, for Egyptians or Cretans.[7]

Returning to the *incipit* of book III, after the Persian events Justin introduces the growing conflict between Sparta and Athens, mentioning Solon and Lycurgus as the lawgivers of the two most powerful *poleis* in Greece.[8] From this association, he begins to summarize the main points of Lycurgus' life, although no chronological indication is provided for the statesman's *akmē*:[9]

> namque Lycurgus cum fratri suo Polydectae, Spartanorum regi, successisset regnumque sibi vindicare potuisset, Charillo,[10] filio eius, qui natus postumus erat, cum ad aetatem adultam pervenisset, regnum summa fide restituit, ut intellegerent omnes, quanto plus apud bonos pietatis iura quam omnes opes valerent. medio igitur tempore, dum infans convalescit tutelamque eius administrat, non habentibus Spartanis leges instituit, non inventione earum magis, quam exemplo clarior: siquidem nihil lege ulla in alios sanxit, cuius non ipse primus in se documentum daret.[11]

> Lycurgus, although he had succeeded his brother Polydektes, king of Sparta, and could claim the royal title for himself, reinstated to the throne with utmost loyalty his brother's son Charillus, born after his father's death, as soon as he became adult, so that everyone might understand how much more, among the good men, the laws of integrity are worth than all possessions. In the meantime, while the infant was growing up, and Lycurgus had the custody of the boy, he

> established the laws for the Spartans who previously had none; he was celebrated no more for their formulation than for his concrete example. Since he has not imposed on anyone by any law, whose example he had not given himself first.

Justin's version of Lycurgus' life begins with a reference to the guardianship of the young Charillus, both his nephew and son of his brother Polydektes. Thus, Lycurgus is assigned to the Eurypontid lineage, following the majority of tradition; this genealogy (with few variants) is the most accepted and is coherent with Plutarch's account.[12] Since Trogus was presumably active during the Augustan age, it is important to note that Plutarch's *Life of Lycurgus*, the fundamental biographical source on the lawgiver, is later than Trogus' *Historiae*. As we shall see, Trogus included several of the significant themes from Hellenistic historiography which Plutarch himself later took into consideration.[13]

The epitomizer implies that the Spartan lawgiver might easily have maintained his royal authority; only because of his high moral stature and deep family loyalty did he decide to relinquish his powers. Likewise, Ephorus and Plutarch report a period of Lycurgus' reign preceding the actual ascension of the nephew to the throne. However, according to Ephorus' fragment and Plutarch's biography, Lycurgus was accused by his political opponents of having planned a plot against the child and, then, he decided to flee to Crete.[14] In contrast, the virtuous Lycurgus described in the *Epitome* does not seem to face any political opposition establishing his legislation and is not forced to escape; thus, he travelled to the Cretan island exclusively to end his life in a voluntary exile. Before briefly examining the laws established by Lycurgus, here is how the 'epitomized' biography ends:

> haec quoniam primo solutis antea moribus dura videbat esse, auctorem eorum Apollinem Delphicum fingit et inde se ea ex praecepto numinis detulisse, ut consuescendi taedium metus religionis vincat. dein ut aeternitatem legibus suis daret, iure iurando obligat civitatem, nihil eos de eius legibus mutaturos, priusque reverteretur, et simulat se ad oraculum Delphicum proficisci, consulturum quid addendum mutandumque legibus videretur. proficiscitur autem Cretam ibique perpetuum exsilium egit abicique in mare ossa sua moriens iussit, ne relatis Lacedaemonem solutos se Spartani religione iuris iurandi in dissolvendis legibus arbitrarentur.[15]

> Since at first he [Lycurgus] saw these laws as severe, as the customs had previously been relaxed, he pretended that Apollo of Delphi was their author and that he had brought them himself at the god's command, so that religious fear would prevail over the frustration of getting used to them. Then, to secure eternal life

> to his laws, Lycurgus binds the city by an oath that they were not to change the laws in any way before he returned, and he pretends to go to the oracle of Delphi to consult on whether anything seemed necessary to be added or modified in his laws. However, in reality, he travelled to Crete and spent his life in permanent exile; he ordered, when he was dying, that his bones be thrown into the sea to avoid that, if they were taken back to Sparta, the Spartans could consider themselves absolved from their oath concerning the alteration in his laws.

Rationalized versions of Lycurgus' divine inspiration are attested by many Greek sources, such as Polybius, Diodorus, Dionysius of Halicarnassus, and Plutarch, becoming a historiographical *topos* for archaic lawgivers. According to these accounts, the relationship between the lawgiver and Apollo was as a 'political lie' being spread to make legislation more acceptable.[16] However, the passage from Trogus' work manifests this rationalistic approach even more explicitly. According to Justin, Lycurgus pretended to have obtained the god's sanction to persuade the Spartans to accept the new rigid lifestyle. Moreover, the political lie does not only apply to just one but two oracle consultations: the first preceding the establishment of the normative *corpus* ('auctorem eorum Apollinem Delphicum fingit', he pretended that Apollo of Delphi was their author), the latter for possible alteration or final approval ('simulat se ad oraculum Delphicum proficisci, consulturum quid addendum mutandumque legibus videretur', he pretends to go to the oracle of Delphi to consult on whether anything seemed necessary to be added or modified in his laws). Furthermore, since he went to Crete instead of Delphi, Lycurgus also lied about his actual destination.

The version of Lycurgus' death in Crete was accepted, in the fourth century BCE, by Timaeus and Aristoxenus and, later, by Aristokrates of Sparta, a local writer quoted by Plutarch.[17] According to Aristokrates' fragment, when Lycurgus died in Crete, his hosts burned his body and scattered the ashes in the sea, since the lawgiver had asked them to prevent even the tiniest shred of his own body from returning to Sparta, which would render the Spartans' oath meaningless.[18] Even though the intention behind Lycurgus' request is the same as in Plutarch, the *Epitome*'s text provides us with a new variant, according to which Lycurgus would have asked to simply throw his bones ('in mare ossa sua moriens iussit', he ordered that his bones be thrown into the sea) without resorting to cremation.[19] Interestingly, in the next paragraph, Justin mentions the scattering of ashes for another Spartan statesman: Phalanthus, the founder of Tarentum.[20]

Before Lycurgus, the Spartans had an extremely relaxed régime (*solutis moribus*, customs relaxed) and did not even possess any form of legislation.[21] Moreover, the ancient lawgiver filled a normative *vacuum* as the sole creator of the constitution, without being inspired by the god Apollo. Lycurgus stands out only by his virtue and moral authority, ordering by law upon others solely what he has given an example of observance in his life.[22]

Why would Justin include these details about Lycurgus' biography? Considering his selection and manipulation methods, he was particularly interested in unusual details, anecdotal accounts, and edifying subjects. Since Justin's aim was to produce a collection of passages he found interesting, we can suppose that the taste for anecdotes and moralistic content is the reason why he preferred Lycurgus' honourable life and his final self-sacrifice, rather than other crucial events on Spartan origins (such as the return of Heraclids or the foundation of the double kingship).

As already stated, Justin reports a list of the major measures passed by the legislator.[23] Each norm is presented in the form of an instruction given by Lycurgus to the Spartans. First, he strengthened the role of state authorities and promoted frugality and moderation among the citizens. Next, he chose to maintain a pre-monetary economy by banishing gold and silver coinage. According to Justin, the only form of economic transaction permitted in Lycurgus' Sparta was the commodities exchange ('non pecunia, sed conpensatione mercium').[24] Interestingly, in this context there is no mention of the iron *nomisma* traditionally attributed since the fourth century to Lycurgus as an alternative to the circulation and possession of precious metals.[25]

Although Justin summarizes only the essential points of Trogus' discourse, he offers precise information on Spartan laws and institutions; most of these measures appear also in Plutarch's *Life of Lycurgus*, almost in the same order of presentation.[26] Justin presents the division of powers and notes the area of competence for each political body: the dual kingship exercises military authority; the magistrates elected annually (the ephors) exercise judicial power; the council of the elders is the guardian of laws; the popular assembly elects magistrates and *gerontes*.[27] After these remarks on political institutions, Trogus – through the mediation of Justin – lists the norms passed by Lycurgus to promote equality and eliminate luxury. As Polybius before him, Trogus ascribed to Lycurgus an equal division of the public land to avoid excessive wealth and property concentration: '[Lycurgus] fundos omnium aequaliter inter omnes divisit, ut aequata patrimonia neminem potentiorem altero redderent' (The lands of the whole state Lycurgus divided equally among all, that equality of possession might leave no one more powerful than another). Furthermore, the lawgiver introduced austere dinners in public messes, not allowing any luxury or ostentatious display.[28]

From the fourth century onwards, the austerity and the contempt for wealth coincided with the standard image of Sparta. It may be interesting to mention a passage of book XX, according to which Pythagoras imitated Lycurgus and introduced a frugal *modus vivendi* in Kroton to prevent the downfall of the state. To learn about Spartan and Cretan constitutions and customs, Pythagoras supposedly travelled to Sparta and the island; then, he returned to Magna Graecia to educate his fellow citizens according to Lycurgus and Minos' teachings.[29]

Returning to Justin's account on Sparta, the epitomizer also summarizes the features of the rigorous education received by the Spartan youth. Following strict rules of behaviour, young Spartans learned how to survive enduring deprivation and hardship:

> iuvenibus non amplius una veste uti toto anno permissum, nec quemquam cultius quam alterum progredi nec epulari opulentius, ne imitatio in luxuriam verteretur. pueros puberes non in forum, sed in agrum deduci praecepit, ut primos annos non in luxuria, sed in opere et in laboribus agerent. nihil eos somni causa substernere et vitam sine pulmento degere, neque prius in urbem redire quam viri facti essent, statuit.[30]

> Lycurgus would not allow the young people to wear more than one dress in a year, nor anyone to appear in public in finer clothes than another, or to dine more luxuriously, lest the imitation of such practices should lead to luxury. He prescribed the boys, once they reached puberty, to be carried not into the *forum*, but into the countryside, that they might spend their early years not indulging in luxury, but in hard labour and struggles. He commanded the boys not to put anything under them to sleep upon or live on highly seasoned food and prohibited them from returning to the city until they reached adulthood.

In Justin's eyes, the education took place outside of the city as a 'primitive' form of initiation. However, Spartan training, described by Xenophon and Plutarch, generally implied that children should constantly live under the watch of the whole community. Thus, even though Justin is clearly referring to general education, this unusual aspect might presuppose a confusion with the *krypteia*.[31] In the infamous *krypteia*, a young Spartan lived a temporary period of hardship hiding in the remote countryside, without the systematic surveillance of the city. According to Plato, *kryptai* did not use footwear during winter and slept without shelter, enduring extremely harsh living conditions.[32] Justin, however, like Plato before him, does not mention the hunting and slaughter of the helots, a practice associated with the *krypteia*, narrated by Aristotle, and condemned by Plutarch.[33]

To catch the Roman reader's attention, Justin and Trogus contrast the Spartans' departure from the city with an allusion to the *deductio* in the forum, well known to the Roman audience ('non in forum, sed in agrum deduci praecepit', to be carried not into the forum, but into the countryside). Although different, both customs can be understood as rites of passage into adulthood: while the Spartan boys were allowed to return as men only after enduring a life of privations, Roman boys' transition to manhood was celebrated at the *forum* (laying down the *toga praetexta* and putting on the *toga virilis*).[34]

At the end of the Lycurgus' account, to ensure that women were chosen for their personal virtues, he introduces the prohibition of dowry for Spartan wives and establishes the most significant honours for the older citizens. Interestingly, Plutarch does not mention the prohibition of the dowry in the *Life of Lycurgus*, although it can be found in the *Apophthegmata Laconica*.[35]

To sum up, Justin's account offers a general description of the laws of Lycurgus, praising the abstention from luxury as well as austerity as distinguishing elements. Although Trogus' sources are unclear, the importance of these themes might originate from general Hellenistic viewpoints upon Sparta or from sources directly connected to the third-century egalitarian reforms.[36] For instance, the author of the *Historiae Philippicae* might have consulted Phylarchus, quoted by Plutarch in the *Lives* of Agis and Kleomenes; another option might be the Ephorus' Ἱστορίαι, interested in both the constitution and the biography of Lycurgus.[37] Furthermore, we might detect some influence of Xenophon: the prohibition of gold and silver, the establishment of common messes, and the youths wearing only one dress throughout the year were all previously accepted by him.[38]

However, several traditional elements of the Spartan constitution are lacking in Justin's summary. As we have already seen, we cannot find any allusion to the brutal killing of helots during the *krypteia*. Moreover, the practice of wife-sharing, the nudity of young men and women in public contexts, and pederasty – all topics discussed, for instance, by Plutarch – are omitted.[39] Rather than unknown, all these traditional elements might have been purposely overlooked because they were perceived as incompatible with the Roman mentality and inconsistent with the positive portrayal of Lycurgus as a political reformer. Thus, by stressing the ancient Spartan morality and equality, Trogus might have only preserved the qualities appreciated within the context of Augustus' cultural restoration to the ancient values.[40]

Furthermore, other paradigms of Roman culture and historiography can be easily recognized. For instance, we can mention the Latin moderation and austerity, the political balance of power between institutions, and the respect for the elders and the Senate.[41] In particular, the concept of *severitas* (strictness) used to describe Spartan customs is essential for the *mos maiorum* (the custom of ancestors) and represents a primary expression of Roman traditional virtue. Like the Spartans, respectable Roman citizens were indeed expected to display a sternness of manner and action, and to behave with integrity and self-discipline.[42]

A comparison with some passages of Valerius Maximus is valuable. Unlike Justin, Valerius Maximus reports an episode of violence against Lycurgus perpetrated by his political enemies. Since the Spartans were so ungrateful to the *vir maior et utilior* (more important and more useful man) of Sparta, Valerius Maximus contrasts the great moral depth and the *summa sinceritas* (the strict uprightness) of Lycurgus with their unjustified act of hostility. The lawgiver was targeted several times by stone throwers, deprived of an eye, and even forced to flee from Sparta. In the end, Valerius Maximus wonders why this city, which claims itself credit for its *gravitas* (seriousness) and *moderatio* (moderation), appears so ungrateful towards such a deserving man.[43] By the same token, in the second book of his *Facta et dicta*, Valerius Maximus praises the austerity of the Spartans and explicitly associates the Spartan and Roman ways of life, in opposition to the softness of Asian peoples:

> idem sensit proxima maiorum nostrorum gravitati Spartana civitas, quac severissimis Lycurgi legibus obtemperans aliquaum diu civium suorum oculos a contemplanda Asia retraxit.

> The Spartan community, which came close to the gravity of our ancestors, felt the same. Obeying the austere laws of Lycurgus, for some long time, it drew the eyes of its members back from gazing at Asia.[44]

Lastly, it is also important to note that Justin's *Epitome* circulated widely during the Medieval Age and was frequently used as a school text.[45] Between the late thirteenth and the early fourteenth centuries, Ptolemy of Lucca, a disciple of Thomas Aquinas, still explicitly mentioned Justin as a primary source on Lycurgus in several passages of the treatise *De Regimine Principum*.[46] Ptolemy even declared that, although various stories of Lycurgus have been told, he decided to follow Justin because of his superior authority in historical matters.[47] Thus, Justin's description played a significant role in Lycurgus' reception during the Roman Empire and in the following centuries, especially when the knowledge of Greek declined in Western Europe.[48]

In conclusion, Justin's *Epitome* testifies the surviving interest in the Greek lawgiver as a model statesman and a moral *exemplum* for the Roman public, appropriate for both Trogus and Justin's epoch. According to the *Epitome of Trogus*, Lycurgus was loyal to the rightful king by renouncing the throne, imposed on the Spartans his morals and ethical views, and even sacrificed himself to preserve the immutability of the laws. Furthermore, the Lycurgan *kosmos* (good order) represents a positive socio-political model that embodied the *severitas*, the *frugalitas* (frugality), and other key virtues of the Roman world.

Notes

1 Several scholars (Malaspina 1976: 134; Yardley and Heckel 1997: 10–15; Borgna 2014: 64–6) date the *Epitome* between the second and the third centuries CE; others (Syme 1988; Mineo 2016: LI–LIX) suggest the second half of the fourth century CE. On the difficulty of determining the chronology of Justin's work, see Santi Amantini 2017: 1–4.

2 For a general overview of Pompeius Trogus' work and chronology, cf. Forni and Bertinelli Angeli 1982: 1298–301; Alonso-Núñez 1987; Mineo 2016: I–XLI; Santi Amantini 2017: 4–28.

3 On the *prologi* and their independence of Justin, cf. Forni and Bertinelli Angeli 1982: 1299; Mineo 2016: LX–LXI; Santi Amantini 2017: 8–10.

4 Cf. Iust., *Prol.* III, 'tertio volumine continentur haec: ut mortuo Xerxe filius Artaxerxes ultus interfectorem patris Artabanum bellum cum defectore Aegypti habuit, primoque dux eius Achaemenes victus est, iterum per Bagabaxum Aegyptus recepta. ut Graecis cum rege pacificatis bella inter ipsos orta sint. inde repetitae Peloponnensium origines: ut ab Herculis posteris Dorico populo sit occupata. deinde bella Argolica et Messania, coalitique Sicyone et Corintho tyranni. bellum Crisaeum et quod Athenienses primo cum Boeotis, dein cum Peloponnesiis gesserunt' (These things are included in the third volume. After the death of Xerxes, his son Artaxerxes, taking revenge on Artabanus, his father's murderer, fought against the one who had instigated Egypt's rebellion; and first, his general Achaemenes was defeated, and then Egypt was recaptured by Bagabaxus. How the Greeks, after the peace with the king of Persia, waged wars among themselves. There are recalled the origins of the Peloponnesians: how they were occupied by the descendants of Hercules, a Dorian people. Next, the Argolian and Messenian wars and the alliance between the tyrants of Sicyon and Corinth. The war of Crisa and how the Athenians fought first with the Boeotians and then with the Peloponnesians). On the contents of the prologue of book III, cf. Bearzot 2014: 101–4.

5 Cf. Bearzot 2014: 104.

6 Cf. Iust., *Praef.* 4.

7 Cf. Forni and Bertinelli Angeli 1982: 1303 and n. 25. For instance, Justin completely suppresses the digressions on the origins of Egypt (prologue I), Thessaly (prologue II), Cyprus (prologue IX), and Crete (prologue XXIX). More in general on Justin's selection methods, see Forni and Bertinelli Angeli 1982: 1301–7; Borgna 2014: 61–3; Mineo 2016: XLVI–LI.

8 Cf. Iust. 3.1 (Artabanus and Artaxerxes); 3.2.1–4 (Sparta against Athens).

9 Comparing Justin with the prologues, the suppression of chronological references, toponyms, eponyms, and onomastic indications seems relatively frequent, cf. Forni Bertinelli Angeli 1982: 1303; Mineo 2016: L.

10 The form Χαρίλλος for the name of the young heir is attested in Aristotle (*Pol.* 2.1271b; 5.1316a), Sosibius (*FGrHist* 595 F2), Plutarch (*Cleom.* 10.8), and Pausanias (2.36.4; 3.7; 4.4; 8.5; 48). Other sources, however, also report the variant Χαρίλαος; for the complete list of attestations, cf. Polito 2001: 53, n. 13.

11 Iust. 3.2.5–8. Unless otherwise indicated, translations are my own.

12 For Lycurgus in the Eurypontids' lineage, cf. Simon. F123 Page = F628 PMG; Dieuch., *FGrHist* 485 F5; Arist., *Pol.* 2.1271b 24–27; cf. Plut., *Lyc.* 1.8; Ael., *VH* 13.23. Lycurgus belongs to the royal family of the Agiads only according to Herdotous (1.65.4) and Pausanias (3.2.3).

13 Hodkinson 2000: 53.

14 Cf. Ephor., *FGrHist* 70 F149 (= Strab. 10.4.19); Plut., *Lyc.* 3.6. In Lycurgus' biography, Plutarch states that he ruled for a total of eight months; in contrast, in the *Life of Solon* (16.2), the author indicates in general terms several years of reign. Other sources, such as Herodotus (1.65) or Aristotle (*Pol.* 4.1296a), include the role of warden only, not mentioning any temporary title of king, cf. also Manfredini and Piccirilli 1990: 223.

15 Iust. 3.3.10–12.

16 Cf. Pol. 10.2.8–12; Diod. Dion. Hal. 2.61.2; Plut., *Num.* 4.12. On divine inspiration as a means of political legitimization in Lycurgus (and Numa), cf. Rodrigues 2012.

17 Cf. Tim., *FGrHist* 566 F128; Aristox., F44 Wehrli^2; Aristocr., *FGrHist/BNJ* 591 F3 (= Plut., *Lyc.* 31.10).

18 Cf. Aristocr., *FGrHist/BNJ* 591 F3 (= Plut., *Lyc.* 31.10).

19 Since it is challenging to establish Trogus' sources and considering the chronological difficulties for both authors, we cannot determine whether Trogus read Aristokrates, as proposed by Zecchini 2016: 186. After the discovery of an unpublished inscription of Tiberius' reign, scholars generally assign Aristokrates of Sparta to the early imperial age, cf. Cartledge and Spawforth 2002: 177; Kennell and Powell 2014 (*BNJ* 591).

20 On the scattering of the ashes of Phalanthus in the agora of Tarentum, cf. Iust. 3.4.13.

21 Cf. Iust. 3.2.7. See supra p. 1.

22 Cf. Iust. 3.2.8.

23 On Justin's summary of Lycurgus' constitution, cf. Hodkinson 2000: 52; Zecchini 2016: 185, n. 86; Santi Amantini 2017: 234–6.

24 Iust. 3.2.9–12.

25 Cf. Xen., *Lac. Pol.* 7; [Plat.,] *Eryx.* 400 a–b; Pol. 6.49.8; Plut., *Lys.* 17.4; *Lyc.* 9.2–5; *Comp. Arist. - Cat. Ma.* 3.2; *Apopht. Lac.* 226d; Poll. 7.105; 9.79. On the Spartan *nomisma* and pre-monetary economy, cf. Christien 2002.

26 Cf. Plut., *Lyc.* 6–10. On the resemblances between Plutarch and the *Epitome*, cf. Hodkinson 2000: 52.

27 Cf. Iust. 3.3.1–2.

28 Cf. Iust. 3.3.1–10. On the division of land in Polybius and Plutarch, cf. Pol. 6.48; Plut., *Lyc.* 8. In contrast, Plato only mentions a land division that predates Lycurgus' measures, cf. Plat., *Leg.* 3.684d–e.

29 Iust. 20.4–5, 'inde [Pythagoras] regressus Cretam et Lacedaemona ad cognoscendas Minois et Lycurgi inclitas ea tempestate leges contenderat. quibus omnibus instructus Crotonam uenit populumque in luxuriam lapsum auctoritate sua ad usum frugalitatis revocavit' (On his return, Pythagoras went to Crete and Lacedaemon to instruct himself in the laws of Minos and Lycurgus, which at that time were in high repute. Then, furnished with all these attainments, he came to Kroton and recovered, by his authority, the people falling into luxury to a temperate and frugal life). On the parallelism between Lycurgus and Pythagoras in this passage, cf. Borgna 2012: 7–8. On Pythagoras fighting against *tryphē* (luxuriousness), see Talamo 2010.

30 Iust. 3.3.5–7.

31 Cf. Birgalias 1999: 75; Ducat 2006: 184–5; Santi Amantini 2017: 236, n. 16. Nevertheless, the fact that Justin conceived Spartan education outside of the city is confirmed by a passage of book 23. According to Justin, the education of the Lucanians conformed to Lycurgus' laws: their training took place in the woods, and the young men had no clothes or bedding, and had to eat the products of their hunt (cf. Iust. 23.1.7–9).

32 Plat., *Leg.* 1.633b–c.

33 Arist. fr. 538 Rose^3 = fr. 543 Gigon; Plut., *Lyc.* 28. On the sources, the purpose, and ideology of the *krypteia*, cf. Ducat 2006: 281–331.

34 However, the *deductio in Forum* does not happen at the start of adolescence. Thus, Ducat 2006: 188 reads in this passage a mere literary effect, without real significance. On the end of childhood in Roman world, cf. Laes 2011: 278–80.

35 Cf. Iust. 3.3.8: '... virgines sine dote nubere iussit ...' (Lycurgus ordered the virgins to be married without dowry); 3, 9: 'maximum honorem non divitum et potentium, sed pro gradu aetatis senum esse voluit ...' (He decreed that the highest respect should be paid, not to the rich and powerful, but the old, according to their degrees of seniority). For the prohibition of dowry in Sparta, cf. Hermipp., *FGrHist* 1026 F6 (= Athen. 13.555c); Plut., *Apopht. Lac.* 227f–228a; Ael., *VH* 6.6.

36 Cf. Hodkinson 2000: 53.

37 Gabba 1957: 202–4 supposes that the notion of the land distribution in Plutarch and Trogus comes from Phylarchus. This hypothesis has been recently considered by Zecchini 2016: 186, who suggests that Aristokrates might have been an intermediate source. In contrast, Tigerstedt 1974: 134 prefers a derivation exclusively from Ephorus. Lastly, Lipka 2002: 40 highlights the resemblances between Justin and Xenophon's accounts; cf. also Forni and Bertinelli Angeli 1982: 1322.

38 Cf. Xen., *Lac. Pol.* 2.4; 5.1–4; 7. On Xenophon's influence on Trogus' account, cf. Lipka 2002: 40.

39 Cf. Plut., *Lyc.* 15.11–13 (wife-sharing); 14.4 and 15.1 (nudity of young men and women); 17.1 (pederasty).

40 On Justin-Trogus omissions in the Spartan account, cf. Zecchini 2016: 185, n. 86.

41 Cf. Santi Amantini 2017: 234, n. 9.

42 On the *severitas* of the Spartan customs and laws, cf., e.g., Val. Max. 2.6.1; Vell. Pat., *Hist. Rom.* 1.6.3; Tac., *Dial. de Orat.* 40.

43 Val. Max. 5.3.ext.2: '. . . quid aliae faciant urbes, ubi etiam illa, quae constantiae et moderationis et gravitatis eximiam sibi laudem vindicat, tam ingrata adversus tam bene meritum extitit?' (What should other cities do when even this one, that claims special credit for perseverance, moderation, and seriousness, proved so ungrateful to so deserving a citizen?)

44 Cf. Val. Max. 2.6.1.

45 On the importance of Justin in the Medieval and Humanistic reception of Lycurgus, cf. Rawson 1991: 108, 126–8.

46 Cf. Ptol., *De Regim. Princ.* 4.9, 'Lycurgus, Spartanorum regis filius, qui Lacedaemoniis iura constituit, ut tradit Iustinus . . .' (Lycurgus, the son of the king of the Spartans, who established laws for the Lacedaemonians, as Justin tells us); 4.16, 'Lacedaemonii igitur, qui Spartiatae sive Spartani, regem habuerunt, in quibus Catellus regnavit, cuius Lycurgus, ut tradit idem Iustinus, in pupillari aetate curam suscepit . . .' (So, the Lacedaemonians, called Spartiates or Spartans, had a king, and among them Charillus reigned, whom Lycurgus, as Justin tells us, tutored in his student days); 4.18. On Ptolemy's *De Regimine Principum*, cf. Blythe 1997: 1–5.

47 Cf. Ptol., *De Regim. Princ.* 4.18, 'et licet diversae historiae de Lycurgo diversimode loquantur, nos tamen relationi eiusdem Iustini magis insistimus, quia praeclarissimus fuit historiarum scriptor antiquus . . .' (Although various stories of Lycurgus have been told, I follow Justin's version for the most part, since he was the most famous writer of histories in Antiquity).

48 Cf. Macgregor Morris 2012: 4, 'the key ancient source for medieval accounts of the Spartan lawgiver was the *Historiarum Philippicarum* of Justin'.

Bibliography

Alonso-Núñez, J. M. (1987), 'An Augustan World History: The "Historiae Philippicae" of Pompeius Trogus', *G&R*, 34: 56–72.

Bearzot, C. S. (2014), 'La "pentecontetia" in Trogo e nell'epitome di Giustino', in C. S. Bearzot and F. Landucci (eds), *Studi sull'epitome di Giustino, I. Dagli Assiri a Filippo II di Macedonia*, 85–124, Milano: Vita e Pensiero.

Birgalias, N. (1999), *L'Odyssée de l'éducation spartiate*, Athènes: Historical Publications St. D. Basilopoulos.

Blythe, J., ed. (1997), *Ptolemy of Lucca. On the Government of Rulers: De Regimine Principum (with portions attributed to Thomas Aquinas)*, Philadelphia, PA: University of Pennsylvania Press.

Borgna, A. (2012), 'Abbiamo davvero bisogno di leggi? Il punto di vista di Pompeo Trogo', *Res Publica Litterarum*, 2: 1–14.

Borgna, A. (2014), 'Uno sguardo originale intorno a Roma: Pompeo Trogo e Giustino', *La Biblioteca di Classico Contemporaneo*, 1: 52–77.

Cartledge, P. and A. Spawforth (2002), *Hellenistic and Roman Sparta: A Tale of Two Cities*, 2nd edition, London: Routledge.

Christien, J. (2002), 'Iron Money in Sparta: Myth and History', in A. Powell and S. Hodkinson (eds), *Sparta: Beyond the Mirage*, 171–90, Swansea: Classical Press of Wales.

David, E. (2007), 'Myth and Historiography: Lykourgos', in G. Herman and I. Shatzman (eds), *Greeks between East and West: Essays in Greek Literature and History in Memory of David Asheri*, 115–35, Jerusalem: Israel Academy of Sciences and Humanities.

Desideri, P. (2002), 'Lycurgus: The Spartan Ideal in the Age of Trajan', in P. Stadter and L. Van der Stockt (eds), *Sage and Emperor: Plutarch, Greek Intellectuals, and Roman Power in the Time of Trajan (98–117 A.D.)*, 315–27, Leuven: Leuven University Press.

Ducat, J. (2006), *Spartan Education: Youth and Society in the Classical Period*, Swansea: Classical Press of Wales.

Forni, G. and M. G. Bertinelli Angeli (1982), 'Pompeo Trogo come fonte di storia', *ANRW* II, 30 (2): 1298–362.

Gabba, G. (1957), 'Studi su Filarco: le biografie plutarchee di Agide e di Cleomene', *Athenaeum* 35, 3–55, 193–239.

Hodkinson, S. (2000), *Property and Wealth in Classical Sparta*, London: Duckworth.

Kennell, N. and A. Powell (2014), 'Aristokrates (591)', in I. Worthington (ed.), *Jacoby Online: Brill's New Jacoby*, Brill: Leiden. Available online: https://scholarlyeditions.brill.com/reader/urn:cts:greekLit:fgrh.0591.bnjo-2-ed-grc:t1-f7?right=bnjo-2-comm3-eng (accessed 20 August 2021).

Laes, C. (2011), *Children in the Roman Empire: Outsiders Within*, Cambridge: Cambridge University Press.

Lipka, M. (2002), *Xenophon's Spartan Constitution: Introduction, Text and Commentary*, Berlin: De Gruyter.

Lupi, M. (2000), *L'ordine delle generazioni: Classi di età e costumi matrimoniali nell'antica Sparta*, Bari: Edipuglia.

Macgregor Morris, I. (2012), 'Lycurgus in Late Medieval Political Culture', in S. Hodkinson and I. Macgregor Morris (eds), 1–42, *Sparta in Modern Thought: Politics, History and Culture*, Swansea: Classical Press of Wales.

Malaspina, E. (1976), 'Uno storico filobarbaro, Pompeo Trogo', *RomBar*, 1: 135–58.

Manfredini, M. and L. Piccirilli, eds (1990), *Plutarco: Le vite di Licurgo e di Numa*, 2nd edition, Milano: Fondazione Lorenzo Valla.

Mineo, B. and G. Zecchini, eds (2016), *Abrégé des 'Histoires philippiques' de Trogue Pompée. 1, Livres I–X*, Paris: Les Belles Lettres.

Mineo, B. and G. Zecchini, eds (2018), *Justin. Abrégé des Histoires Philippiques de Trogue Pompée. Livres XI–XXIII*, Paris: Les Belles Lettres.

Piccirilli L. (1985), 'Suicidio eroico e suicidio politico: Il caso del nomoteta greco arcaico', in F. Broilo (ed.), *Xenia: Scritti in onore di Piero Treves*, 169–71, Rome: L'Erma di Bretschneider.

Polito, M. (2001), *Dagli scritti di Eraclide sulle costituzioni: un commento storico*, Napoli: Arte Tipografica.

Rawson, E. (1991), *The Spartan Tradition in European Thought*, 2nd edition, Oxford: Clarendon Press.

Rodrigues, Á. R. (2012), 'Political Reforms in the Lives of Lycurgus and Numa: Divine Revelation or Political Lie?', in J. R. Ferreira, D. Leão and C. A. de Jesus (eds), *Nomos, Kosmos & Dike in Plutarch*, 67–83, Coimbra: IUC.

Santi Amantini, L., ed. (2017), *Giustino, Storie Filippiche: Epitome da Pompeo Trogo*, Roma: Tored.

Scardigli, B., ed. (2012), *Licurgo e Numa*, Milano: BUR.

Syme, R. (1988), 'The Date of Justin and the Discovery of Trogus', *Historia*, 37: 358–71.

Talamo C. (2010), 'Pitagora e la τρυφή', in C. Talamo (ed.), *Contributi sui Greci d'Asia*, 141–56, Pisa: ETS.

Tigerstedt, E. (1965), *The Legend of Sparta in Classical Antiquity*, vol. I, Stockholm: Almqvist & Wiksell.

Tigerstedt, E. (1974), *The Legend of Sparta in Classical Antiquity*, vol. II, Stockholm: Almqvist & Wiksell.

Yardley, J. C. and W. Heckel, eds (1997), *Justin: Epitome of the Philippic History of Pompeius Trogus: Books 11–12: Alexander the Great*, Oxford: Oxford University Press.

13

Othering the Woman in Augustan Rome: Sophoniba's *Exemplum*

Nuno Simões Rodrigues

Sophoniba was a Carthaginian noblewoman who eventually became queen of the Numidian tribes.[1] Her name, *Sophoniba*, is the Latin form of the Punic *Ṣap̄anbaʿal*, the meaning of which was most likely 'Saphon is *baʿal*', i.e. '[the sacred/divine mountain] Saphon is Lord', an expression echoed in the ancient Phoenician literature of Ugarit,[2] thus reinforcing the quasioriental origins of this character and her name.[3]

The sources providing knowledge on this princess are relatively limited and practically none date back to the same period as this Carthaginian noblewoman. Almost all that is known about the daughter of Hasdrubal Gisco comes from Diodorus Siculus (27.7), Livy (29.23; 30.12.11–15.11), Appian (*Hisp.* 37; *Pun.* 10, 27–28), and Dio Cassius (frg. 57 Zonaras 9.11–13).[4] However, when considering the period in which Sophoniba lived (she died in 203 BCE), these sources emerge from a later period. Nonetheless, allusions to her may be found in Polybius, the princess' contemporary, but the Greek historian never refers to her by her name (14.7). Other indirect and also direct references to her were made by poets, namely Virgil and Silius Italicus.

Sophoniba in Livy

With the exception of the familiar wall painting of the House of Giuseppe in Pompeii, which dates back to the first quarter of the first century and has been interpreted by some historians as a representation of Sophoniba and Masinissa,[5] most of the sources providing knowledge on this Carthaginian princess come from literary texts, including historiography, namely Livy.

Livy elaborates on his account of Sophoniba of Carthage in detail and extensively. Although he only identifies her by name in book 30 of his *opus*, Livy refers to her in the previous book, in the establishment of the alliance between Hasdrubal Gisco and Syphax (29.23). In this passage, the Latin historian states that the alliance with the king of the Masaesyli would be forged with the marriage of a daughter of the Carthaginian general who *nubilis erat uirgo* (29.23.4). Upon realizing the enthusiasm of the Numidian king, who according to the historian *profectus ut accensum cupiditate* (was inflamed with desire – at this point, Livy remarks on the nature of the Numidians, 29.23.4), Hasdrubal hastened the nuptials, ordering his daughter to go to Cirta (Liv. 30.12) in order to marry Syphax. The historiographical narrative continues, allowing the reader to understand that Hasdrubal was unsure about the effectiveness of the alliance, but at the same time had faith in his daughter's abilities to convince her new husband, who was besotted with her, to intercede with Scipio, so that the Romans would not invade Africa. Livy even refers to Syphax's condition as *iunctus* (united) by marriage to a Carthaginian woman (29.23.8). The issue of Syphax being in love with Sophoniba is mentioned again later, and more than once, confirming its importance for Livy in this process (30.3, 11). In Sophoniba's first appearance, the young woman is presented not only as a guarantee of the consolidation of Carthage's alliance with one of the Numidian kingdoms, but also as an agent of this political union process, symbolized by her marriage to the king of the Masaesyli. However, Hasdrubal's political initiative and Syphax's consequent agreement is badly received by Scipio, who immediately makes a point of reminding the king of the warm ties that bound him to Rome (29.24).

Although, in Livy, the narrative of these moments of the Second Punic War focuses on the Numidian kings and their alternating alliances with Rome and Carthage, Sophoniba plays a central role and is again the focus of attention a few paragraphs later. In fact, it is in book 30 of *Ab Vrbe condita* that Sophoniba becomes one of the protagonists of the episode culminating in the role of the Numidian kings in the Punic Wars and which will pave the way for the outcome of the second conflict in 202 BCE. This episode is constructed around two major scenes, in which even direct speeches are attributed to the queen: first, that of the entrance of Masinissa as victor in the palace of Syphax who had settled in Cirta in the meantime, where he is received by the queen (30.12); second, that of Sophoniba's suicide (30.15).

As a result of Masinissa's alliance with Scipio, the Carthaginians and Masaesyli are eventually defeated. The defeat is materialized historiographically at the point where Masinissa takes Syphax's palace and all the goods therein as war spoils. The spoils also include human lives, namely that of the defeated queen. Upon seeing Masinissa, who is notable for his regal bearing (the explicitness of this detail is, in itself, of a romantic nature), Sophoniba throws herself at his feet in supplication, in a scene that appears to echo a passage by Diodorus (et al.).[6] Sophoniba's action is successful and Masinissa not only promises not to hand over the queen to the Romans, he also devises a plan that will not go against the principles of the Roman *fides*, as indeed implied by the agreement entered into with Scipio. Masinissa therefore decides to marry Sophoniba immediately in order to protect her from the military custom which demanded that the spoils of war be handed over to the victors. Thus, the Livian narrative transforms an episode of a private nature, focused on the feelings of the characters, into an event with highly significant public repercussions in the political context of the time. Following their marriage, Masinissa and Sophoniba are surprised by Scipio's envoy, Gaius Laelius, who arrives to collect the spoils and the prisoners who are to be sent to the Roman general. However, Masinissa intervenes and manages to prevent Sophoniba from being handed over to Scipio and convinces Laelius to ask the general to be the judge of which of the two Numidian kings the Carthaginian princess actually belongs to.[7]

Livy then transfers the action to the scene of Scipio, in which Syphax is presented as the defeated king, and this moment becomes an occasion to discuss the case and character of Sophoniba in a narrative loaded with pathetic elements, as will be analysed further ahead (30.13–14). Betraying his wife, who has also betrayed him in the meantime, Syphax warns Scipio of the dangers Sophoniba poses, and the Roman general decides not to be complacent with the queen's wishes, demanding that she be handed over to him as part of the war spoils to be exhibited in Roman triumph. The passage then paves the way for the presentation of the second and final scene in which Sophoniba is the main character.

In this second scene, following Scipio's words, which clearly indicate that he is against allowing Sophoniba to stay with her new husband, Masinissa decides to send a message to the queen, in which he reveals the intentions of the Roman general. He does so by summoning a slave messenger to deliver the message to Sophoniba, in which he explains his inability to fulfil his promise of not handing her over to Rome alive, and his determination to take an alternative option and hand her over dead. To this end, Masinissa also sends the woman a cup of poison. Upon receiving the messenger of death, Sophoniba realizes that she has no other dignified solution and, again in direct speech, she agrees to die with dignity, swallowing the poison presented to her unmoved (30.15). The episode ends with Scipio berating Masinissa, while at the same time paternalistically consoling the

Numidian prince and acknowledging his title of *rex*. He hands him the respective symbols, announcing that with this title he will soon rule over the entire kingdom of Numidia.

The Livian text is therefore full of pathetic elements which go as far as to meet the requirements of Hellenistic tragic-pathetic historiography.[8] The tragic elements are particularly noteworthy and substantiate the influence of Livy's work on the reception of the theme of Sophoniba in Europe, especially from the Renaissance onwards, ranging from lyric poetry to drama and from opera to painting.[9]

Sophoniba, enemy of Rome and *exemplum* of otherness in the first century

Although the information regarding Sophoniba is not restricted to the ancient historiographical narratives, it appears to have been the latter, and that of Livy in particular, which effectively conditioned the portrait of the Carthaginian queen of the Numidians. Indeed, even though authors such as Appian and Dio Cassius (or their reception) contributed to the poetic enrichment of the story of Sophoniba, and even though the political agency of the princess had already been mentioned by Polybius and her psychological portrait sketched by Diodorus Siculus, Livy emerges as the author of a paradigm on which later historians built their representations of the princess. Moreover, the significance of Livy's contribution is twofold, since this author was most likely familiar with the traditions in Diodorus, wrote under the Augustan Principate and, as such, contributed to an image of Rome and its otherness at a key moment in the history of the empire. Hence, the following section will focus on Livy's composition of Sophoniba and its cultural and historical implications.

Several authors have already highlighted the great likelihood of the historical figure of Cleopatra VII being behind Livy's portrait of Sophoniba.[10] Indeed, there are common elements between the two queens and historical contexts that point to this hypothesis, although it has also already been suggested that there is nothing in common between the two queens other than their beauty and charm.[11] This does not appear to be the case. In fact, besides the beauty and charm with which both are described in the sources that bear witness to them, it should be noted that both are foreign queens as far as Rome is concerned, both are located in North Africa, both emerge as obstacles to the achievement of Rome's goals, and the historical existence of one coincides chronologically with the memory of the other. There is, therefore, much in common between

Sophoniba and Cleopatra and, thus, it is not unusual that in terms of representation and memory one has influenced the other, and both are seen to overlap: the *ethos* of the Graeco-Egyptian queen (whose echo is felt in Augustan poetry, for example)[12] most likely influenced the representation of Sophoniba in Livy; Livy's construction of the Carthaginian queen may have influenced Plutarch's composition of the last Egyptian queen in the second century CE, just as it undoubtedly determined the Sophoniba of all the authors who wrote about her after the first century CE.

Similarly, the historical Sophoniba, like Livy's, was most likely behind Virgil's composition of Dido who, like the wife of Syphax and Masinissa, was not only a queen but also a Carthaginian and an obstacle to the achievement of Rome's goals. For this same reason, she also found a way to emulate herself in suicide, rejecting shame and humiliation. Thus, Cleopatra is not the only model on which Virgil's Dido is based.[13]

As already mentioned, the episode of Sophoniba in Livy (especially the final moments, 30.12–15) takes on the contours of a dramatic narrative with a tragic foundation, which meets the principles of pathetic historiography, but also of romantic inspiration, as characterized by M. Braun in his study on relations between ancient novel and historiography almost a century ago.[14] These characteristics of Livy's episode of Sophoniba were also perceived by J. M. K. Martin.[15] This author even pertinently discerned a structure in the narrative according to which five characters are distributed (Masinissa, Sophoniba, Gaius Laelius, Syphax, and Scipio),[16] which also contributes to the perspective of the episode as a small theatrical play, a tragedy integrated in the historiographical work. The distribution of roles among these *dramatis personae* (drama characters) allows the historian to compose characters, through which ideal portraits of heroes and reprehensible portraits of anti-heroes are represented.[17] It thus becomes possible to use the historical personalities whose *ethos* allows for the definition of ideal representations of identity, of the Self, as well as outlines of questionable behaviours of otherness attributable to the 'other'. In this context, the composition of the characters of Sophoniba and Scipio is particularly significant: of Scipio, since it provides for a representation of the citizen and soldier, the ideal Roman; of Sophoniba, as it authorizes the construction of a portrait of the other-woman, the barbarian. In the Roman androcentric worldview, Sophoniba's otherness is therefore doubly representative: of gender and ethnicity.

It is difficult to position Sophoniba and Scipio as opposite characters. Firstly, there is a gender difference that is fundamental to the understanding of their roles. At most, Scipio may stand in contrast to Syphax or Masinissa, and this aspect is explicit in Livy's text.[18] On the other hand, Sophoniba's profile contrasts first with those of the Roman matrons, which is also a theme in Livy's work, as will be seen. However, on a macro-structural level, Scipio unquestionably represents an entire Roman identity while Sophoniba is a metaphor for barbarism.

In fact, as already mentioned, Livy's work includes other female constructions. It should be noted from the outset that women are by no means a major presence in Livy's historiography. They have a far more restrained role when compared to the role of those in Tacitus, for example. In the *Annales*, the compositions of Antonia Minor, Livia Drusilla, Agrippina Major, Agrippina Minor, and Valeria Messalina, just to mention more well-known examples, are unavoidable and almost unparalleled. At various points in Tacitus' work, the political agency of these women is central. In Livy, this is not so much the case, although it is possible to list some names which, nevertheless, have become symbols of Ancient Rome as a result of their presence in *Ab Vrbe condita libri*: Lucretia (1.57–60), Tanaquil (1.34; 39–41; 47), Tullia Menor (1.46; 48; 59.12), Horatia (1.26), and Virginia (3.44–49).[19]

As far as these Livian women are concerned, the use of rhetorical devices based on the tragic and romantic is common in their composition in order to draw the reader's attention to them at particular points of the narrative. It may be noted how the Livian narratives in which females emerge as the main characters are concentrated in book I, but not exclusively, as attested by the case of Virginia. Furthermore, although there are relatively few 'female episodes', they are remarkable for the historiographical and ethical content they represent and convey to the Roman audience. An interpretation of the figures of Lucretia, Tullia Minor, and Tanaquil as representations of ideals and anti-ideals of the female in Rome in the first century has already been proposed by me in a previous study,[20] particularly as regards the work of Livy. Sophoniba appears to contribute to the same ethical representation mechanism, but to the service of otherness. For the Romans, Sophoniba is the essence of the female identity of the other-enemy.

Livy defines Sophoniba as a *matrona Carthaginiensem* (Carthaginian lady; 30.13.11), i.e. at the outset she is an *exemplum* of the *femina peregrina* (foreign woman). In constructing Sophoniba's identity and the otherness she represents, Livy relies on both a physical and psychological characterization. The first of the categories is filled with references to the princess' marriageable age, as well as her virgin status (*nubilis erat uirgo*, the virgin was now marriageable; 29.23.4) when she is promised to Syphax, which is, in fact, decisive to the reaction of the king of the Masaesyli who, characterized as being absolutely delighted with the proposal and one of the Numidians who, more than all the barbarians, abandoned themselves to the power of Venus (*et sunt omnes barbaros Numidae effusi in Venerem*, for the Numidians are, beyond all the other barbarians, violently addicted to Venus, 29.23.4; cf. 30.12.18, *ut est genus Numidarum in Venerem praeceps*, as the Numidians are an excessively amorous race),[21] speeds up the process of allying with Carthage. However, at the point where his defeat to Masinissa is acknowledged, Sophoniba is once again characterized by Livy as being young and of remarkable beauty (*forma erat insignis et florentissima aetas*, she was remarkably beautiful, and in the full bloom of youth; 30.12.16), insisting on these characteristics as central elements for the role she comes to play in the outcome of the Second Punic War.

For the second category (psychological characterization), the creation of a dramatic and even theatrical scenario is essential, insofar as the queen becomes a tragic *ethos*, defined particularly by her psychological characteristics. It is in relation to the latter that the definition of her traits becomes fundamental to her transformation into a model of otherness, representative of all non-Roman women and, above all, enemies of Rome.

Of all Sophoniba's psychological characteristics, the most prominent is her manipulation potential, *perfidia* (perfidy), the antithesis of Roman *fides* (loyalty), her ability to pervert the *temperantia* (self-control) and *continentia* (abstinence) of men.[22] The Carthaginian queen embodies the figure of the *femme fatale*, whose youth and, above all, whose beauty prove fatal to the men who cross her path, namely those, since they are barbarians and unlike the citizens and soldiers of Rome such as Scipio, who are unable to resist her. Syphax and Masinissa are two paradigmatic examples. Indeed, from the very first moment, her beauty, youth, but also her way of speaking and acting prove to be effective means for this woman to control the men with whom she interacts. Livy alludes on several occasions to the weakness of Syphax, but also to that of Masinissa as far as Sophoniba's presence in his life is concerned (29.23; 30.3, 11). The image of a defeated and chained Syphax about to be presented to the Romans is a metaphor for the submissive man under the power of such a manipulative woman as Sophoniba (30.12).[23]

The young woman, in turn, uses the weapons at her disposal to influence the decisions of the men she marries, be they the caresses with which she comforts Syphax (29.23), the affectionate conversation she has with Masinissa (30.12), or the submission, victimization, and female fragility she assumes at the moment she surrenders herself to the king of the Massyli (30.12). It is interesting how

Livy emphasizes both how Syphax is bewitched by Sophoniba's beauty and charm (which later, before Scipio, the king turns into an argument to justify his treasonous behaviour towards Rome), and how the young woman explains and justifies to Masinissa her surrender to her former husband. Both Syphax and Sophoniba confess to being powerless before the potential and influence of these two men, and therefore basically use the same argument to justify themselves to Scipio and Masinissa, respectively.

The scene of her surrender to Masinissa is paradigmatic in this context. Here, Sophoniba appears as a supplicant before someone in a position of power and superiority. The idea of supplicant, the *hiketes* of the Greek, is particularly defined by Livy when he explicitly refers to the attitude of the queen who as *supplex* (suppliant) symbolically touches the *genua* (knees), and *dextera* (right hand), of the victorious king (30.12.12, 14). The scene thus evokes the classical status of submission of the vanquished (Sophoniba) towards the victor (Masinissa), both of whom, however, are alien to the Roman identity. Nevertheless, as Rome's ally, Masinissa contributes to the construction of Sophoniba's image as the vanquished-other. It is precisely this feature, common to the two characters in confrontation, that is raised by Sophoniba when she asks Masinissa not to allow her, as a woman born in the same territory as him (North Africa), to fall into the hands of Scipio and the Romans. The questions of identity, particularly the ethnic, are highly explicit in this passage, in the *oratio recta* or direct speech attributed to the queen by Livy: *si nihil aliud quam Syphacis uxor fuissem, tamen Numidae atque in eadem mecum Africa geniti quam alienigenae et externi fidem experiri mallem* (had I been simply the wife of Syphax I would still choose to trust the honor of a Numidian, born in the same Africa as myself, rather than that of an alien and a foreigner; 30.12.15).

Sophoniba's behaviour is that of a weakened victim who places herself at the mercy of the victor who she still manipulates with affection and caresses. Livy's text reminds Horace's famous verse regarding Greece (*Graecia capta ferum uictorem cepit*, Captive Greece captured, in turn, her uncivilised conquerors; Hor., *Ep.* 2.1.156), when he writes *amore captiuae uictor captus* (he became the slave of his captive; 30.12.18). Even so, the historian does not fail to stress the inferior female condition of the queen, underlined by her objectification, both in relation to her husbands,[24] and the victorious Roman, when he notes that Masinissa questioned Laelius to find out from the Roman authorities which of the two Numidian kings Sophoniba belonged to (30.12.22). In this passage, and also through this objectification, Sophoniba (like Cleopatra in Alexandria and Dido in Carthage) becomes to some extent a metaphor for Carthage, and her identification with the city a synonym for fanaticism of an ethnic and identity nature worthy of *superstitio* (superstition).[25]

In turn, Syphax is rhetorically used by the historian as the male voice that recognizes the female spell of the *femme fatale*. As if freed from the spell to which Sophoniba had subjected him, the Numidian king attributes all the blame for his behaviour to the charms of the young woman, confessing to Scipio that she was the main cause of his folly, which led to a violation of the laws of hospitality, the betrayal of Roman *fides*. *Furia pestisque* (fury and pest) is how Syphax describes Sophoniba (30.13.12), associating her with the idea of *feritas* (wildness), the antithesis or excess of Roman *uirtus* (bravery).[26]

The episode ends with Sophoniba's suicide. Finding himself in a deadlock in view of what he had promised Rome and the queen, Masinissa has no other solution but to send poison to his wife so that she will use it and thus remove herself from the scene. What is surprising in the Livian scene, however, is how the Carthaginian woman accepts death. The Roman historian begins by attributing the task to the Numidian prince of commissioning a servant to deliver not only the poison but also the accompanying words: that Sophoniba remember her father, her Homeland, and the kings she had married (*memor patris imperatoris patriaeque et duorum regum quibus nupta fuisset*, mindful of her father the general, of her country, and of the two kings to whom she had been married; 30.15.6). In other words, as a prelude to the princess' death, Livy lists the factors that grant Sophoniba her status as a noblewoman. For her part, the young woman responds to the challenge and behaves in accordance with the condition she represents. The historian again grants her the honour of *oratio recta*, through which the character of Sophoniba gains even greater prominence in the context of the episode,[27] while resembling a theatrical speech, confirming the aforementioned feature. The dignity of the Carthaginian woman is shown both in how she accepts and swallows the poison – brave, unemotional and unmoved, says Livy (30.15.8), *non locuta est ferocius quam acceptum poculum nullo trepidationis signo dato inpauide hausit* (the spirit with which she spoke was equalled by the firmness with which she took and drained the chalice, without exhibiting any symptom of perturbation) – and in the words with which she leaves the mortal world and makes what can be interpreted as a final declaration of love to Masinissa: 'I accept this wedding gift, no unwelcome one if my husband can do nothing more for his wife. But tell him that I should have died more happily had not my marriage bed stood so near my grave' (30.15.6–7).

Consequently, Scipio recognizes the harshness of the situation and tries to mitigate Masinissa's pain by granting him the title of king (30.15.11), which both humanizes the Numidian prince and contributes to the construction of Scipio as the worthy and just Roman. In fact, it is this passage that perhaps prevents us from stating that, from a general perspective, Sophoniba has the leading role in the whole episode, since this appears not to be the case. Masinissa, in fact, is the main character, followed by Scipio. Sophoniba is presented here with indifference, perhaps even with reproach.[28] Indeed, Livy's main interest lies not in the romantic, but in the political, despite the presence of the former which remains at the service of the political, definitively marking the historiographical treatment. This presence is highlighted by the momentary prominence of Sophoniba, defined by the moment of suicide which ultimately saves her from absolute *damnatio* (damnation) within the context of the figures of ancient literature.

Nevertheless, Sophoniba is portrayed as an enemy of Rome. She is the 'other' or the wife of the 'other', even though this other becomes an ally of the Roman senate and people. Therefore, compared to other Livian figures, such as Lucretia, it is not by chance that Sophoniba reflects the absence of the main virtues of the Roman matron.[29] While Lucretia is the manifestation and embodiment of the virtues appreciated, cultivated, and encouraged by the Romans, such as *pudicitia* (chastity), *pietas* (devotion to the gods), *fides* (loyalty), *concordia* (mutual agreement), *libertas* (freedom), *grauitas* (dignity), *sapientia* (wisdom), *humanitas* (human nature),[30] Sophoniba reflects the opposite or, when she exhibits these same qualities, they are associated with Carthage, Rome's enemy, thus resulting in the same antinomy as far as the dominant power is concerned. Thus, while Lucretia is the prudish and *uniuira* (woman who married only once) woman, Sophoniba changes husbands according to political convenience (although she cannot be blamed fully for this). In fact, it is worth mentioning here the problem of Sophoniba's supposed bigamous marriage, which turns her into the absolute antithesis of the *uniuira* matron. By leading Syphax to betray the values of *fides* implicit in his alliance with the Romans, Sophoniba becomes the trigger of betrayal and sows discord among the people, leading to the loss of freedom of some of them. When she manifests *fides* and *pietas* and respect for the *mos maiorum* (customs of the ancestors) it is for the enemies of Rome, who wish her annihilation. This feature is a symptom of Sophoniba's patriotism, but it is this very patriotism that configures her as a negative *exemplum* when framed in Rome's ideals of women. Lucretia's discretion and wisdom are completely absent in the portrayal of Sophoniba, who proves to be uncontrolled and unwise when she marries Syphax, triggering the betrayal of the Numidian king. Sophoniba's actions only contribute to the state of war and therefore death and destruction, thus contradicting any principle of *humanitas*. Just as Lucretia symbolizes Rome itself, Sophoniba is a symbol of Carthage.[31]

Although Sophoniba is the antithesis of Lucretia's Roman essence, she also reveals traits that are in common with another Roman woman depicted by Livy. This woman is Tullia Minor, who appears in Livy's text as an anti-matron model.[32] The similarities are mainly in terms of their active participation in political life. Like Tullia Minor, Sophoniba manipulates men, leading them to defend her own interests, and those who allow themselves to be led and dragged by a perverse female spirit such as those of these women generally meet with an unhappy ending. This is the fate of Lucius Tarquinius in the case of Tullia, and of Syphax (and also Masinissa in part, who never fails to suffer because of the Carthaginian woman) in the case of Sophoniba. Through their behaviours, both women reflect ideas such as the denial of *uirtus* and *honos* (respect), *concordia*, *modestia*, *temperantia*, and *continentia*.[33] It may be noted, for example, how Sophoniba lives in an environment of Oriental-style luxury, and how pride, akin to the *hybris* of the Greek and contrary to the Roman *maiestas* (grandeur), overrides the modesty that as a woman she should display (30.12). In this regard, Sophoniba is an example of *uanitas* (futility) and the antithesis of the Roman *grauitas*.[34]

As also concluded in a previous study, while Lucretia and Tullia Minor in Livy are representations of ideals and anti-ideals of the female in Augustan Rome, Tanaquil emerges in the Livian text as a compromise solution. Tanaquil is often seen to adopt behaviours that are not fitting for a Roman matron, which are explained by her half foreign origin (she is of Etruscan origin). However, at the same time, one perceives a kind of tacit forgiveness of Tanaquil as her actions, although not in keeping with her female status, are taken for the benefit of Rome and the Romans.[35]

Yet although Sophoniba is undoubtedly a negative representation of the female in a Roman context, the Livian text also appears to give her the benefit of ambiguity as it does with Tanaquil. There are traces of *dignitas* (excellence) in her which, at times, even place her at the level of Lucretia herself. Her suicide, as the final decision for her life, appears to be the moment of this equivalence. This choice also implies a less negative appraisal of the character of the Carthaginian princess as an enemy of Rome.

In fact, Sophoniba's departure from the scene earns her the respect of Livy's readers, as it would certainly have earned the respect of the audience of the time. By preferring death over triumphant public humiliation, by accepting the poison her husband sends her and taking it without complaining or reacting with pain or fear, Sophoniba behaves with remarkable dignity, which can be compared to

Virgil's Dido, Plutarch's Cleopatra, the wife of Hasdrubal, the Boetharch in Appian, and even Tacitus' Boudicca. At the last moment, Sophoniba's courage and dignity bestow *uirtus* and *dignitas* upon her, to the point of making her almost a Stoic heroine, in whom the tranquillity of the soul, the absence of trepidation and ataraxy are reflected.[36] In this regard, Livy almost romanizes Sophoniba in her end.[37] Livy's option to represent her in this manner leads to the question: why does the historian do this?

The answer appears to be obvious. The final dignity of Livy's Sophoniba reinforces her symbolism as Carthage. The noble and aristocratic behaviour of the Carthaginian princess dignifies her city and its inhabitants and natives. In doing so, the historian also dignifies the image of the defeated on one hand, and enhances and exalts the representation of the victors, i.e. the Romans, on the other. Sophoniba thus rediscovers her role and assumes her place as an *exemplum* in Roman historiography of the time of Augustus. Sophoniba was thus further transformed into a tragic heroine in a process that was fuelled by her reception in later times.[38]

Conclusions

As may easily be understood, although the memory of Sophoniba is not restricted to what Livy wrote about her at the time of Augustus, the later testimonies advance little or nothing in comparison to Livy's innovative approach to this character, and therefore add little to our knowledge of her. Appian, Dio Cassius and his epitomist Zonaras, even the poets and other addenda[39] all appear to base their perceptions of Sophoniba on what Livy recorded at the end of the first century BCE, as far as this subject is concerned. Polybius' records, or what has been passed down to us from them, are insufficient to claim that this Greek historian was Livy's model. On the other hand, it should be borne in mind that the dramatic character that the Roman historian imprints on the portrait of the Carthaginian princess may be due to a prior approach to the theme by Ennius, at the epic dramatic level, even if it is only an *argumentum ex silentio*.[40]

The possibility that Livy's Sophoniba owes some of her characterization to historical and factual elements should also be considered, such as those experienced by Cleopatra VII of Egypt, shortly before the publication of the first *Ab Vrbe Condita* books. In fact, this historical character was not strange to Virgil's Dido, she herself also comparable to Sophoniba at several levels.

As observed by Keegan, Sophoniba is essentially a woman.[41] By granting her the importance of being one of the few women he represents, Livy also attributes the category of *exemplum* to Sophoniba who, by *comparatio*, may take her place alongside the *exempla* of the ideal matrons of Rome (such as Lucretia) and their opposites (such as Tullia Minor). In fact, Livy seeks above all to highlight the moral values of the Romans through examples.[42] Thus, as is the case with practically all Livy's females,[43] Sophoniba is also an example: one of opposing otherness or enemy of Rome. The Numidian queen represents the manipulative capacity of the female who, by appealing to the passions, namely the sensorial and affective perceptions of men, leads them to commit acts that go against the rationality and ethics that are typical of the strong-minded, like the good Roman citizens. Such attitudes lead to deviations in behaviour that end in betrayal and disloyalty. Hence, Sophoniba embodies the values that give substance to the image of the vengeful, wicked, treacherous, manipulative, and sorcerous woman. In short, the *femme fatale*, who from the Roman perspective is also the symbol and cause of *feritas*, *superstitio*, *impudicitia*, *uanitas*, *superbia*, *impietas*, and *incontinentia*.

Yet, on the other hand, by accepting death as a path to dignity, by choosing death over humiliation, and by doing so with courage, ataraxy, and even apathy, Sophoniba gains the status of a capable and worthy enemy, for only a loser of this type can also mirror the qualities of the victor. In this case, Rome.[44] Moreover, in line with prior reflections on this subject, from the Roman perspective, the death of a dangerous woman, such as Sophoniba, represents above all a reordering of the world.[45] Another point that should be noted has already been observed by Fabre-Serris, 'in rewriting the Roman history by interpreting the past in the light of current events, Livy appears to be in accordance with the position adopted by Antony's political opponent, Augustus'.[46] In fact, the behaviour of both Syphax and Masinissa suggests something in common with that of Antony in his relationship with Cleopatra VII and in how Plutarch came to characterize him later. Similarly, it may be said that the opposite is also true, leading one to wonder whether Plutarch's characterization of Antony owes anything to Livy's Syphax and Masinissa.

In view of the above, and as demonstrated throughout this essay, it appears clear that it was Livy who anchored and crystallized the representation of Sophoniba as an *exemplum* of gender and ethnic diversity in Roman culture, yet worthy of interacting with Rome and good Roman citizens.

Notes

1 The available factual and historical knowledge on this Carthaginian princess was essentially addressed by Briand-Ponsart 2005 and Dorey 1961.

2 See, e.g., Savignac 1986; Smith and Pitard 2009: 252. Sincere gratitude is extended to Professor José Augusto Ramos for his suggestions and clarifications on this issue.

3 There is a possibility this name means 'Baʿal is shelter' or 'Protected by Baʿal', as noted by Briand-Ponsart 2005: 328. See also Walbank 1967: 426; De Sanctis 1917: 2.532, n. 137.

4 In the early Modern Age, a version of the life of Scipio circulated around Europe, written in Latin and thought to have been the work of Plutarch. Amyot and North included it in their vernacular versions of the *Vitae*. Today, however, philology neither acknowledges it as Plutarchian nor ancient, but rather as apocrypha. Therefore, the statements regarding Sophoniba contained therein are not considered here. On this lost *bios*, see Herbert 1957.

5 However, there is no consensus on this scene being that of Sophoniba's suicide. On this issue, see Kuttner 2013.

6 Referring to the moment when Sisygambis, the mother of Darius III, acknowledges Alexander as victor of the Battle of Issus, kneeling before him and Hephaestion. See D.S., 17.37.5–6, as well as V. Max., 4.7.2; Curt., 3.12.15–17; Arr., *An.* 2.12.6–8.

7 This Livian passage also suggests a parody of the judgment of Paris. Sought by Hera, Athena, and Aphrodite, Paris must decide who is the most beautiful of the goddesses and give her the apple of Eris. This Greek myth is mentioned by several ancient sources, including *Il.* 24.25–30 and D.S., 17.7.4.

8 On Livy and the pathetic, see, e.g., Martin 2015: 260 and esp. Pauw 1991.

9 The bibliography on this issue is most extensive, an example of which is Gonzalbes Cravioto 2018.

10 E.g. Martin 1942: 124; Frabre-Serris 2021.

11 Martin 1942: 124.

12 Lucan's Cleopatra (10.52–171) was also most likely inspired by this context of stereotypical female figures. See also Horace's Cleopatra (*Carm.* 1.37), whose characterization is also in line with that of Sophoniba in Livy. In this regard, 3.11, 4.16. Cf. Haley 1989: 179–80; Frabre-Serris 2021.

13 On the influence of the figure of Cleopatra on Virgil's composition of Dido, see Giusti 2018: 14; Pinheiro 2010: 28, 49, 74; and Moscovich 2015: 28–9. Dido's suicide (see *Aen.* 4.672–692), however, also appears to evoke the death of another woman of Carthaginian nobility who is the main character in an episode related to the Third Punic War, more specifically on the looting and destruction of Carthage (146 BCE). This is the wife of Hasdrubal the Boetharch who, according to the particularly dramatic accounts of Polybius (38.20) and Appian (*Pun.* 27.131), given the imminent defeat of Carthage, threw herself and her two sons into the flames that consumed the city. The full version of the episode only appears in Appian. Polybius' version is incomplete. However, everything points to Appian having recovered the story previously narrated by Polybius. In theory, it could always be argued that Appian's

version might be based on the Virgilian narrative of Dido, but this does not appear to be the case. The episode is referred to in Livy's summaries (*ep.* 51.5), in Dio Cassius/Zonaras (D.C., frgs. 21 = Zon. 9.30), and is also recalled by St. Jerome (*adu. Iou.* 1.43 = PL 23.273). In the ancient authors, Hasdrubal's wife is anonymous, but in the late nineteenth century, Alfred J. Church referred to her as Salamo in a text in which he seeks to recreate the destruction of Carthage and Corinth, *Lords of the World: A Story of the Fall of Carthage and Corinth* (1897). The choice of this name, however, is due to the association with Salammbo, the heroine of Gustave Flaubert's novel (1862), daughter of Hamilcar Barca, who in turn owes her name to a Babylonian goddess of fertility. See Segert 1994: 196–203 and also Walbank 1979: 720–2. On female suicide in a Roman context, see Glendinning 2011.

14 Braun 1938.

15 Martin 1942.

16 Martin 1942: 125.

17 Regarding the theatrical nature of the episode, the moment, when Gaius Laelius appears at the wedding of Masinissa and Sophoniba and almost tears the bride from her wedding bed to bring her before Scipio is an example. The Livian description suggests a theatrical scene, Liv., 30.12.21. The same may be said of the moment when Sophoniba drinks the cup of poison that is handed to her by the servant, Liv., 30.15.7.

18 When referring to the moderation and restraint of Scipio and the erotic incontinence of Syphax and Masinissa. On this issue, see Fabre-Serris 2021: 94; Balmaceda 2017: 152; Haley 1990.

19 On the role of women in Livy's work, see the recent Keegan 2021; also Haouachi 2016; Smethurst 1950.

20 Rodrigues 2022.

21 See Haley 1990.

22 Maillet 2018: 64. On *temperantia*, see Haley 1989: 175–6. See also Haouachi 2016, esp. 123–6.

23 In this regard, the parallelism with Antony and Cleopatra, as represented by Plutarch, is also significant.

24 There is, however, an issue in the narratives around Sophoniba which is never discussed in the sources: that of the princess' alleged bigamy. Indeed, if Sophoniba had been married to Syphax (and no longer considering the possibility of the former promise to Masinissa also being validated as a prior form of marriage), how could she then marry Masinissa without first obtaining a legally valid separation? The sources do not expand on this issue, which, in light of Roman law, is of relevance and may have implications for the validation of the sources. Nevertheless, it is not the purpose of this chapter to develop the question any further.

25 On the objectification of Sophoniba, see also Liv. 30.14. On *superstitio* as a feature of the 'other', see Maillet 2018: 64.
26 Syphax's reneging on Sophoniba contrasts with the love and passion Masinissa maintains for her until the end. Scipio, in turn, contrasts with the two Numidian kings. As noted by Livy, *eo foediora haec uidebantur Scipioni quod ipsum in Hispania iuuenem nullius forma pepulerat captiuae* (all this seemed the more repulsive to Scipio because in Hispania, in spite of his youth, he had himself never been smitten by the beauty of any captive), Liv. 30.14.3. See also Maillet 2018: 64; Fabre-Serris 2021: 109–10.
27 Livy does this here for the second time as far as Sophoniba is concerned. See Liv. 30.12.11–16, where the princess is depicted as a supplicant.
28 In agreement with Martin 1942: 124.
29 Based on an alternative source, another example with the same function that may be cited is that of Turia. On this figure, see Rodrigues 2021.
30 Rodrigues 2022; see also Marques 2013: 39–47.
31 And as already noted, just as Cleopatra is a symbol of Alexandria. On this issue, see Rodrigues 2022: 96 and Rodrigues 2013.
32 Rodrigues 2022.
33 On Tullia Minor and these virtues and their opposites, see Rodrigues 2022: 108.
34 Maillet 2018: 65. As noted by this author, *maiestas* is taken here as a 'forme de supériorité relative à d'autres êtres qui s'inscrit dans une organisation hiérarchique de la société et de ses institutions' (a form of relative superiority to other beings that is part of a hierarchical organization of society and its institutions).
35 This issue is addressed in Rodrigues 2022: 109–13.
36 On Livy and stoicism, see Walsh 1958. It is intriguing how a woman who arouses so many passions ends up as a pillar of ataraxy. However, there is something here that contributes to consolidating the negative representation of Sophoniba as an enemy of Rome. Sophoniba's dignity was also highlighted by González Rolán 2014.
37 Cf. Fentress 2006.
38 There is extensive bibliography on this issue. See, e.g., García Morcillo 2020; González Rolán 2014.
39 Among these addenda is the reference to the promise of marriage between Sophoniba and Masinissa that would have been made before the union with Syphax and which Livy appears to ignore, perhaps intentionally, so as not to dilute the romantic nature of the episode. Cf. D.S., 27.7; App., *Pun.* 10; D.C. = Zon., 9.11, 13. On this matter, see also Fabre-Serris 2021: 95.
40 On this issue, see Walbank 1967: 426; De Sanctis 1917: 2.532; Skutsch 1985: 475, 488, 526. Similarly, some philologists have pointed to the possibility of the historian Lucius Coelius Antipater also having addressed the theme of Sophoniba in the second century BCE, and that his approach may have influenced Livy's. Coelius Antipater was a jurist and historian who wrote a *History of the Second Punic War*

following Hellenistic models, of which, however, only sparse fragments remain. Livy used him as a source for his *opus magnum*. One of the remaining fragments has been presented as a reference to the marriage of Masinissa and Sophoniba (F42, Cornell 2013: II.408–409; III.259). However, the fragment is too laconic to warrant confidence. With regard to this source, see also Briscoe 1980 and García Amutxastegi 2010: 41.

41 Keegan 2021: 130.

42 Fabre-Serris 2021: 93; Chaplin 2000. Haley 1989: 171 and 178 refers to the same 'moral didacticism', which is a rather fitting expression to characterize this function of Livian historiography.

43 See Stevenson 2011.

44 It is noteworthy that, at a certain point, the character of Masinissa takes on qualities similar to those of the Romans, which may be justified by the fact that he is the Numidian king who ends up becoming Rome's ally.

45 García Amutxastegi 2009: 348.

46 Fabre-Serris 2021: 109.

Bibliography

Balmaceda, C. (2017), *Virtus Romana: Politics and Morality in the Roman Historians*, Chapel Hill, NC: University of North Carolina Press.

Barceló, P. (2011), 'Punic Politics, Economy, and Alliances, 218–201', in D. Hoyos (ed.), *A Companion to the Punic Wars*, 357–75, Oxford: Blackwell.

Braun, M. (1938), *History and Romance in Graeco-Oriental Literature*, Oxford: Blackwell.

Briand-Ponsart, C. (2005), 'La mort de Sophonisbe ou le prix à payer pour devenir vassal de Rome?', in S. Crogiez-Pétrequin (ed.), *Dieu(x) et hommes: Histoire et iconographie des sociétés païennes et chrétiennes de l'Antiquité à nos jours. Mélanges en l'honneur de Françoise Thelamon*, 327–43, Mont-Saint-Aignan: Publications des Universités de Rouen et du Havre.

Briscoe, J. (1980), 'Coelius Antipater', *Classical Review*, 30 (2): 208–10.

Chaplin, J. D. (2000), *Livy's Exemplary History*, Oxford: Oxford University Press.

Church, A. J. (1897), *Lords of the World: A Story of the Fall of Carthage and Corinth*, New York: Scribner's.

Cornell, T. J. (2013), *The Fragments of the Roman Historians, vol. II: Texts and Translations; vol. III: Commentary*, Oxford: Oxford University Press.

De Sanctis, G. (1917), *Storia dei romani: III. L'Età delle guerre puniche*, Roma: Fratelli Bocca.

Dorey, T. A. (1961), 'Masinissa, Syphax, and Sophoniba', *Proceedings of the African Classical Associations*, 4: 1–2.

Fabre-Serris, J. (2021), 'Identities and Ethnicities in the Punic Wars: Livy's Portrait of the Carthaginian Sophoniba', in J. Fabre-Serris, A. Keith and F. Klein (eds), *Identities, Ethnicities and Gender in Antiquity*, 93–111, Berlin: De Gruyter.

Fentress, E. (2006), 'Romanizing the Berbers', *Past & Present*, 190: 3–33.

García Amutxastegi, I. (2009), 'Las figuras femeninas en *Púnica* de Silio Itálico: el caso de Sofonisba y de Asbite', *Arenal*, 16 (2): 331–51.

García Amutxastegi, I. (2010), 'La figura de Sofonisba en Silio Itálico', *Estudios Clásicos*, 137: 41–56.

García Morcillo, M. (2020), 'Exotic, Erotic, Heroic? Women of Carthage in Western Imagination', in F. Carlà-Uhink and A. Wieber (eds), *Orientalism and the Reception of Powerful Women from the Ancient World*, 70–85, London: Bloomsbury Academic.

Giusti, E. (2018), *Carthage in Virgil's Aeneid: Staging the Enemy under Augustus*, Cambridge: Cambridge University Press.

Glendinning, E. R. (2011), 'Guilt, Redemption and Reception: Representing Roman Female Suicide', DPhil thesis, University of Nottingham.

Gonzalbes Cravioto, E. (2018), 'Sofonisba, una reina de Numidia entre la Historia, la Literatura y el Arte', in C. Soares, J. L. Brandão, and P. C. Carvalho (coords.), *História Antiga: Relações Interdisciplinares. Fontes, Artes, Filosofia, Política, Religião e Receção*, 197–214, Coimbra: Imprensa da Universidade de Coimbra.

González Rolán, T. (2014), 'La cartaginesa Sofonisba (c. 218–203 a. C.), un ejemplo de patriotismo, fortaleza de ánimo y dignidad personal', *Asparkía*, 25: 145–62.

Haley, S. (1989), 'Livy's Sophoniba', *Classica et Mediaevalia*, 40: 171–81.

Haley, S. (1990), 'Livy, Passion, and Cultural Stereotypes', *Historia: Zeitschrift für Alte Geschichte*, 39 (3): 375–81.

Haouachi, D. (2016), 'Les personnages féminins chez Tite-Live: idéologie et art de la mise en scene', PhD thesis, Université de Strasbourg.

Herbert, K. (1957), 'The Identity of Plutarch's Lost Scipio', *American Journal of Philology*, 78 (1): 83–8.

Keegan, P. (2021), *Livy's Women: Crisis, Revolution, and the Female in Rome's Foundation History*, London: Routledge.

Kuttner, A. (2013), 'Representing Hellenistic Numidia, in Africa and at Rome', in J. R. W. Prag and J. C. Quinn (eds), *The Hellenistic West: Rethinking the Ancient Mediterranean*, 216–72, Cambridge: Cambridge University Press.

Maillet, M. (2018), 'Didon, Sophonisbe, Cléopâtre, Zénobie: fatalia monstra? Représentation des Reines de Méditerranée dans la littérature latine', MA thesis, Université Catholique de Louvain.

Marques, J. (2013), *Tradição e renovações da identidade romana em Tito Lívio e Tácito*, Rio de Janeiro: Apicuri.

Martin, J. M. K. (1942), 'Livy and Romance', *Greece & Rome*, 11 (33): 124–9.

Martin, P.-M. (2015), 'Livy's Narrative of the Regal Period: Structure and Ideology', in B. Mineo (ed.), *A Companion to Livy*, 259–73, Oxford: Wiley-Blackwell.

Moscovich, M. J. (2015), 'Cassius Dio on the Death of Sophoniba', *Ancient History Bulletin*, 11: 25–9.
Pauw, D. A. (1991), 'The Dramatic Elements in Livy's History', *Acta Classica*, 34: 33–49.
Pinheiro, C. S. (2010), *O percurso de Dido, rainha de Cartago, na Literatura Latina*, Coimbra: Imprensa da Universidade de Coimbra.
Rodrigues, N. S. (2013), '*Amimetobiou*, the One "of the Inimitable Life": Cleopatra as a Metaphor for Alexandria in Plutarch', in R. Sousa, M. C. Fialho, M. Haggag and N. S. Rodrigues (eds), *Alexandrea ad Aegyptum: The Legacy of Multiculturalism in Antiquity*, 62–73, Porto-Coimbra: Edições Afrontamento/CITCEM/CECHUC.
Rodrigues, N. S. (2021), 'Túria ou como ser matrona na Roma dos alvores do Principado', in L. M. Barbosa and D. Puga (eds), *Antiguidade e usos do passado. Políticas e Práticas Sociais*, 13–30, Rio de Janeiro: Desalinho.
Rodrigues, N. S. (2022), 'Lucretia, Tullia and Tanaquil: Shaping the Identity of Rome's Women in the Augustan Period', in L. Roig Lanzillota, J. L. Brandão, C. Teixeira and A. Rodrigues (eds), *Roman Identity: Between Ideal and Performance*, 91–120, Turnhout: Brepols.
Savignac, J. de (1986), 'Le sens du terme Sâphôn', *Ugarit-Forschungen*, 16: 273–8.
Segert, S. (1994), 'Crossing the Waters: Moses and Hamilcar', *Journal of Near Eastern Studies*, 53 (3): 195–203.
Skutsch, O. (1985), *The Annals of Q. Ennius*, Oxford: Clarendon Press.
Smethurst, S. E. (1950), 'Women in Livy's "History"', *Greece & Rome*, 19 (56): 80–7.
Smith, M. and W. T. Pitard (2009), *The Ugaritic Baal Cycle, vol. II: Introduction with Text, Translation and Commentary of KTU/CAT 1.3–1.4*, Leiden: Brill.
Stevenson, T. (2011), 'Women of Early Rome as "Exempla" in Livy, "Ab Urbe Condita", Book 1', *Classical World*, 104 (2): 175–89.
Walbank, F. W. (1967), *A Historical Commentary on Polybius, vol. II: Commentary on Books VII–XVIII*, Oxford: Clarendon Press.
Walbank, F. W. (1979), *A Historical Commentary on Polybius, vol. III: Commentary on Books XIX–XL*, Oxford: Clarendon Press.
Walsh, P. G. (1958), 'Livy and Stoicism', *American Journal of Philology*, 79 (4): 355–75.

14

Self-Perception in the Construction of the Other: Case Study of Roman Portrayal of Viriathus, Boudica and Arminius[1]

Rúben Henrique de Castro

When reading the works of the ancient Greek and Roman authors about their enemies, one cannot help but notice how much of the construction of the 'other', of Rome's enemies and neighbours, is dominated by self-perception and self-portrait. We are left with a series of writings on people such as Viriathus, Boudica, and Arminius, three of the most iconic and memorable of Rome's enemies, who occupy in the modern and contemporary collective imagination an in-between position that mixes history and myth.

In the narratives the ancient Greek and Roman authors left us, we are not informed of who those historical figures actually were, instead we are given a somewhat restricted access to how Romans portrayed others and, by doing so, how they portrayed themselves, their empire's expansion, and their civilization. Through a small case study of the portrayals ancient authors provide of Viriathus, Boudica, and Arminius, we hope to give a better understanding of the political, philosophical, and narrative elements in the portraits of those figures, hopefully providing a deeper insight of how self-perception is present in the construction of the 'other' in the Roman world.

While each character in their own right has already received a great deal of attention,[2] few if any attempts have been made to offer a comparative analysis of the three portrayals. This chapter will provide a mini analysis of each of the three characters, before proceeding to a comparative reading of those portrayals.

Viriathus

The most defining trait ancient historians left us of Viriathus' portrayal is his heroization. Such heroization is built upon three axes: his *romanitas*, constructed in opposition to un-roman Roman commanders; his personal excellence; and his construction as a stoic and cynic hero.

Let us start by analysing Viriathus' heroization and his respective association with primitive Roman values. There is consistent recognition of Viriathus' achievements,[3] presented in a positive light by all authors;[4] Florus went as far as to call him *Hispaniae Romulus*.[5] The Lusitanian chieftain is given attributes such as intelligence and cleverness,[6] with expressions such as *ceterum Lusitanos Viriathus erexit, vir calliditatis acerrimae* (the Lusitanians were stirred to revolt by Viriathus, a man of extreme cunning)[7] in Florus, or characterizations such as the following in Cassius Dio.

> τοιούτου δ᾽ αὐτῷ τοῦ σώματος καὶ ἐκ τῆςφύσεως καὶ ἐκ τῆς ἀσκήσεως ὄντος, πολὺ ταῖς τῆς ψυχῆς ἀρεταῖς ὑπερέφερε.ταχὺς μὲν γὰρ πᾶν τὸ δέον ἐπινοῆσαι καὶ ποιῆσαι ἦν ˊτό τε γὰρ πρακτέονἅμα ἐγίγνωσκε, καὶ τὸν καιρὸν αὐτοῦ ἠπίστατὸ, δεινὸς δὲ τά τε ἐμφανέστατα ἀγνοεῖν καὶ τὰ ἀφανέστατα εἰδέναι προσποιήσασθαι.[8]

> And yet, possessed of such a physique, as the result both of nature and training, he excelled still more in his mental powers. He was swift to plan and accomplish whatever was needful, for he not only knew what must be done, but also understood the proper occasion for it; and he was equally clever at feigning ignorance of the most obvious facts and knowledge of the most hidden secrets.

His skill for oratory is also highlighted.[9] Viriathus uses it to acquire his army (App., *Hisp.* 11.62), to reorganize his fleeing troops (App., *Hisp.* 12.67), and even to win Tucca's allegiance through a famous cynic fable (Diod., 33.7.5). To those qualities ancient authors add a sense of justice in distributing the spoils,[10] which explains his inclusion in the *De Officis* by Cicero as a symbol of the importance of justice, valued even among barbarians and bandits[11] (Viriathus was repeatedly portrayed as a *latro* at the start of his career).[12] Also important in ancient narrative is his courage,[13] different from the typically barbarian *ferocitas*, with prudence and rationality added to the mix.[14]

Viriathus is thus presented as an exceptional general,[15] capable of detecting opportunities in the heat of battle,[16] inspiring troops in the most difficult moments,[17] and willing to put himself at risk for his men,[18] something which earned him unwavering loyalty.[19] In the paragraph relating to Viriathus' funeral, Diodorus Siculus mentions all of these traits (33.21a).

Opposite to this positive portrayal of Viriathus, Rome's enemy, was the negative portrayal of the Roman generals.[20] They are often presented, especially by Greek historians, as cowardly, greedy, untrustworthy, incompetent, even cruel leaders.[21]

As Grünewald writes: 'Viriathus was specifically selected as the embodiment of early Roman virtues, to be contrasted with Roman commanders regarded as self-seeking and untrustworthy representatives of the decadent senatorial oligarchy'.[22] Thus, it is clear that there was a process of appropriation of Viriathus by ancient historiography, establishing him as the 'héroe ajeno',[23] a moralizing role model of traditional Roman virtues[24] which had been lost by the Roman elite of his time (the defence of the traditional virtues of Rome in opposition to the Roman present is a constant in Roman historiography).[25]

Because of this, all accounts condemned Servilius Scipio's role in Viriathus' assassination.[26] Valerius Maximus, in his *facta et dicta memorabilia*, is perhaps the author who expresses those feelings the best, saying of Scipio's behaviour that *uictoriamque non meruit, sed emit* (he did not deserve, but bought his victory).[27]

Another impactful element in Viriathus' literary characterization is his image as a stoic and cynic hero, in line with the philosophical concept of the 'good savage'.[28] Both stoicism and cynicism had an enormous influence in the Classical World. Originating from Greece, they expanded to Rome, where stoicism would become one of the most defining[29] and dominating philosophical tendencies.[30] Cynicism never reached the same level, probably because of its more radical way of life[31] (incompatible with public life[32] due to the active condemnation of the *nomos* and *nomisma*)[33] and because of the similarities between stoic ideals and traditional Roman values.[34]

The main element of Viriathus' characterization, fitting both stoic and cynic beliefs, is his way of life according to nature. Diodorus[35] and Cassius Dio (influenced by Posidonius)[36] are the two authors who reveal his harmony with the natural world.

Dio's description of Viriathus' way of life is one of the best examples of the cynic nature of his character (22.73.2): a frugal eating regime (also valued, even if differently, by stoics)[37] determined by what he was able to gather from nature;[38] and living the life of a homeless nomad[39] which strengthened his body and spirit, allowing him to find satisfaction from whatever was at hand[40] (this state of contentment and adaptability was also strongly valued by stoics).[41] All those elements are to be found in cynicism and, in a more moderate fashion, in stoicism.[42]

Similarly, Viriathus criticized customs and money,[43] *nomos* and *nomisma*, considered 'the twin corrupters of nature'[44] by cynics. The thought he offers on wealth at his wedding is quite close to cynic doctrine[45] (as indeed the whole episode is).[46] Two elements of cynic philosophy are present: his disdain for wealth and his criticism of its illusory and transitory nature. Alongside this contempt of the *nomisma* typical of cynicism, the occasion of Viriathus' wedding also offers an image of his feeling of disdain for the *nomos* (that which Liv Yarrow calls 'his lack of social graces').[47] Not only is his frugality on display in Diodorus, but also a strong disregard for what was socially expected, abstaining from eating with guests and from showering (Diod., 33.7.2–3), something common in cynicism.[48] The taking of his wife to the mountains shows also a clear parallel with the story of Hipparchia and Crates,[49] as others have stated.[50]

The typology of his speech is also another important element of his cynic characterization, with Diodorus (Diod., 33.7.5–7) telling us that his oratory was direct and natural, unaltered by formal education, and filled with metaphors (elements of cynic inspiration).[51]

While our analysis has attempted to show the closeness of Viriathus' portrayal with the cynic doctrine, there are some elements of his characterization that undermine a full identification with the cynics: he got married; he participated in religious rites;[52] and he was a military chieftain.[53] All those elements were condemned by cynic philosophers.[54] Despite his stoic and, mainly, cynic, conception, Viriathus' portrayal was above all else that of the noble savage, a virtuous, righteous, primitive being uncorrupted by the vices and temptations stoics and cynics found in their own civilizations.

Boudica

Just like the Viriathus that lives in the pages of his enemies' history, Boudica's portrayal was also tainted by the cultural, literary, and philosophical conceptions of the authors who wrote of her. However, the portrayal of Boudica, even if different in the two main sources, is clearly negative. As Carolyn Williams highlighted, 'Dio's approach to the character of Boudica is almost entirely different from Tacitus'. Instead of partly presenting her as a wronged Roman matron (as Tacitus does), Dio stresses Boudica's monstruous, barbarian features'.[55]

Unlike that of Viriathus, the characterization of Boudica is determined by the actions of her army, with no attempt by the ancient sources to differentiate between the queen and her followers. On the contrary, there is many affirmations of Boudica's culpability,[56] her responsibility for instigating[57] and commanding[58] the rebellion.

The portrayal that both Cassius Dio and Tacitus (in his *Annales* and *De Vita Iulii Agricolae*) present of the rebellion is negative, invoking the alleged barbarity of her army (the use of the word barbarian to classify Britons is a constant throughout their history).[59]

Both authors describe regularly and vividly the violence perpetrated by her army, whom *nec ullum in barbaris saevitiae genus omisit ira et victoria* (in their rage and their triumph, they spared no variety of a barbarian's cruelty).[60] Those portrayals go from the generic statement of the destruction caused by the rebellion – δύο τε γὰρ πόλεις ἐπορθήθησαν, καὶ μυριάδες ὀκτὼ τῶν τε Ῥωμαίων καὶ τῶνσυμμάχων αὐτῶν ἐφθάρησαν, ἥ τε νῆσος ἠλλοτριώθη (two cities were sacked, eighty-thousand of the Romans and of their allies perished, and the island was lost to Rome)[61] – to the specific mention of the terrible mortality caused by episodes such as the fall of Londinium – *neque enim capere aut venundare aliudve quod belli commercium, sed caedes patibula ignes cruces, tamquam reddituri supplicium at praerepta interim ultione, festinabant* (for it was not on making prisoners and selling them, or on any of the barter of war, that the enemy was bent, but on slaughter, on the gibbet, the fire and the cross, like men soon about to pay the penalty, and meanwhile snatching at instant vengeance).[62]

Cassius Dio goes as far as to offer a detailed description of the torture inflicted on massacred civilians, sometimes linking such violence to the performance of native religious rituals (D.C. 62.7.2–3). So, there is use of native religion (specifically the practice of human sacrifices) to forge the estrangement between the reader and the Britons.

The barbarization of Boudica and her rebellion is more visible in Cassius Dio than in Tacitus.[63] Cassius Dio provides a more violent portrayal of the rebellion, offering details of tortures whose occurrence is merely stated by Tacitus; increasing the death toll,[64] and associating the violence of the rebellion with native religion (while Tacitus limits the reference to human sacrifices to the isle of Nola,[65] never a mention in relation to Boudica's rebellion). But the barbarization of Boudica is also present in Dio's physical description of the queen. She was tall and robust, a common feature of 'barbarians', striking terror in others just by her looks, with her ferocious gaze, rough (*trachu*) voice, and long loose hair (D.C. 62.2.3–4).

It is interesting how Cassius Dio, who comes from a very patriarchal society, describes Boudica, giving her one trait that suggests a partial masculinization of her character: her voice. As Carolyn Williams has intelligently pointed out, the word chosen to characterize her voice, *trachu*, is usually applied in the adjectivization of adolescent boys, thus her voice is 'transgressing the bounds of proper femininity, yet lacking the legitimate authority of mature manhood'.[66]

There is constant emphasis in our sources of the fact that the rebellion's leadership is in the hands of a woman.[67] Tacitus regularly mentions the irrelevance of gender in the laws of succession of her people.[68] Cassius Dio, with maximum expression of the strangeness of the Roman world to such reality, writes that ἀναπείσασα, τῆς τε προστατείας αὐτῶν ἀξιωθεῖσα καὶ τοῦ πολέμουπαντὸς στρατηγήσασα, Βουδουῖκα ἦν, γυνὴ (possessed of greater intelligence than often belongs to women),[69] considering simultaneously that the shame caused by the temporary success of the defeat was exacerbated by its female leadership.[70]

While both authors place considerable emphasis on Boudica being a woman, they do so in different ways.[71] Tacitus uses Boudica's gender as a basis for the portrayal of the abuses she suffered, promoting, at an early stage of his narrative, a sympathetic view of her through her partial transformation into a 'wronged Roman matron'.[72] Cassius Dio highlights her gender especially through the incorporation in her speeches of a series of philosophical elements tending towards the creation of a dichotomy between the corruptive nature of civilization and the idealized primitive purity of the Bretton world.[73]

Boudica's rebellion is used by both authors for the elaboration of a critical reflection on Roman expansionism and rule. But they do it in different ways, with Cassius Dio exploring, philosophically, the dichotomy of the two worlds, and Tacitus putting its focus on the abuse suffered by the locals at the hands of Rome.

Tacitus' portrayal is made in two different stages of his literary career (in his early career with the *De Vita Iulli Agricolae* and in his late career with the *Annales*). Such a time gap allows for small differences in his exploration of the events.[74] For example, in the biography of Agricola, Tacitus does not go into detail on the offences suffered by Boudica (which are to be found in Tac., *Ann.* 14.31 and 14.35), opting instead for vague allusions to abuses on the life and property of the Britons.[75] But even in that context, he seems to mitigate the accusations by writing that the Britons *conferre iniurias et interpretando accendere* (compared their wrongs, and exaggerated them in the discussion).[76] This situation matches the difference of his perspective on Roman rule in the two works, with the *Agricolae* (and the Histories, in a certain way) being more positive, and the *Annales* offering a negative and critical vision.[77]

While in the *Agricolae* the only apparent criticism of Roman rule is the speech made by Calgacus to its troops, in the *Annales* Boudica's rebellion is used to provide a wholly negative view of Roman expansionism. This initially sympathetic view of the queen and her suffering changes as the violence of the rebellion is exposed by Tacitus, and the Britons become unhinged barbarians: *quod uberrimum spolianti et defendentibus intutum* (who delighted in plunder and were indifferent to all else).[78] Still, both Tacitus and Cassius Dio criticize Roman rule,[79] with the denunciation of the rapacity that allegedly gave birth to the empire;[80] an assertion of the abuses perpetrated by Roman troops;[81] of the cowardliness[82] and incompetence[83] of the Romans, with a clear opposition between the pre-Roman freedom and the oppression of Roman rule[84] (which, according to Cassius Dio's Boudica, was worse than slavery).[85] The very speech of Suetonius Paterculus to his soldiers before the decisive battle seems to prove Tacitus' accusation of Roman greed, with the general having to ask his soldiers to focus on the fight and not on plunder before the enemy was destroyed, *praedae immemores: parta victoria cuncta ipsis cessura* (without a thought of plunder: when once the victory had been won, everything will be in your power).[86]

Cassius Dio presents, through Boudica's speeches, an image of the natives strongly marked by philosophical conceptions like the ones that dominated Viriathus' portrayal. In those speeches, Cassius Dio's Boudica constructs a utopic portrayal of life before Rome, 'linked to a vision of pre-Roman Britain as an idyllic golden age, free from the vicissitudes of "civilized" life'.[87] Tacitus also contributed to this idealized vision based on stoic and cynic ideals.[88]

The establishment of a clear link between romanization and the loss of freedom is present throughout the texts of both authors,[89] but let us focus on an excerpt from Tacitus (Ann. 21.3):

> inde etiam habitus nostri honor et frequens toga; paulatimque discessum ad delenimenta vitiorum, porticus et balinea et conviviorum elegantiam. idque apud imperitos humanitas vocabatur, cum pars servitutis esset.
>
> step by step they were led to things which dispose to vice, the lounge, the bath, the elegant banquet. All this in their ignorance, they called civilization, when it was but a part of their servitude).

The text refers to the corruptive nature of civilization (expressed in the words *paulatimque discessum ad delenimenta vitiorum*), destructive of virtue, purity, and freedom, elements which the Roman elite associated with primitive societies. As we have also seen for Viriathus, classic literature tends to the adoption of philosophical conceptions that make the civilization a synonym of fragility, not only moral but also physical.[90] Cassius Dio is particularly useful in this regard. His text from 62.5.2 to 65.5.6 includes in the speech of Boudica a series of considerations regarding the moral and physical superiority of the Britons, exactly because of their primitive and uncorrupted state. It is this philosophical conception that is at the heart of Boudica's claim which has obvious similarities with the portrayal of Viriathus.

ἔν τε οὖν τούτοις παρὰ πολὺ ἡμῶν ἐλαττοῦνται, καὶ ἐνἐκείνοις, ὅτι οὔτε λιμὸν οὔτε δίψος, οὐ ψῦχος οὐ καῦμα ὑποφέρουσιν ὥσπερἡμεῖς, ἀλλ᾽ οἱ μὲν καὶ σκιᾶς καὶ σκέπης σίτου τε μεμαγμένου καὶ οἴνου καὶἐλαίου δέονται, κἂν ἄρα τι τούτων αὐτοὺς ἐπιλίπῃ διαφθείρονται, ἡμῖν δὲ δὴπᾶσα μὲν πόα καὶ ῥίζα σῖτός ἐστι, πᾶς δὲ χυμὸς ἔλαιον, πᾶν δὲ.[91]

There is also the fact that they cannot bear up under hunger, thirst, cold, or heat, as we can. They require shade and covering, they require kneaded bread and wine and oil, and if any of these things fails them, they perish; for us, on the other hand, any grass or root serves as bread, the juice of any plant as oil, any water as wine, any tree as a house.

The highlighting of the disparity of wealth between Romans and Britons[92] corresponds not only to an attempt to highlight the alleged Roman avarice,[93] but also a certain philosophical defence of Boudica's society, poor but free. It is in that line of thought that Cassius Dio places Boudica telling her troops that ἐγνώκατε δὲ ὅσῳ καὶ πενία ἀδέσποτος πλούτουδουλεύοντος (and you have come to realize how much better is poverty with no master than wealth with slavery),[94] just like Tacitus had Calgacus mentioning the uselessness of wealth against strength,[95] two visions shared by cynical philosophers.

Arminius

If Viriathus' portrayal is positive, despite the accusation of banditry, and if Boudica's characterization is mostly negative, that of Arminius is surely a more complex one. While all other authors offer a clearly negative portrayal, in Tacitus' *Annales*, the main source, there is a mixed image, with the progressive growth of positive aspects of Arminius as the narrative nears its end, with an entirely negative portrayal during the Battle of Teutoburg Forest evolving to a more complex image afterwards.

The first mention of the famous massacre of the Teutoburg Forest is made by Ovid in two of his poems, one written some months after the event,[96] the other after about a year.[97] At around the same time Marcus Manilius published the poem *Astronomica*, which mentions the battle.[98] These three compositions mark the beginning of the negativity which will characterize Roman narratives, with a criticism of the events, of Germans in general, and of Arminius in particular.[99] German actions are permanently seen as treason by all authors,[100] and the violence of the battle results in expressions such as *fera Germania*.[101] In line with the *feritas* and *ferocia* of Germans (a typically barbarian trait),[102] there is denouncement of their brutality during the battle itself by Ovid (*Tr.* 4.2.29–38) and Manilius (*Astr.* 1.899–900). The characterization that Ovid gives of Arminius is illustrative of the negativity that is shown by all authors at this early stage:

> ille ferox et adhuc oculis hostilibus ardens
> hortator pugnae consiliumque fuit.
> perfidus hic nostros inclusit fraude locorum,
> squalida promissis qui tegit ora comis
> illo, qui sequitur, dicunt mactata ministro
> saepe recusanti corpora capta deo.[103]

> This fierce fellow with hostile eyes still ablaze was at once the instigator and planner of the fight. This traitor here trapped our men in a treacherous place – the one who now conceals his unkempt face with his long hair. That one following him they say was the priest who sacrificed captives to a god who often refused them.

The two last verses are especially interesting because, just as we verified for Boudica, they link the native religion to the perceived violence of the natives' actions, something Tacitus also does.[104]

The attempt to create a negative image of Arminius and his followers by emphasizing their violence is consistent among all authors. Cassius Dio writes that they provoked great destruction.[105] Florus highlights the brutality of the massacre and the tortures inflicted upon the Romans (2.30.36–37). Velleius Paterculus mentions the extermination of every Roman captured by the Germans (Vell. 2.119.2) and details the mangling of Varus' corpse (Vell. 2.119.5). The abhorrence in Roman culture of the mutilation of a dead person's body, and its religious implications for life after death, make Paterculus' portrayal of the German violence quite shocking for his readers. The negative image of the Germans (the words 'savage' and 'barbarian' are regularly found in the texts)[106] is very impactful in the narratives of the Battle of Teutoburg Forest, even if Varus is also a target of criticism, qualified as an incompetent, proud, greedy, and cruel man.[107]

Upon being introduced to the reader, Arminius is presented as the instigator and leader of the rebellion,[108] a true *turbator Germaniae* (troubler of Germany),[109] and an instigator of the tortures suffered by Romans.[110] Thus, he is said to be clever and treacherous[111] (or *perfidus*, as Ovid calls him)[112] – matching the characterization of his people as ferociously belligerent.[113] Tacitus tells us of his *insitam violentiam* (naturally furious temper)[114] and *ferocitas*,[115] which is also pointed out by Ovid[116] and Velleius Paterculus.[117] His *insitam violentiam* leads to his ferocity in battle, his violent reaction at the capture of his wife,[118] and his famous discussion with his brother.[119] Even his physical appearance matches the appearance of a barbarian in the Roman imagination, with a ferocious gaze and unkempt long hair (Ov., *Tr.* 4.2.31–33).

In Tacitus,[120] and in part in Velleius Paterculus[121] there is the progressive presentation of a positive portrayal of Arminius. So, Arminius can be included in a certain Roman historiographical tradition where 'one sees a developing fascination with paradoxical characters, individuals in whom great virtues and great vices coexist'.[122] So, Arminius is seen as the defender of the traditions and ancestral freedom of his people (Tac., *Ann.* 2.10), freedom counterposed by the servitude of the Romans.[123] Tacitus inserts the subject of German freedom in Arminius' speeches to his troops[124] (we are told that Arminius was a gifted speaker)[125] and in the argument with his Roman-loyalist brother;[126] and he writes it explicitly: *liberator haud dubiae Germaniae* (undoubtedly the liberator of Germany);[127] *Arminium pro libertate bellantem fauor habebat* (Arminius aroused enthusiasm as the champion of liberty).[128] Velleius Paterculus also mentions Arminius' *ultra barbarum promptus ingenio* (possessing an intelligence quite beyond the ordinary barbarian),[129] thus placing him above his countrymen. Such intelligence, *ultra barborum*, allowed him, on certain occasions, to refrain from his *insitam violentiam*, as is verifiable in his disagreement with Inguiomerus about the best strategy to adopt against that portion of the Roman army they had been able to isolate.[130] Against Inguiomerus' proposed full frontal assault, which would eventually lead to the Germans' defeat, Arminius offers a cautious and risk-adverse strategy.

Another positive concession to the character of Arminius is the apparent parallel Tacitus tries to draw between Arminius and Germanicus. Besides the existence of a similar narrative rhythm,[131] Tacitus, as Rhiannon Ash highlights,[132] associates both characters with the idea of *libertas* (making them symbols in the fight 'against the forces of tyranny').[133] This association with the concept of *libertas*[134] makes both characters, in a certain measure, anachronistic figures, representative of ancient Roman virtues. Such reality places them against their respective families: while Arminius is placed in opposition to Segestes (his father-in-law),[135] Inguiomerus (his uncle),[136] and Maroboduus,[137] Germanicus is placed in opposition to Tiberius, his uncle. But the 'popular young hero, fighting wars in an old-fashioned way, is ultimately no match for the older, less attractive, but very shrewd modern manipulator'.[138] And so, they both fall.

The portrayal Tacitus provides of Arminius' death is the zenith of his positivity (2.88); if he was introduced as *turbator Germaniae*, he now departs as a *liberator haud dubiae Germaniae*.

Comparative analysis

Having completed a brief study of each of the portrayals in question, let us now offer a comparative analysis.

Of all the portrayals, the positivity of Viriathus' representation stands out. Thomas Grünewald, however, believes that Viriathus did not fit the category of respected enemy of Rome, even if he admits the positivity inherent to his presentation as noble bandit, 'exemplifying the morally admirable'.[139] While excluding Viriathus, Grünewald does include Arminius in the list of the most respected enemies of Rome.[140] A similar focus on the positive dimensions of the portrayal of Arminius is offered by Rhiannon Ash,[141] probably because her study focused solely on the work of Tacitus. The analysis offered in the previous pages prevents adherence to such conclusions. Thomas Grünewald highlights the gradual manner in which the positivity of Viriathus' characterization is built.[142] He ignores, however, that same representation for the portrayal of Arminius.

Viriathus' characterization is gifted a stronger and more encompassing positivity than that of Arminius, and less negativity, restricted to his classification as a bandit. We should not overstress the positivity of Arminius' portrayal in Tacitus to the point of ignoring the negativity of all the other accounts, and even of Tacitus' account at the Battle of Teutoburg. While the 'barbarization' of Arminius has as background the massacre of Roman soldiers in Teutoburg, Viriathus is presented as a noble barbarian, the ideal stoic-cynic man. The negative dimensions of Viriathus' characterization are ambiguous and can be seen as partly positive: his promotion of a guerrilla warfare is presented as *latrocinium* (banditry) and simultaneously as a proof of his alleged military genius. So, we have a positive portrayal of Viriathus, built upon his alleged personal excellence (true *exemplum bonum*),[143] and on his status as a symbol of traditional Roman virtues and values. This last element, allied to his presentation as a prototype of stoic and, especially, cynic ideals, consubstantiate in his quasi-utopian transformation as noble savage and noble bandit.

Boudica is clearly the target of the most negative portrayal, even if her rebellion is used by Cassius Dio and Tacitus to criticize Roman rule. While the barbarization of Viriathus is tinted by a positive philosophical construction, and that of Arminius is partially diminished by the evolution of Tacitus' narrative, neither argument can be fully used for Boudica.

We can thus claim that the three analysed portrayals present different degrees of positivity and/or negativity: Viriathus' characterization is clearly positive; Arminius' portrayal is gifted of a strong complexity and ambiguity, a mixed image; and Boudica's depiction is the one with the clearest negativity, even if inserted in a narrative that strongly criticizes Roman behaviour towards the queen and Roman rule.

Despite those differences, there are evident similarities between the portrayals. All three characters are barbarized; there is in all three characterizations a dialectic between the enemies of Rome and the Romans themselves, with a certain presentation of the enemies as representative of primitive Rome and a criticism of contemporaneous Rome and its leaders; and there is the centrality and omnipresence of philosophical conceptions of cynic-stoic influence, which tend to see the state of Roman civilization as corrupt and weak. So, there is in the studied sources a clear auto-reflection, a colonizing treatment of enemy nations by classical historiography.[144] There is what we may call a dichotomous and self-centred interpretation of the 'other' by Roman historiography, seen in the light of classical civilization and classical philosophy.

Viriathus' portrayal is the only one in which his 'barbarian' nature (as it was understood by Romans) is not linked to negative conceptions. The personality that ancient authors constructed for him is different from the classical representation of a 'barbarian'; certain traits such as *feritas*, *ferocitas*, *auaritia*, cruelty, and irrationality are not ascribed to him. The very presentation of his *barbaritas* at the light of the cynic and stoic idealizations of 'noble savages' leads to an almost utopic presentation of Viriathus. Quite the opposite is the 'barbarization' of Arminius and Boudica, with an attempt by the ancient sources to emotionally distance the reader from said characters, except in very specific moments. For both characters there is not only a clear barbarization of the peoples they lead (by highlighting their cruelty and its link to their religion), but also of themselves. The role religion played in both accounts is very interesting. It is one of the instruments used by classical authors to reinforce the barbarity of the two nations in question (thus reinforcing the emotional distance between the reader and the peoples portrayed). This use of religion and human sacrifice to provide 'otherness' to Celtic and Germanic tribes is a common element in classical historiography, being observable not only for the studied characters, but also for the peoples of Gaul[145] and Hispania[146] (even if, for Hispania, not during the portrayal of Viriathus' war).

During our analysis of Boudica, we noted the importance that her gender assumes. Her gender is used as an exacerbating tool for the cultural disparities between the worlds of the Romans and the Britons, but it is not limited to the Iceni queen. Despite the exceptionality of Boudica, there are parallels between the characterization of Briton, Germanic, and Hispanic women as transgressive of the gender boundaries of the historians' own societies. It is in such light that we should understand Boudica's claim that women were as courageous as men.[147] The same courage is attributed by Tacitus to Arminius' wife, who was capable of maintaining a stoic attitude after being captured by the Romans.[148]

As Tomás Aguilera Durán explained in his study of the pre-Roman barbarian stereotype, the positive version that is occasionally given by ancient authors of Rome's northern enemies 'deriva de ciertas tendencias filosóficas y políticas que se valen de la imagen idealizada del primitivo como contrapunto para la crítica de determinadas políticas y personajes romanos' (derives from certain philosophical and political tendencies that use the idealized image of the primitive as a counterpoint to the criticism of certain Roman policies and characters).[149] Concomitantly with this statement there is, in the analysed portrayals, the existence of a certain dialectic between the enemies of Rome and the generals and emperors who fought them, with a critical reflection not only of certain Roman figures, but also of the moral state of the empire. In the case of Viriathus there is a demonization of the Roman generals who fought against him, and a dichotomic presentation of the vices of these Romans against the moral and personal virtues of the Lusitanian chief. Tacitus and Cassius Dio, as we have seen, use the narrative of Boudica's rebellion to elaborate a negative image of Rome's rule and its decadence. Also, in the portrayal of the Battle of Teutoburg Forest, there is strong criticism of Varus and his role in the Roman defeat.

In addition to the criticism that is made of Rome, there is also a certain 'romanization' of the studied characters. This 'romanization' did not associate the three characters with the Rome they were fighting, instead attempting to turn them into flawed representatives of the traditional values of that lost Urbe of which Livy writes with wistfulness (Liv., 1.pr.11), in opposition to the morally degraded Rome of his days (Liv., 1.pr.9).

It is in considering the transversality of the idea of moral decay of the contemporary Urbe that we must frame the association of some of Rome's enemies with a long-lost virtuous archaic Rome.[150] As Rhiannon Ash puts it, 'that old Rome is to be found in the most remote parts of the Empire, or even beyond the empire's bounds'.[151] It is in such a category of adversaries 'more Roman than the Romans'[152] that characters such as Viriathus must be included. In the case of Boudica's portrayal, such characterization is not verifiable beyond the partial and transitory romanization subjacent to her presentation as 'wronged Roman matron'[153] by Tacitus. In the case of Arminius, such presentation is more problematic, even if verifiable. That association with the noble Roman past is made, in Arminius' portrayal, through two elements: by the parallel Tacitus seems to attempt to build between Arminius and Germanicus, and by a generational conflict present in the *Annales*, in which the younger leaders are representative of an idealized past in opposition to older leaders, better examples of moral decay.

Regarding the positive traits of the studied figures, it is important to highlight the recurrent acknowledgment of attributes such as courage, persuasiveness, defence of freedom, and sagacity. These elements are not only present in the portrayal of Viriathus and Arminius, but also in the portrayal of Boudica.[154]

To understand the levels of positivity and negativity of each character, it is important to acknowledge the degree of separation between the portrayal of the studied figures and their respective peoples. Arminius is presented to the reader as sharing several traits with his people, still, he had the *ultra barbarum promptus ingenio* that made him the ideal leader. In contrast, Boudica's portrayal tends to dilute her personality into that of her people. For Viriathus we are offered a mixed portrayal in this regard. Just like his people, he is shown as a primitive and brave bandit. But unlike the *ferocitas* of his people,[155] his courage is linked to his intellect and military genius, clearly superior to that of his fellow countrymen in several instances.[156]

The process of association of the studied characters to traditional Roman values is linked to the subjacency of the noble savage's conception, glorifier of a simple and virtuous life, associated by Roman historiography with the beginnings of Rome. As Liv Yarrow explains, the concept of noble savage provides a way to glorify a simpler past, with the moral strength of such a way of life being regularly glorified as the reason for Rome's rise to power in the Mediterranean.[157] It is in conformity with such historiographical reality that we must understand the regular contamination of Roman histories with philosophical conceptions conducive to an expression of the alleged corruptive character of civilization, in opposition to a virtuous primitivism in line with the image of noble savage.

Of all the three studied characters, Viriathus is the one who more clearly expresses that contaminative action of classical authors, presented as a true prototype of cynic and stoic ideals, a true noble savage whose heroism is contraposed to the morally corrupted Roman generals. The speeches of Cassius Dio's Boudica are an even clearer expression of this opposition between the physical and moral superiority of primitive nations and the contrasting physical and moral decay subjacent to the process of romanization. In her speeches it is not just Boudica who is shown as fitting the concept of the idealized savage, but her entire people, with the presentation of an unspoiled and utopian image of the Britons in opposition to a negative Roman image.

While Arminius' portrayal does not share the omnipresence of philosophical conceptions like those of Viriathus and Boudica's characterizations, his people play an important role in the construction of such conceptions in classical historiography, taken as one of the best examples of the fortifying nature of life in accordance with the natural world. Authors as varied as Julius Caesar,[158] Tacitus,[159] and Cassius Dio[160] create a hierarchy of braveness and strength of several peoples, with Germans occupying a position of primacy. Julius Caesar compares several times the Gauls, Britons, and Germans, comparisons in which the Germans are presented as superior due to the greater primitivism of their societies,[161] with a similar thought process being followed by Tacitus (Tac., *Ag.* 11).

Conclusion

It is important to conclude this analysis by restating the imagistic, thematic, and conceptual wealth of the portrayal constructed for three of Rome's biggest western enemies. It is true that our records of ancient Rome are contaminated in terms of 'historical truth'. It is also true that such contamination is nothing but an opportunity to understand how ancient authors and their societies understood not only their own world, but that of the 'other', how they portrayed themselves and their past when they attempted to portray their enemies. Hopefully, we have made evident the self-reflective and, in a way, colonizing treatment of foreign peoples and their leaders by ancient historiography.

We have attempted to understand the similarities and dissimilarities between the different portrayals, with their respective degrees of positivity and negativity. Viriathus is presented as the prototype of the noble savage; for Arminius we are left with a complex, ambiguous image; and Boudica is clearly the portrayal in which there is a a pre-eminence of negative barbaric elements, even if framed by a narrative quite critical of Rome's civilization and Rome's rule. Despite the differences highlighted during the short case study of each character, we have attempted to show the reader how there is evidence, in all portrayals, of the transversality (even if to different degrees) of narrative, political, literary, and philosophical elements such as the expression of the barbaric nature of all three characters; the framing of Boudica in the transgressive nature of 'gender frontiers' assumed by 'barbaric' women; and the dialectic built between the studied characters and the Romans they fought, a relationship which tends to express the association of certain enemy leaders with an idealized image of archaic Rome, in opposition to the corruptive nature of Roman civilization and the consequent negativity of the present Roman leaders.

Through our small case study, we hope to have contributed to a better understanding of the similarities and differences between the narrative and philosophical elements present in each characterization and, by doing so, maybe we have provided a clearer insight on how self-perception is present in the construction of the 'other' in the Roman world.

Notes

1 The research for this paper was funded by Fundação para a Ciência e para a Tecnologia (scholarship SFRH/BD/146403/2019).

2 For Boudica, the following works were found impactful: Adler 2008; Williams 2009; Ash 2012. For Arminius, Wells 2003; Benario 2004; Ash 2012. And for Viriathus, Alvar Ezquerra and Blázquez Martínez 1997; Pastor Muñoz 2003; Grünewald 2004; Pérez Abellán 2006; Yarrow 2006; and Gorges 2009. For an analysis of the portrayal of Iberians, I recommend the following works: Thollard 1987; Gómez Fraile 1999; Cruz-Andreotti 2002; García Moreno 2002; Gorges 2009; ar 2011, 2012; Sánchez Moreno and Aguilera Durán 2013.

3 For example, see: D.C. 22.73.1–3; App., *Hisp.* 11.62, 12.67, 12.69; Cic., *Off.* 2.40; *Amm.* 14.11.33; Sil., *Punica.* X.215–234; Vell., 2.90.3; Diod., 33.1.5, 33.21a; etc.

4 The same was stated by Grünewald 2004: 36 and Pastor Muñoz 2003: 203.

5 Flor., *Epit.* 1.33.15.

6 Flor., *Epit.* 1.33.15; D.C. 22.73.3; App., *Hisp.* 12.69–70; Diod., 33.7.7.

7 *Epit.* 1.33.15.

8 D.C. 22.73.3.

9 That is why Diodorus (33.7.7) tells us that τοῦ δὲ εἰπόντος ὅτι πολλῶν εἰδότων οὐδεὶς ἐπεβάλετο λαβεῖν ἢ αἰτῆσαι, Τί οὖν, εἶπεν, ἄνθρωπε, διδόντων σοι τὴν ἄδειαν καὶ τὴν ἀσφαλῆ τούτων ἀπόλαυσιν τῶν κρατούντων, καταλιπὼν τούτους ἐπεθύμησας τῆς ἐμῆς ἀγραυλίας καὶ ἀγενείας οἰκεῖος γενέσθαι; ἦν δὲ οὗτος κατὰ τὰς ὁμιλίας εὔστοχος, ὡς ἂν ἐξ αὐτοδιδάκτου καὶ ἀδιαστρόφου φύσεως φέρων τοὺς λόγους· (He is said to have made many other pithy remarks as well, for though he had had no formal education, he was schooled in the understanding of practical affairs. For the speech of one who lives according to nature is concise, being a by-product of virtuous pursuits; and when a thing is stated simply, briefly, and without frills, the speaker is credited with a pointed saying, while the hearer has something to remember).

10 See App., *Hisp.* 12.75.

11 Cic., *Off.* 2.40.

12 D.C. 22.73.1; App., *Hisp*. 12.71; Diod. 33.1.2, 33.1.3 or 33.1.5; Vell., 2.1.3; Liv., *Per.* 52.8; Cic., *Off.* 2.40; Flor., *Epit*. 1.33.15.

13 App., *Hisp.* 12.75.

14 App., *Hisp.* 12.70 and App., *Hisp*. 12.69.

15 See Diod., 33.21a, 33.1.2, 33.1.5; App., *Hisp.* 11.62, 12.67, 12.69.

16 E.g., Diod., 33.21a or App., *Hisp.* 12.67.

17 E.g., App., *Hisp*. 11.62.

18 E.g., App., *Hisp*. 12.67.

19 Diod., 33.1.5.

20 App., *Hisp.* 10.59, 10.60, 11.61, 11.63, 12.74; D.C., 22.74.1, 22.74.2, 22.77.1, 22.78.1; Vell., 2.1.3, 2.90.3; Flor., *Epit.* 1.33.17; Val. Max., 6.4 and 9.6.

21 App., *Hisp.* 10.59, 10.60, 11.61, 11.63, 12.74; D.C., 22.74.1, 22.74.2, 22.77.1, 22.78.1; Vell., 2.1.3, 2.90.3; Flor., *Epit.* 1.33.17; Val. Max., 6.4 and 9.6.

22 Grünewald 2004: 35.

23 Alvar Ezquerra and Blázquez Martínez 1997: 139.

24 Grünewald 2004: 35–44; Pastor Muñoz 2003: 203; keark 2014: 139.

25 Grünewald 2004: 35; Ash 2012: 58–64.

26 Diod., 33.1.4 and 33.21a; App., *Hisp.* 12.74; Flor., *Epit.* 1.33.17; Val. Max., 9.6.

27 Val. Max., 9.6.

28 Two works are of importance to this subject and highly impacted our own analysis: Pastor Muñoz 2003 and Lens Tuero 1986.

29 Sedley 2004: 238.

30 Ibid., 165, 204.

31 Desmond 2008: 101.

32 Ibid., 110–11.

33 Ibid., 99.

34 Sandbach 2001: 142; Sedley 2004: 202.

35 Diod., 33.1.1–2.

36 Grünewald 2004: 42.

37 Pastor Muñoz 2003: 188.

38 Desmond 2008: 77.

39 Ibid., 80.

40 Ibid., 83–4; Pastor Muñoz 2003: 188–91.

41 Long 2006: 391.

42 Sandbach 2011: 21; Desmond 2008: 77, 78, 80, 101.

43 App., *Hisp.* 12.75; Diod. 33.21a, 33.1.5; Cic., *Off.* 2.40.

44 Desmond 2008: 99.

45 Diod., 33.7.1.

46 Pastor Muñoz 2003: 189; Gorges 2009: 12.

47 Yarrow 2006: 335.

48 Desmond 2008: 77–8.
49 Desmond 2008: 189.
50 Pastor Muñoz 2003: 189–90.
51 Desmond 2008: 77–8, 148.
52 See Diod., 33.7.2.
53 D.C., 22.73.4.
54 Desmond 2008: 78, 92, 111–12.
55 Williams 2009: 181.
56 D.C., 62b.1.1, 62b.2.2, 62b.7.1.
57 Tac., *Ann.* 14.35; Tac., *Ag.* 16.1; D.C., 62b.2.2, 62b.2.3, 62b.7.1.
58 D.C., 62b.1.1, 62b.2.2, 62b.2.3, 62b.6.4, 62b.7.1; Tac., *Ag.* 16.1.
59 Tac., *Ag.* 5.9, 16.1, 11, 33.1; Tac., *Ann.* 12.35, 14.32, 14.33, 14.36; D.C., 39.51.3, 60.20.2, 62b.12.1.
60 Tac., *Ag.* 16.1–2.
61 D.C., 62b.1.1.
62 Tac., *Ann.* 14.33.
63 Adler 2008: 189.
64 Williams 2009: 37.
65 Tac., *Ann.* 14.30.
66 Ibid., 61.
67 Tac., *Ag.* 16.1, 31; Tac., *Ann.* 14.31, 14.35; D.C. 62b.1.1, 62b.2.2, 62b.2.3, 62b.6.4.
68 Tac., *Ag.* 16.1; Tac., *Ann.* 14.35.
69 D.C., 62b.2.2.
70 D.C., 62b.1.1.
71 Williams 2009: 120.
72 Ibid., 181.
73 Adler 2008: 190–4.
74 Ash 2012: 182.
75 Ash 2012: 182.
76 Tac., *Ag.* 15.
77 Ash 2012: 183–4.
78 Tac., *Ann.* 14.33.
79 See Tac., *Ann.* 14.31, 14.32, 14.35, 14.36; D.C., 62b.2.1, 62b.3.2, 62b.4.2, 62b.6.4.
80 E.g., D.C., 62b.3.4 or Tac., *Ag.* 15.
81 Tac., *Ann.* 14.31.
82 Tac., *Ann.* 14.32.
83 Tac., *Ag.* 15.
84 Tac., *Ag.* 11, 21.3, 24.3, 30; Tac., *Ann.* 12.37, 14.31, 14.35; D.C., 62b.3.1, 62b.4.3, 62b.6.4.
85 D.C., 62b.3.3.

86 Tac., *Ann.* 14.36.

87 Adler 2008: 192.

88 Ibid., 194.

89 For such dichotomy between the freedom of the primitive world and the oppression subjacent to the process of romanization, I recommend reading the following excerpts: Tac., *Ann.* 14.31; Tac., *Ag.* 13.1, 30; D.C., 62.3.1, 62.4.3, 62.3.1, 62.4.3.

90 See Caes., *Gall.* 1.39, 5.14, 6.21, 6.24; Tac., *Ag.* 11; D.C., 40.39.2.

91 D.C., 62b.5.5.

92 D.C., 23.3, 31, 60.33.3c, 62b.3.1.

93 E.g., D.C., 62b.3.4 or Tac., *Ag.* 15, 30.

94 D.C., 62.3.1.

95 Tac., *Ag.* 32.

96 Ov., *Tr.* 3.12.45–48.

97 Ov., *Tr.* 4.2.1–2, 4.2.29–38.

98 Man., *Astr.* l.896–900.

99 Wells 2003: 37–41.

100 Ov., *Tr.* 3.12.47–48, 4.2.34.35; Man., *Astr.* I.888–889; Vell., 2.118.1; D.C., 56.18.4, 56.19.5.

101 Man., *Astr.* l.896–900.

102 Dauge 1981: 424–36.

103 Ov., *Tr.* 4.2.31–36.

104 In the narrative of the battle (Tac., *Ann.* 1.61) and in a previous debate between Arminius and his brother (Tac., *Ann.* 2.10).

105 D.C., 56.19.5.

106 E.g., Flor., *Epit.* 2.30.36; Ov., *Tr.* 4.2.1; Tac., *Ann.* 1.57, 1.65, 1.68; Vell., 2.118.2, 2.119.5; or D.C., 38.47.5.

107 D.C., 56.18.3; Flor., *Epit.* 2.30.34; Vell., 2.118.1.

108 Tac., *Ann.* 1.55, 1.57, 1.58, 1.61.

109 Tac., *Ann.* 1.55.

110 Tac., *Ann.* 1.61.

111 See Tac., *Ann.* 2.17; Vell., 2.118.2; D.C., 56.19.2; Ov., *Tr.* 4.2.34.

112 Ov., *Tr.* 4.2.34.

113 Tac., *Ger.* 4; Tac., *Ann.* 1.68; Vell., 2.118.1; D.C., 38.35.2, 38.45.4; App., *Gall.* 1.3; and Man., *Astr.* I.896–900. Tac., *Ann.* 1.55, 1.57, 1.68, 2.44; Flor., *Epit.* 2.30.32. Tac., *Ann.* 1.57.

114 Tac., *Ann.* 1.59.

115 Tac., *Ann.* 1.59, 2.10, 2.19.

116 Ov., *Tr.* 4.2.31–34.

117 Vell., 2.118.2.

118 E.g., Tac., *Ann.* 2.17.
119 Tac., *Ann.* 2.10.
120 Ash 2012: 308.
121 Vell., 2.118.2.
122 Marincola 2007: 106.
123 Tac., *Ann.* 1.59, 2.9, 2.15.
124 Tac., *Ann.* 2.15.
125 Ov., *Tr.* 4.2.29–38; Tac., *Ann.* 1.55, 1.59, 1.61, 2.45; Vell., 2.118.3.
126 Tac., *Ann.* 2.10.
127 Tac., *Ann.* 2.88.
128 Tac., *Ann.* 2.44.
129 Vell., 2.118.2.
130 Tac., *Ann.* 1.68.
131 Ash 2012: 308.
132 Ibid., 306–9.
133 Ibid., 306.
134 Ibid.
135 Tac., *Ann.* 1.59.
136 Tac., *Ann.* 2.45.
137 Tac., *Ann.* 2.44.
138 Ash 2012: 307.
139 Grünewald 2004: 163.
140 Ibid., 33.
141 Ash 2012: 308–9.
142 Grünewald 2004: 36–7.
143 Ibid., 37.
144 Marincola 2007: 48; Alvar Ezquerra and Blázquez Martínez 1997: 140; Habinek 2001: 100; Ash 2012: 95; Dauge 1981: 250.
145 E.g., Caes., *Gall.* 6.16, 6.17.
146 Sánchez Moreno and Aguilera Durán 2013: 229.
147 D.C., 62.6.4.
148 Tac., *Ann.* 1.57.
149 Aguilera Durán 2012: 545.
150 Pastor Muñoz 2003: 193; Ash 2012: 59–65.
151 Ash 2012: 59.
152 Ibid., 64–5.
153 Adler 2008: 181.
154 See Tac., *Ann.* 14.35 ; D.C., 62.2.2, 62.6.4, 62.8.2.
155 Dauge 1981: 78–9; Aguilera Durán 2012: 545.
156 Diod., 33.21a, 33.1.2, 33.1.5; App., *Hisp.* 11.62, 12.67, 12.69.

157 Yarrow 2006: 334.

158 See Caes., *Gall.* 1.39, 5.14, 6.21, 6.24.

159 E.g., Tac., *Ag.* 11.

160 See the presence of such idea on Cassius Dio in the excerpt 40.39.2.

161 See Caes., *Gall.* 1.39, 5.14, 6.21, 6.24.

Sources

Ammianus Marcellinus (1950), *Rerum Gestarum*, trans. J. Rolfe, Cambridge, MA: Harvard University Press.

Appian (1899), *Historia Romana*, trans. H. White, New York: Macmillan.

Cassius Dio (1914), *Historia Romana*, trans. E. Cary, Cambridge, MA: Harvard University Press.

Cicero (1913), *De Officiis*, trans. W. Miller, Cambridge, MA: Harvard University Press.

Diodorus Siculus (1967), *Bibliotheca historica*, trans. F. Walton, Cambridge, MA: Harvard University Press.

Florus (1929), *Epitome*, trans. E. S. Forster, Cambridge, MA: Harvard University Press.

Julius Caesar (1869), *De Bello Gallico*, trans. W. S. Bohn, New York: Harper.

Livy (1959), *Periochae*, trans. A. Schlensinger, Cambridge, MA: Harvard University Press.

Marcus Manilius (1992), *Astronomica*, trans. G. P. Goold, Cambridge, MA: Harvard University Press.

Ovid (1939), *Tristia*, trans. A. L. Wheeler, Cambridge, MA: Harvard University Press.

Silius Italicus (1961), *Punica*, trans. J. D. Duff, Cambridge, MA: Harvard University Press.

Suetonius (1889), *De Vita Caesarum*, trans. A. Thomson, Philadelphia, PA: Gebbie.

Tacitus (1942), *Annales*, trans. A. J. Church, New York: Random House.

Tacitus (1942), *De Vita Iulii Agricolae*, trans. A. J. Church, New York: Random House.

Tacitus (1942), *De Origine et Situ Germanorum Liber*, trans. A. J. Church, New York: Random House.

Valerius Maximus (1935), *De Factis Dictisque Memorabilibus*, trans. P. Constant, Paris: Librarie Garnier Frères.

Velleius Paterculus (1924), *Historiae*, trans. F. Shipley, Cambridge, MA: Harvard University Press.

Bibliography

Adler, E. (2008), 'Boudica's Speeches in Tacitus and Dio', *Classical World*, 101: 173–95.

Aguilera Durán, T. (2011), 'La utopía del bárbaro: Imágenes idealizadas del pasado prerromano en la España contemporánea', *El Futuro del Pasado*, 2: 371–87.

Aguilera Durán, T. (2012), 'Una visión historiográfica alternativa: la deconstrucción del estereotipo del bárbaro prerromano', *Antesteria*, 1: 543–55.

Alvar Ezquerra, J. and Blázquez Martinez, J. M., eds (1997), *Héroes y antihéroes en la antigüedad clásica*, Madrid: Cátedra.

Ash, R. (2012), *Tacitus*, Oxford: Oxford University Press.

Benario, H. (2004), 'Arminius into Hermann: History into Legend', *Greece & Rome, Second Series*, 51: 83–94.

Clark, J. H. (2014), *Triumph in Defeat: Military Loss and the Roman Republic*, Oxford: Oxford University Press.

Clarke, C. (2002), *Between Geography and History: Hellenistic Constructions of the Roman World*, Oxford: Clarendon Press.

Cruz-Andreotti, G. (2002), 'Iberia e Iberos en las fuentes Histórico-Geográficas griegas: una propuesta de análisis', *Mainake*, 24: 153–80.

Dauge, Y. A. (1981), *Le barbare: recherches sur la conception romaine de la barbarie et de la civilización*, Brussels: Latomus.

Desmond, W. (2008), *Cynics*, Stocksfield: Acumen Publishing.

Feldherr, A. and G. Hardy, eds (2011), *The Oxford History of Historical Writing, vol. 1: Beginnings to AD 600*, Oxford: Oxford University Press.

García Moreno, L. (1989), 'Hispaniae tumultus: rebelión y violencia indígena en la España romana de época republicana', *Polis: revista de ideas y formas políticas de la Antigüedad Clásica*, 1: 81–107.

García Moreno, L. (2002), 'Polibio y la creación del estereotipo de lo Hispano en la etnografía y la historiografía Helenísticas', *Polis: revista de ideas y formas políticas de la Antigüedad Clásica*, 14: 127–46.

Gómez Fraile, J. (1999), 'Los conceptos de Iberia y Ibero en Estrabón', *SPAL: revista de prehistoria y arqueología de la Universidad de Sevilla*, 8: 159–88.

Gorges, Jean-Gérard (2009), *Lusitânia romana: entre o mito e a realidade*, Cascais: Câmara Municipal de Cascais.

Grünewald, T. (2004), *Bandits in the Roman Empire: Myth and Reality*, London: Routledge.

Habinek, T. (2001), *The Politics of Latin Literature: Writing, Identity, and Empire in Ancient Rome*, Princeton, NJ: Princeton University Press.

Lens Tuero, J. (1986), 'Viriato. Héroe y Rey Cínico', *Estudios de Filología Griega*, 2: 253–72.

Long, A. (2006), *From Epicurus to Epictetus: Studies in Hellenistic and Roman Philosophy*, Oxford: Clarendon Press.

Marincola, J. (2007), *A Companion to Greek and Roman Historiography*, vol. 1, Malden, MA: Wiley-Blackwell.

Méry, L. (2005), 'Barbares et civilisés chez les auteurs romains du 1er s. av. J.-C.', *Cahiers Kubaba*, 7: 153–85.

Neves, M. (2010), 'Entre nacional e local, entre história e memória: estratégias para uma patrimonialização identitária de Viriato', *Sphera publica: revista de ciencias sociales y de la comunicación*, 2010 (spec. issue): 211–29.

Nice, A. (1993), 'Superstition and Religion in Tacitus' and Dio's Accounts of the Boudican Revolt', *Pegasus*, 36: 15–18.
Pastor Muñoz, M. (2003), *Viriato: a luta pela liberdade*, Lisboa: Ésquilo.
Pérez Abellán, J. (2006), 'Problemática en torno al estudio de la figura de Viriato', *Panta Rei: revista de ciencia y didáctica de la historia*, 5: 45–56.
Sánchez Moreno, E. and T. Aguilera Durán (2013), 'Bárbaros y vencidos, los otros en la conquista romana de Hispania', in C. López and G. Fernandes (eds), *Debita verba: Estudios en homenaje al profesor Julio Mangas Manjarrés*, vol. 1, 225–44, Oviedo: Universidad de Oviedo.
Sandbach, F. (2001), *The Stoics*, London: Duckworth.
Sedley, D. (2004), *The Cambridge Companion to Greek and Roman Philosophy*, Cambridge: Cambridge University Press.
Thollard, P. (1987), *Barbarie et civilisation chez Strabon: étude critique des livres III et IV de la Géographie*, Besançon: Presses universitaires de Franche-Comté.
Wells, P. (2003), *The Battle that Stopped Rome: Emperor Augustus, Arminius, and the Slaughter of the Legions in the Teutoburg Forest*, New York: W. W. Norton.
Williams, C. (2009), *Boudica and Her Stories: Narrative Transformations of a Warrior Queen*, Newark, DE: University of Delaware Press.
Yarrow, L. (2006), *Historiography at the End of the Republic: Provincial Perspectives on Roman Rule*, Oxford: Oxford University Press.

15

Othering the Emperor in Suetonius

José Luís Brandão

Suetonius' biography, by focusing on the scrutiny of the Caesars' *ethos* (the true character) and illustrating it with examples of their virtues and vices, sometimes ends up describing extreme cases that go beyond what is acceptable. In the case of the worst emperors, Suetonius ends up describing behaviours that border on fiction and that transform the emperor into something else, into a pattern of what an emperor, a citizen or a Roman should not be. In these cases, it is identity and identity identifiers that are called into question.

A great example of this alienation is the description of Caligula's clothing, introduced by a striking gradation: 'In his clothing, his shoes, and the rest of his attire he did not follow the usage of his country and his fellow-citizens; not always even that of his sex; or in fact, that of an ordinary mortal'.[1] This description recalls that of Locri's legate when, in Livy, describing the tyrannical behaviour of Pleminius, the propraetor who reconquered the city from Hannibal, equates him with a monster from myth (*belua immanis*).[2]

The introduction to Caligula's *habitus* (the attire) underlines the result of a metamorphosis, where some of Suetonius' procedures are more or less implicit: the connection of *eidos* (the external appearance) to *ethos*; the anticipation of *ethos* to facts; the adoption of speech topics against tyranny and the influence of dramatic culture. In this chapter, we will focus on these procedures, regarding the metamorphosis operated on some emperors, as well as their results.

Othering by the connection of *eidos* to *ethos*

The attention that Suetonius pays to dress, often treated together with physical portraits and often presented as a visual reflection of the other aspects of life, shows the importance that the visual has for the definition of *ethos*.[3] Moreover,

Suetonius was the author of a *De genere Vestium*, which makes him an expert on the subject.[4] The description of Caligula's clothes and trappings denotes first of all the rejection of patriotic and civilian dress.

The biographer stresses the transgression of the norm and lists clothes and adornments considered effeminate (*manulatus et armilatus*; *sericatus et cycladatus*); eastern clothes and footwear (*crepidae*); footwear of the Hellenistic kings and of the tragic actor (*coturni*); military footwear (*speculatoria caliga*); women's footwear and of the comic actors (*soccus muliebris*); attributes of the gods, golden beard, thunderbolt, trident, and *caduceus* (*aurea barba*;[5] *fulmen tenens aut fuscinam aut caduceum*); Venus clothing; triumphal clothes and the breastplate of Alexander the Great,[6] which makes one suspect a will of *imitatio* and *aemulatio*.[7] It is a list of props that seem to be somehow linked to his histrionic activities. The description is a moral lesson in the negative: one must respect the habits of the fatherland and of the citizens, not give in to philhellenism.

It represents the opposite of the attitude of Augustus who had sought to encourage the wearing of the toga (*Aug.* 40.5). This is about the affirmation through clothing of the lack of *ciuilitas* (the quality of what is suited to a citizen), an essential virtue for the good *princeps*, lest he become a tyrant. If wearing women's clothes is morally reprehensible from the point of view of the Roman aristocracy,[8] the use of divine attributes corresponds to the highest point of *inciuilitas*, to say nothing of *impietas* (impiety).[9] The fact that Suetonius does not indicate the contexts in which Caligula used each of the attributes may contribute to increasing the transgression, as Wardle[10] points out. In fact, there are precedents that by being contextualized do not take on such a serious meaning and may even justify Caligula's behaviour. For example, Tiberius exchanged the *patrius habitus* for *pallium* (the Greek cloak) and *crepidae* (slippers) in his retreat on the island of Rhodes.[11] And Augustus promotes an exchange of *habitus* (*togae* and *pallia*) and language between Romans and Greeks, but in Campania, which affects neither identity nor dignity (*Aug.* 98.3).[12] On the contrary, these cases of controlled experiences emphasize plainly that dress and speech codes could be shifted, but only in private, controlled spaces and times, which Caligula's uncontrolled deregulated dress violated.[13]

Additionally, the use of divine attributes has many parallels with the activities of Hellenistic kings. Even Augustus himself was accused (by Antony and in subversive verses) of dressing as Apollo at a banquet called *dodekatheos* (*Aug.* 70.1). That said, the context of political invective used as a source makes us at least doubt the veracity of this episode.[14] But Caligula trespasses the traditional barriers of civic, constitutional, moral, and human behaviour. Thus, where Augustus hesitates, Caligula continues.[15] We must not lose sight of the fact that in this part of the *Life*, Suetonius is describing a monster (*Cal.* 22), as we will see. This pattern of civic 'monstrification' is reinforced and nuanced in several lives.

The description of Nero's way of presenting himself in public, for example, is not limited to the mention of the aforementioned elements, but expands that portrait through other violations of dress and behaviour and 'taste' codes (*Nero* 51):

> He was utterly shameless in the care of his person and in his dress, always having his hair arranged in tiers of curls, and during the trip to Greece also letting it grow long and hang down behind; and he often appeared in public in a dining-robe, with a handkerchief bound about his neck, ungirt and unshod.

There is in this description a clear moral judgement, which reminds us of Nero's *probra* ('shameful deeds'), anticipated by the biographer in the *diuisio* by which he structures the *Life* of this emperor between positive and negative parts (*Nero*, 19.3). Among the *probra* are Nero's activities as actor and *auriga* – widely described in the biography and unacceptable to the more traditionalist aristocracy – and which seem to be suggested by the clothes described and the style of his hair.[16] Suetonius mentions the *citharoedicus habitus* ('the guise of a lyre-player') (*Nero* 25.2), on statues and coins of Nero,[17] as well as the *scaenicus habitus* ('stage costume') in the supposed performance before the burning city (*Nero* 38.2). And, the fact that he displays female roles makes Nero cross gender boundaries.[18] The fact of the emperor becoming an actor constituted, for the Roman mentality, not only social but also moral degradation, thus calling into question the *dignitas* (dignity of status) of the emperor and *maiestas* (majesty) of the Roman Empire.

As for Caesar, the negative note of the portrait's rubric is in the excessive zeal with the physique, and the extravagant way he wears his clothes (*Jul.* 45.2–3):

> He was somewhat overnice in the care of his person, being not only carefully trimmed and shaved, but even having superfluous hair plucked out, as some have charged. . . . They say, too, that he was remarkable in his dress; that he wore a senator's tunic with fringed sleeves reaching to the wrist, and always had a girdle over it, though rather a loose one.

By these habits, Caesar becomes something other than a traditional Roman.[19] Such care of the body and such manner of dress suggested effeminacy and orientalism or a supposed aspiration to a monarchy, as Cassius Dio (43.43.2) suggests when he relates the style of his clothes to that of the kings of Alba Longa from whom Caesar claimed to be descended.[20] This portrait contrasts with the one presented by Plutarch (*Caes.* 17.2), which is much soberer and without such connotations.[21]

The image of Caesar, always crowned with laurels, made him the perpetual *imperator*,[22] and seems to symbolize his regal aspirations (*Jul.* 79), an abominable ambition for a Roman citizen which is illustrated with Caesar's *facta* and *dicta* (actions and words) that render his death just (*Jul.* 76.1) and which is ultimately presented as the cause of his murder (*Jul.* 80). But the laurel wreath, transformed into Caesar's personal adornment, is also the symbol of the progeny of the Caesars, which will end with Nero, as is accentuated in the introduction to the *Life of Galba* (*Gal.* 1), and of a new kind of sovereignty, to which Julius Caesar gives his name.

The effeminate habits are common to Caesar and Otho, but in the former they are attenuated by physical vigour and in the latter by a transformation that occurred *in extremis*. The weak physique and unorthodox manners of Othon's costume are presented in contrast to the unexpected courage shown in death (*Otho* 12.1):

> Neither Otho's person nor his bearing suggested such great courage ... but almost feminine in his care of his person.... Moreover, they say that he used to shave every day and smear his face with moist bread ... so as never to have a beard; also that he used to celebrate the rites of Isis publicly in the linen garment prescribed by the cult.

Besides his bodily habits, which were alien to a traditional Roman, Otho adds the cult of a foreign religion which was also persecuted by Tiberius.[23] For all this, the biographer concludes the portrait with the sentence that heroic death was not consonant with his life.[24] In fact, the association with Nero, with whom he had become a close friend, because of the compatibility of habits, and even, according to the rumour, because of their reciprocal carnal relations, was a taint.[25] In this way, the biographer suggests that death was the *miraculum* (marvel) which, by contrast with the life he led, reveals his true essence, in accordance with conventional Roman identity.

The continuity (or not) between the portraits and the character of each emperor contributes to ensure the unity of each *Life* and supports Suetonius' compositional technique and purposes.

Othering by the subordination of facts to *ethos*

By virtue of the structure organized by rubrics, Suetonius puts forward the categories of character to which he subordinates the facts and sayings of the protagonists in order to illustrate the *ethos*. This subordination of the facts to character description often makes the facts, when given, appear out of context, overemphasized or minimized depending on the aim of each rubric he uses. This is purposefully arranged according to a pre-defined image.[26]

Suetonius begins by presenting the beginning of Tiberius' Principate characterized by manifestations of *ciuilitas* (*Tib.* 26.1), and then goes on to point out his trajectory towards autocracy.[27] But it is Tiberius' spatial move to the island of Capri that motivates an ethical change – a fictional transformation/revelation organized by the biographer on the basis of rumours equated with real historical sources:[28] 'Moreover, having gained the licence of privacy, and being as it were out of sight of the citizens, he at last gave free rein at once to all the vices which he had for a long time ill-concealed . . .' (*Tib.* 42.1).

With the statement *uitia male diu dissimulata* ('vices ... long time ill-concealed'), the biographer suggests that the entire previous life has to be seen in a new light: the vices already existed, but were purposely hidden by Tiberius. Therefore, in order to highlight the emperor's dissimulation, the biographer had proceeded to provisionally conceal the information. Now the biographer introduces an analepsis (or a series of analepses) to treat the various vices, introduced by the expression *ab exordium referam* ('I shall give a detailed account from the beginning').[29] The removal of the mask – Tiberius' characteristic dissimulation – is illustrated with a scandalous staging in the depths of his retreat:

> On retiring to Capri, he devised a pleasance for his secret orgies: teams of wantons of both sexes, selected as experts in deviant intercourse and dubbed analists, copulated before him in triple unions to excite his flagging passions. . . . boys and girls got up as Pans and nymphs solicited outside bowers and grottoes: people openly called this 'the old goat's garden', punning on the island's name.[30]

Although he says it all takes place in the secrecy of the island, the biographer describes the whole scene using the perfect as if he had witnessed it, which seems suspicious. The penchant for scandal makes Suetonius give in to the bawdier versions arising from slander[31] and inspired by the Philhellenism of the emperor.[32] The case of Malonia, which illustrates the tyrant's abuse of the women of the aristocracy, resumes Tiberius' association with the goat (*Tib.* 45).[33] Caligula, too, is associated with a goat in the physical portrait rubric, where it is said that it was forbidden to utter the word goat next to him (*Cal.* 50.1). From the description of the retreat in Capreae, another Tiberius is revealed. From now on, the other vices of Tiberius are treated in a crescendo.[34]

It is well known the *diuisio* that Suetonius establishes in the *Life of Caligula*, when he says that until now he spoke *quasi de principe* (as if about a prince),[35] and who will then talk *de monstro* (as if about a monster).[36] The monster's behaviour radically subverts morals and customs. The description of Caligula *qua* monster[37] begins precisely with the assumption of royal and divine honours that Augustus and Tiberius refused, demonstrating *ciuilitas*.[38] Caligula exceeds the barriers established by Augustus and approaches Julius Caesar (*Jul.* 36.1).[39] But he does not stop there, for he shows himself insolent even towards the gods (*Cal.* 22.4). And the peremptory presumption that Caligula committed incest with all his sisters (*Cal.* 24.1) – to focus on the privileged relationship with Drusilla – aims to assimilate him with the monster the biographer intends to recreate, but may be inspired by the emperor's desire to assimilate himself to a Hellenistic theocratic monarchy.[40] This is followed by a series of vices as *saeuitia ingenii* ('his innate brutality') (*Cal.* 27 ff.), *impudicitia* (unchastity) and the abuse of matrons and freemen (*Cal.* 36), sumptuousness (*Cal.* 37), and rapine (*Cal.* 38–42).

Among the Caligula-monster's behaviour is the radical subversion of the Roman constitutional model, manifested in his disrespect for the senate (*Cal.* 26.2) and the *superbia* (insolence) and *uiolentia* (brutality) with which he treats the orders (26.4). It was rumoured that he wanted to make his horse consul (*Cal.* 55.3), a joke in bad taste by himself or others, or arising from the exaggerated (and considered improper) dedication he had to the art of the *auriga* (*Cal.* 54.1) and the care he showed for the horse, Incitatus, but which Suetonius places at the climax of his eccentricities and immediately before the report of his murder.

Caligula's life takes place in a kind of Bacchic delirium, in an intermediate state between madness and reality, which precipitates his death.[41] But, according to his biographer, he died when he was planning even bigger crimes (*Cal.* 49.2): the aim was to eliminate the most distinguished members among the senators and knights (cf. *Nero* 37.3).

Similar to the process established for Caligula, Suetonius transforms Nero into the opposite of a *princeps*, enhancing certain traits and elevating rumours to the category of historical fact.[42] In fact, Suetonius introduces in this biography a division similar to the one he had established in the *Life of Caligula*. To the good deeds he had just presented, Suetonius counterposes ignominies and crimes (*probra ac scelera*) (*Nero* 19.3).[43] However, this change does not correspond at all to the real chronology but is an arrangement of the biographer according to his characterological objectives.[44] Indeed, Suetonius goes on to describe the ignominies that undermine Nero's *dignitas* (especially his dedication to the performing arts, considered unthinkable for a certain traditional elite)[45] and the crimes that turn him into a criminal artist.[46]

Nero is associated with Greekness based on his artistic behaviours, so he lives and dies more like an artist than a Roman emperor.[47] When the freedman Helius writes to him to say that the *urbicas res* demand Nero's presence in Rome, he replies: '... you ought rather to counsel me and to hope that I may return worthy (*dignus*) of Nero' (*Nero* 23.1). There is thus an inversion of the Roman concept of *dignitas*, which takes on a personal interpretation different from that of the traditional aristocracy: Nero's criterion for his own *dignitas* is the success of his art.

The same degradation takes place with regard to the values of *amicitia* (friendship) and *laus* (merit or glory): their criterion of friendship or enmity is the lavish or meagre praise they gave to the emperor's talent (*Nero* 25.3). Therefore, the praise that Nero desires concerns his histrionic abilities, in short, the praise of his own degradation, his *probra* that so depart from the permitted self-fashioning of a Roman emperor.

To the *probra* Suetonius adds the *scelera* ('criminal deeds') (as he had announced) – grouped under ethical characteristics stated in epigraph (*Nero* 26.1), *petulantia*, *libido*, *luxuria*, *auaritia*, *crudelitas* ('wantonness, lust, extravagance, avarice and cruelty'), stressing that they were *naturae uitia* ('defects of his character') and not proper to the age. The gradation is accentuated with the information that such vices were exercised, at first, *sensim ... et occulte* ('gradual and secret').[48] The corollary of this is that, as in the case of Caligula, some anecdotes border on nonsense. For example, the gradation in the treatment of the *libido* reaches its apogee in his prostitution of his own *pudicitia* as a sort of game (*lusus*). Suetonius insists on the theatrical aspect of the rite (*Nero* 29). The biographer thus presents, from the perspective of moral degradation, two mimetic representations of the emperor: one that recreates the fate of those condemned to beasts, but in which Nero himself metamorphoses into the fierce beast that carries out the punishment;[49] and another in which he mimics a situation that, by its obscenity and the search for realism, reminds us of a mime scene (as *imitatus* suggests).[50]

A scene that shows the action of the criminal artist is that of Agrippina's death, in which Nero becomes impious and confesses himself the target of divine persecution. Once the three attempts at murder with poison have failed, the attempts become more over the top, contrived, and above all theatrical: he commissions a mechanism that would make the ceiling of the room fall on her and a prepared boat in which she would die either by the collapse of the cabin or by shipwreck.[51]

For Suetonius, Nero, bringing together artistic and criminal propensities, clearly becomes the author of the fire of 64, although the parallel tradition is not so assertive.[52] Rumours about Nero's guilt may have arisen later from the care put into the reconstruction and the quality of the buildings.[53] Later Suetonius will say that Nero, in his eagerness for immortal fame, planned to rename Rome (*Neropolis*) from his name (*Nero* 55), giving credence to a rumour (*uidebatur*) that Tacitus (*Ann.* 15.40.3) mentions in connection with the fire. But beyond aesthetic criteria, Nero's guilt in the crime is also based on the emperor's histrionic tastes and illustrated with yet another theatrical performance, in which reality is assimilated into myth: '. . . he sang the whole of the "Sack of Ilium" in his regular stage costume' (*Nero* 38.2). Suetonius, yielding to the more Romanesque version, presents as fact what the sources refer to as a possibility, since Tacitus presents the episode as a *rumour* that, moreover, took away merit from the emperor's efforts.[54] In Suetonius' version, the myth combines with reality by the hands and voice of the *artifex* (art creator) Nero, who can now experience the feelings of Priam, watching Troy burn. But, the contrast between the public calamity and the rejoicing (*laetatus*) of the emperor, singing of the destruction he himself had caused, contributes to accentuate an image of monstrosity bordering on madness. This is not only *mimesis*, but also *poiesis*: the author of the poem will also be the author of the sung matter, for, in his megalomania, he needed to create a realistic, grandiose, and terrible scenario, tailor-made for his work.[55]

Thanks to the effect of Suetonius' non-chronological technique, Nero, who had been praised for the *forma urbis noua* (the 'new form for the buildings of the city') and, in particular, for the construction at his own expense of porticoes to facilitate firefighting (*Nero* 16.1), is now accused of starting the fire that caused the *urbs noua*.[56]

Like Caligula (*Cal.* 49.2), Nero intended to eliminate the most illustrious of the higher orders (*Nero* 37.3). On the advice of an astrologer and based on a custom of kings, Nero plans the death of all the noblest citizens, to ward off the omen of the appearance of a comet (*Nero* 36.1).[57] Thus, Suetonius, instead of describing the conjures perpetrated against Nero,[58] turns the deaths of the conspirators into expiatory sacrifices performed by the emperor.

As with Caligula, Nero's unreasonable and dangerous behaviour proves equally fatal for him. The departure from moral and constitutional norms could only be absolved with death, according to the statement of those condemned to death themselves (*Nero* 36.2).[59]

If Nero destroys even the walls of the homeland, he is a danger to the entire world. It is not only Rome, not only Italy, but the whole *orbis terrarum* that discards Nero, after enduring him for fourteen years (*Nero* 40.1).[60] Yet even at the moment of his death, he continues to portray himself as a consummate artist through the famous exclamation *Qualis artifex pereo!* ('What an artist the world is losing!').[61] There seems to be a certain parallel with Augustus, who on his deathbed asks whether he has represented the *mimus* of life well and asks for applause (*Aug.* 99.1).[62] But the implicit approval granted to the unmasked performance of Augustus, contrasts blatantly with the orb's condemnation of Nero's actions, who assumed monstrous mythical masks, a kind of metonymy for cruel and tyrannical behaviour. Therefore, while Augustus remains the same as himself in his performance, as the mirror he asks for at the moment of death seems to symbolize,[63] the *artifex* Nero is transformed into something else and makes the histrionic connection completely explicit.

The biographer makes Nero himself acknowledge the unworthiness of his life before giving himself up to death (*Nero* 49.3).[64] The atrocities attributed to Nero recall that of the *monstrum* Caligula. A bodily trait at the moment of Nero's death recalls the idea of the monster: after expiring, Nero's rigid gaze instils horror and astonishment in those present (*Nero* 49.4).

The Life of Domitian presents a division approximating those referred to in the *Lives* of Caligula and Nero, through which a contrast is established between a positive part and another dealing with the vices (*Dom.* 3.2).[65] After presenting the positive part, the biographer reminds the reader: 'But he did not continue this course of mercy or integrity, although he turned to cruelty somewhat more speedily than to avarice' (*Dom.* 10.1.). In doing so, Suetonius highlights the chronological progression of his character or its descent.[66]

As with Caligula and Nero, there follows descriptions of executions of senators and even former consuls. To prove that Domitian is a cruel tyrant, Suetonius expressly accentuates the futility of pretexts,[67] the overreaction on the basis of simple distrust,[68] and a worsening of Domitian's susceptibility to paranoia, who, in contrast to his father Vespasian, cannot bear even slight hostile allusions to his person.[69]

The technique adopted accentuates Domitian's guilt, considering the crimes of the condemned to be light, minor or even futile.[70] The confrontation between the execution of Helvidius Priscus, in Vespasian's principate (*Ves.* 15), and that of the younger Helvidius (killed for supposedly having censored in a farce the separation of Domitian and Domitia, under the names of Paris and Oenone) throws on the biographer the suspicion of partiality (*Dom.* 10.4).[71]

Domitian's cruelty appears associated with hypocrisy and Black humour. A sentence, however terrible, was preceded by a clement preface 'to abuse men's patience the more insolently'.[72] The context in which Suetonius quotes the words of Domitian (*Dom.* 11.3) accentuates the cruel and arbitrary manipulation of the senate.[73]

The *Life* reaches its climax when Domitian becomes hated by all. As with Caligula and Nero, tyrannical behaviour becomes lethal. At this point, as with those two, Suetonius introduces the account of his death.[74] What is certain is that three Caesars (Julius Caesar, Caligula, and Domitian) have a similar bloody end. In the former and in the latter, the acts of arrogance are associated, by proximity, with the account of death, which brings us to the next chapter.

Othering by the adoption of speech topics against tyranny

The examples used by Suetonius in the *Lives of the Caesars* to document certain vices, as well as the terms in which these are expressed, seem to be part of the traditional discourse against tyranny. We are confronted with the evidence that, in the direct or indirect description of the worst emperors, commonplaces normally connoted with the idea of tyrant are used, as presented in theatre, philosophy, history, forensic speeches, and schools of rhetoric. Such coincidence raises the suspicion that many *exempla* that illustrate the species of the *Lives* may be modelled on the attitudes that are supposed to exist in a monarch in the Oriental manner, more by association of ideas or characters than by historical evidence.

The traditional description of Hellenistic tyrants points to proverbial wealth, linked to sumptuousness, rapacity, and a type of pleasure that derives from being able to do as one pleases with impunity.[75] In the rhetoric against tyranny, *superbia, crudelitas, auaritia, libido* become conventional elements,[76] of the kind used, for example, by Livy in describing Tarquinius Superbus (1.49 ff.) or Hieronymus of Syracuse (24.5.3–6), of whom, besides arrogance and cruelty, other significant elements are mentioned, such as the wearing of sumptuous costumes, the ostentation of bodyguards, and the propensity for an unprecedented *libido*.[77] These are terms also used by Cicero to classify the activities of Verres, Clodius, Piso, Gabinius or Antony,[78] and also by one of Suetonius' sources, Pliny the Elder, in the biographical elements he transmits about the emperors.[79] Such ideas would have been framed in Roman political invective at the end of the Republic and gained momentum with the assassination of Caesar.[80] The punishment for whomever wished to seize power was death; and several *declamationes* dealt with the subject of the *praemium* to be awarded to the slayer of a tyrant.[81] Caligula's death itself imitates the ritual of sacrifice.[82]

Suetonius presents Caligula and Nero as drunk on power, on license: they acted this way because they could.[83] This is tantamount to saying that they are moving away from the model of the principate established by Augustus, based on moderation, calibrating towards a declared autocracy that does not respect the value of *libertas* (freedom) prized by the senate. Departure from the norm is manifested in arrogance and aspirations to a divine cult[84] – a behaviour designated by tradition as *inpotentia* (unbridledness) or *arrogantia* or *superbia*, terms defining tyrannical behaviour.[85]

Among the characteristics of tyrants, *crudelitas* or *saeuitia* stands out.[86] In Tiberius, Caligula, Nero, and Domitian, the tyrannical spirit is aggravated by cruelty.[87] The term *atrocitas*, referred to in the *Lives* of Tiberius, Caligula, Nero, and Domitian, suggests very adverse situations of fortune,[88] but also the monstruous actions and words of the protagonists.[89] The lack of moderation is further expressed by the *immanitas* (enormity) of Caligula's acts and of Nero's behaviour[90] and *natura* itself.[91] The fact that, in Caesar, the tyrannical spirit does not appear associated with *saeuitia* (cruelty), but mitigated by a remarkable *clementia* (*Jul.* 75.1), makes Suetonius' judgement on the dictator more balanced.

Cruelty carried to the point of parricide, when the conquest of power is at stake, occurs in the declamations of the Latin schools of rhetoric.[92] The idea that the tyrant is by nature parricidal has a tragic model in Oedipus.[93] In seeking to endow Nero with the characteristics of the typical tyrant, Suetonius makes him, to say the least, complicit in the death of Claudius (*Nero* 33.1), whereas, in the account of the death of this emperor (*Cl.* 44), the complicity of his successor was not hinted at, but only the action of Agrippina.

A frequent characteristic of tyrants, and often the motivator of acts of cruelty, is *auaritia* (greed). Tiberius' greed is presented in a gradation: being *pecuniae parcus ac tenax* ('in money matters . . . frugal and close') (*Tib.* 46) before becoming emperor, he then progresses to extortion (*Tib.* 49.1). This model of evolution towards *rapinae* also suits Caligula, Nero, and Domitian[94] to the point of reaching extremes of ridicule. Such vice is also associated with *impietas* when it implies temple robbery, another typical crime of the rhetorical tyrant[95] perpetrated by Nero and, before him, by Caesar.[96] Moreover, *impietas*, with religious and cultural dimensions, is manifested both in a contempt for traditional religion and for familial duty; it is a constant among the bad emperors.[97]

Sumptuousness is another typical feature of tyrants: in Tiberius, and similarly in Galba (*Gal.* 12.1), *rapinae* are the consequence of avarice; in Caligula, Nero, and Domitian, they are the result of lavishness.[98] Caligula and Nero become heralds of the inversion of values, when they praise lavishness and waste of resources as the most recommendable attitudes in a prince.[99] The height of Nero's extravagance is the expensive construction of the *Domus Aurea* (*Nero* 31.1), the description of which seems to be based on the topics of the diatribe against lavishness.[100]

Sexual invective was commonplace, as evidenced by the attacks on Caesar by his political enemies (*Jul.* 49–52). Caesar's *impudicitia* and *libidines* are exposed in the verses of the soldiers at the triumph of Gaul (*Jul.* 49.4, 51). Mark Antony accuses Augustus of abusing free women (*Aug.* 69). But the seduction of married noblewomen by Caesar and Augustus[101] does not assume the Black tones of the outrage at illustrious matrons perpetrated by Tiberius (*Tib.* 45), the humiliating scrutiny of women carried out by Caligula in the triclinium (*Cal.* 36.2), or the orgies attributed to Nero (*Nero* 27.3). Tiberius' abuse of the women of the aristocracy is illustrated with the harassment of Malonia (*Tib.* 45), a fact not mentioned by other sources. Nonetheless, the episode may have been modelled on that of Lucretia, victim of the sexual tyranny of Sextus Tarquinius.[102]

As is typical of tyrants, Domitian displays an exacerbated *libido.*[103] Indeed, the last of the Flavians has an unmeasured and amoral sexual appetite, which manifests itself in the way in which, despite having refused marriage to Julia, his brother's daughter, he seduces her after marriage, to the point of later causing her death by forcing her to have an abortion.[104] Such a relationship was considered incestuous: Claudius' marriage to his niece Agrippina therefore had to be ratified by the senate (*Cl.* 39.2). Incest was typical of eastern Hellenistic tyrants and kings, who married within their own families sometimes. Accusations of incest were also made against Caligula and Nero, as we have seen (*Cal.* 24; *Nero* 28.2).

The rumour of Domitian swimming among the vilest courtesans (*Dom.* 22) seems to inscribe itself in the *topos* of eroticism in the pool, explored in epigrammatic poetry and in the diatribe against tyrants, and already present in the rumours about prostitution of young boys, whom Tiberius called *pisciculi*, and who swam around him to excite his senses (*Tib.* 44.1).[105] Licentiousness includes passive homosexuality, known as *impudicitia*, which is often invoked in political invective.[106] Such accusations seem to denote, in Suetonius, an implicit expedient in the rise of the future tyrant's career.[107]

Another element of convention breaking among tyrants and emperors, discussed above, is affectations of appearance.[108] The terrifying facial expression of the tyrant is also explored in rhetorical exercises, perhaps an influence of the fierce expression of the tyrant's mask in tragedy.[109] The motive seems to be present in the news that Caligula worked his face (*natura horridus ac taeter*, 'naturally forbidding and ugly'), in front of the mirror, so as to provoke *terror ac formido* (horror and astonishment) (*Cal.* 50.1), and in the note on Nero's impressive rigid gaze as he died, which equally instils *horror* and *formido* in those present (*Nero* 49.4).

And the rhetorical animalistic quality of the tyrant, because of his lasciviousness and cruelty, as in the case of Pleminius *immanis belua* (Liv. 29.17.12; cf. 29.8.8–9),[110] is an association that can be linked to several bad emperors also, for example, through the association of Tiberius (*Tib.* 43, 45) and Caligula (*Cal.* 50.1) with goats,[111] and Nero with a wild animal (*Nero* 29).

Othering by the influence of dramatic genres

Linked to that visual and performative aspect, is the potential influence or contamination of the dramatic genre, as Livy himself already complained of (5.21.9), or even the transposition of scenes from tragedy, comedy, or mime to historical-biographical accounts.[112]

The doctrinal substance about the tyrant in the Greek fashion may have been introduced into Roman society through tragedy.[113] The truth is that various tragic quotations are sometimes used in the *Lives of the Caesars* as a way of illustrating the propensity for tyranny of those who utter them. Caligula's character appears denounced in the repetition of a phrase from Atreus of Accius: *oderint, dum metuant* ('let them hate me, so they but fear me'),[114] which had become a kind of emblem of tyrannical cruelty[115] and is also attributed, with variation, to Tiberius.[116]

In fact, like tragedy, biography represents the actions of intrepid men,[117] who often have an unfortunate end. Suetonius does not aim primarily at a rigorous enquiry into historical facts, with their causes and consequences, but, like Plutarch, presents a process of personality-building that departs from the historical-narrative genre to approach the dramatic representation of human life.[118]

Biography, as an imitation of life, can be related to the Aristotelian concept of *mimesis* of *praxis*, that is, of persons in action,[119] through which the hero reveals the character.[120] The hero's action leads them to happiness or unhappiness.[121] If we take into account that, according to Aristotle, the passage from happiness to unhappiness is more tragic,[122] there are several examples where the actions of the protagonists of the *Lives* lead them to ruin. However, in Suetonius, ruin seems to be largely the result of the hero's guilt,[123] not so much in the Aristotelian sense of *hamartia* (failure or tragic error),[124] but more narrowly in the sense of characterological vice.

The biographer deduces the character from the man in action; and the characters take on the designation of the Roman virtues of the *mos maiorum* (forefathers' customs) and the vices opposed to them. In this sense, under the influence of Roman mentality, a link is established between the intrinsically moralizing discourse, which accentuates virtues and vices, and the end that Aristotle attributed to tragic representation – *katharsis pathematon* – if we restrict this notion to a moral value.[125]

There seems to be an assimilation of Nero to the roles he plays on stage:[126] the masks of heroes and gods, of heroines and goddesses have their own traits or those of women who have their favour, thus neutralizing the gap between representation and reality.[127] Through the roles that Suetonius relates ('Canace in Labor', 'Orestes the Matricide', 'The Blinding of Oedipus', and the 'Frenzy of Hercules'), he seems to suggest that such myths would shed light on Nero's actual behaviours, mentioned later.[128] In this sense, those masks are metaphors for Nero's deviant behaviour.[129]

We can see in the episode of the death of Agrippina (*Nero* 34.2–4) dramatic connections. If we accept the version *papillas quoque exosculatus* ('kissing her breasts'), at the moment when Nero says goodbye to his mother,[130] Suetonius makes an amalgam of two crimes, one explicit and one suggested: matricide and incest, both widely explored in this *Life* and in the tragic tradition. For now the biographer goes on to confirm the suspicion of incest by immediately adding facts that he declares more nefarious (*atrociora*), based on *nec incerti auctores* ('trustworthy authorities'): Nero ran to contemplate his mother's corpse, palpated its limbs, critiqued some, praised others and, as he felt thirsty in the meantime, drank (*Nero* 34.4.).[131] Suetonius, in accordance with the ethical profile he intends to create, pursues Nero's transformation beyond the point where Tacitus hesitates: from this author we know that such acts were only a rumour.[132] On the other hand, the act of drinking in the presence of corpses causes Suetonius repulsion more than once.[133] There is a purpose to accentuate the *impietas* as much as possible in order to reinforce the tragic connection.

Like Orestes, Nero is a polluted being and will be pursued by the avenging Erinyes. But Suetonius goes further: he makes Nero himself acknowledge the transposition of the ghosts of that tragedy into his own life (*Nero* 34.4).[134] Such persecution combined with the vain attempt to placate Manes, a fact that neither Tacitus nor Cassius Dio mentions, contributes to make Nero's tragic existence and 'method' acting, given Nero's inability to purify himself. Nero is thus transformed into a cursed man: a bad citizen, a bad son, a danger to the human race.

Besides the tragic elements, the biographer sometimes uses comic deformation, which is more in line with his language and style.[135] Claudius' ascension to the throne and the role reversal that takes place throughout his life brings him closer to a *senex* of comedy, dominated by women and freedmen (Cl. 25.5, 29.1).[136] In contrast, in Vespasian, comedic elements are used to favour the affable image (*comitas*) of the emperor: a character who maintains humour until the hour of death becomes sympathetic to the reader (*Ves.* 23.4).[137]

The realism, the obscenity, the blood on the scene are situations that are closer to the plot of a genre that was widely spread at the beginning of the empire and that takes up, among others, some of the arguments of the *palliata*: the mime.[138] Indeed, the hint of *mimus* appears at times in Suetonius, as we have seen.[139] It cannot be excluded that Suetonius was influenced by such a popular genre and that it seems to have affinities with the biographer's objectives. In this genre, the content of the *mimesis* is life, in all that it contains that is licit and illicit,[140] an object that offers a clear resemblance to Suetonian biography. In the mime, the imitation of dirty deeds implies or suggests a moral condemnation.[141]

Fate and *Fortuna* (*tyche*) are present on a parallel plane to the idea of merit or personal guilt.[142] Fate seems to determine the character of the emperor, with moral consequences. Tiberius is, from the start, chained to his *saeua ac lenta natura* ('cruel and cold-blooded character') (*Tib.* 57.1), Caligula to his *natura saeua atque probrosa* ('natural cruelty and viciousness') (*Cal.* 11), Nero to *infelicitas* (unhappiness) (*Nero* 6.2), Vitellius to a bad horoscope (*Vit.* 3.2). Emperors seem ultimately to be the playthings of the gods. Although tyrants may ultimately be punished for their vices,[143] one gets the idea that they could hardly act otherwise. If they try to escape their fate, *natura* eventually speaks louder and the initial period of happiness is replaced by a regime of terror.

Concluding remarks

In composing each life, Suetonius continually shapes, in a dynamic process, the depiction of his characters and highlights their moral development, from the treatment of each emperor's ancestors to the description of reactions to death. The development of each character, disconnected from chronological evolution, is organized according to the intensity of the facts described. Moreover, Suetonius includes in the *Lives* accounts from various sources and, in general, does not make a clear distinction between credible and dubious sources, which are mostly referred to generically, using expressions such as *sunt qui putent* (there are some who think), *ut quidam putant* (as some think), *multi* (many), *alii* (others), *quidam* (a certain), *nonnulli* (some).

By previously establishing the rubrics with the various aspects of the personality, the biographer establishes a graph that he then fills with decontextualized examples in order to highlight the image he wants to portray. The inclusions or omissions he makes aim to present a coherent picture of each Caesar, accentuating some traits or mitigating others, as we see by comparison with other sources. Thus, he does not try to rank the facts according to their historical relevance; rather, he tends to give in to the more novelistic versions, often resulting from calumny.[144] By opting for the more intense versions, Suetonius presents narratives which may be no more than rumours, but which accentuate the characters described, according to the objectives of the biography (cf. Plu., *Alex.* 1). This leads him to recreate the emperors, transforming them sometimes into exemplary figures of *romanitas*, sometimes into strange and sinister ones capable of provoking horror.

Given the importance of portraiture and dress, Suetonius tends to establish a relationship between visual appearance and character, to the point of expressing surprise when this is not possible, as in the case of Otho. In this sense, the deviations from the norm correspond to an alienation of identity.

Taken up by the biographer, the characteristics of the tyrants applied to the Caesars allow contemporary audiences to make macroscopic character connections easier through identification with well-known historical personality types.[145] This is certainly based on a fund of truth, framed by a typified vocabulary and illustrated with examples sometimes taken from analogous situations or even from theatrical fictions, with exaggerations or distortions of reality, operated by the author or already by his sources.

From the doctrinal point of view, taking the Hellenistic monarchs as an example, every tyrant would at the outset show *inciuilitas*, *saeuitia* or *crudelitas*, *luxuria*, *rapacitas*, *libido exacerbada* e *impietas* against the gods, the fatherland, and the family. And if he did not present these traits, one concludes that he concealed them: a skilful way of explaining, without contradicting, the favourable beginnings of emperors like Tiberius, Caligula, Nero, and Domitian.

Notes

1 *Vestitu calciatuque et cetero habitu neque patrio neque ciuili, ac ne uirili quidem ac denique humano semper usus est* (Suet., *Cal.* 52). Translations by J. C. Rolfe, *LCL* 31 (1913–14).

2 Liv. 29.17.11–12: . . . *nec hominis quicquam est, patres conscripti, praeter figuram et speciem neque Romani ciuis praeter habitum uestitumque et sonum Latinae linguae; pestis ac belua immanis, quales . . . fabulae ferunt.* See Dunkle 1971: 17.

3 See Brandão 2004: 83–113; 2009: 341–56.

4 Wardle 1994: 191–2.

5 An attribute of the gods: cf. Cic., *N.D.* 3.83; Varro, *R.* 1.1.4.

6 At Baiae: cf. D.C. 59.17.3.

7 See Wardle 1994: 336–41; Hurley 1993: 186–9; Guastella 1992: 272–3.

8 Cf. Sen., *Ep.* 122.7.

9 Wardle 1994: 336.

10 Wardle 1994: 337.

11 *Tib.* 13.1.

12 Dench 2005: 295–6.

13 See Dench 2005: 277–8; Brandão 2022: 197–8.

14 See Wardle 2014: 444. Such allegations would therefore often be made by political enemies.

15 As Wardle 1994: 340 notes.

16 A sign of Philhellenism. See Bradley 1978: 284–5.

17 A representation of Nero as Apollo *Citharoedus*. See Bradley 1978: 152; Warmington 1999: 53.

18 As Schulz 2019: 289 points out.

19 Cf. *Jul.* 45.3; D.C. 43.43.4; Plu., *Caes.* 4.4.

20 See Weinstock 1971: 338–40; Gascou 1984: 733; Pelling 2011: 213–15; Brandão 2009: 341–2, 353–4.

21 See Gascou 1984: 733; Brandão 2009: 341–2, 353–4.

22 See Martin 1991: 51–2, quoting Carcopino 1968.

23 Cf. persecution of Egyptian (Isis) and Jewish cults as *externae caerimoniae* (*Tib.* 36); the ritual of Isis is here described as *superstitio*, as in *Dom.* 1.2.

24 *Otho* 12.2: *mors eius minime congruens uitae maiore miraculo fuerit.* Cf. Pl., *Oth.* 18.3; Tac., *Hist.* 2.50.1; D.C. 64.15.2. See Gascou 1984: 311–12; Cizek 1977: 130–2.

25 Suet., *Otho* 2.2. Cf. C.D. 64.8. Suet., *Otho* 7.1. Plu., *Gal.* 19.2–5.

26 A 'process of dissolution and reconstitution', according to Wallace-Hadrill 1984: 13; 'fragmentation and re-contextualization', according to Schulz 2019: 273–7.

27 *Tib.* 33: *Paulatim principem exeruit* . . .

28 Gascou 1984: 705.

29 See Giua 1978: 331. On hypocrisy in Suetonius and Tacitus, see Lindsay 1995: 14; Giua 1975: 53, 352–63.

30 *Tib.* 43. Cf. Tac., *Ann.* 6.1.

31 Gascou 1984: 438–9; Martin 1991: 153–7.

32 See Dupont and Éloi 2001: 293–306; Wallace-Hadrill 1984: 183–4; Brandão 2005b: 92–4.

33 *feminarum quoque, et quidem illustrium . . . 'hircum uetulum capreis naturam ligurire'.*

34 *Tib.* 46, 49.1, 50.1, 57.1, 61.1; *Tib.* 62.1, 63.1; *Tib.* 67.

35 *Cal.* 22, *hactenus quasi de principe, reliqua ut de monstro narranda sunt.* About his *quasi*, see Wardle 1994: 9.

36 *Monstrum* is etymologically associated with *moneo.* Cf. *Gal.* 18.1. See Guastella 1992: 157; Schulz 2019: 309.

37 *Cal.* 22.2–3.

38 Cf. *Aug.* 51–52; *Tib.* 26.1.

39 See Hurley 1993: 86; Wardle 1994: 205–8.

40 See Martin 1991: 331; Colin 1954: 408; Lambrechts 1953: 226–8 and n. 2; Guastella 1992: 171–2; Wardle 1994: 224–6.

41 *Cal.* 56.1, *Ita bacchantem atque grassantem non defuit plerisque animus adoriri.*

42 See Gascou 1984: 703–6.

43 *haec partim nulla reprehensione, partim etiam non mediocri laude digna in unum contuli, ut secernerem a probris ac sceleribus eius, de quibus dehinc dicam . . .*

44 See Gascou 1984: 369–71.

45 See Warmington 1999: 48; Schulz 2019: 309–10.

46 See Frazer 1966: 17–20.

47 Schulz 2019: 288–90.

48 See Lounsbury 1991: 3752.

49 *suam quidem pudicitiam usque adeo prostituit ut contaminatis paene omnibus membris nouissime quasi genus lusus excogitaret, quo ferae pelle contectus emitteretur e cauea uirorumque ac feminarum ad stipitem deligatorum inguina inuaderet . . .*; maybe a distorted reference to the punishments suffered by Christians in 64 CE, who, according to Tacitus (*Ann.* 15.44.4), were covered in animal skins and torn apart by dogs. See Bradley 1978: 164. Brandão 2022: 202–3.

50 *et, cum affatim desaeuisset, conficeretur a Doryphoro liberto; cui etiam sicut ipsi Sporus, ita ipse denupsit, uoces quoque et heiulatus uim patientium uirginum imitates.* Cf. Tac., *Ann.* 15.37.4 and D.C. 63.13.2. See Verdière 1975: 19–20; Bradley 1978: 164–5; Cizek 1982: 41–2; Martin 1991: 160, 169–71; Fernández Uriel 1994: 111–24.

51 *Nero* 34.2–3. See Lounsbury 1991: 3768–70. The artistic character of Nero appears associated with the criminal character also in the parallel sources: see Frazer 1966: 17–20. Cf. D.C. 61.12.2; Tac., *Ann.* 14.7.6.

52 *Nero* 38.1, *incendit urbem tam palam . . .* According to Tacitus (*Ann.* 15.38.1), the trickery (*dolus*) of the princeps is only one of the versions that ran on equal footing with that of a fortuitous accident.

53 In fact, Nero seems to have made efforts to fight the fire or mitigate its effects, as Holson 1976: 37–44 points out. See Bradley 1978: 230–1.

54 Tac., *Ann.* 15.39.3. Cf. D.C. 62.18.1. See Holson 1976: 43; Gascou 1984: 442–4.

55 See Brandão 2009: 191–2.

56 'Une presentation purement impressioniste', as Gascou (1984: 371) calls it.

57 Cf. D.C. 61.18.2–3.

58 In contrast to the long account of the Pisonian conspiracy in Tacitus, *Ann.* 15.48–74. Cf. Baldwin 1983: 178.

59 *nonnulli etiam imputarent, tamquam 'aliter illi non possent nisi morte succurrere dedecorato flagitiis omnibus.* Suetonius is, as usual, generalizing. Those words, according to Tacitus (*Ann.* 15.68.1), were pronounced only by Sulpicius Asper. Cassius Dio (62.24.2) says that another conspirator, Subrius Flavius, adds that he could not be a slave of a lyre player and *auriga*.

60 *talem principem . . . terrarum orbis tandem destituit . . .*

61 *Nero* 49.1. See Lorenzo 1981: 523–35.

62 See Fornaro 1988: 155–67; Wardle 2014: 550; Brandão 2009: 271–3; Power 2014: 68–9.

63 As Hulls 2014: 190–1 notes.

64 *viuo deformiter, turpiter.* See Gascou 1984: 797.

65 *circa administrationem autem imperii aliquamdiu se uarium praestitit, mixtura quoque aequabili uitiorum atque uitutum, donec uirtutes quoque in uitia deflexit: quantum coniectare licet, super ingenii naturam inopia, rapax, metu saeuus.*

66 See Baldwin 1983: 487; Gascou 1984: 696; Schulz 2019: 310, 316–18.

67 *Dom.* 10.2–4.

68 *quasi molitores rerum nouarum* (*Dom.* 10.2); *quasi . . . diuortium suum cum uxore taxasset* (*Dom.* 10.4).

69 As stated by Martin 1991: 295–6.

70 See Southern 1997: 110–18; Galli 1991: 81–4; Jones 1996: 84–97; Jones and Milns 2002: 145–9.

71 See Southern 1997: 113–14.

72 *Dom.* 11.2.

73 As Murphy 1991: 3788 notes.

74 *Dom.* 14.1, *per haec terribilis cunctis et inuisus, tandem oppressus est . . . amicorum libertorumque intimorum simul et uxoris.* Cf. *Cal.* 56.1; *Nero* 40.1. See Croisille 1970: 78, n. 5. Cf. D.C. 67.15.1–2.

75 See McGlew 1993: 26 ff.

76 Cf. Quint., *Decl.* 329. See Tabacco 1985: 87 and 131.

77 As Dunkle 1971: 16–17 shows.

78 Dunkle 1967: 151–71; Erskine 1991: 113–14, 118–20.

79 See Oliveira 1992: 23–43; 1995: 67–84; 1997: 119–38.

80 See Erskine 1991: 106–20.

81 See Tabacco 1985: 14 ff.

82 *. . . alii tradunt adloquenti pueros a tergo Chaeream ceruicem gladio caesim grauiter percussisse praemissa voce: 'hoc age!' Hoc age* was a cry with which the priest was invited to strike the victim to carry out the sacrifice; cf. Ov., *Fast.* 1.321–322; Sen., *Contr.* 2.3.19; Plu., *Numa* 14.5, *Cor.* 25.2. See Guastella 1992: 300; Hurley 1993: 209–10; Wardle 1994: 364; Ailloud 1931: n. 38.

83 *Nero* 37.3, *elatus inflatusque tantis uelut successibus negauit quemquam principum scisse quid sibi liceret*'; *Cal.* 29.1: '*memento*', *ait*, '*omnia mihi et in omnis licere*'.

84 Cf. *Jul.* 76.1; *Cal.* 22; *Dom.* 13.2.

85 See Oliveira 1992: 26–7.

86 Dunkle 1971: 14–15 notes that, from Cicero's later years, the term *crudelitas* begins to be replaced by *saeuitia* in the popular description of the tyrant; and it primarily refers to the ferocity of wild animals. In Suetonius, *saeuitia* prevails. See Tabacco 1985: 89–116.

87 *Tib.* 57–62; *Cal.* 27–33; *Nero* 33–38; *Dom.* 10–11. See Gascou 1984: 723 and 725.

88 Cf. *Tib.* 23; *Tib.* 48.1; *Cal.* 6.2.

89 *Tib.* 58; *Tib.* 59.1; *Tib.* 75.1; *Cal.* 12.2; *Cal.* 29.1; *Cal.* 48.1; *Nero* 34.4; *Dom.* 11.1; *Dom.* 11.3.

90 *Cal.* 29.1.

91 *Nero* 7.2; 43.1.

92 Cf. Quint., *Decl.* 322. See Tabacco 1985: 111.

93 And in Altemenes, Catreus' son: cf. Apollod. 3.2.1–2; D.S. 5.59.

94 *Cal.* 38.1; *Nero* 32.1; *Dom.* 12.1.

95 Cf. Quint., *Decl.* 329; Sen., *Con.* 5.8, 9.4; Quint., *Inst.* 3.6.78; Plato, *R.* 9.573d–575; cf. Arist., *Pol.* 1305b39 ff. See Tabacco 1985: 28–29, 118, n. 327.

96 *Nero* 32.4. Cf. *Jul.* 54.3.

97 Neglect of gods and auspices: *Jul.* 59; *Jul* 81.4; *Tib.* 69.1; *Cal.* 51.1; *Nero* 56; *Vit.* 11.2 and 1.3. Impious attitudes: *Nero* 32.4; *Tib.* 61.5.

98 *Cal.* 38.1; *Nero* 32.1; *Dom.* 12.1.

99 *Cal.* 37.1–2; *Nero* 30.1–2.

100 *Nero* 31.2. Cf. Tac., *Ann.* 15.42–43. See Morford 1968: 158–79; Blaison 1998: 617–24.

101 *Jul.* 50.1; *Aug.* 69.1.

102 Cf. Liv. 1.58. See Martin 1991: 133.

103 *Dom.* 22. Cf. D.C. 67.6.3–4.

104 Cf. Juv. 2.29–33; Plin., *Ep.* 4.11.6; D.C. 67.3.1. Jones 1996: 151 doubts that Domitian's relationship with Julia was the one described by tradition, given what is said in Martial, 6.3.5. See Jones and Milns 2002: 167.

105 See Gascou 1984: 438; Martin 1991: 153–7; Dupont and Éloi 2001: 293–306; Brandão 2005b: 92–4.

106 Already Cicero (*Phil.* 2.44) had accused Antony of prostituting himself.

107 Cf. *Jul.* 2, 49.1, 49.4; *Aug.* 68; *Dom.* 1.1; *Vit.* 3.2 vs. Tac. *Hist.* 3.86.1; *Otho* 2.2: cf. C.D. 64.8.3; see Martin 1991: 166; Carney 1968: 11–12.

108 See Dunkle 1967: 170; 1971: 18–19.

109 Cf. Sen., *Con.* 2.5.4. See Dunkle 1967: 170.

110 See Dunkle 1971: 17; Dupont and Éloi 2001: 264.

111 See Hurley 1993: 179–80; Gascou 1984: 609–10; Wardle 1994: 329; Dupont and Éloi 2001: 298–306.

112 See Brandão 2005a: 159–93 and 2009: 317–25. Cf. Lefkowitz 1981 and the creation of artistic lives from plotlines, as the depiction of Socrates in Aristophanes' *Clouds* (90, 93). These lives provide excellent fodder for biography writing, as do the works of Diogenes Laertius and Plutarch.

113 See Dunkle 1967: 153–4; 1971: 12–13.

114 *Cal.* 30.1. The *Atreus* of Accius features the earliest extant Latin usage of the word *tyrannus*. Caligula's monarchical aspiration is also expressed (*Cal.* 22.1) by the Homeric quotation 'let there be one chief, let there be one king!' (*Il.* 2.204–205); and the first hemistich of the same verse 204 – 'it is not good that power be distributed among many' – is put into Domitian's mouth (*Dom.* 12.3).

115 Cic., *Sest.* 48.102, *Phil.*1.14.34, *Off.* 1.28.97; Sen., *Ira* 1.20.4, *Cl.* 1.12.4, 2.2.2. Expression attributed to Sulla. See Hurley 1993: 122; Wardle 1994: 256.

116 *Tib.* 59.2, 'oderint, dum probent'. The biographer notes, quoting Cicero (*Off.* 3.82), that Caesar repeated some verses from Euripides' *Phoenician Women*, in which ambition was placed before *ius* and *pietas* (*Jul.* 30.5): Cf. Eur. *Ph.* 524. See Canfora 2000: 153.

117 Cf. Aristotle, *Po.* 1449b 9–10. As notes Foucher (2000: 777), 'Or la tragédie est aussi la représentation des actions des grands hommes, dans une forme littéraire qui revêt la même unité que la biographie, laquelle fédère une pluralité d'événements'.

118 As Tagliasachi 1960: 131–2 says about Plutarch.

119 Cf. Arist., *Po.* 1450b 3–4. See Fialho 1977: 385.

120 Cf. Arist., *Po.* 1454a 16–20; 33–36.

121 Cf. Arist., *Po.* 1450a 15–22. See Fialho 1977: 381.

122 Cf. Arist., *Po.* 1453a 25 ff.

123 According to Tagliasachi 1960: 138–41, the concept of moral guilt occurs in Plutarch and is justified by several instances in Attic tragedy.

124 Arist., *Po.* 1453a 3–12. Fialho 1977: 384 notes that Christian authors who translate it by *peccatum*.

125 As Foucher 2000: 778 suggests.

126 Cf. fanciful constructions of the lives of the Greek poets based on the plots of their plays; see Lefkowitz 1981 *passim*.

127 Cf. D.C. 63.9.4–6. This author says that the masks had the features of Poppaea.

128 *Nero* 21.3. Lounsbury 1991: 3775 suggests that each of these roles is a mask of Nero himself: while deflowered by Doryphorus (29), murderer of his mother (34.1–4), incestuous with his mother (28.2); murderer of friends and wives (35.2–3, 5). Cf. Martin 1991: 264. Cf. the literary life of Euripides modelled on such works as the *Bacchae* and *Hippolytus*: see Lefkowitz 1981: 2, 93–9, 110.

129 According to Bartsch 1994: 46 and 51–2, Nero plays the role of himself.

130 *hilare prosecutus atque in digressu papillas quoque exosculatus reliquum.* Verdière 1960: 774–6 proposes the correction of *papillas* by *pupillas*; cf. *oculi* (Tac., *Ann.* 14.4.4) and *ommata* (D.C. 61.13.2): see Verdière 1975: 14; contra Benediktson 1992: 161–3. Lounsbury 1991: 3760 places *exosculatus* in parallel with *exosculans* (*Nero* 28.2), which characterized Nero's behaviour towards the eunuch Sporus.

131 For Baldwin 1979: 380–1, this passage denotes Nero's histrionic tastes: the touching of the limbs of a royal body recalls the scene of Agave and Pentheus in Euripides' *Bacchae*. Contra Bartsch 1994: 61–2.

132 Cf. *Ann.* 14.9.1. Cf. D.C. 61.14.2. See Verdière 1975: 13.

133 Cf. *Vit.* 10.3.

134 See Martin 1991: 264.

135 See Brandão 2009: 76–81. Comedy presents men worse than they are: cf. Arist., *Po.* 1448a 17.

136 See Guastella 1999: 9–10, 33–4.

137 Vespasian himself used humour for this purpose: to break the tension generated by unorthodox ways of obtaining revenue (*Ves.* 23.1).

138 Cf. Ov., *Tr.* 2.497–498. See Giancotti 1967: 65 ff; Fantham 1989: 157–8; Panayotakis 1995: xvii.

139 *Aug.* 99.1; *Tib.* 24.1; *Cal.* 45.2; *Otho* 3.2. See Power 2014: 68–9.

140 See Giancotti 1967: 28; Panayotakis 1995: xiii.

141 See Giancotti 1967: 27, 295; Dupont 1985: 298; Panayotakis 1995: xvii.

142 E.g. *Fatum*: *Aug.* 65.1, 94.12; *Tib.* 69; *Tit.* 9.1. *Fortuna*: *Nero* 23.3; *Tit.* 1; *atrox fortuna*: *Tib.* 23. Suetonius often stresses the coincidences of fate: *Cal.* 60; *Nero* 6; *Nero* 40.4; *Nero* 57.1; *Gal.* 6.1; *Cl.* 2.1; *Tit.* 11; *Tit.* 1; *Tit.* 5.2; *Tit.* 11.

143 *Ves.* 1.1, ... *licet Domitianum cupiditatis ac saeuitia merito poenas luisse*. Cf. *Jul.* 76.1; *Cal.* 56.1; *Nero* 40.1; *Galba* 16.1; *Vit.* 17.2; *Dom.* 14.1.

144 See Gascou 1984: 438; Martin 1991: 153–7.

145 See Dupont and Éloi 2001: 263–9.

Bibliography

Aiardi, A. (1978), 'Per un'interpretazione della Domus Aurea', *PP*, 33: 90–103.

Ailloud, H. (1931), *Suétone. Vie des douze Césars*, texte établi et traduit, vols I–III (2nd edition, 1989: vol. I; 1993; vol. II; 1980: vol. III), Paris: Les Belles-Lettres.

Baldwin, B. (1979), 'Nero and His Mother's Corpse', *Mnemosyne*, 32: 380–1.

Baldwin, B. (1983), *Suetonius*, Amsterdam: Hakkert.

Bartsch, S. (1994), *Actors in the Audience: Theatricality and Doublespeak from Nero to Hadrian*, Cambridge, MA: Harvard University Press.

Benediktson, D. T. (1992), 'Nero and Agrippina's Goodbye Kiss: *papillas* or *pupillas*?', *Maia*, 44: 161–3.

Blaison, M. (1998), 'Suétone et l' *ekphrasis* de la *Domus Aurea*', *Latomus*, 57: 617–24.

Bradley, K. R. (1978), *Suetonius' Life of Nero: An Historical Commentary*, Brussels: Latomus.

Brandão, J. L. (2004), 'Retratos dos Césares em Suetónio', in A. Pérez Jiménez, J. R. Ferreira and M. C. Fialho (eds), *O retrato e a biografia como estratégia de teorização política*, 83–113, Coimbra-Málaga: Imprensa da Universidade de Coimbra/Universidade de Málaga.

Brandão, J. L. (2005a), 'Suetónio e drama: da tragédia ao mimo', *Humanitas*, 57: 159–93.

Brandão, J. L. (2005b), 'Suetónio e o fascínio do Oriente', in F. Oliveira (ed.), *Génese e consolidação da ideia da Europa III: O mundo romano*, 81–102, Coimbra: Imprensa da UC.

Brandão, J. L. (2009), *Máscaras dos Césares: Teatro e moralidade nas Vidas suetonianas*, Coimbra: Imprensa da UC.

Brandão, J. L. (2022), 'Performing Roman Identity in Suetonius' *Caesars*', in L. Lanzillota, J. Brandão, C. Teixeira and A. Rodrigues (eds), *Roman Identity: Between Ideal and Performance*, 185–223, Turnhout: Brepols.

Canfora, L. (2000), *Giulio Cesare: Il dittatore democratico*, 5th edition, Rome: Laterza.

Carney, T. F. (1968), 'How Suetonius' *Lives* Reflect on Hadrian', *PACA*, 11: 7–24.

Cizek, E. (1977), *Structure et idéologie dans les* Vies des douze Césars *de Suétone*, Paris: Les Belles Lettres.

Cizek, E. (1982), *Néron*, Paris: Fayard.

Colin, J. (1954), 'Les consuls du césar-pharaon Caligula et l'héritage de Germanicus', *Latomus*, 13: 394–416.

Croisille, J. M. (1970), 'L'art de la composition chez Suétone d'après les *Vies* de Claude et de Néron', *AIIS*, 2: 73–87.

Dench, E. (2005), *Romulus' Asylum: Roman Identities from the Age of Alexander to the Age of Hadrian*, Oxford: Oxford University Press.

Dunkle, J. R. (1967), 'The Greek Tyrant and Roman Political Invective of the Late Republic', *TAPhA*, 96: 151–71.

Dunkle, J. R. (1971), 'The Rhethorical Tyrant in Roman Historiography: Sallust, Livy and Tacitus', *CW*, 65: 12–20.

Dupont, F. (1985), *L'acteur-roi ou le théâtre dans la Rome antique*, Paris: Les Belles Lettres.

Dupont, F. and T. Éloi (2001), *L' érotisme masculin dans la Rome antique*, Paris: Belin.

Erskine, A. (1991), 'Hellenistic Monarchy and Roman Political Invective', *Classical Quarterly*, 41 (1): 106–20.

Fantham, R. (1989), 'Mime: The Missing Link in Roman Literary History', *CW*, 82: 153–62.

Fernández Uriel, P. (1994), 'Tácito, *Annales* XV, 37,8 y Suetonio, *Nero* XXVIII y XXIX: Interpretación sexual o religiosa?', in J. Alvar, C. Blánquez and C. Wagner (eds), *Sexo, muerte y religión en el mundo clásico*, 111–24, Madrid: Ediciones Clásicas.

Fialho, M. C. (1977), 'Algumas considerações sobre o homem trágico', *Biblos*, 53: 375–88.

Fornaro, P. (1988), 'Una vita senza maschera, Suet. *Aug.* XCIX, l', *CCC*, 9: 155–67.

Foucher, A. (2000), 'Nature et formes de l''histoire tragique' à Rome', *Latomus*, 59: 773–801.

Frazer, R. M. (1966), 'Nero the Artist-Criminal', *CJ*, 62: 17–20.

Galli, F., trans. (1991), *Svetonio, Vita di Domiziano*, Rome: Ateneo.

Gascou, J. (1984), *Suétone historien*, Paris: de Boccard.

Giancotti, F. (1967), *Mimo e gnome: Studio su Decimo Laberio e Publilio Siro*, Florence: Anna.

Giua, M. A. (1975), 'Tiberio simulatore nella tradizione storica pretacitiana', *Athenaeum*, 53: 352–63.

Giua, M. A. (1978), 'Sulla biografia suetoniana di Tiberio: Tradizione e struttura', *Athenaeum*, 56: 329–45.

Guastella, G., trans. (1992), *Gaio Svetonio Tranquillo, La vita di Caligola*, Rome: La Nuova Italia Scientifica.

Guastella, G. (1999), *Gaio Svetonio Tranquillo: L'imperatore Claudio*, Venice: Marsilio.

Holson, P. (1976), 'Nero and the Fire of Rome: Fact and Fiction', *Pegasus*, 19: 37–44.

Howard, A. A. and C. N. Jackson (1922), *Index uerborum C. Suetoni Tranquili stilique eius proprietatum nonnullarum*, Cambridge, MA: Harvard University Press.

Hulls J.-M. (2014), 'The Mirror in the Text: Privacy, Performance and the Power of Suetonius' *Domitian*', in T. Power and R. Gibson (eds), *Suetonius the Biographer: Studies in Roman Lives*, 178–96, Oxford: Oxford University Press.

Hurley, D. W. (1993), *An Historical and Historiographical Commentary on Suetonius' Life of C. Caligula*, Atlanta, GA: Scholars Press.

Jones, B. W., ed. (1996), *Suetonius: Domitian*, London: Bristol Classical Press.

Jones, B. and R. Milns (2002), *Suetonius: The Flavian emperors, a Historical Commentary*, London: Bristol Classical Press.

Lambrechts, P. (1953), 'Caligula dictateur littéraire', *BIBR*, 28: 219–32.

Lefkowitz, M. (1981), *The Lives of the Greek Poets*, Baltimore, MD: Johns Hopkins University Press.

Lindsay, H., ed. (1995), *Suetonius: Tiberius*, London: Bristol Classical Press.

Lorenzo, E. di (1981), 'A proposito dell'espressione neroniana *qualis artifex pereo* (Suet., *Nero* 49)', in I. Gallo (ed.), *Studi salernitani in memoria di R. Cantarella*, 523–35, Salerno: Pietro Laveglia Editore.

Lounsbury, R. C. (1991), '*Inter quos et Sporus erat:* The Making of Suetonius' *Nero*', *ANRW II*, 33 (5): 3748–79.

Martin, R. (1991), *Les douze Césars: du mythe à la réalité,* Paris: Les Belles Lettres.

McGlew, J. F. (1993), *Tyranny and Political Culture in Ancient Greece*, Ithaca, NY: Cornell University Press.

Morford, M. (1968), 'The Distortion of the *Domus Aurea* Tradition', *Eranos*, 66: 158–79.

Murphy, J. P. (1991), 'The Anecdote in Suetonius' Flavian *Lives*', *ANRW II*, 33 (5): 3780–93.

Oliveira, F. (1992), *Les idées politiques et morales de Pline l'Ancien*, Coimbra: INIC/CECH.

Oliveira F. (1995), 'Biografia dos imperadores em Plínio o Antigo', *Biblos*, 71: 67–84.

Oliveira, F. (1997), 'La imagen del gobernante ideal en Plinio el Viejo', in J. A. Sánchez Marín, J. Lens Tuero, and C. López Rodríguez (eds), *Historiografía y biografía*, 119–38, Madrid: Ediciones Clásicas.

Panayotakis, C. (1995), *Theatrum Arbitri: Theatrical Elements in the* Satyrica *of Petronius*, Leiden: Brill.

Pelling, C., trans. (2011), *Plutarch: Caesar*, Oxford: Oxford University Press.

Power, T. (2014), 'The Endings of Suetonius' Caesars', in T. Power and R. K. Gibson (eds), *Suetonius the Biographer: Studies in Roman Lives*, 58–77, Oxford: Oxford University Press.

Rolfe, J. C. (1913–14), *Suetonius*, vols I and II, Loeb Classical Library (1979 reprint), Cambridge, MA: Harvard University Press.

Schulz, V. (2019), *Deconstructing Imperial Representation: Tacitus, Cassius Dio and Suetonius on Nero and Domitian*, Leiden: Brill.

Southern, P. (1997), *Domitian: Tragic Tyrant*, London: Routledge.

Tabacco, R. (1985), 'Il tiranno nelle declamazioni di scuola in lingua latina', *Memorie della Accademia delle Scienze Morali, Storiche e Filologiche di Torino II: Classe di Scienze Morali, Storiche e Filologiche*, 5 (9): 1–141.

Tagliasachi, A. M. (1960), 'Plutarco e la tragedia greca', *Dioniso*, 34: 125–42.

Verdière, R. (1960), 'Le baiser d'adieu de Néron', in P. Grimal (ed.), *Hommages à Léon Herrmann*, 774–6, Brussels: Latomus.

Verdière, R. (1975), 'À verser au dossier sexuel de Néron', *PP*, 30: 5–22.

Wallace-Hadrill, A. (1984), *Suetonius: The Scholar and His Caesars*, New Haven, CT: Yale University Press.

Wardle, D. (1994), *Suetonius: Life of Caligula: A Commentary*, Brussels: Latomus.

Wardle, D., trans. (2014), *Suetonius: Life of Augustus*, Oxford: Oxford University Press.

Warmington, B. H., ed. (1999), *Suetonius: Nero*, 2nd edition, London: Bristol Classical Press.

Weinstock, S. (1971), *Divus Julius*, Oxford: Clarendon Press.

16

Zenobia: The 'Exceptional Other' in the *Historia Augusta*

Cláudia Teixeira

The biography of Septimia Zenobia Sebaste,[1] written by the biographer of the *Historia Augusta*, transforms the queen of Palmyra into one of the most intriguing historical subjects of the third century CE.

Broadly speaking, Zenobia acted in a very particular political framework. After the capture of Valerian by the Persians, the resistance to the Sassanid Persians and Goths of the Black Sea was largely led by Odenathus. Gallienus rewarded him with the title of *Corrector totius Orientis* (governor of the entire East), legitimizing his rule over that area of the empire. After his assassination in 267 or 268 CE, along with his first-born son, the power passed to his youngest son, Vabalathus. Notwithstanding, it was Zenobia who, as regent, ruled the region. The aspiration to legitimize Vabalathus[2] led Zenobia to an armed campaign and diplomatic manoeuvres, by means of which Palmyra came to integrate, under its power, various cities of Cilicia, Cappadocia, and Mesopotamia as well as the territory between Syria and Egypt.[3] Aurelian regained Palmyra in 272.[4] Zenobia, who had refused to surrender, was captured on her way out of the city, which capitulated in the aftermath. Unlike most of her advisors and generals, according to some sources, she escaped a death sentence and spent the rest of her life in Tibur.[5]

The *Historia Augusta*, the source which gives us the most detailed information about Zenobia, significantly expands on this information.[6] The narrative, historically unreliable,[7] gives primacy, in adjustment to the biographical model developed by Suetonius, to the mores of the biographees, which constitute the criterion for selection or exclusion of discursive material. In the case of Zenobia's biography, the narrative is particularly dominated by the description of her leadership qualities, her exceptional beauty, her outstanding chastity, her enormous charisma, bravery, and political intelligence. Being a woman and foreigner, a usurper and the cause of one of the secessions that took place in the empire during the third century, this account challenges not only the conceptualization that the author of the *Historia Augusta* frequently makes of the female gender throughout the work, but also the traditional conception of the ethnic 'other'.

In recent years, a vast literature has drawn attention to the dangers and detours generated by the application of the theoretical apparatus about the 'other' to the ancient world, designed as it was to identify, analyse, and respond conceptually to contemporary problems.[8] The warning naturally extends to the use of this apparatus in literary analysis. As happened in the literature of later periods, the literary representations of the 'other', in ancient literature, took shape in a plurality of discourses, from those that today we may consider essentialist, to those marked by the actualization of cultural stereotypes and prejudices, to others that, although still very far from the knowledge of what would be defined, many centuries later, as multiculturalism, revealed, in some way, more tangible sensibilities concerning the understanding of difference.[9] These representations, with rare exceptions,[10] hardly reflect accurate and impartial images of the 'other(s)', either as individuals or as group(s), let alone ordinary others, historically situated in objective realities and moving daily within the framework in which various cultures intersected. The image of the 'other' in literature is, on the contrary, a construction mediated by the non-objectifiable perceptions of the writer and conditioned by the cultural system from which it emerges.[11] The same applies to the processes of othering, that is, the mechanisms by which the 'other' is ordered, classified, valued, or devalued. These processes hardly echo or represent the way the 'others' were positioned or positioned themselves in the various cultural networks that emerged in the Roman world, defined by the intersection between the culture that became dominant and the various cultures of origin, nor represent the distinct processes of negotiation and renegotiation of identities that developed within the framework of this intersection.[12] Thus, literature offers us perceptions and perspectives, emanating from the centre of the cultural system or, in other words, from the dominant culture. In this sense, 'literary others', as well as the processes by which they are transformed into 'others', must be seen as discursive constructions mediated by motivations, values, operational concepts, and programmatic intentionalities. In view of these assumptions, the aim of this chapter is to analyse Septimia Zenobia Sebaste's literary depiction in the *Historia Augusta*, arguing that her conceptualization as a powerful and respected 'other' is compromised by the programmatic agenda that underlies the narrative as well as by three discursive devices used by the author to develop it: exceptionality, hybridity, and dualization.

Programmatic agenda

Latin literature, including biography, created typologies of women that, similar to men's, were divided rhetorically into three main paradigmatic models: models of moral virtue; models that, on the contrary, evidence the disruption of the moral order; and mixed models.[13] Obviously, the individual characterizations made within the frameworks of this paradigmatic segmentation are not homogeneous and are subject to a variability imposed by situations and contexts.[14] However, generally speaking, women who adjust their actions to the moral standards associated with the roles traditionally played by their gender, namely those of wife and mother, fall into the first typology; women who, on the contrary, go beyond the limits imposed by these roles, namely intervening in the political arena, are generically integrated into the second typology. Moreover, their 'off-limits' behaviour is often substantiated as such in the discourse through ethically immoral expedients such as intrigue, betrayal, and manipulative sexuality.

The description of Zenobia in the *Historia Augusta* challenges this framework. Her performance takes place in a political and military environment traditionally closed to the female gender, but the biographer exempts her from the degradation into which several empresses fell, precisely because of their involvement and intervention in political affairs.

However, in *Tr. Tyr.* 31.7, the biographer presents the reason that led him to include the biographies of women in the work. This inclusion is clearly stated as subject to a programmatic agenda, which aims to demote the emperor Gallienus:

> studiose in medio feminas posui ad ludibrium Gallieni, quo nihil prodigiosius passa est Romana res publica . . .
>
> It was with deliberate purpose that I included the women, namely that I might make a mock of Gallienus, a greater monster than whom the Roman state has never endured . . .[15]

The achievement of this programmatic agenda is done, in the particular case of Gallienus, by two distinct but related narrative blocks. The first is constituted by his own biography which follows the pattern of imperial biography. In this case, Gallienus' biography does not bring anything new. The narrative constitutes a repository of the emperor's *uitia* (vices), articulating the public and private spheres of his life, in order to create and reinforce the idea of his inadequacy, both moral and political, to rule the empire. For example, a lack of respect and faithful affection for his father (*pietas*),[16] frivolity,[17] lust,[18] self-indulgence,[19] cruelty,[20] etc., are repeatedly addressed, either directly or indirectly, throughout his *uita* and developed in order to demonstrate his negligence,[21] contempt for public affairs,[22] and preference for a luxurious and irresponsible life at the expense of the wellbeing of the state.[23]

The second narrative block is constituted by a significant part[24] of the biographies that form part of the section dedicated to the *Triginta Tyranni*, a set of biographies of usurpers, who emerged in the political and military climate of the third century CE. These figures are used by the biographer to develop his programmatic agenda, as he depicts them as champions of an empire that was crumbling under Gallienus' leadership, as the author of the *Historia Augusta* explains several times.[25] Thus, in this section, the biographer significantly expands the discursive mechanism typically used to form the traditional Caracalla and Geta mirroring-type biographies, that is, biographies in which the vices of one historical figure are reinforced through comparison with the virtues of another acting in the same historical reality.

However, the inclusion, among these usurpers, of Zenobia, a figure that represents a genre to which the political and military leadership of the empire is not traditionally allowed, broadens even further the scope of this discursive mechanism, as it opens space for the design of an 'other' that extrapolates not only her feminine condition, but also her condition of subaltern implied in the system of the power relations that developed in the empire between the provincial elites and the imperial power.

In this sense, the first question that arises from the biographer's discursive enunciation in *Tr. Tyr.* 31.7 is the following: as the stated programmatic intention, which aims to deride and discredit Gallienus, justifies the inclusion of women's *uitae* in this section of the *Historia Augusta*, does it also justify the positive portrayal of Zenobia? Or, on the contrary, do the qualities developed throughout her biography express the genuine belief that gender is not an obstacle when it comes to obtaining and exercising leadership skills?

As already mentioned, many of the narratives dealing with usurpations are used situationally to criticize or praise leaderships. Zenobia's leadership, like that of Postumus, is indisputably developed in adjustment to this purpose, to the point that the biographer transforms the secessionist movement of Palmyra, and also that of Gaul, into a providential expedient that guaranteed both the protection of the empire and the safeguard of the dignity of imperial power,[26] debased by Gallienus.[27] And this reason is sufficient for the biographer, when conceiving these biographies, to instrumentalize discourses and narratives, including the narratives of otherness, introducing various degrees of distortion into them. In this regard, the implications that result from the programmatic agenda enunciated by the author are important for us to understand his view on gender identities, namely on the dialectic underlying the construction of the male/female gender relationship. In fact, by announcing that he has included the biographies of women *ad ludibrium Gallieni* ('to make a mock of Gallienus'), it is nonetheless significant that, in his perception, the good *exemplum* provided by these women is what produces the emperor's greatest deflation – a demotion that does not result from the fact that they have better qualities than him, but from the fact that they have those better qualities, being women.

Exceptionality

The literary conceptualization of Zenobia as an example of political and moral qualities begins in the biography of Gallienus (13.2–3, 13.5), is emphasized in Odenathus' *uita* (*Tr. Tyr.* 15.2, 15.7–8), and is definitively established, as already explained, in her own biography. In this text, the exceptional status of the queen of Palmyra is attested at its the very beginning (*Tr. Tyr.* 30.1–2):

> omnis iam consumptus est pudor, si quidem fatigata re publica eo usque perventum est ut Gallieno nequissime agente optime etiam mulieres imperarent. et quidem peregrina enim, nomine Zenobia, ... post Odaenathum maritum imperiali sagulo perfuso per umeros ... diutius quam femineus sexus patiebatur imperavit.

> Now all shame is exhausted, for in the weakened state of the commonwealth things came to such a pass that, while Gallienus conducted himself in the most evil fashion, even women ruled most excellently. For, in fact, even a foreigner, Zenobia ... proceeded upon the death of her husband Odaenathus to cast about her shoulders the imperial mantle.

The biographer clearly conveys the superiority of the Palmyrene queen over Gallienus. It is she who, in the biographer's perspective, guarantees the survival of the empire that has been perverted under the rule of a negligent and incapable emperor. Furthermore, her qualities, which the biographer subsequently describes, fit 'the old Roman philosophical opinion (which developed under the Republic) that only virtuous politicians were entitled to rule'.[28] In fact, both her moral and physical perfection, which protects her from any potential negative appraisal similar to that produced by the influence of physiognomy, attest to her excellence and exceptionality.[29]

However, Zenobia's status as 'exceptional', which apparently ennobles her as an 'other' both from an ethnic and gender point of view, presents problems in terms of representation. In fact, the expressions *etiam mulieres* (even women) and *quidem peregrina* (even a foreigner) make Zenobia emerge in the narrative as an exception arising from two implied generalizations concerning women and foreigners. In other words, Zenobia's exceptionality is constructed not only against her identity base (woman and Syrian) but also against the universal base that includes 'all women' and 'all foreigners'. Thus, in the perception of the author of the *Historia Augusta*, Zenobia surely represents an 'other', but an 'exceptional other' that emerges, in her singularity, precisely because she has been departed from her collective base.[30] In this way, by creating her in opposition to her identity base, the author not only negotiated on her behalf the characteristics that allowed her to emerge from that base, but, more than that, developed the implication that those characteristics did not result from the realization of any potential existing in that base and which, as such, could potentially extend to all of its members. This, ultimately, makes her exceptionality fall into the condition of exceptionalism.

Hybridity

As we have seen, although the portrait of Zenobia is framed by a programmatic intentionality that aims, above all, to reinforce, by contrast, the negative characterization of Gallienus, the truth is that this does not conflict with the fact that the description of her qualities has required on the part of the biographer a proper treatment with regard to issues of gender and ethnicity.

Despite being a woman and a foreigner, Zenobia possesses exceptional characteristics that are highly valued by the biographer. These qualities, both political and moral, converge in the creation of a charismatic leader, not only capable but also endowed with the type of political intelligence that allows her to perceive, in the manner of a wise ruler, the contexts, adapting her actions to the demands of each circumstance (*Tr. Tyr.* 30.16): *severitas, ubi necessitas postulabat, tyrannorum, bonorum principum clementia, ubi pietas requirebat* ('her sternness, when necessity demanded, was that of a tyrant, her clemency, when her sense of right called for it, that of a good emperor').

However, and despite all this, the biographer also conceives her as a hybrid 'other', namely by mitigating cultural elements arising from her lineage and by saddling her cultural behaviour with traces of Romanness, which casts shadows on the genuineness of the encomiastic character of her description.

Lineage

The biographer presents Zenobia (*Tr. Tyr.* 30.2) as a queen who boasted of descending *Cleopatrarum Ptolemaeorumque gente* ('from the family of the Cleopatras and the Ptolemies') and who used to adorn herself with the robes of Dido (*habitu Didonis ornata*). The mention of these rebellious queens, the historical Cleopatra and the fictional Dido, would need no further explanation considering that both would be very well known in the Roman world. However, if, on one hand, Cleopatra[31] links Zenobia to an illustrious lineage, on the other, both Cleopatra and Dido were inscribed in the Roman imagination as symbols of 'foreign danger'. The conceptualization of this danger materialized, in Cleopatra's case, in a war against Rome, which could have resulted in the destruction of the Roman state itself. Moreover, her relationship with Marc Antony, managed through a manipulative and emasculating hypersexuality,[32] called into question, at least in the texts of the Augustan propaganda, the basis of the Roman social system that regulated the relations between men and women. Dido, despite her later crystallization as 'chaste',[33] had also established herself in the Roman imaginary as the passionate and *furens* (raving) woman who jeopardized the mission of Aeneas,[34] one of the founding fathers of Roman civilization, and was also – a subject developed in Virgil's *Aeneid* – at the mythical origin of the conflict between the Romans and their arch-enemies, the Carthaginians (*En.* 4.622–629).

Zenobia is, however, skilfully rescued by the biographer from this model of femininity (*Tr. Tyr.* 30.12):

> cuius ea castitas fuisse dicitur ut ne virum suum quidem scierit nisi temptandis, conceptionibus. nam cum semel concubuisset, exspectatis menstruis continebat se, si praegnans esset, sin minus, iterum potestatem quaerendis liberis dabat.
>
> Such was her continence, it is said, that she would not know even her own husband save for the purpose of conception. For when once she had lain with him, she would refrain until the time of menstruation to see if she were pregnant; if not, she would again grant him an opportunity of begetting children.'

The biographer's almost graphic insistence on Zenobia's chastity makes her an idealized model of female purity, strongly connected with marital fecundity. *Pudicitia* (chastity), as Langlands states, 'was instrumental in regulating this system [the positioning of the individual within a network of hierarchical social relations], keeping some individuals apart, drawing boundaries and emphasising differences and distances between individuals – between, for instance, Roman and foreign, free and slave, male and female, young and old, plebeian and patrician'.[35]

In the biography of Zenobia, *pudicitia* assumes similar functions, namely because it allows her to redefine the relationship with her own lineage. Lineage constitutes an important *species* in imperial biography,[36] not only because it associates family and power, but also because it provides identity substance that makes the subjects collectively recognizable within the cultural community. And, in this sense, the biographer's categorical affirmation of Zenobia's chastity operates a segmentation that distances her from the identity substance that emanates, as far as sexuality is concerned, from the women who precede her in her purported lineage.[37] And, more importantly, the drawing of her chastity ultimately transfers her into the homogenized cultural cycle of female virtue in the Roman world, composed of figures like Lucretia. By making her more Roman and less Oriental, or at least less Cleopatra-like, the biographer manipulates Zenobia's identity, inscribing her within an acceptable pattern of hybridity, in which the potentially most disruptive traits of her orientality are eliminated. As we shall see below, the construction of Zenobia as an acceptable hybrid extends to virtually every facet of her cultural characterization.

Cultural behaviour

Roman historical and literary discourse conveys ideas and beliefs about both what it means 'to be Roman' and what it means 'to be the other'. The cultural representations of these beliefs are usually done through a system of oppositions that extends from physical stereotypes to social practices.[38] The depiction of Zenobia in the *Historia Augusta* balances between the two poles of this system of oppositions. If the introduction in the narrative of her *pudicitia* (chastity) already denoted this, the biographer will amplify even further her status as inter-polar individual, by depicting her as someone engaged in social practices that express oscillation between East and West: her dress was oriental (30.2), but in assemblies she dressed in the manner of the Roman emperors (30.14); she drank with her generals, but was sober (30. 18); she socialized with Persians and Armenians, but only to show them her superiority; she preferred to be worshipped according to Persian customs (30.13–14), but her political behaviour revealed the traits of the behaviour of the Roman *principes* (30.16); she expressed herself badly in Latin, although she was not totally ignorant of the language, but made sure that her children learned it.

The way the biographer describes her oscillation between East and West, between local culture and Romanness, would probably not be too far from the way the various historical 'others' were understood and would understand themselves within the context of the diverse cultural spectra that emerged in the Roman world as the result of processes of negotiation and renegotiation of identities. Cultural hybridization phenomena would be common in regions in which the dominant culture and local cultures intersect. Zenobia's biography offers us the possibility to see how this phenomenon is perceived from the biographer's perspective.

Zenobia's description clearly denotes that her hybrid status results from the incorporation of two cultures and that hybrid-others are able to act and intervene politically in the new cultural space that was created by this intersection of cultures. However, the outcome of her confrontation with Aurelian expresses the limitations that exist within the framework of the relationships established between hybridity and dominant culture. In fact, her subsequent reduction to the status of Roman matron illustrates not only the hegemonic culture's ability to standardize itself by nullifying the difference, whether pure or hybrid, represented by individuals or groups who do not conform to the norms of the socially and culturally dominant group, but also that hybrid identities are contingent and fragile; in the confrontation with hegemonic systems, these identities tend to be obliterated and replaced by something more acceptable to the dominant group, which ultimately proves that, within the framework of the tensions between sameness and otherness, the sovereign structure of Roman culture has not ceased to function.

Dualization and unification

In addition to materializing her as an example of cultural hybridity, Zenobia's gender identity also swings between typically masculine and feminine patterns. Among the characteristics typically associated with the female gender, besides her chastity, her beauty stands out (*Tr. Tyr.* 30.15):

> fuit vultu subaquilo, fusci coloris, oculis supra modum vigentibus nigris, spiritus divini, venustatis incredibilis. tantus candor in dentibus ut margaritas eam plerique putarent habere, non dentes.
>
> Her face was dark and of a swarthy hue, her eyes were Black and powerful beyond the usual wont, her spirit divinely great, and her beauty incredible. So white were her teeth that many thought that she had pearls in place of teeth.

Zenobia's beauty is of an idealized femininity, which contrasts with other stereotypical masculinizing characteristics: Zenobia was engaged in several military campaigns, displayed military skills, presented herself in assemblies dressed like the Roman emperors, used the chariot and horse and rarely a female chariot; she often drank with her generals, marched with her foot soldiers for three or four miles, hunted like the Spaniards; her voice was clear as a man's voice; she managed the public treasury better than anyone else. These characteristics place her in the conceptual framework of the 'good ruler'. Although in Antiquity the characteristics associated with 'good leadership' were not divided by gender, not least because there was never any normativization of female leadership models, there are two elements that attest that the biographer wanted to place these characteristics in the masculine plane. The first lies in the way the biographer describes Zenobia's rise to power. Although he tells us that she used to accompany Odenathus on military campaigns[39] (*Tr. Tyr.* 15.2), it is only when her status as wife dies along with her husband that she inaugurates herself at the command of the *imperium*, assuming the masculinizing characteristics of a political and military leader (*Tr. Tyr.* 30.2): *post Odaenathum maritum imperiali sagulo perfuso per umeros* ('proceeded upon the death of her husband Odaenathus to cast about her shoulders the imperial mantle'); the second element is developed by Aurelian when, rebuked for wanting to show off a woman in his triumph, makes it clear that, although she is a woman, her judgement and sentence should depend on her military and political qualities (*Tr. Tyr.* 30.5–8):

> audio, patres conscripti, mihi obici, quod non virile munus impleverim Zenobiam triumphando. ne illi, qui me reprehendunt, satis laudarent, si scirent quae illa sit mulier, quam prudens in consiliis, quam constans in dispositionibus, quam erga milites gravis, quam larga, cum necessitas postulet, quam tristis, cum severitas poscat. possum dicere illius esse quod Odaenathus Persas vicit ac fugato Sapore Ctesiphonta usque pervenit. possum adserere tanto apud orientales et Aegyptiorum populos timori mulierem fuisse ut se non Arabes, non Saraceni, non Armenii commoverent. nec ego illi vitam conservassem, nisi eam scissem multum Romanae rei publicae profuisse, cum sibi vel liberis suis orientis servaret imperium.

> I have heard, Conscript Fathers, that men are reproaching me for having performed an unmanly deed in leading Zenobia in triumph. But in truth those very persons who find fault with me now would accord me praise in abundance, did they but know what manner of woman she is, how wise in counsels, how steadfast in plans, how firm toward the soldiers, how generous when necessity calls, and how stern when discipline demands. I might even say that it was her doing that Odaenathus defeated the Persians and, after putting Sapor to flight,

> advanced all the way to Ctesiphon. I might add thereto that such was the fear that this woman inspired in the peoples of the East and also the Egyptians that neither Arabs nor Saracens nor Armenians ever moved against her. Nor would I have spared her life, had I not known that she did a great service to the Roman state when she preserved the imperial power in the East for herself, or for her children.

Wisdom, discipline, rationality, generosity, competence, and firmness are elements of the culturally shared image that represents masculine achievements. Aurelian sees Zenobia in total conformity with this image, further validating her catalogue of virtues with the following statements: it was by her agency that Odenathus had defeated the Persians and it was thanks to her that imperial power in the East had been preserved.

However, the circumstances of her defeat by Aurelian will bring some reformulation to this imbalance. Zenobia will undergo a process of feminization, as if the biographer wanted to make her empirical evidence that leadership is, above all, a male appanage.

In Aurelian's biography we learn the circumstances leading up to Zenobia's defeat and imprisonment. At first, the emperor writes her a letter (*Aur.* 26. 7–9), demanding that she surrender and hand over her goods – *gemmae, aurum, argentum, sericum, equi, cameli* ('your jewels, your gold, your silver, your silks, your horses, your camels') – to the Roman treasury, promising, however, that he would spare her life and that the people of Palmyra would have their rights preserved. The reply of the queen of Palmyra[40] maintains the masculinizing register. On one hand, her reply confirms the masculine imaginary in which Aurelian's first letter (*Tr. Tyr.* 5–8) placed her, since she summons *virtus* (valour)[41] as the main value to be taken into account in their dispute. As observed by Jones, this concept '. . . brings to mind gender-appropriate behaviour. *Virtus* encompasses strength, bravery, courage, and excellence. The root, *vir*, of course, implies that these are qualities that apply to the male gender.'[42] But, on the other hand, she directly and expressively assumes her female lineage by summoning the death of Cleopatra as a sort of political statement emanating from a female-rebellious authority, who had appropriated the outcome of her own destiny, subtracting it from the sphere of male power.[43]

However, Aurelian's victory in the end will challenge the almost 'hegemonic masculinity' in which the biographer has placed Zenobia's leadership qualities, since it will translate, as far as the duality of male-female gender is concerned, her total reduction to the role of woman. After being decoratively displayed in a triumphal procession, Zenobia was reduced, until the end of her days, to the unified and structuring model of Roman femininity (*Tr. Tyr.* 30.27): *ferturque vixisse cum liberis matronae iam more Romanae* ('they say that thereafter she lived with her children in the manner of a Roman matron').

The movement of reduction and unification undergone by the male-female gender duality also extends to the power relations that are established between leaderships.[44] The final part of Aurelian's letter to the Senate explains the way he and the biographer conceptualize Zenobia's power (*Tr. Tyr.* 30.10–11):

> nam si vicisse ac triumphasse feminam non est decorum, quid de Gallieno loquuntur, in cuius contemptu haec bene rexit imperium? quid de divo Claudio, sancto ac venerabili duce, qui eam, quod ipse Gothicis esset expeditionibus occupatus, passus esse dicitur imperare? idque consulte, ac prudenter, ut illa servante orientalis fines imperii ipse securius quae instituerat perpetraret.

> For if it is not meet to vanquish a woman and lead her in triumph, what are they saying of Gallienus, in contempt of whom she ruled the empire well? 11 What of the Deified Claudius, that revered and honoured leader? For he, because he was busied with his campaigns against the Goths, suffered her, or so it is said, to hold the imperial power, doing it of purpose and wisely, in order that he himself, while she kept guard over the eastern frontier of the empire, might the more safely complete what he had taken in hand.

Aurelian's remarks illuminate, once again, how he, or rather the biographer, conceptualizes the relationship between political authority and gender. By assigning instrumental functions and purposes to Zenobia's leadership – she reigned under Gallienus just to promote his 'contempt'; under Claudius, she was tolerated because her keeping the East safe allowed the emperor to devote himself to the campaign against the Goths –Aurelian, or rather the biographer, is saying nothing more than that the power allowed and open to women is an accidental and temporary power-type. In Zenobia's case, the circumstances which dictated her ascension confirm this: she comes to power, not by herself, but through family ties; her husband's murder created both a power vacuum and the opportunity for her ascension, all the more so since she was the only person in the family who met the age requirements to occupy it.[45] In this sense, what the biographer tells us is that Zenobia was indeed a great leader, but an accidental and temporary leader, who governed a region during a leadership vacuum, in the context of an immeasurably larger world that was in crisis.[46] Her power was, therefore, a functional power, instrumentalized in her purposes and strategically maintained according to the urges and emergencies suffered within the scope of the 'great, central, masculine and Roman political framework'. Therefore, when this situation rebalances itself, returning to its condition of a stable political environment, this leadership reaches its existential limit.

Zenobia, from the biographer's perspective, fails this understanding. Leadership typically entails two principles: relational and self-recognition. Zenobia recognizes and perceives herself as leader, but she fails to understand how she is recognized in the larger framework of relationships between leaders. This dual aspect is reduced and finally unified, at the end of her biography, before being taken in Aurelian's triumphal procession (*Tr. Tyr.* 30.23):

> cum illam Aurelianus cepisset atque in conspectum suum adductam sic appellasset, 'quid est, Zenobia? ausa es insultare Romanis imperatoribus?' illa dixisse fertur: 'imperatorem te esse cognosco, qui vincis, Gallienum et Aureolum et ceteros principes non putavi. victoriam mei similem credens in consortium regni venire, si facultas locorum pateretur, optavi.'

> When Aurelian had taken her prisoner, he caused her to be led into his presence and then addressed her thus: 'Why is it, Zenobia, that you dared to show insolence to the emperors of Rome?' To this she replied, it is said: 'You, I know, are an emperor indeed, for you win victories, but Gallienus and Aureolus and the others I never regarded as emperors. Believing Victoria to be a woman like me, I desired to become a partner in the royal power, should the supply of lands permit.'

The perception that Zenobia had revealed in the letter previously sent to Aurelian, which is transcribed by the biographer in *Aur.* 27.2–5, is now reversed in her discursive utterance. In that letter, she refused to surrender, recalled the agency of her ancestor Cleopatra when faced with similar circumstances, mentioned her many allies[47] and questioned the strength and competence of Aurelian's army.[48] Now she recognizes Aurelian as true *Princeps* (Emperor) because he *uincit* (wins), and states that she dared *insultare* (to show insolence) to the power of Rome, represented by Gallienus, Aureolus, and *ceteri*, because she never recognized them as emperors. This statement allows us to understand how Zenobia conceptualizes power and, consequently, to understand the shift that takes place in her self-perception as a leader. Zenobia clearly has a 'charismatic conception' of power (in this respect it does not differ from that of the biographer), in which power is derived and legitimized by the intrinsic qualities of the leader. So while she had as opponents men with no qualities, she self-perceived herself as legitimately enthroned. In the first letter, Zenobia also perceives Aurelian within this framework. Now her perception changes, recognizing that Aurelian possesses the qualities she values after all. And this forces her to readjust her position within the framework of inter-leaderships relations, recognizing Aurelian as the true emperor and, consequently, acknowledging that her leadership has lost its *raison d'être*. The biographer objectifies the consequences of this transformation in *Aur.* 33.4–34.3:

> Blemmyes, Axomitae, Arabes Eudaemones, Indi, Bactriani, Hiberi, Saraceni, Persae cum suis quique muneribus; Gothi, Alani, Roxolani, Sarmatae, Franci, Suebi, Vandali, Germani, religatis manibus captivi. praecesserunt inter hos etiam Palmyreni qui superfuerant principes civitatis et Aegyptii ob rebellionem. ducta sunt et decem mulieres, quas virili habitu pugnantes inter Gothos ceperat, cum multae essent interemptae, quas de Amazonum genere titulus indicabat – praelati sunt tituli gentium nomina continentes. inter haec fuit Tetricus chlamyde coccea, tunica galbina, bracis Gallicis ornatus, adiuncto sibi filio, quem imperatorem in Gallia nuncupaverat. incedebat etiam Zenobia, ornata gemmis, catenis aureis, quas alii sustentabant.

> There were Blemmyes, Axomitae, Arabs from Arabia Felix, Indians, Bactrians, Hiberians, Saracens and Persians, all bearing their gifts; there were Goths, Alans, Roxolani, Sarmatians, Franks, Suebians, Vandals and Germans – all captive, with their hands bound fast. There also advanced among them certain men of Palmyra, who had survived its fall, the foremost of the State, and Egyptians, too, because of their rebellion. There were led along also ten women, who, fighting in male attire, had been captured among the Goths after many others had fallen; these a placard declared to be of the race of the Amazons – for placards were borne before all, displaying the names of their nations. In the procession was Tetricus also, arrayed in scarlet cloak, a yellow tunic, and Gallic trousers, and with him his son, whom he had proclaimed in Gaul as emperor, and there came Zenobia, too, decked with jewels and in golden chains, the weight of which was borne by others.

Her last image, chained up and paraded in the triumphal Aurelian procession, along with an immense plethora of men and women from distant places of the empire, elucidate her destruction, both as woman-leader and ethnic-leader – and, consequently, also makes explicit that the interior of the male-patriarchal-system, despite the profound changes that occurred in leadership during the third century,[49] still remains, after all, a zone where difference and complexity are eliminated.

Conclusion

The *Historia Augusta* has been systematically rejected as a historically reliable source. The subjugation of historical matters, such as major military and political events, to the individual narrative of the biographee, the enormous degree of subjectivity imposed by the author to the treatment of historical subjects and agents, the absence of a precise methodology, the development of subsidiary and irrelevant information, the use of unreliable sources and forged documents constitute, among others, elements that have relegated the work to an umbratic status, placed between history and fiction. In this regard, Zenobia's biography is no exception. The author's account does indeed have a historical basis: Zenobia is a documented historical figure; the *termini a quo* (her rise to power after the death of Odenathus) and *ad quem* (her defeat in the confrontation with Aurelian) of her rule, as well as the conflicting circumstances that marked her control over the East, are also confirmed by other sources. Everything else, from her unsurpassed beauty, chastity, habits, mores, and actions to the articulation of these elements within the narrative, seems to be the product of a literary construction.

However, literary constructions also express perceptions about contextualized socio-cultural practices and values. In fact, from this perspective, Zenobia's biography is a particularly eloquent document, in that it concerns the treatment of the 'other'.

From a general perspective, Zenobia is drawn by the biographer as an 'exceptional other'. However, the biographer seems not to admit the same 'achievement potential' for the 'others' she represents both from a gender and ethnic point of view. Zenobia is also drawn as a hybrid-other, but not to highlight the historical transformations resulting from the intercultural dynamics that emerged in the empire. On the contrary, the biographer manipulates this segmentation, maintaining the ambivalence of her cultural identity, which simultaneously invalidated the possibility of describing her both within a framework of an 'authentic' otherness and of full belonging to the Romanness. The biographer also depicts her as a dualized subject, oscillating between masculinity and femininity, between the status of a political and military leader and one of a defeated captive – an oscillation which, however, he subjected to a unifying movement that, ultimately, dissolved her complexity within the traditional and univocal paradigm of Roman femininity.

Zenobia's biography attests to the creation of an 'other' in which multiple levels of diversity intersect. Her story shows both the schemes and the limits that exist in the biographer's perception regarding the full-realization potential of this diversity as well as the constraints that prevent the full understanding of difference.

Notes

1 Southern 2008: 2–3: 'Zenobia is the name by which she is known to modern audiences, but there are variations of her name in the ancient sources. According to Arab sources, Zenobia was the daughter of a chief of the 'Amlaqi or 'Amalaqi tribe, and her name was Na'ilah. In Manichaean documents, she is Queen Tadi. Sometimes

she is called Nafsha, but this is also the name of Zenobia's sister, whose existence is doubtful. In the city of Palmyra, Zenobia is attested on inscriptions in Palmyrene script, which transliterates as *sptymy'btzby*, or Septimia Bat-Zabbai. The name by which she is known on her coinage is Septimia Zenobia Sebaste.'

2 Potter 2004: 266–7: 'The point at issue was surely the position that Odaenathus had held as *corrector totius orientis*. Zenobia claimed this title, as if it were hereditary, for her son, Vaballathus. . . . For a Roman the status conferred by the holding of an office might be passed on, but not the office itself.' On the same subject, Watson 2003: 61: 'Zenobia began to press her claim to exercise control over those parts of the empire which had lain within her husband's competence, and increasingly expected compliance from the Roman administration in the region. This included not just the Syrian desert and Arabia, but the whole region from Asia Minor to Egypt. She was fully conscious that she possessed the military might to back her claim, and also that, at least south of Cappadocia, she could count on considerable local support for her cause.'

3 On the status of the Palmyrene Empire, see Downey 1950; Stoneman 1992; Ball 2000; Southern 2008; Potter 2004; Hekster 2008; Kulikowski 2016; Andrade 2018; Dirven 2021.

4 See Watson 1999.

5 HA, *Tr. Tyr.* 30.27.

6 On Zenobia's literary sources, see Schneider 1993: 34–52; on iconographic sources, see Senden 2008; Bland 2011.

7 Southern 2008: 10: 'The author of the *Historia Augusta* significantly devotes more words to Zenobia than to her husband Odenathus, but the quantity of verbiage hardly represents quality of information.' On this subject, see Dessau 1889; Mommsen 1890; Momigliano 1954; Syme 1971, 1983; Adams 1972; Zahran 2003; Hengst 2010; Rohrbacher 2016. For the different positions regarding the date of composition of the *Historia Augusta*, see Honoré 1987.

8 E.g., Isaac 2017: 13: 'In other words, when interpreting names we need to take into account that ideas concerning ethnicity in the Roman Near East were highly flexible and not necessarily what they might seem to us. The reason for this is not far to seek: in the ancient texts we are faced with what was in many respects a different approach to group identity from our contemporary concepts. Categories and definitions that seem clear to us often do not apply in antiquity.' Dench 2010: 267–8: 'More broadly, it is important also to recognize the danger of using modern sociological definitions prescriptively, importing conditions peculiar to the modern nation-state, or maintaining rigid categories that would exclude "social", "religious", or "political" identity from one's enquiry. It is also perhaps the case that we interpret the 'subjective' quality of ethnicity in modern liberal terms, overestimating the degree to which people's identities in ancient societies might be a matter of 'choice', with the result that we can be more interested in complex self-scrutiny exercised in literature

than in legal and tax categories. On the other hand, we should be receptive to ideas in antiquity that will sound a little like thoroughly modern concepts such as nationhood or race, without expecting these ideas to work in the same way.'

9 See Gruen 2011, 2020.

10 E.g. Tacitus' *Germania.*

11 See Introduction of this volume.

12 On this subject, see Revell 2009; Woolf 1992, 1994, 2004.

13 On the subject, see Adams 2013.

14 On the concept of situational ethics, see Langlands 2011: 100–22.

15 This programmatic agenda is stressed by Burgersdijk 2005, 149–50: 'The balanced narrative (a female leader, but a skilled one) serves the rhetorical goal to depict the very effeminate bad emperor Gallienus. The opposition of good and bad emperors explains an historical incorrectness: Gallienus only reigned until 268, the year that Zenobia ascended to the throne. The idea can be formulated thus: under he bad emperor Gallienus, even women were able to reign, while Aurelian was able to defeat this very capacious female general.' The *Historia Augusta*'s translations presented in this paper are by Magie 1953–4.

16 *Gall.* 1.1, 3.8–9, 9.6–8, 10.5, 17.1.

17 *Gall.* 3.7, 4.3.

18 *Gall.* 4.3, 5.7, 10.1; *Tr. Tyr.* 3.4, 5.1, 5.6, 8.13, 9.1, 9.5.

19 *Gall.* 3.7, 7.4, 9.3, 14.5, 16.1.

20 *Gall.* 7.2–3, 18.1; *Tr. Tyr.* 9.3, 9.3, 9.5, 9.6, 26.1–2.

21 *Gall.* 1.2, 10.3.

22 *Gall.* 6.3–7.

23 *Gall.* 5.1; *Tr. Tyr.* 2.3.2.1.

24 The *Triginta Tyranni* includes the biographies of two usurpers who challenged the imperial power in the reigns of Maximinus and Claudius Gothicus, as stated by the biographer in *Tr. Tyr.* 31: 7: . . . *duos etiam nunc tyrannos quasi extra numerum, quod alieni essent temporis, additurus, unum qui fuit Maximini temporibus, alterum qui Claudii, ut tyrannorum triginta vitae, hoc volumine tenerentur* ('now I will add two pretenders besides, supernumeraries, so to speak, for they lived each at a different period, since one was of the time of Maximinus, the other of the time of Claudius, my purpose being to include in this book the lives of thirty pretenders').

25 E.g., *Tr. Tyr.* 3.1, 5.1, 5.5, 11.3.

26 On the imperial authority during the third century, see Ziolkowski 2011: 113–33.

27 Moreover, outside this narrative block, the territorial unity of the empire is at the centre of the author's attention. See, for instance, *Aur.* 1.5, 32.4, 37.4.

28 Dmitriev 2004: 214.

29 See Schneider 1993: 34.

30 Isaac 2017: 180 explains racism as follows: 'The essence of racism is then that it regards individuals as superior or inferior because they are believed to share imagined physical, mental, and moral attributes with the group to which they are deemed to belong, and it is assumed that they cannot change these traits individually.' The opposite position, developed by the author of the *Historia Augusta*, that is, that only a 'few exceptionals' can effectively change these traits individually, falls in a similar prejudice.

31 On the creation of the genealogical link between Cleopatra and Zenobia, see Burgersdijk 2005: 144, and Dirven 2021: 263.

32 See, for instance, Plut., *Ant.* 25.

33 See Lord 1969.

34 Vir., *Aen.* 6.698: *Quam metui ne quid Libyae tibi regna nocerent!* (How I feared the kingdom of Libya would do you harm!).

35 Langlands 2006: 365.

36 On the importance of lineage during the third century, see Dmitriev 2004.

37 A similar statement could be made regarding many other women in the *Historia Augusta*. The biographer places great emphasis on female infidelities, namely by creating doubts about the paternity of several emperors.

38 On this subject, see Hall 2000. Burgersdijk (2005) discusses structuring topics of Zenobia's portrait, such as culture and language, as well as lineage, beauty, chastity, etc., in relation to other literary models, in order to clarify its fictional character.

39 In this biography, Zenobia is mostly depicted as a follower, and in the same plane as the children: *Tr. Tyr.* 15.2: *quare adsumpto nomine primum regali cum uxore Zenobia et filio maiore, cui erat nomen Herodes, minoribus Herenniano et Timolao collecto exercitu contra Persas profectus est* ('he assumed, therefore, as the first of his line, the title of King, and after gathering together an army he set out against the Persians, having with him his wife Zenobia, his elder son, whose name was Herodes, and his younger sons, Herennianus and Timolaus').

40 *Aur.* 27.2–5, *Zenobia regina orientis Aureliano Augusto. Nemo adhuc praeter te hoc quod poscis litteris petiit. virtute faciendum est quidquid in rebus bellicis est gerendum. deditionem meam petis, quasi nescias Cleopatram reginam perire maluisse quam in qualibet vivere dignitate. nobis Persarum auxilia non desunt, quae iam speramus, pro nobis sunt Saraceni, pro nobis Armenii. latrones Syri exercitum tuum, Aureliane, vicerunt. quid si igitur illa venerit manus quae undique speratur, pones profecto supercilium, quo nunc mihi deditionem, quasi omnifariam victor, imperas* ('from Zenobia, Queen of the East, to Aurelian Augustus. None save yourself has ever demanded by letter what you now demand. Whatever must be accomplished in matters of war must be done by valour alone. You demand my surrender as though you were not aware that Cleopatra preferred to die a Queen rather than remain alive, however high her rank. We shall not lack reinforcements from Persia, which we are even now expecting. On our side are the Saracens, on our side, too, the Armenians. The brigands of Syria have defeated your

army, Aurelian. What more need be said? If those forces, then, which we are expecting from every side, shall arrive, you will, of a surety, lay aside that arrogance with which you now command my surrender, as though victorious on every side').

41 Jones 2016: 227.

42 *Tr. Tyr.* 27.2: *virtute faciendum est quidquid in rebus bellicis est gerendum* ('whatever must be accomplished in matters of war must be done by valour alone').

43 Jones 2016: 222: 'By comparing herself to Cleopatra VII, Zenobia not only likens herself to a woman who was a ruler and a powerful political figure who posed a threat to Rome, but she also aligns herself with an individual who challenged Roman notions of gender, power, and East versus West . . .'

44 On the subject of power and status in the Roman Empire, see Mennen 2011.

45 *Gall.* 13.2: *tum Zenobia, uxor eius, quod parvuli essent filii eius qui supererant, Herennianus et Timolaus, ipsa suscepit imperium* ('then Zenobia, his wife, since the sons who remained, Herennianus and Timolaus, were still very young, assumed the power herself').

46 On the third century crisis, see Potter 2004; de Blois 2007: 497–507; Liebeschuetz 2007: 11–20; Hekster 2008; Drinkwater 2008: 28–66; Ziolkowski 2011: 113–33; Hebblewhite 2016; Kulikowski 2016.

47 *Aur.* 27.4: *nobis Persarum auxilia non desunt, quae iam speramus, pro nobis sunt Saraceni, pro nobis Armenii* ('we shall not lack reinforcements from Persia, which we are even now expecting. On our side are the Saracens, on our side, too, the Armenians').

48 *Aur.* 27.5: *latrones Syri exercitum tuum, Aureliane, vicerunt* ('the brigands of Syria have defeated your army, Aurelian').

49 On this subject, see Mennen 2011.

Bibliography

Adams, G. W. (2013), *Marcus Aurelius in the* Historia Augusta *and Beyond*, Lanham, MD: Lexington Books.

Adams, J. N. (1972), 'On the Authorship of the *Historia Augusta*', *CQ*, 22: 186–94.

Andrade, N. J. (2018), *Zenobia: Shooting Star of Palmyra*, Oxford: Oxford University Press.

Ball, W. (2000), *Rome in the East: The Transformation of an Empire*, London: Routledge.

Bland, R. (2011), 'The Coinage of Vabalathus and Zenobia from Antioch and Alexandria', *Numismatic Chronicle*, 171: 133–86.

Breytenbach, M. (2005), 'A Queen for all Seasons: Zenobia of Palmyra', *Akroterion*, 50: 51–66.

Burgersdijk, D. (2005), 'Zenobia's Biography in the *Historia Augusta*', *Talanta, Proceedings of the Dutch Archaeological and Historical Society*, 36/37: 139–51.

De Blois, L. (2007), 'The Military Factor in the Onset of Crises in the Roman Empire in the Third Century AD', in L. De Blois and E. Lo Cascio (eds), *The Impact of the Roman Army (200 BC–AD 476): Economic, Social, Political, Religious and Cultural Aspects*, 497–507, Leiden: Brill.

Dench, E. (2010), 'Roman Identity', in A. Barchiesi and W. Scheidel (eds), *The Oxford Handbook of Roman Studies*, 266–80, Oxford: Oxford University Press.

Dench, E. (2018), *Empire and Political Cultures in the Roman World*, 226–80, Cambridge: Cambridge University Press.

Dessau, H. (1889), 'Über zeit und Persönlichkeit der *Scriptores Historiae Augustae*', *Hermes*, 24: 337–92.

Dey, H. W. (2011), *The Aurelian Wall and the Refashioning of Imperial Rome, AD 271–855*, Cambridge: Cambridge University Press.

Dirven, L. (2021), 'Zenobia of Palmyra', in E. D. Carney and S. Müller (eds), *The Routledge Companion to Women and Monarchy in the Ancient Mediterranean World*, 256–67, London: Routledge.

Dmitriev, S. (2004), 'Good Emperors and Emperors of the Third Century', *Hermes*, 132: 211–24.

Downey, G. (1950), 'Aurelian's Victory Over Zenobia at Immae, AD 272', *Transactions and Proceedings of the American Philological Association*, 81: 57–68.

Drinkwater, J. (2008), 'Maximinus to Diocletian and the "Crisis"', in A. Bowman, P. Garnsey and A. Cameron (eds), *The Cambridge Ancient History, vol. XII: The Crises of Empire A.D. 193–337*, 28–66, Cambridge: Cambridge University Press.

Gruen, E. (2011), *Rethinking the Other in Antiquity*, Princeton, NJ: Princeton University Press.

Gruen, E. (2020), *Ethnicity in the Ancient World: Did it matter?*, Berlin: de Gruyter.

Hall, S., ed. (2000), *Representation: Cultural Representations and Signifying Practices*, Thousand Oaks, CA: Sage.

Hebblewhite, M. (2016), *The Emperor and the Army in the Later Roman Empire, AD 235–395*, London: Routledge.

Hekster, O. (2008), *Rome and Its Empire, AD 193–284*, Edinburgh: Edinburgh University Press.

Hengst, D. (2010), *Emperors and Historiography: Collected Essays on the Literature of the Roman Empire by Danièel Den Hengst*, Leiden: Brill.

Honoré, T. (1987), 'Scriptor Historiae Augustae', *JRS*, 77: 156–76.

Huskinson, J. (2013), *Experiencing Rome: Culture, Identity and Power in the Roman Empire*, London: Routledge.

Isaac B. (2017), *Empire and Ideology in the Graeco-Roman World: Selected Papers*, Cambridge: Cambridge University Press.

Jones, P. (2016), 'Rewriting Power: Zenobia, Aurelian, and the *Historia Augusta*', *Classical World*, 109: 221–33.

Kleijn, G. de (2013), *Integration in Rome and in the Roman World*, Leiden: Brill.

Kulikowski, M. (2016), *The Triumph of Empire: The Roman World from Hadrian to Constantine*, Cambridge, MA: Harvard University Press.
Langlands, R. (2006), *Sexual Morality in Ancient Rome*, Cambridge: Cambridge University Press.
Langlands, R. (2011), 'Roman *exempla* and Situation Ethics: Valerius Maximus and Cicero *De Officiis*', *JRS*, 101: 100–22.
Lawrence, R. and J. Berry (1998), *Cultural Identity in the Roman Empire*, London: Routledge.
Liebeschuetz, W. (2007), 'Was there a Crisis of the Third Century?', in O. Hekster, G. de Kleijn, and D. Slootjes (eds), *Crises and the Roman Empire: Proceedings of the Seventh Workshop of the International Network Impact of Empire, Nijmegen, 20–24 June*, 11–20, Leiden: Brill.
Lord, M. L. (1969), 'Dido as an Example of Chastity. The Influence of Example Literature', *Harvard Library Bulletin*, XVII: 216–32.
Magie, D. (1953–4), *The Scriptores Historiae Augustae*, vol. 3, Cambridge, MA: Loeb Classical Library.
Mennen, I. (2011), *Power and Status in the Roman Empire, AD 193–284*, Leiden: Brill.
Millar, F. (1971), 'Paul of Samosata, Zenobia and Aurelian: The Church, Local Culture and Political Allegiance in Third-Century Syria', *Journal of Roman Studies*, 61: 1–17.
Momigliano, A. (1954), 'An Unsolved Problem of Historical Forgery: The *scriptores Historiae Augustae*', *Journal of the Warburg and Courtauld Institutes*, 17: 22–46.
Mommsen, T. (1890), 'Die Scriptores *Historiae Augustae*', *Hermes*, 25: 228–92.
Potter, D. S. (2004), *The Roman Empire at Bay, AD 180–395*, London: Routledge.
Revell, L. (2009), *Roman Imperialism and Local Identities*, Cambridge: Cambridge University Press.
Rohrbacher, D. (2016), *The Play of Allusion in the* Historia Augusta, Madison, WI: University of Wisconsin Press.
Roselaar, S. T. (2015), *Processes of Cultural Change and Integration in the Roman World*, Leiden: Brill.
Schneider, E. E. (1993), *Septimia Zenobia Sebaste*, Rome: L'Erma.
Senden, A. (2008), 'Zenobia in nummis', *Talanta*, 40/41: 137–50.
Southern, P. (2008), *Empress Zenobia: Palmyra's Rebel Queen*, London: Continuum.
Spivak, G. C. (1985), 'Can the Subaltern Speak?', *Wedge*, 7 (8): 120–30.
Stoneman, R. (1992), *Palmyra and its Empire: Zenobia's Revolt Against Rome*, Ann Arbor, MI: University of Michigan Press.
Syme, R. (1971), *Emperors and Biography: Studies in the Historia Augusta*, Oxford: Clarendon Press.
Syme, R. (1983), *Historia Augusta Papers*, Oxford: Clarendon Press.
Watson, A. (1999), *Aurelian and the Third Century*, London: Routledge.
Woolf, G. (1992), 'The Unity and Diversity of Romanization', *Journal of Roman Archaeology*, 5: 349–52.

Woolf, G. (1994), 'Becoming Roman, Staying Greek: Culture, Identity and the Civilizing Process in the Roman East', *Proceedings of the Cambridge Philological Society*, 40: 116–43.

Woolf, G. (2004), 'Cultural Change in Roman Antiquity: Observations on Agency', *Kodai*, 13/14: 157–67.

Zahran, Y. (2003), *Zenobia between Reality and Legend*, Oxford: BAR Publishing.

Ziolkowski, A. (2011), 'The Background to the Third-Century Crisis of the Roman Empire', in J. P. Arnason and K. A. Raaflaub (eds), *The Roman Empire in Context: Historical and Comparative Perspectives*, 113–33, Malden, MA: Wiley-Blackwell.

17

Novel Gifts: Imperial Self-Fashioning from Non-Normative Bodies

Serena Connolly

An Indian king once sent to Augustus an embassy that was accompanied by a collection of extraordinary gifts chosen to dazzle, delight, and interest the emperor. Nicolas of Damascus' eyewitness account, preserved by Strabo (15.1.73, C719), captures what must have been an arresting sight:[1]

> Εἶναι δὲ τὰ δῶρα τόν τε Ἑρμᾶν, ἀπὸ τῶν ὤμων ἀφῃρημένον ἐκ νηπίου τοὺς βραχίονας, ὃν καὶ ἡμεῖς εἴδομεν, καὶ ἐχίδνας μεγάλας καὶ ὄφιν πηχῶν δέκα καὶ χελώνην ποταμίαν τρίπηχυν πέρδικά τε μείζω γυπός.
>
> The gifts were Hermas, whose arms had been removed at the shoulders in youth – whom I saw – and large vipers, a snake ten pecheis in length, a river tortoise of three pechei, and a partridge larger than a vulture.
>
> trans. Roller

In 1977, in a survey of gifts to and from emperors, Fergus Millar observed that, 'The most surprising, if also least important in economic terms . . . are a number of freaks and curiosities, human, animal and inanimate, which were brought to various emperors, and afterwards shown by them at games, or put on permanent display at imperial residences.'[2] In 1988, Millar urged a study of such gifts to the emperors, writing: 'The presentation of freaks and curiosities to the Emperor would be an interesting sidelight on Imperial history, worth exploring for itself.'[3] Yet despite Millar's encouragement, there has been little exploration of these gifts. I will argue in this chapter that Roman emperors' receipt and display of gifts of non-normative form, such as those described by Strabo, provided an opportunity for imperial self-fashioning: in their response to such gifts, emperors were keen to present themselves as intellectually curious and discerning recipients.

Scholarship on emperors and their responses to non-normativism has been concerned largely with monstrosity. Robert Garland, most notably, has argued that emperors were interested in 'monsters': standing outside normal socio-political typologies, emperors identified with those who similarly stood outside natural physical typologies.[4] I argue that emperors' interest in non-normative bodies was rooted not in commonality or identification, but rather in a desire for a public-facing cultivation of intellectualism through discerning appreciation of their otherness. Moreover, the existence of observable types among these non-normative gifts strongly suggests that there were acceptable (and unacceptable) targets for emperors' intellectual curiosity.

Roman emperors' curiosity has implications for the history of scholarship on non-normativism. Historians once proposed that intellectual responses to non-normativism developed in a linear fashion from the medieval period, when non-normativism was regarded as monstrous, degenerate, and even portentous and non-normative bodies provoked visceral responses (i.e. driven by emotion and/or religious sensibilities), including horror, revulsion, fascination, and amusement, through to the sixteenth century, when those responses gave way steadily to intellectually derived curiosity. More recent work has offered important correctives: scholars now posit a less linear development from the medieval period through the early modern period and point out that intellectual curiosity emerged, but then fluctuated in prominence across time and space; they also acknowledge that visceral responses to non-normativism did not disappear, but rather coexisted within societies along with intellectual curiosity. Roman emperors' advertisement of an intellectually curious response to non-normativism complicates further this new history of responses to non-normative bodies. I argue that intellectual curiosity did not emerge in the early modern period, but existed already in Rome of the first century; moreover, the two attitudes towards non-normativism – intellectual and visceral – coexisted in that time.

The chapter opens with a survey of non-normative gifts to emperors, first inanimate and then animate. I identify among those gifts typologies that reveal emperors' discerning interest in the natures and ranges of non-normativism. I turn then to the emperors' responses to the gifts and their display of them to show that they advertised their intellectual approaches to them. This intellectualism was, I claim, one facet of imperial self-presentation. Yet, as I finally argue, these gifts could be misrepresented in our sources, in order to malign their recipients. I close by newly situating emperors' interests within the broader history of responses to non-normativism.

In 17 CE, when an earthquake levelled cities in the Black Sea region, cracks in the ground revealed large fossil remains, which locals interpreted as belonging to a hero.[5] They sent the emperor, Tiberius, a sample tooth at least 30 cm long, with the offer of the remaining bones, should he want them. Tiberius refused the offer to avoid any charge of sacrilege, though he was determined to know the hero's size. According to Phlegon of Tralles (*Mir.* 14, Stramaglia ll. 557–564), the emperor devised an ingenious way to satisfy his curiosity:

> γεωμέτρην γάρ τινα τῶν οὐκ ἀφανῶν, Ποῦλχρον ὀνόματι, τιμώμενον ὑπ' αὐτοῦ διὰ τὴν τέχνην, καλέσας πρόσωπον ἐκέλευσε πλάσαι πρὸς τὸ μέγεθος τοῦ ὀδόντος. ὁ δὲ σταθμησάμενος ἡλίκον ἂν γένοιτο τό τε σύμπαν σῶμα καὶ τὸ πρόσωπον αὐτοῦ τῷ τοῦ ὀδόντος ὄγκῳ, ἐργασάμενος διὰ ταχέων ἐκόμισε τῷ αὐτοκράτορι. κἀκεῖνος εἰπὼν ἀρκεῖσθαι τῇ θέᾳ ταύτῃ ἀποπέμπει τὸν ὀδόντα ἐκεῖσε ὅθεν καὶ ἐκομίσθη.

> He summoned a certain geometer, Pulcher by name, a man of some renown whom he respected for the man's skill, and bade him fashion a face in proportion to the size of the tooth. The geometer estimated how large the entire body as well as the face would be by means of the weight of the tooth, hastily made a construction, and brought it to the emperor. Tiberius, saying that the sight of this was sufficient for him, sent the tooth back to where it had come from.
>
> trans. Hansen

Tiberius seems to have been captivated by the extraordinary size of the tooth, even going so far as to employ a geometer to construct a model that would satisfy his intellectual curiosity.[6] The model could further function as an ersatz display that would advertise both the find and Tiberius' interest.

Later in his reign, Tiberius ordered the rebuilding of the Naumachian bridge, after it had burned, and according to the Elder Pliny (*Nat.* 16.190), specified Rhaetian larches for the re-build. Larchwood was a practical choice: it is strong, consistent, fire-resistant, and also has some resistance to rot. Larches had only recently entered the Roman consciousness: they are first attested in a Roman context in Vitruvius, who tells us that larch was first encountered by Julius Caesar on campaign in the Alps.[7] Rhaetia, an inaccessible area, had been a Roman province for only fifty years.

Of the lumber brought to Rome, one trunk was unusually long (36 metres) and wide (consistently half a metre); it cannot have been accidental that such a trunk was included in the shipment: larches will grow to 45 metres (and occasionally a little taller), though in the high elevations of Rhaetia, fewer will have done so. The chief lumbermen seem to have understood that this abnormally large specimen would impress the emperor and make for a fine display. Tiberius, in turn, appreciating its extraordinary size, picked out the trunk for display on the bridge, where it inspired wonder (Plin., *Nat.* 16.200):

> amplissima arborum ad hoc aevi existimatur Romae visa, quam propter miraculum Tiberius Caesar in eodem ponte naumachiario exposuerat advectam cum reliqua materie, duravitque ad Neronis principis amphitheatrum. fuit autem trabs ea e larice, longa pedes CXX, bipedali crassitudine aequalis, quo intellegebatur vix credibilis reliqua altitudo fastigium ad cacumen aestimantibus.

> What has been judged the largest tree up to this point in time was shown at Rome; brought along with the rest of the timber, Tiberius Caesar displayed it as a marvel on the same bridge of the Naumachia, and it stayed there up until the amphitheater of Nero. It was the trunk of a larch, 120 feet in length, with a consistent diameter of two feet, and from those measurements people estimating its total height from base to top have scarcely believed it.

A final gift was an unusually tall man. In 37 CE, Tiberius concluded peace negotiations with Artabanus II. Among the Parthian king's gifts to the emperor was, according to Josephus (*AJ* 18.4.5), 'a Jewish man measuring seven cubits, Eleazar by name; he was called the Giant because of his size' (ἄνδρα ἑπτάπηχυν τὸ μέγεθος Ἰουδαῖον τὸ γένος Ἐλεάζαρον ὄνομα: διὰ μέντοι τὸ μέγεθος Γίγας ἐκαλεῖτο). The gift, a gesture of goodwill and confirmation of good faith, was also politically significant: Artabanus had successfully and peacefully put to an end a recent rebellion by Jewish inhabitants of Babylonia, and specification of the man as Jewish signalled the king's territorial control. But the tall man was an object of intellectual curiosity too, chosen from the Babylonian Jewish population on account of his extraordinary size. The emperor appreciated that fact, as did those who saw him: Columella, writing about unusually tall humans, explains that the Germans are a tall people, but then notes (*Rust.* 3.8.2): 'I myself have been able to see recently among the items in the parade at the Circus games a man of the Jewish people taller than the tallest German' (*nuper ipsi videre potuimus in apparatu pompae Circensium ludorum Iudaeae gentis hominem proceriorem celsissimo Germano*). With the negotiations set in the final year of Tiberius' reign, it is unclear whether he or Gaius received the gifts.[8] Yet the recipient's identity was irrelevant: the practice of giving gifts of outsized inanimate items and humans and animals with non-normative bodies, gifts that had begun under Augustus and Tiberius, would continue with successive emperors.

Emperors did not simply have a broad fascination with 'freaks', but cultivated collections of non-normative bodies that fell into certain types: deficient or supernumerary body parts, extremes of size, and abnormal physical processes.[9] So, for example, among gifts with either deficient or supernumerary body parts, there was a young Antiochene girl about to wed in 45 CE: suffering extreme abdominal pain, according to Phlegon (*Mir.* 6, Stramaglia ll. 396–416), 'suddenly male genitals burst forth from her, and the girl became a man. Some time later she was brought to the Emperor Claudius in Rome' (ἄφνω αὐτῇ ἀρσενικὰ μόρια προέπεσεν, καὶ ἡ κόρη ἀνὴρ ἐγένετο. μετὰ δὲ χρόνον εἰς Ῥώμην ἀνηνέχθη πρὸς Κλαύδιον Καίσαρα; trans. Hansen).[10] According to Pliny (*Nat.* 11.262), Gallic hermaphrodite horses were gifted to Nero, who was sufficiently impressed that he had them draw his own chariot. In addition, Phlegon (*Mir.* 20; Stramaglia ll. 595–596) reports that 'a child was brought to Nero that had four heads and a proportionate number of limbs' (παιδίον πρὸς Νέρωνα ἐκομίσθη τετρακέφαλον, ἀνάλογα ἔχον καὶ τὰ ἄλλα μέλη; trans. Hansen). Finally, Hermas, who was presented to Augustus in the Indian embassy, was notable for his lack of arms.

Emperors also welcomed gifts of non-normative size: the Babylonian-Jewish man, tooth, and tree trunk, all sent to Tiberius, were abnormally large. Pliny, giving examples of tall people of times past, reports that (*Nat.* 7.75) 'under the Divine Augustus, there had been ones a half-foot taller, whose bodies were kept on display to be a source of wonder in the repository of the Sallustian Gardens; their names were Pusio and Secundilla' (*fuere sub Divo Augusto semipede addito, quorum corpora eius miraculi gratia in conditorio Sallustianorum adservabantur hortorum; Pusioni et Secundillae erant nomina*). Indeed, Augustus was so interested in exceptionally large bones that, according to Suetonius (*Aug.* 72.2–3), he stocked one of his properties 'with objects notable for their age or rarity, such as the enormous limbs of huge beasts and wild animals from Capri, which are known as the bones of giants' (*rebusque vetustate ac raritate notabilibus, qualia sunt Capreis immanium beluarum ferarumque membra praegrandia, quae dicuntur gigantum ossa*). According to Pliny (*Nat.* 7.74), 'it was under the Divine Claudius that our age saw the tallest of men, Gabbaras by name, who was brought from Arabia and measured nine feet and as many inches' (*procerissimum hominum aetas nostra Divo Claudio principe Gabbaram nomine ex Arabia advectum novem pedum et totidem unciarum vidit*).[11] Augustus received, as part of the Indian embassy, gifts of an oversized snake, tortoise, partridge, and vipers. A deficit in size seems to have been equally interesting to emperors: for example, Tiberius is said (Suet., *Tib.* 61.6) to have had someone of exceptionally short stature (*quodam nano*) at his court.[12]

There are examples of abnormal physical processes too. For example, Trajan was presented with an Alexandrian woman and her quintuplets, whom he then supported financially; the following year, she produced triplets (Phlegon, *Mir.* 29; Stramaglia ll. 630–34).[13] Hadrian would be shown a superannuated member of his household, who had apparently reached the astonishing age of 136; the paradoxographer Phlegon, who was one of Hadrian's freedmen, witnessed the presentation (*Long.* 4; Stramaglia ll. 116–118). Finally, Pliny, remarking that nothing is more fertile than wheat (*tritico nihil est fertilius*), especially in ideal conditions such as in Byzacium (in modern Tunisia), goes on to report (*Nat.* 18.94–95) that 'the procurator sent from that place to the divine Augustus, and it is hard to believe I am writing this, just shy of 4000 shoots from a single seed, and his letters on that very subject survive. In similar fashion, he sent to Nero 360 stalks from one seed' (*misit ex eo loco divo Augusto procurator eius ex uno grano, vix credibile dictu, CCCC paucis minus germina, exstantque de ea re epistulae. misit et Neroni similiter CCCLX stipulas ex uno grano*). Realization of the economic potential of such yields may have prompted correspondence with Augustus; the procurator's subsequent presentation to Nero might have been the result of efforts to improve the wheat yet further. But alongside acknowledgement of the crop's economic value, the procurators' correspondence and presentations may have been occasioned by their knowledge of emperors' intellectual appreciation of a natural phenomenon.

Human-animal hybridity seems also to have been an acceptable source of imperial intellectual curiosity: Claudius was gifted a hippocentaur that had lived less than one day (Plin., *Nat.* 7.35; the same story is told in Phlegon, *Mir.* 34; Stramaglia ll. 646–660). Though a human-horse hybrid, its status as a creature in myth may have placed it outside the regular dichotomy of human and animal and made it suitable for an emperor's intellectual curiosity. The creature was a fake, though our ancient sources do not suggest that this was suspected at the time; its preservation in honey, which has limited effectiveness, may have helped to disguise the deception. Augustus and Tiberius had also taken an interest in tritons, nereids, and other creatures of myth, according to Pliny (*Nat.* 9.9–10).

Exoticism was not itself a typology of non-normative bodies. Gifts to emperors often have an exotic origin, which our sources specify.[14] For example, Eleazar hailed from Babylonia and Gabbaras from Arabia; the hermaphrodite bride was Antiochene and the mother of quintuplets (and triplets) was Alexandrian. Nero's hermaphrodite horses were born in Gaul; the outstanding wheat was grown in African Byzacium; the larch was sent from Rhaetia; and the hero's tooth was found in Pontus. A gift's exotic origins could certainly accentuate its extraordinary nature and accord it additional value thanks to its inaccessibility and therefore rarity.[15] Yet not all gifts to emperors of non-normative bodies had exotic origins: for example, the superannuated man in Hadrian's household was a Sabine.[16] Specification of origin for all gifts is more likely driven by generic tradition: it was an organizing principle in some early paradoxographical texts, such as Callimachus' *Collection of Wonders That Are on the Whole Earth Arranged by Place*.[17] Crucially, emperors received human individuals who were non-normative one-offs, the crème-de-la-crème of non-normativism; they were not sent representatives of the extraordinary peoples listed by Pliny.[18]

A lack of proportion was an 'otherness' that was excluded from intellectual interest. It might explain the absence of extraordinary peoples from imperial gifts: their strangeness often derives from, variously, disproportion and asymmetry. We know that disproportionate dwarfism was unacceptable to Augustus: Suetonius (*Aug*. 83) tells us that 'he was repelled by those who were disproportionate dwarfs, and by everyone of that sort, as mockeries of nature and of evil portent' (*pumilos atque distortos et omnis generis eiusdem ut ludibria naturae malique ominis abhorrebat*).[19] The phrase *ludibria naturae* (mockeries of nature) reveals that the precise cause of Augustus' revulsion is disproportionate dwarfism. A person with proportionate dwarfism adheres to the size typology, but otherwise resembles a normative human and can be a source of intellectual interest. By contrast, a person with disproportionate dwarfism does not bear such a resemblance and is thus considered to be disfigured; that individual is a source of visceral revulsion.

Our ancient sources explain the difference as arising from the fact that disproportionate and similarly disfigured individuals could resemble animals more than humans.[20] Only a close adherence to human normativism is intellectually acceptable and therefore suitable for presentation to an emperor. This is confirmed by Suetonius, who tells us that Augustus (*Aug*. 43.3) 'displayed a young Lycian man of noble birth, only so that he might show off something that was less than two feet in height, weighing seventeen pounds and of a very deep voice' (*adulescentulum Lycium honeste natum exhibuit, tantum ut ostenderet, quod erat bipedali minor, librarum septemdecim ac vocis immensae*). The detail that the man's voice was deep is revealing: he most likely had proportionate dwarfism, in which a person's body is markedly smaller than average, but within normative proportion; their voice is also normative for their sex and maturity. By contrast, individuals with one of the various types of dwarfism that results in disproportion, especially of the limbs, often have unusually high-pitched voices. Suetonius' reader, unaware of the significance of the man's voice, probably assumed that he had disproportionate dwarfism because, among forms of dwarfism, the most prevalent are achondroplasia and hypochondroplasia, both of which are disproportionate.[21] Moreover, most depictions of dwarfism among our visual evidence present disproportionate forms.[22]

Emperors perhaps recognized that an interest in disproportionate non-normativism was, at least for some, grounds for censure. Evidence for this comes from Plutarch (*Mor.* 520C), who claims that there was a market that sold humans with non-normative bodies (τὴν τῶν τεράτων ἀγορὰν): people with stunted legs or arms (τοὺς ἀκνήμους καὶ τοὺς γαλεάγκωνας, literally 'calf-less and weasel-armed'), with three eyes (τριοφθάλμους), and with microcephaly (στρουθοκεφάλους, literally 'ostrich-headed').[23] The context is instructive: Plutarch has urged that to avoid meddlesomeness (πολυπραγμοσύνη, which he defines at *Mor.* 515D as a yearning to learn about others' misfortunes), the reader should be interested only in those persons who are unblemished in appearance; meddlesome individuals, by contrast, are fascinated with persons who exhibit non-normativism, specifically – as Plutarch's examples make clear – disproportion.[24]

The repeated and continued presentation of gifts to emperors of non-normative bodies that followed typologies and therefore stimulated intellectual curiosity suggests that they were welcomed. We know they were displayed at the Pompa Circensis (Columella, *Rust.* 3.8.2), the Saepta on the Campus Martius and the Comitium in the Roman Forum (Suet., *Aug.* 43.4), and the Sallustian Gardens (Plin., *Nat.* 7.75). When emperors displayed gifts at such heavily frequented locations and in parades, they were also advertising that intellectual curiosity. Indeed, such advertisement was sufficiently important that, despite – or because of – the difficulties of preserving and displaying these gifts, whether alive or dead, emperors retained personnel to manage just this task: Pausanias (8.46.5) refers to 'those in charge of marvels' (οἱ ἐπὶ τοῖς θαύμασιν).[25]

Some of our sources misplace gifts outside of the typologies presented above in order to malign their recipients as sympathetically monstrous or deviant, or as frivolous, more interested in the gifts than in matters of state. For example, as we saw above, Suetonius mentions that Augustus had displayed a Lycian man with dwarfism, though he had obscured the fact that the dwarfism was proportionate. The broader context of the episode further helps to distort the intellectual curiosity that Augustus presumably had in the man: Suetonius had reported (*Aug.* 43.3) that the emperor sometimes used equestrians to participate in theatrical and gladiatorial events, but was stopped by the Senate, who deemed the entertainment inappropriate; apparently piqued by this obstruction, he thereafter exhibited only the Lycian man. Suetonius' arrangement of his material encourages the reader to understand the Lycian man as another source of inappropriate entertainment; his wording underscores the point: though well born (*honeste natum*), the Lycian was shown only in order that (*tantum ut*) his non-normativism might be displayed. But Suetonius continues (43.4) that if anything previously unseen and worthy of understanding was brought to the city, the emperor would put it on display for the people; examples included a rhinoceros, a tiger, and a very large snake. As we have seen, according to the apparent imperial typological preferences, the Lycian man would have belonged with this group, as a source of intellectual curiosity; but Suetonius' displacement of him in the text to be a replacement for actors and gladiators instead renders him a source of criticism of the emperor.[26]

The inclusion of other accounts of such gifts in paradoxographical texts might also mislead. Paradoxographical texts report a wide variety of surprising phenomena, such as extraordinary flora and fauna, including humans. Dismissed as absurd, irrational, and nonsensical, these texts aroused the ire of ancient commentators such as Aulus Gellius (*NA* 9.4.12): 'when I was reading these things, a loathing gripped me for writing that lacks respectability and that contributes nothing to enriching or sustaining enjoyment of life' (*cum ea scriberemus, tenuit nos non idoneae scripturae taedium nihil ad ornandum iuvandumque usum vitae pertinentis*). Some modern scholars have been similarly scornful: Emilio Gabba, for example, describes paradoxographical literature as reflecting the interest of 'middle-brow culture' in the 'miraculous and fantastic' and claims that 'the result for the most part was a pseudo-historical literature, popular and escapist'.[27] Yet as paradoxography is becoming better appreciated in the context of ancient Mediterranean scientific thought, modern readers may more clearly realize the gifts – and other examples – presented by Phlegon as not just entertaining, but also intellectually interesting.[28]

Scholars' terminology might also mislead. For example, Millar uses many of the foregoing examples to illustrate his point that 'freaks and curiosities, human, animal and inanimate' were 'significant for the tone of the exercise of monarchy in the empire'.[29] He mentions neither typologies nor emperors' discerning intellectual interests in them: they were not his immediate interest in *The Emperor in the Roman World*, in a chapter titled 'The Imperial Wealth: Gifts and Exactions'. But the examples he chooses – and those he omits – suggest that he was perhaps nevertheless aware of them. Still, his phrasing has not aged well: most scholars today would be unlikely to use 'freaks' outside of a quotation or critical discussion of (earlier) terminology.[30] Reading Millar, they might imagine that emperors lumped together all types of non-normativism without discernment or intellectual appreciation.

Finally, amid a widespread contemporary distaste for the objectification of human bodies, modern readers might be disinclined to elevate emperors' interest in some types of non-normativism to the level of intellectual, even in an ancient Mediterranean context. Indeed, for all their intellectualism, those emperors may still have dehumanized the human gifts given to them: their anticipated fascination would often have led to the relocation, presumably involuntary, of these individuals, who might then be put on public display.

The stories presented above of gifts of non-normative bodies suggest that Roman emperors, of the Julio-Claudian period at least, were either intellectually curious or keen to present themselves as such. Of course, there are caveats to this claim: emperors may not all have had the same degree of intellectual curiosity; nor may they have had the same intellectual tastes. Even if emperors signalled an intellectually curious response to gifts of non-normative bodies, that apparently did not preclude some of them from sometimes reacting to non-normativism in non-intellectual ways.[31] Finally, emperors' responses to non-normativism, even if intellectually motivated, were not free of ideology or prejudice. And yet, even if an emperor was not personally interested in, for example, outsized turtles from India, nevertheless the imperial court advertised, primarily by establishing precedents of enthusiastic acceptance and subsequent display, that such gifts were welcome. The identification of types among the gifts they received points to a broad consensus at the imperial court of what constituted acceptable targets for intellectual curiosity.

That curiosity, which seems broadly consistent and sustained across the reigns of the Julio-Claudians, is striking given the wide range of opinions about non-normativism in the wider population. For example, as Mary Beagon has noted, responses to hermaphroditism did not develop uniformly and consistently across the population: there were 'changes in social attitudes in the first century CE, when negative religious interpretations of physical anomaly are in decline, at any rate among the trend-setting wealthy of Rome; though there was no simple temporal or social shift either now or many centuries later and attitudes even in the early modern era remained complex'.[32] We might extend that observation to responses to non-normativism more generally. It is in that context that we see emperors balancing their own display of intellectual curiosity with others' religiously informed responses: when Claudius received the gift of a hermaphrodite, he respected the conventions of public religion by building an altar on the Capitoline to Jupiter the Averter of Evil.[33]

Julio-Claudian emperors' display of intellectual curiosity in non-normativism and the responses to it challenge two notions: first, that non-normativism generated solely visceral responses among rulers, scientists (or natural philosophers), and the general population through the Renaissance (or later), and second, that intellectually curious responses then developed among those same groups in a linear fashion into the eighteenth century and beyond.

The first notion was set out in Lorraine Daston and Katherine Park's seminal 1981 article, in which they offered an attractively clear and uncomplicated narrative of development from emotion to intellect: 'In the early years of the Reformation, the tendency to treat monsters as prodigies – frightening signs of God's wrath dependent ultimately or solely on his will – was almost universal. By the end of the seventeenth century only the most popular forms of literature – ballads, broadsides and the occasional religious pamphlet – treated monsters in this way ... By the end of the eighteenth century, the canon of prodigies had been dissolved.'[34]

Yet long before, Roman emperors had adopted a response to non-normativism of intellectual curiosity. Indeed, we might push the starting point for the change even earlier: Roman imperial self-fashioning through a display of intellectual curiosity had its origins in the Hellenistic period, when kings kept exotic animals for display.[35] Hanno of Carthage is said also to have displayed the skins of humans (or creatures with some human-like features) that he captured off the coast of West Africa.[36] The practice was picked up by prominent Romans: Pompey, for example, displayed at his theatre statues of biological wonders, such as women of unusual fecundity.[37] Emperors' intellectual interest in non-normativism was perhaps also inspired by contemporary natural philosophers such as Pliny, whose own interest, as John Healy notes, 'may, in a sense, constitute a logical, preliminary stage on the way to genuine "scientific" curiosity'.[38]

The second notion, that of a linear development, has been complicated in more recent work, notably by Daston and Park themselves. Their 1998 book traces two responses to non-normativism: the visceral and the intellectually curious, which at various times, as philosophical and scientific ways of responding to the natural world have changed, have overlapped or run counter to each other, but always co-existed – even as intellectual curiosity has become predominant among learned and expert communities.[39] The book, despite its magisterial scope, looks back only to Late Antiquity; if it had looked back further, it would have seen those two responses at play even under the Julio-Claudian emperors.

The Julio-Claudian emperors stand in a long line of rulers who received gifts of non-normative bodies. Dwarfs, giants, and individuals with hypertrichosis, for example, were gifted to European rulers of the early modern period. Some subsequently served in court positions, where they attracted visceral responses.[40] But others were included in royal collections of corporeal non-normativism, where they attracted the intellectual curiosity of rulers such as Henry II, sixteenth-century king of France; Rudolf II, Holy Roman emperor of the late-fifteenth and early-sixteenth centuries; and most notably Peter I, Russian Tsar of the late-seventeenth and early-eighteenth centuries, who for a time kept a small number of living individuals for display and to work at his cabinet of curiosities.[41] Their precise responses to the gifts they received, their motivations for collecting, and the types of non-normativism they preferred may have differed. Nevertheless, the advertisement of their interests in non-normative bodies suggests that an intellectual curiosity in certain types of otherness was a means of self-presentation adopted by rulers across time and space.[42]

These rulers' predilections are a part of the complex and nuanced history of humans' responses to otherness. As the early modern period gave way to modernity, so teratology – the study of physical abnormality – was born.[43] Yet even as non-normative bodies were becoming specimens, objects of study and intellectual inquiry to be measured, catalogued, and classified in order to explain the various manifestations of abnormalities and their physical causes, so they could still be met with horror, revulsion, fascination, and amusement, among other responses.

Over the past century, attitudes towards non-normativism have developed dramatically. Scientists have been moving away from research that is ideologically driven and seeks to 'correct' or 'fix' non-normativism, towards study that is absent from ideologies of bodily ideals. Public attitudes continue to change too, away from a perception of non-normative bodies as inferior and as sources of entertainment, towards a growing acknowledgement of alterity without prejudice. Yet work remains to be done, as disability rights scholars and activists continue to urge the general population towards due regard for their needs and rights and towards an embrace of more capacious notions of normal.[44]

Notes

1 On the embassy, see Roller 2018: 871–2, as well as Schwarz 1985 and Bosworth 2013.

2 Millar 1977: 139–40; the survey is on pp. 133–63.

3 Millar 1988: 374.

4 Garland 1995, who has found broad support: for example, Gervaert and Laes 2013: 222–3. Bodily non-normativism in the ancient Mediterranean world has been well explored in recent scholarship: on emperors and non-normativism, see esp. Barton 1993 and Dench 2005: 285–90. On monstrous creatures, including humans, see Healy 1999; Naas 2002: 243–393; Beagon 2005, 2007, 2014. More generally, see most

recently Chappuis Sandoz 2008; Doroszewska 2015; Gerolemou 2018; Kazantzidis 2019; Felton and Joyce 2021. On non-normativism and disability, see esp. Laes 2017, 2018; Draycott 2018. On imperial collections, which comprised mostly paintings and sculpture, as well as examples of physical non-normativism, see Rutledge 2012. On collecting as a means of self-expression, see Bounia 2014. This chapter focuses on the Julio-Claudian emperors, for whom our evidence is fullest. There seems no reason why emperors of the second century, at least, should not have continued to receive gifts of non-normative bodies and responded to them with similar curiosity, but our evidence for them is sparser and, especially in the case of the *Historia Augusta*, more difficult.

5 The appearance of enormous bones in a seismic fissure and their identification as heroic is paralleled by another story set in Crete and recorded by Plin., *Nat.* 7.73.

6 Tiberius liked to draw on expert help for intellectual matters, such as the mortality of Pan (Plut., *Mor.* 3.419B–E) and words of doubtful Latinity (Dio 57.17.1–3; Suet., *Gramm.* 22.2).

7 Vitr., *De arch.* 2.9.14–17.

8 Our sources are unclear: Josephus attributes the negotiations to Tiberius, but does not specify whether the gifts were sent to Tiberius or Gaius; Suetonius sets the negotiations and gifts in Gaius' reign in *Calig.* 14.3 and 19.2, but does not specify the receiving emperor at *Vit.* 2.4; Dio (59.27) and Columella offer no help. Ziegler 1964: 62, n. 125 and Hurley 1993: 42–3 survey the sources more fully.

9 Chappuis Sandoz 2008: 26–9 identifies among ancient characterizations of entire peoples the typologies of human-animal hybridity, abnormal anatomy (including absence, excess and disproportion), remote context and longevity. Emperors embraced these typologies among their gifts as intellectually worthwhile, though with some discernment: they abhorred disproportion (see below). A remote context does not seem to have been a typology for non-normative imperial gifts (see further below).

10 On this story, see Doroszewska 2015: 100–1; Moralee 2018: xi–xii.

11 Gabbaras' height of nearly 3 metres should not be read literally, but as connoting extraordinary size.

12 Doroszewska 2015: 158, presumably inferring from Suetonius' *quodam*, claims that Tiberius 'had many dwarfs at his court', but we lack evidence to confirm this. On records of and attitudes to dwarfism in the ancient Mediterranean, see esp. Dasen 1993; Weiler 1995.

13 The story is also told, with some differences, in *Dig.* 34.5.7pr. (Gaius) and 46.3.36 (Julianus).

14 Emperors received, kept, and displayed rarely seen animals from distant locations (see Jennison 1937: 99–136 *passim*), some of them gifts (for helpful approaches, see Becker 2014 on Late Antiquity).

15 On Romans' acquisition of recherché objects and creatures at the furthest reaches of their territory and beyond, see Carey 2003: 32–40 and 75–101; Murphy 2004: 129–64; Beagon 2007; Pollard 2009; Naas 2011; Rutledge 2012: 193–220. See also generally Romm 1992. Expeditions by imperial family members included the search for exotic *mirabilia*: for example, Tacitus (*Ann.* 2.61) describes Germanicus' tour of Egypt, which took in the statue of Memnon, an inanimate object that nevertheless resounded with a human voice when hit by the sun's rays, great pyramids, a huge man-made lake, and extraordinarily deep gorges. Augustus' grandson Gaius Caesar, accompanied by Juba II, explored Arabia, as discussed in Roller 2003: 212–26.

16 The exceptionally large bones from Capri collected by Augustus might be considered exotic: though geographically close to Rome, Capri was an island and, as Gabba 1981: 57–60 discusses, with reference to the fifth book of Diodorus Siculus, 'an island was always considered as a privileged location for the occurrence of natural phenomena, the emergence of unusual human situations, the development of the exotic and the miraculous' (p. 56).

17 Suda K 227, Θαυμάτων τῶν εἰς ἅπασαν τὴν γῆν κατὰ τόπους ὄντων συναγωγή.

18 In *Nat.* 7.6–32, Pliny discusses far-off peoples who present group (i.e. phenotypic) non-normativism; at 7.32–36, he turns to individual non-normativism within otherwise normative groups, e.g. hermaphrodites, who are presented as gifts. Beagon 2005: 162 helpfully provides a clear demarcation between the two discussions of them.

19 I take the phrase as a hendiadys in which the second substantive, *distortos*, limits or specifies the first, *pumilos*: 'dwarfs, with disproportion'. Examples of similar hendiadyses in Suetonius' *Augustus* include 'weak from illness' (*invalidus atque aeger*; 13) and 'by the precedent from rank' (*more atque ordine*; 35). On the use of hendiadys to express specificity, see Panagl 2005. Led by *abhorrebat* and following Edwards and Graves, I translate *ludibria* negatively here as 'mockeries'; at Plin., *Nat.* 7.32, it is construed more positively (and with altered syntax) by Beagon as 'to amuse', though as she reminds us (2005: 162), 'the theme of nature at play . . . is often redolent of the capricious power of the Olympian gods'.

20 On disproportion as a source of approbation, see esp. Dasen 2008: 51–2; for a review of the ancient Mediterranean preference for proportion, see Vlahogiannis 1997: 21–3. Vlahogiannis also observes that symmetry was valued; the gift of Hermas may have been acceptable to Augustus because he lacked both arms, rather than only one, while the rest of his body was presumably unremarkable.

21 Dasen 1988: 276.

22 Dasen 1988: 274–5.

23 A supernumerary eye is unattested in humans, and it is unclear to what ophthalmic condition or phenomenon Plutarch is referring.

24 Quintilian is similarly critical: at *Inst.* 2.5.11, he notes that just as there is a vogue for speech that departs from what is right and according to nature, so some people prize

distorted and portentous bodies. See also *Inst.* 1.1.2 and 8 pr. 33. Quintilian is drawing on the general notion that a distorted style is the product of a distorted body and that both are a source of interest to a misguided audience (e.g. Hor., *Ars. P.* 27, and [Longinus], *Subl.* 3.4). Sen., *Ep.* 50.2, Plin., *Ep.* 9.17 and Plut. *Mor.* 726A (*Quaest. conv.* 8.6.1) refer scornfully to 'clowns' (*fatua*, *morio* and γελωτοποιός respectively) kept for amusement in elite households, but it is unclear what physical condition, if any, is being referenced. (On the treatment of enslaved individuals with intellectual disabilities, see Gevaert 2002.) The imagery of a market is found also in Quint., *Inst.* 5.12.17–19, which likens some orators' search for exaggerated delicacy to the search for eunuchs, another example of bodily distortion that appealed to some. Finally, [Longinus], *Subl.* 44.5 reports, with some hesitation, the claim that dwarfs were kept in cages in order to stunt their growth.

25 On this passage, see Bosak-Schroeder 2019: 87–8. On the administration of collections of and gifts to the emperors, see Liverani 2014: 72–7. According to Pliny (*Nat.* 7.34), Pompey had avoided the technical difficulties of preservation and long-term display of animate objects of intellectual interest by choosing to render them as statues. Trajan had a different solution: he advertised that he had undertaken financial support of the Alexandrian woman's quintuplets.

26 Suetonius reports (*Nero* 37) that Nero was gifted a man who would eat raw animal flesh and anything else offered, an example of an abnormal physical process; the emperor wished to give him live human flesh, a perversion of the process. The story is probably a fabrication, as Suetonius' introductory words 'it is even believed' (*creditur etiam*) acknowledge, though the denial functions as apophasis and thus still maligns the emperor.

27 Gabba 1981: 53.

28 On paradoxography and scientific thought, see Schepens and Delcroix 1996; Geus and Guthrie King 2018; Kazantzidis 2019; Shannon-Henderson 2020. Phlegon's companions in paradoxography – Callimachus, Cicero and Nicolaus of Damascus, among others – were intellectually respectable, and indeed, Phlegon himself also wrote a universal history, a work on Sicily and a study of Roman festivals, among other works, on which see Hansen 1996: 17.

29 Millar 1977: 140. Among his examples (pp. 139–40), Millar adds the presentation of a giant turbot to Domitian, described in Juv. 4. While an outsized fish fits the typology of an intellectually interesting non-normative gift, I regard the event as Juvenal's fiction, written to comment (following the reading of Stewart 1994: 321–30) on the emperor's exercise of his role as pontifex maximus.

30 Similarly, Gabba 1981: 53, 'the scientific interests of Aristotle and Theophrastus necessarily involved the study of freaks and remarkable phenomena in the world of nature.'

31 According to Stat., *Silv.* 1.6.57–64, Domitian used dwarfs to stage a mythological fight between pygmies and cranes. For a sensitive discussion of the event, see Gevaert and Laes 2013: 225–6.

32 Beagon 2016: 59.
33 Phlegon, *Mir.* 6 (Stramaglia ll. 396–416). Santangelo 2019 argues that prodigies continue to be an important part of public religion in the Principate, a fact reflected in Claudius' reported action.
34 Daston and Park 1981: 24 and 53.
35 On Hellenistic kings' interest in the exotic and their intellectual curiosity about scientific matters, see esp. Berrey 2017: 122–5, though note the caution in Romm 1989.
36 Plin., *Nat.* 6.200, on which see esp. Bosak-Schroeder 2019.
37 Plin., *Nat.* 12.20. On Pompey's collection, see Dench 2005: 286–7. The subjects in Pompey's discerning collection comprised examples from the typologies presented earlier, as well as human-animal hybrids, though a woman who had apparently birthed an elephant was also included.
38 Healy 1999: 70.
39 Pender 1996 first sketched out the co-existence of two attitudes. Following his and others' work, Daston and Park revised and expanded their work into their 1998 book.
40 On early modern courtiers with non-normative bodies, see Ghadessi 2011; Cheng 2012; O'Bryan 2012; Ravenscroft 2006; Wells 2018. Dasen 1993: 157–8 notes that dwarfs had served as courtiers under Egyptian pharaohs.
41 On Henry II of France, see Wiesner-Hanks 2009: 97 and 103. On Rudolf II, see Mauriès 2002: 109; Wiesner-Hanks 2009: 216. On the enormous collection of Peter I, which included around 2000 human specimens or body parts, see Neverov 1985; Anemone 2000.
42 See, for example, DaCosta Kaufmann 1978, who notes that the collection of Rudolf II was organized according to contemporary natural philosophical principles and classifications.
43 The modern scientific discipline of teratology is said to begin in the nineteenth century with Isidore Geoffroy Saint-Hilaire.
44 Garland Thomson 2017.

Bibliography

Anemone, A. (2000), 'The Monsters of Peter the Great: The Culture of the St. Petersburg Kunstkamera in the Eighteenth Century', *Slavic and East European Journal*, 44: 583–602.

Barton, C. (1993), *The Sorrows of the Ancient Romans: The Gladiator and the Monster*, Princeton, NJ: Princeton University Press.

Beagon, M. (2005), *The Elder Pliny on the Human Animal: Natural History, Book 7*, Oxford: Clarendon Press.

Beagon, M. (2007), 'Situating Nature's Wonders in Pliny's *Natural History*', *BICS*, 50 (S100): 19–40.

Beagon, M. (2014), 'Wondrous Animals in Classical Antiquity', in G. Lindsay Campbell (ed.), *The Oxford Handbook of Animals in Classical Thought and Life*, 115–30, Oxford: Oxford University Press.

Beagon, M. (2016), 'Variations on a Theme: Isidore and Pliny on Human and Human-Instigated Anomaly', in A. Fear and J. Wood (eds), *Isidore of Seville and His Reception in the Early Middle Ages*, 57–74, Amsterdam: Amsterdam University Press.

Becker, A. (2014), 'La girafe et la clepsydre: Offrir des cadeaux diplomatiques dans l'Antiquité tardive', *Monde(s)*, 5: 27–42.

Berrey, M. (2017), *Hellenistic Science at Court*, Berlin: De Gruyter.

Bosak-Schroeder, C. (2019), 'Making Specimens in the Periplus of Hanno and its Imperial Tradition', *AJPh*, 140: 67–100.

Bosworth, A. (2013), 'Strabo, India and Barbequed Brahmans', in V. Troncoso and E. Anson (eds), *After Alexander: The Time of the Diadochi (323–281 BC)*, 71–83, Oxford: Oxbow.

Bounia, A. (2014), 'Archetypes of Collecting in the Roman World: Antiquarianism, Gift Exchange, Identity and Time-Space as Parameters of Value', in M. Gahtan and D. Pegazzano (eds), *Museum Archetypes and Collecting in the Ancient World*, 78–90, Leiden: Brill.

Carey, S. (2003), *Pliny's Catalogue of Culture: Art and Empire in the* Natural History, Oxford: Oxford University Press.

Chappuis Sandoz, L. (2008), 'La survie des monstres: ethnographie fantastique et handicap à Rome, la force de l'imagination', *Latomus*, 67: 21–36.

Cheng, S. (2012), 'The Cult of the Monstrous: Caricature, Physiognomy, and Monsters in Early Modern Italy', *Preternature*, 1: 197–231.

DaCosta Kaufmann, T. (1978), 'Remarks on the Collections of Rudolf II: The Kunstkammer as a Form of Representatio', *Art Journal*, 38: 22–8.

Dasen, V. (1988), 'Dwarfism in Egypt and Classical Antiquity: Iconography and Medical History', *Medical History*, 32: 253–76.

Dasen, V. (1993), *Dwarfs in Ancient Egypt and Greece*, Oxford: Clarendon Press.

Dasen, V. (2008), '"All Children are Dwarfs": Medical Discourse and Iconography of Children's Bodies', *OJA*, 27: 49–62.

Daston, L. and K. Park (1981), 'Unnatural Conceptions: The Study of Monsters in Sixteenth- and Seventeenth-Century France and England', *Past & Present*, 92: 20–54.

Daston, L. and K. Park (1998), *Wonders and the Order of Nature, 1150–1750*, Berkeley, CA: University of California Press.

Dench, E. (2005), *Romulus' Asylum: Roman Identities from the Age of Alexander to the Age of Hadrian*, Oxford: Oxford University Press.

Doroszewska, J. (2015), *The Monstrous World: Corporeal Discourses in Phlegon of Tralles'* Mirabilia, Frankfurt: Peter Lang.

Draycott, J. (2018), *Prostheses in Antiquity*, London: Routledge.

Felton, D. and D. Joyce, eds (2021), *The Supernatural and Uncanny in Classical Antiquity*, Special issue of *Preternature*, 10 (1), Pennsylvania, PA: Penn State University Press.
Gabba, E. (1981), 'True History and False History in Classical Antiquity', *JRS*, 71: 50–62.
Garland, R. (1995), *The Eye of the Beholder: Deformity and Disability in the Graeco-Roman World*, London: Duckworth.
Garland Thomson, R. (2017), *Extraordinary Bodies: Figuring Physical Disability in American Culture and Literature*, New York: Columbia University Press.
Gerolemou, M., ed. (2018), *Recognizing Miracles in Antiquity and Beyond*, Berlin: De Gruyter.
Geus, K. and C. Guthrie King (2018), 'Paradoxography', in P. Keyser and J. Scarborough (eds), *The Oxford Handbook of Science and Medicine in the Classical World*, 431–44, Oxford: Oxford University Press.
Gevaert, B. (2002), '*De morionibus, stultis et fatuis* . . . Mentaal gehandicapte slaven in het Romeinse Rijk', *Kleio*, 31: 98–111.
Gevaert, B. and C. Laes (2013), 'What's in a Monster? Pliny the Elder, Teratology and Bodily Disability', in C. Laes, C. F. Goodey and M. L. Rose (eds), *Disabilities in Roman Antiquity*, 211–30, Leiden: Brill.
Ghadessi, T. (2011), 'Inventoried Monsters: Dwarves and Hirsutes at Court', *Journal of the History of Collections*, 23: 267–81.
Hansen, W. (1996), *Phlegon of Tralles' Book of Marvels*, Exeter: University of Exeter Press.
Healy, J. (1999), *Pliny the Elder on Science and Technology*, Oxford: Clarendon Press.
Hurley, D. (1993), *An Historical and Historiographical Commentary on Suetonius' Life of C. Caligula*, Atlanta, GA: Scholars Press.
Jennison, G. (1937), *Animals for Show and Pleasure in Ancient Rome*, Manchester: Manchester University Press.
Kazantzidis, G., ed. (2019), *Medicine and Paradoxography in the Ancient World*, Berlin: De Gruyter.
Laes, C., ed. (2017), *Disability in Antiquity*, London: Routledge.
Laes, C. (2018), *Disabilities and the Disabled in the Roman World: A Social and Cultural History*, Cambridge: Cambridge University Press.
Liverani, P. (2014), 'The Culture of Collecting in Roma: Between Politics and Administration', in M. Gahtan and D. Pegazzano (eds), *Museum Archetypes and Collecting in the Ancient World*, 72–7, Leiden: Brill.
Mauriès, P. (2002), *Cabinets of Curiosities*, London: Thames & Hudson.
Millar, F. (1977), *The Emperor in the Roman World: 31 BC–AD 337*, London: Duckworth.
Millar, F. (1988), 'Government and Diplomacy in the Roman Empire during the First Three Centuries', *International History Review*, 10: 345–77.
Moralee, J. (2018), *Rome's Holy Mountain: The Capitoline Hill in Late Antiquity*, Oxford: Oxford University Press.
Murphy, T. (2004), *Pliny the Elder's Natural History: The Empire in the Encyclopedia*, Oxford: Oxford University Press.

Naas, V. (2002), *Le projet encyclopédique de Pline l'Ancien*, Rome: École française de Rome.

Naas, V. (2011), 'Imperialism, *mirabilia*, and Knowledge: Some Paradoxes in the *Naturalis Historia*', in R. Gibson and R. Morello (eds), *Pliny the Elder: Themes and Contexts*, 57–70, Leiden: Brill.

Neverov, O. (1985), '"His Majesty's Cabinet" and Peter I's *Kunstkammer*', in O. Impey and A. MacGregor (eds), *The Origins of Museums: The Cabinet of Curiosities in Sixteenth- and Seventeenth-Century Europe*, 54–61, Oxford: Clarendon Press.

O'Bryan, R. (2012), 'Grotesque Bodies, Princely Delight: Dwarfs in Italian Renaissance Court Imagery', *Preternature*, 1: 252–88.

Panagl, O. (2005), 'Linguistisches und Stilistisches zum Hendiadyoin', *Journal of Latin Linguistics*, 9: 877–84.

Pender, S. (1996), '"No Monsters at the Resurrection": Inside Some Conjoined Twins', in J. Cohen (ed.), *Monster Theory: Reading Culture*, 143–67, Minneapolis, MN: University of Minnesota Press.

Pollard, E. (2009), 'Pliny's *Natural History* and the Flavian *Templum Pacis*: Botanical Imperialism in First-Century C. E. Rome', *Journal of World History*, 20: 309–38.

Ravenscroft, J. (2006), 'Invisible Friends: Questioning the Representation of the Court Dwarf in Hapsburg Spain', in W. Ernst (ed.), *Histories of the Normal and the Abnormal: Social and Cultural History of Norms and Normativity*, 26–52, New York: Routledge.

Roller, D. (2003), *The World of Juba II and Kleopatra Selene: Royal Scholarship on Rome's African Frontier*, New York: Routledge.

Roller, D. (2018), *A Historical and Topographical Guide to the Geography of Strabo*, Cambridge: Cambridge University Press.

Romm, J. (1989), 'Aristotle's Elephant and the Myth of Alexander's Scientific Patronage', *AJPh*, 110: 566–75.

Romm, J. (1992), *The Edges of the Earth in Ancient Thought: Geography, Exploration, and Fiction*, Princeton, NJ: Princeton University Press.

Rutledge, S. (2012), *Ancient Rome as a Museum: Power, Identity, and the Culture of Collecting*, Oxford: Oxford University Press.

Santangelo, F. (2019), 'Prodigies in the Early Principate?', in L. Driediger-Murphy and E. Eidinow (eds), *Ancient Divination and Experience*, 154–77, Oxford: Oxford University Press.

Schepens, G. and K. Delcroix (1996), 'Ancient Paradoxography: Origin, Evolution, Production and Reception', in O. Pecere and A. Stramaglia (eds), *La letteratura di consumo nel mondo greco-latino: atti del convegno internazionale, Cassino, 14–17 settembre 1994*, 373–460, Cassino: Università degli studi di Cassino.

Schwarz, F. (1985), 'Diplomatie und Selbstverbrennung: Strabon über die Indiengesandtschaft an Augustus', *Wissenschaftliche Zeitschrift der Wilhelm-Pieck-Universität Rostock*, 34: 51–5.

Shannon-Henderson, K. (2020), 'Constructing a New Imperial Paradoxography', in A. König, R. Langlands, and J. Uden (eds), *Literature and Culture in the Roman Empire, 96–235: Cross-Cultural Interactions*, 159–78, Cambridge: Cambridge University Press.

Stewart, R. (1994), 'Domitian and Roman Religion: Juvenal, *Satires* Two and Four', *TAPhA*, 124: 309–32.

Trentin, L. (2013), 'Exploring Visual Impairment in Ancient Rome', in C. Laes, C. F. Goodey and M. L. Rose (eds), *Disabilities in Roman Antiquity*, 89–114, Leiden: Brill.

Vlahogiannis, N. (1997), 'Disabling Bodies', in D. Montserrat (ed.), *Changing Bodies, Changing Meanings: Studies on the Human Body in Antiquity*, 13–36, London: Routledge.

Weiler, I. (1995), '*Hic audax subit ordo pumilorum* (Stat. *Silv* 1.6.57). Überlegungen zu Zwergen und Behinderten in der antiken Unterhaltungsliteratur', *GB*, 21: 121–45.

Wells, C. (2018), 'Court "Monsters": Deformity in the Western European Royal Courts between 1500 and 1700', *Preternature*, 7: 182–214.

Wiesner-Hanks, M. (2009), *The Marvelous Hairy Girls: The Gonzales Sisters and Their Worlds*, New Haven, CT: Yale University Press.

Ziegler, K. (1964), *Die Beziehungen zwischen Rom und dem Partherreich; ein Beitrag zur Geschichte des Völkerrechts*, Wiesbaden: F. Steiner.

Index

www.ingramcontent.com/pod-product-compliance
Ingram Content Group UK Ltd.
Pitfield, Milton Keynes, MK11 3LW, UK
UKHW032241010225
454413UK00003B/28

9 781350 353985